Multilevel Analysis for Applied Research

Methodology in the Social Sciences
David A. Kenny, Series Editor

This series provides applied researchers and students with analysis and research design books that emphasize the use of methods to answer research questions. Rather than emphasizing statistical theory, each volume in the series illustrates when a technique should (and should not) be used and how the output from available software programs should (and should not) be interpreted. Common pitfalls as well as areas of further development are clearly articulated.

Multilevel Analysis for Applied Research

It's Just Regression!

Robert Bickel

SERIES EDITOR'S NOTE by David A. Kenny

THE GUILFORD PRESS
New York   London

©2007 The Guilford Press
A Division of Guilford Publications, Inc.
72 Spring Street, New York, NY 10012
www.guilford.com

Printed in the United States of America

This book is printed on acid-free paper.

Last digit is print number: 9 8 7 6 5 4 3

Library of Congress Cataloging-in-Publication Data
Bickel, Robert.
  Multilevel analysis for applied research : it's just regression! / Robert Bickel.
    p. cm. — (Methodology in the social sciences)
  Includes bibliographical references and index.
  ISBN-13: 978-1-59385-191-0 (pbk.: alk. paper)
  ISBN-10: 1-59385-191-X (pbk.: alk. paper)
  ISBN-13: 978-1-59385-429-4 (hardcover: alk. paper)
  ISBN-10: 1-59385-429-3 (hardcover: alk. paper)
  1. Social sciences—Research—Mathematical models.   2. Multilevel models
(Statistics)   3. Regression analysis.   I. Title.
  H61.25.B53 2007
  001.4'22—dc22
                                                      2006103283

To Tanya, Molly, Byll, Sid, Lady, and Buffy,
my best friends for many years

About the Author

Robert Bickel, PhD, is Professor of Advanced Educational Studies at Marshall University in Huntington, West Virginia, where he teaches research methods, applied statistics, and the sociology of education. His publications have dealt with a broad range of issues, including high school completion, teen pregnancy, crime on school property, correlates of school size, neighborhood effects on school achievement, and the consequences of the No Child Left Behind Act of 2001 for poor rural schools. Before joining the faculty at Marshall University, Dr. Bickel spent 15 years as a program evaluator and policy analyst, working in a variety of state and local agencies.

Series Editor's Note

Social science data are typically multilevel: Children are in classrooms, workers are in departments or organizations, and people live in neighborhoods. Even laboratory data are often multilevel in that the unit, whether it is a person or a Norwegian rat, is very often measured over time, creating the levels of time and unit. Despite the nearly universal presence of multilevel data, data analysis methods have historically focused on a single level, usually the individual. The reasons for such a focus are many. Some are practical: Single-level models are much simpler than multilevel models. Some are philosophical: Western culture focuses so much on the individual that higher-level units recede to the background. Whatever the reasons, single-level data analysis tools have dominated social research, which is ironic in that social science is inherently multilevel.

The days of data analysis being limited to a single level are dwindling. Multilevel analysis has dramatically burst on the scene, and we now have the statistical tools to study phenomena at multiple levels. However, many researchers think that they cannot conduct such analyses because they are too complicated and they require specialized, expensive software. Fortunately, as this book shows, both of these beliefs are mistaken.

First, multilevel analysis is not all that complex, as conveyed in the subtitle of the book: "It's Just Regression." If the reader understands multiple regression, the fundamental statistical model in the social sciences, it is a relatively simple step to learn about multilevel analysis. Typically, books on multilevel analysis emphasize how it is different from standard methods of analysis. This book builds on the researcher's prior knowledge and shows how multilevel analysis is an extension of multiple regression. In fact, learning multilevel analysis should help one better understand regression. The focus is usually on the coefficients in regression—what is called the "fixed piece" in multilevel analysis. However there is also the "random piece," which is the error variance. In multilevel analysis, there are multiple random effects.

Second, multilevel analysis need not require specialized software. Certainly excellent pieces of stand-alone, expensive software that can conduct multilevel analysis are available. However, as this book shows with numerous examples, one can use software that is currently present on most readers' computer desktops to conduct multilevel analyses—that software being SPSS. The commands in SPSS are very similar to those of regression. It must be said that some of the output of multilevel analysis (e.g., log likelihoods) does not look like the output from a multiple regression. However, the author presents that complicated output and explains carefully what it means and how to use it in making decisions about the model.

Some researchers may plan to eventually use complicated software like the programs HLM or MLwiN. However, these researchers would still benefit in their understanding of multilevel analysis by seeing the similarities between multilevel analysis and regression.

The book provides several different examples of multilevel analysis, which start simply. In one case the model is just the simple mean of the outcome variable. These models expand to become much more complicated, with interactions and cross-level effects. Readers can follow along and try things out on their own. In the process they will learn not only how to conduct a multilevel analysis, but also how to build complex, theoretically rich models. I would strongly recommend that readers analyze their own data as they read the book. The practical lessons of statistics are never clearer than when you see them illustrated in your own data!

In 1968, Jacob Cohen wrote the seminal paper showing how analysis of variance is really multiple regression. This book follows in that tradition and should educate a new generation of social scientists that multilevel analysis is an extension of multiple regression.

DAVID A. KENNY

Preface

Multilevel regression models have become commonplace in published research in education, political science, public health, sociology, and a variety of other disciplines. Textbooks and other instructional accounts of multilevel modeling, however, are difficult to follow for most applied researchers, program evaluators, policy analysts, and graduate students (Greenland, 2000; Singer & Willett, 2003; Rumberger & Palardy, 2004). Furthermore, instructional materials are rarely geared toward enabling prospective users to employ widely available, general-purpose, user-friendly statistical software such as SPSS in estimating and testing multilevel models (cf. SPSS, 2005a).

A pervasive source of difficulty in becoming a self-taught user of multilevel analysis is textbook authors' inclination to minimize rather than emphasize parallels between multilevel modeling and widely understood statistical techniques, notably multiple regression analysis. My account of multilevel modeling takes the position that *it's just regression* under a specific set of circumstances. I assume, moreover, that most researchers who use multilevel modeling will be primarily interested in relationships between an individual-level dependent variable and explanatory contextual factors used in conjunction with individual-level predictors.

My account is made concrete with examples taken from research on educational achievement, income attainment, voting behavior, and other timely issues. A detailed analysis of county-level data from the U.S. presidential election of 2004 is used to illustrate the claim that multilevel regression is best used when the power and versatility of ordinary least squares (OLS) regression and its established correctives have been exhausted. From start to finish, the presentation is meant to be accessible and interesting for readers with a broad range of substantive interests.

One perhaps surprising judgment illustrated by many of my examples is that there is usually little difference between the unstandardized regression coefficients estimated with conventional OLS regression and multilevel regression (Kreft, 1996). This observation may lead some readers—not just the most cynical!—to wonder if multilevel regression is worth the effort. Many of us for whom research methods and statistics do not come easily have long suspected that state-of-the-art developments in quantitative techniques are best seen as convenient covers for the substantive thinness of social and behavioral research. In short, there seems to be much ado about very little.

In the case of multilevel regression, it sometimes seems that not much is promised beyond marginally improved estimates of standard errors, and identification of the correct numbers of degrees of freedom for inferential tests. Contextual variables and even cross-level interaction terms are sometimes assumed to be peculiar to multilevel regression models, and completely beyond the scope of OLS regression. In truth, however, these terms have long been incorporated into conventional OLS multiple regression equations, even though OLS regression is inherently single level. The standard errors of regression coefficients may very well be deflated, resulting in misleading tests of significance, but this too may be corrected through the use of comparatively simple adjustments that do not entail mastery of multilevel regression analysis (Bickel & Howley, 2000).

However, many analytical tasks that are beyond the scope of OLS can be accomplished with multilevel regression. Intercepts and slopes may be permitted to vary from group to group, reflecting, for example, the facts that mean achievement levels may vary from school to school, and that the relationship between measured achievement and explanatory factors such as socioeconomic status may also vary from school to school. In addition, contextual sources of variability in intercepts and slopes may be identified and actually incorporated into multilevel regression models. Beyond that, varying intercepts and varying slopes may turn out to be correlated in substantively interesting ways. These relationships too may have measurable contextual sources that can be used as additional independent variables.

Nevertheless, the frequently occurring similarity of the values of unstandardized regression coefficients estimated using OLS and multilevel procedures is a useful reminder that multilevel analysis is aptly construed as just one among many extensions of regression analysis. It is easy to lose sight of this fact as we get caught up in discussion of specification and testing of multilevel models. As I read over the material that follows, I can see that I have lapsed into this oversight many times, in effect exaggerating the substantive uniqueness of multilevel regression.

Perhaps the most important difference between OLS regression and multilevel regression is the thorough theoretical and substantive knowledge base needed to properly specify a multilevel model. In the absence of such a base, an analyst may be wise to acknowledge the limitations of OLS, use readily available correctives for standard errors and degrees of freedom, and forgo the opportunities provided by multilevel regression. After all, the use of OLS procedures with contextual variables and cross-level interaction terms to simulate what we now call multilevel regression has been with us for three decades.

In spite of these disclaimers, multilevel regression analysis is a statistical tool whose time has come. Undue reliance on adjustments to OLS regression in an effort to approximate multilevel regression results more closely is sure to raise objections. Furthermore, the ideas, procedures, language, and software that constitute multilevel regression analysis have been thoroughly institutionalized in academic and professional journals, colleges and universities, governmental agencies, and private consulting firms throughout the world (cf. Alford, 1998). Let's make an effort, therefore, to identify the strengths and limitations of this comparatively new statistical technique. Let's learn to identify the analytical opportunities it presents and the constraints it imposes. Ultimately, it is worth the effort.

Some readers may find the presentation that follows unduly conversational and wordy. I acknowledge that my approach to multilevel regression and other topics in statistics is conceptual and verbal rather than mathematical, and that this may be an inefficient way to proceed. I suspect, however, that the nonmathematical approach is the one taken by most applied researchers, policy analysts, and program evaluators—people such as myself.

Some readers may also be troubled by the fact that new concepts are sometimes introduced and briefly explained, but fully developed only later. This is the way I taught myself to understand and use multilevel regression, and I have proceeded as if others, especially fellow autodidacts, may also find this way of handling new and difficult material useful.

I may have used far too many examples and too many different data sets, illustrating too freely while directly explaining too little. However, my experience with the multilevel regression literature has persuaded me that it relies too heavily on one or a few data sets and contains too few accessible and realistic examples. This is especially true of ideas and procedures such as estimates of covariance parameters and residual covariance parameters, which are unfamiliar to many experienced users of OLS regression.

Some examples are used to answer questions or address issues that technically astute readers may find obvious or trivial. My initial encounters with the literature on multilevel models, however, were extremely confusing and left me certain of very little. As a result, seemingly simple questions such as "Can a multilevel model have fixed and random coefficients at the same level?" were sources of a good deal of anguish.

Throughout, however, I have tried to bear in mind that this book is meant to be a pedagogical tool. It is meant to make learning how to interpret and use multilevel regression no more difficult than is necessary. As such, the book has three ideal readers: the overwhelmed graduate student who is supposed to be good at this stuff but seems not to be measuring up; the isolated academic in a small to midsized college or university who, largely by default, has been cast in the role of local statistics person; and the policy analyst or program evaluator whose position is ill defined but who invariably, it seems, is expected to be able to read, interpret, and respond to everything ever published, especially if it involves numbers. Having played all these roles at one time or another, I know how tough things can get.

OVERVIEW OF CHAPTERS

The first chapter, a brief one, seeks illustratively to place multilevel regression into a useful historical and conceptual context. Multilevel regression is treated as one part of a sustained, long-term effort to make regression analysis applicable even if well-known OLS assumptions have been violated. Like established correctives with longer histories, multilevel regression is a set of sophisticated tools designed to broaden the scope of regression analysis, making it more versatile and informative. I emphasize the admonition "It's just regression!" under specific circumstances, and we see again that OLS and multilevel regression results are often less different than we might expect.

In Chapter 1 I also begin providing instruction in using SPSS with the Windows interface to estimate multilevel regression models. Since we do not yet have a working knowledge of the basic concepts that make up multilevel regression, much of the SPSS output will be unfamiliar. Running optional SPSS routines before we have mastered interpretation of the statistical procedures is intended to provide mechanical facility and confidence that we can make the software work. As we learn more about multilevel regression, the SPSS output will become more interpretable.

Chapter 2 represents an effort to clarify the meaning of the fundamental concept of *nesting*. Numerous examples illustrate the meaning and consequences of nesting, which may correctly be construed as the primary reason for developing and mastering the tools that constitute multilevel regression. Not just the simple truth that nesting is ubiquitous, but the fact that nesting commonly reflects and produces group homogeneity, prompts special analytical consideration. Within any group, observations become correlated or dependent, thereby violating an important assumption of conventional regression analysis.

There is nothing complicated about nesting itself: Students are nested within schools, employees are nested within occupational groups, patients are nested within wards, and wards are nested within hospitals. Nevertheless, nesting is sometimes easy to overlook, and it has important conceptual implications and methodological consequences.

When we use multilevel regression to give proper attention to nesting, we invariably work with two or more levels—say, individual students at level one and school characteristics, such as size and grade-span configuration, at level two. Quite often, analysis of nested data involves measures of the same variable, such as socioeconomic status, at more than one level. For example, in comparing public and private schools in terms of effectiveness and equity, we typically measure both individual students' socioeconomic status and schools' average socioeconomic status, with each serving as an independent variable in the same analysis.

Combining individual-level and group-level variables in this way has been done with profit by analysts using OLS. However, the uniqueness of multilevel analysis becomes apparent when we see that variables at different levels in a multilevel framework are not simply add-ons to the same single-level equation. Instead, variables at different levels are clearly linked together in ways that make explicit the simultaneous existence of distinct level-one and level-two regression equations. In routine ways, these different equations are then combined into one, and the result is a full equation that, in appearance and interpretation, makes long-time users of OLS multiple regression feel very much at home.

Chapter 3 includes a long discussion of a crucial concept made necessary by nesting: *contextual variables*. Contextual variables take a variety of forms. Some are aggregates (typically means or percentages), computed using lower-level variables, such as the percentage of students in a school who belong to an ethnic minority group. Some are characteristics of an organization, such as for-profit or not-for-profit hospitals, or extractive, manufacturing, or service industry firms. Still other contextual variables may refer to location, including values on the commonly used U.S. Department of Agriculture's urban–rural continuum (sometimes referred to as Beale Codes).

Whatever their specific form, the need for contextual variables can be traced directly to the pervasive and consequential phenomenon of nesting. Without nesting there are no contexts of substantive or methodological importance; there are just innocuous naming conventions called categories. The reality of nesting, however, assures that contexts differ from one another, and that they can be measured in ways that permit creation of contextual variables.

The quality of rural neighborhoods, for example, can be conceptualized and measured in a variety of interesting ways, sometimes focusing on the degree to which neighbors are like-minded and routinely supportive yet unobtrusive. Rural residents who participate in the same neighborhood—who are nested in the same context—become like each other and different from residents of other neighborhoods. Measured levels of neighborhood quality, as a result, can be used to constitute a contextual variable.

Contextual factors are used as independent variables in multilevel models to explain variability in a level-one dependent variable. In this sense, they function exactly like level-one independent variables. Neighborhood quality, for example, is often used to help explain student-to-student variability in school achievement from one classroom to another.

In addition, contextual variables contribute to explaining variability in random intercepts and random slopes. They help to explain *why* relationships differ from group to group. Variability in neighborhood quality, for example, may help account for variability in the relationship between ethnicity and dropping out of school. Contextual variables, in short, are used in an effort to explain the substantive consequences of nesting.

Finally, when contextual factors are used in an effort to account for group-to-group variability in random slopes, they imply the existence of cross-level interaction terms. Cross-level interaction terms are conceptually the same as conventional same-level interaction terms, but they are created using variables from different levels. An example that occurs frequently in this presentation involves creating a cross-level interaction term using individual students' ethnicity and the ethnic composition of schools.

As with contextual variables, cross-level interaction terms contribute to explaining variability in a level-one dependent variable, and they also help to account for the variances of varying slopes. Cross-level interaction terms make it unmistakably clear that differing levels are linked together in one analysis.

In Chapters 4 and 5 we finally get past just talking about and illustrating multilevel regression models. We actually start acquiring the statistical tools needed to specify, estimate, test, and reformulate them. I continue providing instruction in using SPSS with the Windows interface to estimate random coefficient and multilevel regression models. Fundamentally, multilevel regression models are applications and extensions of random coefficient regression models. The term *random* as used here refers to the fact that coefficient values are not fixed, but are selected from a probability distribution of values. That probability distribution is referred to as a random variable; hence random coefficient regression models.

With models such as this, the intercept and the slopes for lower-level variables may be permitted to vary from context to context. Mean measured achievement levels, for example, may vary enormously from school to school, and this is reflected in the way a random intercept is conceptualized and measured. Furthermore, the association between, say, measured reading achievement and an independent variable such as family income may vary from school to school. In some schools, family income differences may be more consequential for achievement than in others. This is reflected in the way a random coefficient representing the achievement-by-income relationship is conceptualized and measured.

In addition, a random intercept and a random slope may be correlated, and the same may be true for two random slopes. For example, from one school to another, higher mean achievement levels may tend to occur with stronger associations between achievement and family income. Excellence, in a sense, is acquired at the cost of equity. This set of circumstances may give rise to a positive correlation between the random intercept and the random slope for socioeconomic status. Just as random coefficient regression models permit coefficients to vary from context to context, they may also permit them to vary together.

The variance of random coefficients and the covariances among them may be of real substantive interest, as in the excellence–equity example. Furthermore, when random coefficient regression models are used in a multilevel framework, the variances and covariances may be treated as functions of contextual variables and cross-level interaction terms. In a school setting where differences in reading achievement are being studied, a random intercept and random slope may be functions of school size, varying together as a result. School size, then, is introduced as a contextual factor—a school-level independent variable used to help explain variability in reading achievement *and* to help account for the variances and covariances of the random coefficients. In this way, a random coefficient regression model takes on a specific and very instructive form, becoming a *multilevel* regression model.

If slopes and intercepts were the same for all schools, there would be no need for random coefficient regression. If there were no need for random coefficient regression, multilevel regression would be an abstract mathematical exercise. Once again we see that the ubiquitous phenomenon of nesting gives rise to the need for random coefficient and multilevel regression models. And once again we see the value of contextual variables, along with implied cross-level interaction terms, as explanatory factors.

Determining whether a random coefficient regression model is needed, or whether conventional OLS regression will suffice, can be done using a statistic called the *intraclass correlation coefficient*. The numerical value of the coefficient tells us the proportion of variance in the dependent variable that occurs between groups, such as classrooms or schools, rather than within groups. The intraclass correlation coefficient, then, tells us whether or not nesting makes a difference. If it does, random coefficient regression and multilevel regression may be productively applied.

Once an informed decision is made to use random coefficient or multilevel regression, OLS ceases to be the most useful estimator of intercepts, slopes, and especially standard errors. The most commonly used alternatives that fit neatly into situations where nesting is consequential are maximum likelihood and restricted maximum likelihood estimators. In substantive terms, fortunately, the alternative estimators provide coefficient values that are interpreted in exactly the same way as OLS coefficients.

The distinction between fixed and random *components* of random regression *coefficients* is explained and illustrated. The roles of contextual variables and cross-level interaction terms in linking together the levels of a multilevel regression model are clarified with numerous examples. The nature of the more complex error term required by multilevel models with one or more random coefficients is discussed in detail. Emphasis is given to the increasing complexity of the error term as more random coefficients are introduced.

Decisions as to how to center or rescale explanatory variables turn out to be quite consequential for substantive results. Centering is used as a way to make coefficients more readily interpretable and as a very effective means of minimizing the consequences of multicollinearity when cross-level interactions are included. I explain procedures for centering explanatory variables with respect to the grand mean, and I discuss the consequences of group-mean centering.

Centering is a topic that turns out to be less innocuous and straightforward than one might imagine. Instead, the type of centering employed is an important issue in multilevel regression model specification. For most applications it is well covered by a simple admonition: "Always use grand-mean centering." Nevertheless, some questions of real theoretical and substantive importance may require use of alternatives such as group-mean centering.

Other issues in regression model specification—Which coefficients should be fixed and which should be random? Which contextual factors and cross-level interaction terms should be employed? Should we constrain random components to be uncorrelated or permit them to vary together?—are examined in detail. Increasingly complex multilevel regression models are estimated, evaluated, and given substantive interpretations. The distinction between fixed and random components is developed a bit further, and ways of interpreting random components are illustrated.

In Chapter 5 especially, the notion that multilevel analysis is just regression analysis under specific circumstances remains an important organizing principle. Parallels with conventional OLS regression become particularly clear as I repeatedly illustrate development of the full multilevel regression model. This is the equation that actually provides the estimates of the fixed components—the intercept and slopes—for our regression coefficients. As with OLS regression, most of our substantive interest is in fixed components, often called fixed effects.

In contrast to other instructional sources, I delay introducing the notational conventions peculiar to multilevel regression until Chapter 5. This is consistent with my emphasis on highlighting parallels with OLS regression. When the conventions are finally introduced, however, I give them more attention than other sources. I am especially concerned with subscript conventions, which other sources take for granted, but which readers may very well find quite confusing.

While emphasizing parallels between OLS regression and multilevel regression, I use numerous examples to illustrate the exaggerated complexity of specifying a multilevel model. In the absence of informative theoretical or substantive literature that provides a good deal of guidance, multilevel regression model specification is fraught with ambiguity and very difficult judgment calls. As a result, multilevel regression can easily devolve into uninformed data dredging.

Chapters 6 and 7 are based on development of a lengthy example to illustrate the judgment that multilevel regression is best understood as a set of procedures that come into play only after the power and versatility of conventional OLS procedures have been exhausted. This places multilevel regression more firmly in the same broad category as other correctives that are employed when one or more of the usual regression assumptions are violated. To illustrate this, I use a national county-level data set to study the results of the 2004 U.S. presidential election.

I identify commonalities and differences between OLS and multilevel approaches, and illustrate the added complexity of proper specification of a multilevel regression model. After repeated and fruitful applications of increasingly refined OLS models, I explain why use of multilevel analysis with random coefficients, contextual variables, and cross-level interaction terms makes sense. As is often the case, the values of the coefficients estimated for OLS and multilevel regression equations are very similar. Nevertheless, consequential differences between results of application of the two techniques emerge. This is especially conspicuous with regard to tests of significance for random slopes and the slopes of contextual variables and cross-level interaction terms.

Difficulties in making important specification decisions in multilevel modeling become painfully apparent, especially with regard to which coefficients should be fixed, which should be random, and which state-level variables should be used to explain the variances and covariances of random components. Difficult decisions as to how best to measure vaguely defined concepts, notably "traditional family values," are common to OLS and multilevel regression analyses. Much the same is true as to specification of the proper functional form of relationships between vote and three of my four county-level ethnicity measures.

Given the choices I have made, the results are illuminating and, especially with regard to one high-profile relationship, surprising: With controls in place, county-level median family income turns out to be *negatively* related to the percentage of county residents who voted for George W. Bush. Throughout this exercise, avoiding the ecological fallacy of making inferences about individuals from grouped data is an ever-present danger. Like so many other issues, this is a concern that OLS regression and multilevel regression share.

Chapter 8 consists of a brief introduction to multilevel models with more than two levels. I use a Kentucky data set that includes measures on nearly 50,000 students, 347 schools, and 135 districts. Students are treated as nested within schools and within districts.

Conceptually, this is a straightforward extension of the two-level model. In practice, however, three-level models bring with them a dramatic increase in complexity, with seemingly minor changes in model specification yielding a proliferation of random components and requiring much more computer time. SPSS instructions for estimating a three-level model using the Windows interface are also included.

The possibility of formulating three-level models also introduces important specification questions not previously encountered. As a specific example, should we treat students as nested within *both* schools *and* districts, permitting one or more level-one coefficients to vary across both higher-level units? Furthermore, should we permit one or more school-level coefficients to vary across districts? I use the ongoing school size controversy to illustrate specification, respecification, and evaluation of multilevel models with three levels.

Chapter 9 is organized around application to three-level models of the intraclass correlation coefficient, the $R_1{}^2$ summary statistic, the deviance and deviance difference statistics, and information criteria. In the process of presenting this material, I include a more detailed and focused discussion of each of these measures. The chapter is brief because I have already applied and interpreted each of the statistics with respect to two-level models, and extension to higher-level models is quite straightforward.

Chapter 10 is an effort to use what I term *OLS-engendered commonsense* to address the complex issue of suitable sample size in a multilevel model. Students of multilevel regression show far more interest in sample size and statistical power than most users of OLS regression analysis. In part, this may be due to the fact that multilevel regression requires acknowledgment of at least two sample sizes: the sample size at level one, perhaps a specified number of students, and the sample size at level two, perhaps the number of schools in which students are nested. Beyond that, each level-two group may be construed as having a sample size of its own.

Moreover, when observations at level one are nested within groups at level two, dependence among level-one observations is likely to diminish the *effective* level-one sample size. When regression coefficients for level-one independent variables are permitted to vary across groups, the number of groups, not the number of level-one observations, is used in tests of significance for level-one slopes. To make matters even more complex, cross-level interaction terms are likely to have unstable coefficients and uncertain inferential properties unless there is a comparatively large number of cases at both levels one and two.

While there are commonly invoked rules of thumb, such as the frequently cited 30/30 standard, for sample size at the various levels of a multilevel regression model, they are offered with reservations and turn out to be of dubious value. The best advice one can give on collecting data for multilevel analysis is to maximize the number of higher-level groups relative to lower-level observations.

Most of us, of course, do secondary analyses with data collected by others, often for purposes other than those that interest us. Under these circumstances, the most we can do is be sure that the questions we ask are consistent with the strengths and limitations of the data set.

In Chapter 11 I introduce still another consequential form of nesting: *observations nested within individuals*. For readers accustomed to working with repeated measures, this is nothing new. Nevertheless, the idea of construing individual elementary school students as constituting the second level in a multilevel analysis does seem contrary to commonsense. When we work with multilevel regression growth models, however, this is exactly what we do.

Growth models in a multilevel regression framework enable us to do justice to achievement data collected annually on a cohort of rural children during their first 4 years of elementary school. Similarly, growth models enable us to make best use of national certification exam pass rates reported periodically over the course of a decade for all the nursing education programs in an Appalachian state.

The growth model itself describes a trajectory—a pattern of change—for each observational unit. The explanatory variables in a multilevel regression growth model explain why individual units differ with regard to change. In the case of linear relationships, instead of doing a simple before-and-after or pretest–posttest analysis, we are able to acknowledge unit-to-unit differences in intercepts and slopes, and explain why these occur. There is nothing intrinsic to either repeated measures growth models or multilevel regression that inevitably ties the two together. In conjunction, however, they may be much more informative than either would be alone.

In my presentation, I have tried to emphasize common features of multilevel regression growth models and more conventional multilevel models. This includes avoiding the common practice of using different notation for growth models. Furthermore, residual covariance parameters, not introduced before discussion of growth models, are presented as displaying the same patterns as covariance parameters for random components in commonplace multilevel regression analyses.

Complete datasets and other useful information for *Multilevel Analysis for Applied Research: It's Just Regression!* are now available at *www.itsjustregression.net*

Acknowledgments

Alison Bianchi at Kent State University, Julia McQuillan at the University of Nebraska–Lincoln, and Lesa Hoffman and Jonna Kulikowick at The Pennsylvania State University provided invaluable comments on this book. Without their assistance, the chapter on models with more than two levels would have remained unreadable.

My editor, C. Deborah Laughton, was patient, resourceful, good humored, and gracious throughout a long and tedious process.

David Kenny, Series Editor, was unobtrusive and patiently instructive, enabling me to learn from my mistakes.

My copy editor, Marie Sprayberry; cover designer, Paul Gordon; and production editor, Anna Nelson, were simply brilliant. They turned a cluttered and homely manuscript into a really nice-looking and readable book.

My mother, Arlene Bickel Yaw, came up the hard way and never quit. She has my love and admiration, earned many times over.

My brother, Perry Bickel, is a *mensch*, a good man in a hard world. When I think of family, he is the first person who comes to mind.

My niece, Kia Rebecca Bickel, and my stepson, Eli Riter, are the most genuine and good-hearted people I have ever known. It's good to see that they are enjoying their lives.

My wife, Lisa Higgins, is a treasure and my soulmate. She has my love, devotion, and gratitude for the duration.

Contents

9 • Familiar Measures Applied to Three-Level Models   248

10 • Determining Sample Sizes for Multilevel Regression   266

11 • Multilevel Regression Growth Models   285

1

Broadening the Scope of Regression Analysis

1.1   CHAPTER INTRODUCTION

Much of the material in the first three chapters is devoted to explaining reasons for using multilevel regression analysis. One answer is that nesting poses methodological problems and presents analytical opportunities that otherwise would be dealt with in less satisfactory fashion. Another answer is that the history of regression analysis can be written in terms of tests and procedures used to detect and correct for violations of the usual ordinary least squares (OLS) assumptions. Still another answer is that multilevel regression has now been thoroughly institutionalized in the academic and technical–professional worlds, obliging those who would participate in these settings to understand it.

The three answers offered for "Why do we use multilevel regression?" are complementary. Whichever one(s) we prefer, it is important to bear in mind that, in the abstract, multilevel regression is no different from a large number of other correctives that have been offered over the past 100 years to make regression analysis more useful. When one or more of the usual OLS assumptions are violated and we hope to make regression more generally applicable, such procedures are developed. Over time the use of such correctives becomes routine, and regression analysis is made more informative.

It is true, however, that learning the basic principles of conventional regression analysis is usually a lot less difficult than mastering needed correctives. As with multilevel regression, explanations of the correctives are often expressed in densely technical language, including new concepts and unfamiliar terminology, as well as distinctively forbidding notation. It is easy to get lost in technical details, losing sight of our objective: finding ways to make regression analysis more generally applicable and useful.

Once we have mastered and applied the new material, we may be surprised (and perhaps even a bit exasperated) to find that regression results with and without correctives are nearly the same. When comparing OLS and multilevel regression results, we may find that differences among coefficient values are inconsequential, and tests of significance may lead to the same decisions. A great deal of effort seems to have yielded precious little gain.

Nevertheless, taken together and over the long term, we trust that even modest improvements in specification, estimation, and inference make our statistical work more informative. We continue to benefit from the power and versatility of regression analysis, and we learn to do it better. Multilevel regression is part of this process; it is one of many useful correctives that have been developed to make regression analysis more broadly applicable and illuminating.

1.2   WHY USE MULTILEVEL REGRESSION ANALYSIS?

Our introductory discussion of basic issues in multilevel regression analysis may seem much too long. Results of numerous examples will be presented for illustrative purposes, but specification and testing of the statistical models and procedures that generated the results will be delayed until basic issues have been explained. All this may prompt the reader to wonder when—if ever!—we will get to construction and evaluation of multilevel regression models.

Admittedly, getting through this introductory material takes time. Working through basic issues, however, will make our presentation of multilevel regression analysis more accessible and useful.

Throughout this discussion it is important to bear in mind that multilevel analysis is best construed as one among many extensions of OLS multiple regression. In the tables in Chapters 6 and 7, our long statistical account of county-level data concerning the 2004 U.S. presidential election illustrates the claim that multilevel regression is most useful *after* the power and versatility of OLS regression have been exhausted in specific ways. We will begin, therefore, with the most fundamental sort of question: **Why bother?** Why use multilevel regression analysis in the first place?

Many of us doing applied work in the social and behavioral sciences learned to use and understand statistical methods by reading material written by the late Hubert Blalock (e.g., Blalock, 1960, 1972). In one of his first and most influential textbooks, Blalock matter-of-factly observed that the laws of social science, insofar as they can be formulated, are manifest in partial regression coefficients (Blalock, 1964). Blalock did most of his work before the importance of contextual variables and the nested nature of much social science data were widely appreciated. However, the search for partial regression coefficients that give interpretably consistent results from time to time and from place to place inevitably leads in this direction (Kunovich, 2004).

The importance of contextual factors in social and behavioral research is fairly obvious, and contextual effects have a good deal of intuitive appeal (Blau, 1960, 1994; Lazarsfeld & Menzel, 1969; Barr & Dreeben, 1983; Coleman & Hoffer, 1987; Riordan,

2004). When we are studying reading achievement among middle school students, for example, it is important to acknowledge explicitly that values of the dependent variable may be affected by independent variables at both the individual level *and* at one or more contextual or group levels. As a result, it is useful to know the gender, ethnicity, and family income of each student, *and* it is also useful to know the gender composition, ethnic composition, and median family income of the schools they attend (Iversen, 1991; Hox, 1995). The possibility of individual-level effects *and* contextual effects in the same analysis is one compelling reason why multilevel modeling has become so conspicuous in the study of student achievement.

Contextual variables can be used along with individual-level factors in conventional OLS multiple regression analyses. Analyses of this kind have been reported at least since the 1970s, and they have merit (Boyd & Iversen, 1979; Iversen, 1991). A good case can be made, however, that such work can be done more accurately, elegantly, and persuasively by using alternatives to conventional OLS regression (Kreft, 1996).

In spite of its importance and intuitive appeal, however, the prospect of using multilevel modeling to complement individual-level explanatory variables with contextual factors may leave many applied researchers feeling obsolete and confused. Earlier methodological developments, such as path analysis, log-linear analysis, and structural equation modeling, have had similar consequences. When they were introduced, however, these techniques seemed easier to ignore as issue-specific, of uncertain value, and perhaps even faddish (Coser, 1975; Duncan, 1975, pp. vii–viii; Cliff, 1983; Freedman, 1987; Smelser, 2001).

One sometimes gets the impression, moreover, that the most fervent proponents of new techniques have never really appreciated the power and flexibility of established procedures, especially OLS multiple regression analysis. Given some historical sense and the statistical maturity that comes with experience, it seems reasonable to surmise that champions of novel quantitative techniques would be less inclined to dismiss demonstrably useful methods as analytically naïve, technically deficient, or simply old-fashioned.

Nevertheless, the sometimes overstated claim that analysis of student achievement and other outcomes may be misleading unless consequences of group membership are evaluated by using alternatives to OLS multiple regression analysis has to be acknowledged. Otherwise, the credibility of a wide variety of statistical analyses will be diminished (Raudenbush & Bryk, 2002). Understanding multilevel regression and its legitimate place in empirical work, therefore, seems undeniably important to policy analysts, program evaluators, and others who produce or consume applied research.

1.3   LIMITATIONS OF AVAILABLE INSTRUCTIONAL MATERIAL

Available texts, instructional articles, and tutorials on multilevel analysis are difficult for most readers. Resources produced for beginners seem only tenuously related to things they may already understand, especially multiple regression analysis. Even Singer's (1998) often-cited article-length account of applying the general purpose software SAS in multilevel modeling is limited in this regard. The online *Multilevel Modelling Newsletter*, while timely and informative, reads as if it were written by and for technically astute insiders—and that, no doubt, is as intended.

In large measure, failure to draw all but the most abstract parallels between multilevel analysis and conventional regression analysis may be due to authors' understandable desire to make clear the distinctiveness of multilevel modeling by highlighting its peculiar virtues, limitations, and demands. After all, multilevel regression is a technique that raises unusually complex issues in regression model specification, and it works best when pertinent theory is well developed and substantive literature is rich.

Whether or not this explains the absence of emphasis on obvious parallels, some of the best-known, most influential authors of material on multilevel modeling seem to be impatient with those who judge their offerings to be needlessly dense (cf. Goldstein, 2000; De Leeuw, 2003). Occasional efforts to make their applied work accessible to a broader readership, though no doubt offered in good faith, seem oddly lacking in persuasiveness (see, e.g., Yang, Goldstein, Rath, & Hill, 1999).

It is true that some of the best-known and most influential texts seem much more clearly related to widely used, better-understood regression-based procedures *after* readers have acquired a fairly thorough understanding of multilevel regression (see, e.g., Bryk & Raudenbush, 1992; Raudenbush & Bryk, 2002; Heck & Thomas, 2000). Typically, however, discussions of parallels are presented in *very* condensed form; new concepts, such as cross-level interaction terms, are sometimes introduced with only an off-handed acknowledgment that they may indeed be unfamiliar to the reader. As a result, acquiring facility in working with new ideas and never-before-seen notation remains the brutally difficult part.

Missing from existing accounts, moreover, is explicit recognition of the fact that development of regression analysis over the last 100 years consists largely of efforts to find ways to make OLS multiple regression applicable to increasingly complex questions, even when its basic assumptions have been violated (see, e.g., Haavelmo, 1943; Ezekiel & Fox, 1959; Blalock, 1964; Goldfield & Quandt, 1972; Belsley, Kuh, & Welsh, 1980; Hosmer & Lemeshow, 1989; Kmenta, 1997; Kennedy, 1998, 2003; Campbell & Kenny, 1999; Hoffmann, 2003; Kline, 2005; Aguinis, 2004; Santos & Freedman, 2004). Moreover, whatever adjustments are made to accommodate violations of well-known regression assumptions, analysts know that they are still doing regression analysis (Wooldridge, 2006).

1.4   MULTILEVEL REGRESSION ANALYSIS IN SUGGESTIVE HISTORICAL CONTEXT

Some of the best known statistical tests, such as the Durbin–Watson, Hausman, Chow, and Breusch–Pagan tests, were developed to detect violations of assumptions that undergird OLS multiple regression analysis (Mirer, 1995). Commonly used correctives, such as estimated generalized least squares, two-stage least squares, logistic regression, and generalized Tobit, were devised in an effort to permit efficient estimation of unbiased regression coefficients when fundamental assumptions do not hold (Heckman, 1979; Hausman, 1998; Fox, 1991; Berry, 1993; Menard, 2002).

By way of illustration, we will use a data set containing school-level reading achievement data for 1001 Texas high schools for the school year 1996–1997 (Bickel, Howley, Williams, & Glascock, 2001). Using OLS multiple regression analysis, we try to account for mean reading achievement differences from school to school.

We use a conventional complement of school-level independent variables: percentage of students who are Black (X_{BLACK}), percentage who are Hispanic ($X_{HISPANIC}$), percentage sufficiently poor to be eligible for free/reduced cost lunch (X_{POOR}), student–teacher ratio (X_{STR}), expenditure per pupil in units of $1000 ($X_{EPP}$), and school enrollment units of 100 students (X_{SIZE}). The results of the OLS regression analysis are reported in Table 1.1.

When we divide the unstandardized regression coefficients by their standard errors (in parentheses), we get t values showing that X_{BLACK}, $X_{HISPANIC}$, and X_{POOR} have statistically significant coefficients. For each 1% increase in X_{BLACK}, mean school reading achievement decreases, on average, by 0.029 test score points. For each 1% increase in $X_{HISPANIC}$, mean school reading achievement decreases, on average, by 0.020 test score points. For each 1% increase in X_{POOR}, mean school reading achievement decreases, on average, by 0.044 test score points. Each of these relationships holds, moreover, while we are controlling for all the other independent variables in the multiple regression equation.

We then run routine tests for violation of OLS assumptions, including the Koenker–Bassett (KB) test for heteroscedasticity (Gujarati, 2003). The test is easy to use:

1. Run the regression equation as in Table 1.1.
2. Save the residuals and the predicted values.
3. Regress the squared residuals on the squared predicted values.
4. A statistically significant regression coefficient for the variable represented by squared predicted values tells us that standard errors of regression coefficients may be inflated because the variance of the residuals is a function of one or more independent variables.

The results of the KB test appear in Table 1.2. With a t value of 4.50 and 999 degrees of freedom, we conclude that the assumption of homoscedasticity has been violated.

TABLE 1.1. Mean Reading Achievement in Texas High Schools

$$Y = 41.754 - 0.029X_{BLACK} - 0.020X_{HISPANIC} - 0.044X_{POOR} - 0.014X_{STR} + 0.023X_{EPP} - 0.005X_{SIZE}$$
$$(0.655)\ (0.004)\quad\ (0.004)\quad\quad\ (0.005)\quad\quad\ (0.036)\quad\ (0.060)\quad\ (0.011)$$

$$R^2 = 36.7\%$$
$$N = 1001$$

TABLE 1.2. The KB Test for Heteroscedasticity

$$Y_{\text{RESIDUALS}}^2 = 16.718 - 0.009X_{\text{PREDICTED}}^2$$
$$(0.002)$$

One source of heteroscedasticity may be the relationship between the residual variance and school size, as illustrated in Figure 1.1. Even though school size does not have a statistically significant relationship with the reading achievement dependent variable, it seems quite clear that the residual variance behaves as if it were a function of school size: As school size increases, residual variance is diminished.

Given these results—a statistically nonsignificant coefficient for school size and the apparent implication of school size in generating heteroscedasticity—a reasonable response might be simply to delete the school size variable (Wittink, 1988). For present purposes, however, we will proceed as if there is a compelling substantive or theoretical reason to keep school size in the regression equation to avoid specification error.

Does this mean that heteroscedasticity will necessarily render our regression results dubious? Of course not. There are various correctives for heteroscedasticity, including an easy-to-use procedure called *estimated generalized least squares* (EGLS) (Wooldridge, 2002). The EGLS procedure works as follows:

1. Run the regression equation as above and save the residuals.
2. Square the residuals and take their natural logarithms.
3. Use the natural logarithm of the squared residuals as a new dependent variable, run the regression equation, and save the predicted values.
4. Create a new variable by exponentiating the predicted values. In other words, raise the base of natural logarithms, 2.71828, to the power represented by each of the predicted values. Then take the reciprocal of the exponentiated predicted values.
5. Run the regression equation from item 1, but use the new variable from item 4 as a regression weight.
6. With EGLS, the regression analysis has now been approximately corrected for violation of the assumption of homoscedasticity.

The EGLS results appear in Table 1.3.

The OLS regression coefficient estimates in Table 1.1 and EGLS regression coefficient estimates in Table 1.3 are not exactly the same. Differences are due to greater precision in estimating regression coefficients after heteroscedasticity has been corrected; after all, inflated

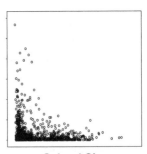

FIGURE 1.1. Heteroscedasticity: Residual variance by school size.

TABLE 1.3. EGLS Correction for Heteroscedasticity

$$Y = 41.922 - 0.028X_{\text{BLACK}} - 0.022X_{\text{HISPANIC}} - 0.047X_{\text{POOR}} - 0.030X_{\text{STR}} + 0.037X_{\text{EPP}} - 0.008X_{\text{SIZE}}$$
$$(0.593)\ (0.004) \qquad (0.004) \qquad\quad (0.004) \qquad\quad (0.030) \qquad (0.059) \qquad (0.008)$$

$$R^2 = 43.7\%$$
$$N = 1001$$

standard errors mean less precise estimates. Nevertheless, differences between the two sets of coefficients are small. This is often the case when correctives for violation of assumptions are invoked, and it holds in most applications of multilevel regression.

We see, however, that five of the seven standard errors are smaller in Table 1.3 after corrections for heteroscedasticity. Again, this is what we would expect, since heteroscedasticity yields inflated standard errors of OLS regression coefficients. These differences too are small. Furthermore, decisions as to the statistical significance of unstandardized regression coefficients are the same for both corrected and uncorrected analyses.

The most conspicuous difference between the two analyses is manifest in R^2 values, with R^2 substantially larger for the EGLS equation. Over the past 30 years, however, regression analysts have become a good deal less interested in R^2 increments, giving most of their attention to identification of relationships that are comparatively stable or explicably different from time to time and from place to place (Blalock, 1964; Duncan, 1975; Wittink, 1988).

Finally, if we compare the scatterplot in Figure 1.2 with the scatterplot in Figure 1.1, we see that the EGLS procedure for correcting for heteroscedasticity, while effective, is far from perfect. Heteroscedasticity is less strikingly evident in Figure 1.2, but we still find that the residual variance, on average, diminishes as school size increases. This is an approximate correction, but a correction nonetheless.

In general terms, what did we just do? We acknowledged that OLS regression has a set of assumptions that must be satisfied if we are to get defensible parameter estimates. We detected violation of one of the assumptions in the form of heteroscedasticity. We used one of the easiest-to-apply procedures to make an approximate correction for that violation, and we estimated an equation with suitably precise parameter estimates (Kennedy, 2003, pp, 133–156). We noted, moreover, that the differences between corrected and uncorrected results were small.

Throughout this process, there was never any doubt that we were doing regression analysis. We were just trying to make regression applicable

Residual Variance

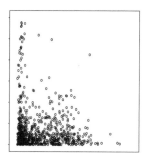

School Size

FIGURE 1.2. Heteroscedasticity approximately corrected: Residual variance by school size.

to a broader range of specific circumstances. When we finished, we acknowledged that consequences of invoking the EGLS correctives were not large, and reasonable observers might be skeptical concerning claims that much of anything was gained. Given the tentative and coarse-grained nature of knowledge in the social and behavioral sciences, perhaps we erred in the direction of undue precision–but perhaps not.

Whatever the long-term value of remedial measures such as EGLS, they exemplify the sort of corrective process we engage in when we employ multilevel regression analysis. Viewed in this way, multilevel analysis is rightly understood as but one part of a long-term effort to permit more effective use of multiple regression analysis when one or more of its assumptions have been violated.

1.5   IT'S JUST REGRESSION UNDER SPECIFIC CIRCUMSTANCES

Consistent with this tradition, multilevel modeling can be usefully viewed as a better way of doing regression analysis under specific circumstances. The circumstances are those in which observations, such as students, are *nested* or grouped in identifiable contexts, such as classrooms, schools, and districts.

Grouping may give rise to interesting contextual effects and cross-level interaction effects, as well as easy-to-miss but consequential methodological problems (Iversen, 1991). As such, explicitly acknowledging grouping through the use of multilevel regression analysis provides both improved analytical opportunities and a means of effectively addressing troublesome statistical difficulties, such as dependence among nested observations and correlated residuals.

Recognition of the importance of nesting is not new in the social and behavioral sciences. A conspicuous example from the early 1980s is Barr and Dreeben's insightful and widely read 1983 book *How Schools Work*, in which IQ is treated both as a characteristic of individual students and, in the aggregate, as a characteristic of ability groups in which students are nested.

To gauge the independent effects of IQ at the individual and group levels, Barr and Dreeben constructed manifest variable path models, with standardized regression coefficients estimated via OLS. This is a perfectly legitimate approach, so long as the inherently single-level nature of OLS regression is consistent with the analytical task at hand. In Barr and Dreeben's research, however, that was not the case.

An inherently single-level analysis means that *both* individual IQ *and* aggregated group IQ will be treated as characteristics of *individual students*. Nesting is nominally acknowledged in the form of group mean IQ, *but*, wittingly or not, nesting is effectively ignored by simply plugging both individual-level and group-level variables into the same OLS regression equation where both variables have the same analytical status.

While acknowledging the powerfully suggestive value of early research such as that reported in *How Schools Work*, we need a more informative and methodologically defensible way to deal with nesting. At this point, multilevel analysis becomes a valuable technique for broadening the applicability of conventional regression analysis.

1.6   JUMPING THE GUN TO A MULTILEVEL ILLUSTRATION

For a moment, we'll get *way* ahead of ourselves. We will use Tables 1.4, 1.5, and 1.6 to illustrate the meaning of multilevel analysis for data organized into nested levels, with individual observations thereby rendered dependent. Our objective is much the same as with Tables 1.1 and 1.3, used to illustrate the consequences of EGLS for heteroscedasticity. Specifically, when a regression assumption has been violated—in this case, independent observations—what happens when correctives are brought to bear?

Using data from the Child Development Supplement of the Panel Study of Income Dynamics (Institute for Social Research, 2003), we want to identify factors that explain variability in total family income. We begin by calculating the intraclass correlation coefficient, a statistic that measures the degree of dependence among observations nested within states. There is, of course, a huge conceptual, social, and geographical gap between the individual and the state (Belanger & Eagles, 2005). In the absence of intervening units such as counties, however, we will work with what is available.

The intraclass correlation coefficient tells us the proportion of income variability that occurs between states rather than within states. Though the numerical value of the coefficient in this instance is small ($r = 0.051$), we shall learn that even a very weak intraclass correlation can substantially deflate standard errors of regression coefficients (Singer, 1987; Kreft & De Leeuw, 1998).

In spite of the existence of nesting-engendered intraclass correlation, for illustrative purposes we begin with a conventional OLS multiple regression analysis. Total family income in units of $1000 ($Y_{INCOME}$) is the dependent variable, and we have just two independent variables: race of the household head simplified into two categories, Black or White (X_{BLACK}, coded 1 if Black and 0 if White); and years of educational attainment of the household head ($X_{EDUCATION}$). This is an inadequate specification, to be sure, but it is a useful point of departure.

The results reported in Table 1.4 are simple enough: Families headed by someone who is Black have, on average, an annual income of $29,213 less than families headed by someone who is White, and each level of educational attainment for the family head corresponds, on average, to an additional $22,880 annually. (Standard errors are in parentheses.)

TABLE 1.4. OLS Family Income Function

$$Y_{INCOME}{}^a = 84.156 - 29.213X_{BLACK1} + 22.880X_{EDUCATION1}$$
$$\quad\quad\quad (2.464)\quad (9.688)\quad\quad\quad\quad (1.966)$$

$$R^2 = 9.2\%$$
$$N = 1524$$

Note. ^{a}For the sake of simplicity, in this example we have not sought to compensate for the rightward skew of family income, so we are not using natural logarithms of Y_{INCOME}.

We may suspect, however, that not only individual characteristics of family heads are important; contextual variables may make a difference as well. Still with OLS, and with the state as the context or group, X_{BLACK1} is aggregated to the state level to give the percentage of family heads in each state who are Black (X_{BLACK2}), and $X_{EDUCATION1}$ is aggregated to the state level, yielding the state-level mean for level of educational attainment for household heads, $X_{EDUCATION2}$.

Beyond that, we may surmise that there may be specific interaction effects at work in accounting for annual income differences among families. The relationship between $Y_{INCOME1}$ and X_{BLACK1} may vary with the percentage of Black household heads in the state, and the relationship between $Y_{INCOME1}$ and $X_{EDUCATION1}$ may vary with the mean educational level of household heads in the state. In response, two multiplicative interaction terms are created: $X_{BLACK2} * X_{BLACK1}$ and $X_{EDUCATION2} * X_{EDUCATION1}$. The respecified OLS regression equation is reported in Table 1.5.

Three explanatory factors have statistically significant unstandardized coefficients: $X_{EDUCATION2}$, $X_{EDUCATION1}$, and X_{BLACK2}. With a more adequate OLS regression model specification, we see that families headed by a Black have, on average, an annual family income \$39,373 less than families headed by a White; each additional year of educational attainment by the household head yields, on average, an annual family income increment of about \$25,232; and for each increment in a *state's* mean educational level for household heads, annual family income increases, on average, by \$8351.

At this point, we decide to take another step toward proper regression model specification. We explicitly acknowledge that we are working with hierarchically organized, nested data, and we abandon OLS in favor of the soon-to-be-familiar tools of multilevel regression. The concrete results of this change in analytical approach are reported in Table 1.6.

To obtain the multilevel results in Table 1.6, you can just look at your computer screen and follow the steps outlined in SPSS Routine 1.1. Much of the output will be uninterpretable to readers who are new to multilevel regression. This SPSS routine is included with our jumping-the-gun example for those who like to begin analyzing data as soon as possible, even with a very imperfect understanding of the procedure being used. Some of us gain confidence from the knowledge that once we have mastered concepts and statistical procedures, we will not be stymied by inability to use pertinent software. Other readers may choose to skip over this until later, coming back to use it as a step-by-step guide for doing conventional multilevel analyses with SPSS.

TABLE 1.5. OLS Family Income Function Respecified

$$Y_{INCOME1} = 87.490 - 39.373X_{BLACK1} + 25.232X_{EDUCATION1} - 2.10X_{BLACK2} + 8.351X_{EDUCATION2}$$
$$(2.507)\ (12.633) \qquad\quad (2.188) \qquad\qquad (25.122) \qquad (3.056)$$

$$+\ 116.377X_{BLACK2} * X_{BLACK1} - 0.083X_{EDUCATION2} * X_{EDUCATION1}$$
$$(82.276) \qquad\qquad\qquad (1.268)$$

$$R^2 = 11.8\%$$
$$N = 1478$$

TABLE 1.6. Multilevel Regression Analysis of Family Income

$$Y_{INCOME1} = 85.328 - 39.712X_{BLACK1} + 24.030X_{EDUCATION1} - 2.706X_{BLACK2} + 5.038X_{EDUCATION2}$$
$$\phantom{Y_{INCOME1} = }(3.921)\quad(12.448)\qquad\quad(2.739)\qquad\qquad(34.115)\qquad\quad(4.319)$$

$$+\ 113.164X_{BLACK2} * X_{BLACK1} - 0.072X_{EDUCATION2} * X_{EDUCATION1}$$
$$(82.147)\qquad\qquad\qquad(1.514)$$

$$R_1^2 = 7.0\%$$
$$N_1 = 1478$$
$$N_2 = 49$$

Near the bottom of the SPSS output, values for the intercept and slopes, along with their standard errors, appear in the ESTIMATE and STD. ERROR columns of the box labeled ESTIMATES OF FIXED EFFECTS. This is the information reported in Table 1.6.

The additional output, especially ESTIMATES OF COVARIANCE PARAMETERS, is new to users of OLS regression and essential to understanding multilevel regression. As we proceed through our presentation, we will learn to understand and apply the additional information. For now, however, we will focus exclusively on the intercept and the slopes, which are interpreted just as the intercept and slopes in OLS regression are.

SPSS Routine 1.1. Multilevel Regression Analysis of Family Income

1. Open the SPSS data file and click on ANALYZE.
2. Go to MIXED MODELS and click on LINEAR.
3. Since the state is the level-two grouping variable in which individuals are nested, insert the state identifier into the SUBJECTS box.
4. Click on CONTINUE; insert family income as the dependent variable into the DEPENDENT VARIABLE box; and insert the independent variables X_{BLACK1}, $X_{EDUCATION1}$, X_{BLACK2}, and $X_{EDUCATION2}$, and the cross-level interaction terms X_{BLACK2} * X_{BLACK1} and $X_{EDUCATION2}$ * $X_{EDUCATION1}$, into the COVARIATE(S) box.
5. Click on FIXED at the bottom of the screen. In the small box in the middle of the screen, change FACTORIAL to MAIN EFFECTS. Move the independent variables and cross-level interaction terms from the FACTORS AND COVARIATES box to the MODEL box.
6. Click on CONTINUE.
7. Click on the RANDOM button at the bottom of the screen. The state identifier is already in the SUBJECTS box, and now we also insert it into the COMBINATIONS box.
8. In the small box in the middle of the screen, change FACTORIAL to MAIN EFFECTS.
9. Near the top of the screen, click on INCLUDE INTERCEPT, and move the independent variables X_{BLACK1} and $X_{EDUCATION1}$ into the MODEL box.
10. Just above INCLUDE INTERCEPT, select UNSTRUCTURED.
11. Click on CONTINUE, and then click on the STATISTICS button.
12. On the left, under MODEL STATISTICS, select PARAMETER ESTIMATES and TESTS FOR COVARIANCE PARAMETERS.
13. Click on CONTINUE and click on OK.

Researchers who became comfortable with SPSS using syntax language may do their analyses in that way, simply by clicking on the PASTE button to the right of the DEPENDENT VARIABLE box. Begin by entering a dependent variable in the DEPENDENT VARIABLE box, click on PASTE, and there it is! Analysts who prefer working with the Windows interface but who would like to see what their SPSS routine looks like in syntax language may click on PASTE any time after entering a dependent variable.

With so many more explanatory factors serving simultaneously as controls, it is to be expected that the coefficients and standard errors for the independent variables in Table 1.4 will be substantially different from corresponding measures in Tables 1.5 and 1.6. It may seem surprising, however, to see that the regression coefficients in Tables 1.5 and 1.6 are, for the most part, quite similar. After all, in ways that we shall discuss at length, the multilevel regression model is conceptually and statistically much better suited to the analysis at hand. In contrast to OLS regression, multilevel regression has an inherently hierarchical structure, and it is designed to deal with nested data.

Recall, however, that when we compared the OLS and EGLS analyses from Tables 1.1 and 1.3, the regression coefficients were nearly the same, but the standard errors were, on average, smaller with EGLS. When comparing Tables 1.5 and 1.6, we see that the OLS and multilevel coefficients are, for the most part, nearly the same, but the multilevel regression standard errors, on average, are larger. This becomes especially clear and consequential when we compare the slopes for $X_{EDUCATION2}$ in the OLS and multilevel models: The $X_{EDUCATION2}$ slope is statistically significant in the OLS analysis but not in the multilevel analysis.

When comparing OLS and multilevel regression results, we will *often* find just what we have found here: small coefficient differences coupled with typically larger standard errors for the multilevel estimates. As with this example, we will see that statistically significant results are harder to find with multilevel regression.

At this point, nevertheless, one may understandably feel obliged once again to raise the all-important question: Why bother? Why use multilevel regression analysis in the first place? The gains, at least to some well-informed and experienced analysts, may seem small indeed. In response, let's remember that, as with EGLS, established regression correctives are often disappointing in just the same way that multilevel regression may be: A lot of additional effort leads to analytical improvements that are less compelling than we may have expected. Beyond that, we should ask ourselves just how important it is to gain a bit of precision in coefficient estimation, to avoid deflated standard errors, and to avoid misleading results from tests of significance. After we have completed our account of multilevel regression, we will be in a position to give better-informed answers to questions such as these.

1.7   SUMMING UP

Regression analysis, as we commonly understand that procedure, has been used in applied work for nearly a century. The first edition of Ezekiel and Fox's (1959) classic text *Methods of Correlation and Regression Analysis* was published by Ezekiel in 1930, and the 1930 volume contains references to applications of regression published as early as 1917.

With subsequent editions and printings, this seminal statement got longer and manifested a shift in emphasis from correlation to regression. The third edition contained a heuristic introduction to the very contemporary topic of simultaneous equation models (Ezekiel & Fox, 1959). Since simultaneity results in the error term's being correlated with an explanatory factor, all coefficients are estimated with bias. The development of instrumental variable methods for estimating simultaneous equations is but one more example of a regression corrective being developed to deal with a violation of one or more of the usual OLS assumptions, enabling regression analysts to address interesting questions that otherwise would be off limits.

Simultaneous equation models are often used in rigorous causal analyses, sometimes taking the form of path models, with nonexperimental data. Many of us who were students or practitioners in the late 1960s and throughout the 1970s trace the development of path analysis to Duncan's influential article (Duncan, 1966) and widely read textbook (Duncan, 1975). As Duncan and others have conspicuously noted, however, the first applications of recursive path models were made much earlier by Wright (Office of the Secretary, 1994; Wolfle, 2003). Wright's first published path model on the heritability of patterns of coloration among guinea pigs has a startlingly contemporary look and interpretation (Wright, 1920). But what was Wright doing? Simply trying to find a way to make regression analysis more informative by constructing testable causal models.

In the 1960s and 1970s, however, the social science literature on path analysis did nothing quite so well as obscure the fact that path analysis was simply a system of OLS regression equations organized and interpreted in a specific way (see, e.g., the collection edited by Borgatta & Bohrnstedt, 1969). Today, however, some of the same authors who 40 years ago rendered path analysis hopelessly obscure to experienced users of multiple regression have managed to make it sufficiently accessible to be included in usable form in introductory texts (Knoke, Bohrnstedt, & Mee, 2002).

Statistical tools may have a natural history that spans the range from new, overused, and hopelessly obscure, all the way to established, applied as needed, and reasonably accessible. This certainly is the case with structural equation modeling, a melding of principles taken from simultaneous equations, path modeling, and modern measurement theory. To see the transition from obscurity to accessibility, one need only compare Joreskog's seminal papers (e.g., Joreskog, 1973) and earlier versions of LISREL software with Kline's 2005 text and Byrne's (2001) *Structural Equation Modeling with Amos*. Nevertheless, even in recently published, reader-friendly treatments, the fact that structural equation modeling is best construed as but one of many correctives permitting more informative use of multiple regression analysis is understated, disguised, or completely unacknowledged.

The purpose of our account of multilevel regression is to facilitate the process whereby a mathematically arcane, difficult-to-use, and sometimes overvalued statistical procedure becomes routinely available for judicious application by applied researchers asking interesting questions. We have taken the tack that this can best be accomplished by emphasizing rather than giving short shrift to parallels with OLS multiple regression analysis. In fact, we have construed multilevel analysis as just another way of doing regression analysis under specific circumstances. The circumstances are those in which data are nested, and nesting produces within-group homogeneity.

Multilevel analysis enables us to accommodate dependent observations and correlated residuals, while providing analytical opportunities in the form of contextual variables and cross-level interaction terms. These additional terms were used in conventional OLS regression equations long before multilevel regression came along. In most instances, the two procedures yield similar coefficient estimates with comparable interpretations. With nesting, however, OLS estimators have deflated standard errors, making tests of significance misleading. OLS software, moreover, routinely employs an incorrect number of degrees of freedom for contextual variables and cross-level interaction terms.

Multilevel regression, in other words, is but one of the many correctives developed over the past century to enable regression analysts to make their work more informative. The farther we stray from this fundamental fact, the more difficult it becomes to learn multilevel regression.

1.8   USEFUL RESOURCES

Ezekiel, M., & Fox, K. (1959) *Methods of Correlation and Regression Analysis: Linear and Curvilinear* (3rd ed.). New York: Wiley.

For readers with little or no knowledge of regression analysis, this old text can still be useful. Though now out of print, it is available through Amazon.com and other online vendors. Some of the examples are so dated as to be quaint, and the book is replete with the kind of short-cut computational formulas that were routinely employed before high-speed digital computers became widely available. Nevertheless, the authors present a good deal of valuable material in easy-to-read form. If the reader ignores the formulas and focuses on conceptual development, this is a good introduction to the rudiments of simple and multiple regression analysis. Most of the badly outdated and extraneous material can be avoided by covering just Chapters 1–9, 11, 17, 21, 22, and 25. When the book is read in this way, Ezekiel and Fox enable the reader to focus on the nature of regression analysis without getting lost in narrowly specific technical details.

Gujarati, D. (2006) *Essentials of Econometrics*. New York: McGraw-Hill.

Up-to-date and reasonably comprehensive, this may be the most accessible regression text for the modern reader who has completed a first course in statistics. It is easier to read than the same author's *Basic Econometrics* (Gujarati, 2003) but covers less material. Comparing the text by Gujarati with the one produced by Ezekiel and Fox powerfully reinforces the judgment that the history of regression analysis has been largely a process of finding correctives and procedures to make OLS regression applicable to a broader range of interesting issues without violating essential assumptions. As with most of the econometrics texts commonly used to teach and learn regression analysis, Gujarati's work requires little or no knowledge of economics. The statistical techniques introduced are applicable to a broad range of disciplines.

Wooldridge, J. (2002) *Introductory Econometrics* (2nd ed.). Cincinnati, OH: South-Western.

This volume is a bit more mathematical than Gujarati's text, but still far more readable than most introductions to regression analysis. Wooldridge gets to useful applications of *multiple* regression more quickly than Gujarati, and this enhances the value of his book, especially for students who are just starting out. As Gujarati does, Wooldridge often uses examples that include sets of predictors spanning more than one level of analysis. Nevertheless, neither Wooldridge nor Gujarati acknowledges the value of random coefficient regression or multilevel regression. This anomaly is consistent with the view that applied statistics varies in important ways from one discipline to another. Nevertheless, much of the credit for developing random coefficient regression models rightly goes to econometricians such as Swamy (1971).

Schroeder, L., Sjoquist, D., & Stephan, P. (1986) *Understanding Regression Analysis: An Introductory Guide*. Beverly Hills, CA: Sage.

Lewis-Beck, M. (1980) *Applied Regression: An Introduction*. Beverly Hills, CA: Sage.

Retherford, R., & Choe, M. (1993) *Statistical Models for Causal Analysis*. New York: Wiley, pp. 1–68.

Heck, R., & Thomas, S. (2000) *An Introduction to Multilevel Modeling Techniques*. Mahwah, NJ: Erlbaum, pp. 37–52.

The two easy-to-read Sage monographs are useful as preliminary or ancillary readings in first courses in regression, and much the same is true of the first two chapters of Retherford and Choe's text. For students who are having trouble with Gujarati, Wooldridge, or other standard introductory texts, the material contained in these brief accounts may be helpful. Each provides the sort of overview that enables students to place detailed treatments of specific topics in a coherent context. This helps students understand just what we are trying to accomplish with all the tests, correctives, and relatively advanced analytical procedures that make up the bulk of textbooks such as those by Gujurati and Wooldridge. Heck and Thomas's very brief, elegantly written overview of multiple regression can be read with benefit, along with any or all of the other three volumes listed above.

Kennedy, P. (2003) *A Guide to Econometrics* (5th ed.). Cambridge, MA: MIT Press.

This fifth edition of Peter Kennedy's very useful volume is 623 pages long. The first edition (Kennedy, 1979), published 24 years earlier, ran 175 pages. Throughout the various editions and a 250% increase in page length, *A Guide to Econometrics* has remained what it was at the outset: a *catalogue* of regression analysis correctives. The author explicitly acknowledges that his objective has been to compile an accessible repository of the rapidly growing list of tests and procedures available to make regression analysis more generally applicable and informative.

Though Kennedy does not acknowledge multilevel regression as such, the following passage is instructive:

> Not all instances of autocorrelated errors relate to time series data. Suppose you have micro [individual-level] data on wages and other characteristics of workers located in several different industries. You are interested in the impact of different characteristics on wages and so add measures of industry characteristics to the set of regressors. Workers in the same industry are likely to have correlated errors because they all share the influence of unmeasured characteristics of that industry. (Kennedy, 2003, p. 150)

This is an unambiguous acknowledgment of one important consequence of the nesting of individual observation within groups: Correlations among residuals may artificially deflate standard errors of regression coefficients, rendering tests of significance unreliable. There is nothing remarkable about this quotation except that, in sharp contrast to the existing literature on multilevel regression, it uses conventional language—expressions such as "autocorrelated errors"—to identify a primary consequence of nesting.

One might respond by judging this to be excruciatingly obvious. To those just learning to make sense of multilevel regression, however, it may not be obvious at all. By emphasizing the distinctiveness of multilevel analysis and failing to make use of opportunities to discuss it in well-known and broadly applicable language, authors needlessly mystify their material.

2

The Meaning of Nesting

2.1   CHAPTER INTRODUCTION

The nesting of observations within groups is fundamental to multilevel modeling. In fact, nesting is the primary reason for doing multilevel analysis. Without nesting, grouping, or clustering, multilevel analysis loses its reason for being. As it turns out, whether by design or as an intrinsic or emergent quality, nesting is ubiquitous, taking an inexhaustible variety of forms.

Whatever its methodological consequences, nesting is a concept that should be of first importance to students of any discipline that gives attention to contextual factors, rather than focusing exclusively on individual-level variables. Nevertheless, the obvious importance of nesting is often overlooked. This is due in part to the peculiar world views that pervade different disciplines, providing both conceptual tools and unacknowledged assumptions, with the assumptions sometimes serving as blinders (Alford & Friedland, 1985; Halsey, Lauder, Brown, & Wells, 1997; Alford, 1998).

Ironically, mainstream American economics, which has yielded so many important developments in regression-based statistical procedures, is largely indifferent to the methodological difficulties and substantive opportunities occasioned by nesting. The high-profile public policy-making tool known as *human capital theory* is a case in point (see, e.g., Mincer, 1974; Farkas, 1996; Woodhall, 1997).

The literature on human capital is often technically demanding, but the basic causal process is quite simple:

$$\text{EDUCATION} \rightarrow \text{PRODUCTIVITY} \rightarrow \text{INCOME}$$

In other words, people who work for a living invest in themselves by improving their levels of educational attainment. As a result, they become more productive in the workplace. Productivity is rewarded with increased income.

Seminal affirmations of human capital theory have placed near-exclusive emphasis on characteristics of individuals (Schultz, 1960; Becker, 1964, 1993; Heckman & Krueger, 2003). With rare exceptions, consequences of investments in oneself have been treated as independent of variability in the social, political, and economic contexts in which people are located (cf. Carnoy, 2001).

One consequence of this individual-level orientation has been fairly relentless "school bashing" by American economists (see, e.g., McMurrer & Sawhill, 1998). When, as during the past 30 years in the United States, expectations engendered by human capital theory are not met, the simple casual chain becomes problematic. Since the PRODUCTIVITY → INCOME connection has become sacrosanct in mainstream economic theory (Becker, 1993), the break must occur at the EDUCATION → PRODUCTIVITY nexus. Public education is presumed to be a lazy monopoly, incapable of producing a productive workforce without thoroughgoing reform.

Schwarz (1997), however, has offered evidence that human capital theory works much as expected *only* if working people have the institutionalized political resources to secure payoffs for productivity. In western Europe, human capital theory works pretty well. In the United States, by contrast, levels of educational attainment are not matched by levels of income attainment, and exacerbation of economic inequality is one result (Newman, 1994, 1999; Uchitelle, 2006).

If ever there were a theoretical perspective that demanded emphasis on nesting, human capital theory is it! The simple causal chain that undergirds this perspective is a useful point of departure, but obvious and important contextual factors— manifestations of *nesting*!—determine the nature and strength of the relationships among the variables in the model. With multilevel regression analysis, these factors can be explicitly incorporated. Regression coefficients themselves, such as the slope that measures the PRODUCTIVITY → INCOME relationship, may be treated as functions of overarching contextual factors, especially measurable changes in the occupational distribution. Failure to acknowledge nesting and its consequences results in a misspecified model.

There is nothing new about the judgment that contemporary economics gives insufficient attention to contextual factors. Moreover, some commonplace econometric tools such as the Chow test (Gujarati, 2003) were developed in recognition of contextual differences. However, when the number of categories of a contextual variable (e.g., labor markets nested in very different countries) becomes large, usual methods of dealing with interaction effects are rendered hopelessly cumbersome. At this point, the virtues of multilevel regression analysis become conspicuous.

By way of illustration, we will use a U.S. data set reported by Card (1995) that permits evaluation of human capital theoretic causal processes (Wooldridge, 2002). Respondents' education is measured in years of schooling completed, and income is expressed in terms of hourly wage. Because individual-level productivity is notoriously difficult to measure (Thurow, 1983; Lowery, Petty, & Thompson, 1995; Boudreau & Boswell, 1997), we will use respondents' score on a standardized test of knowledge of the world of work as a crude proxy for productivity. Given these operational definitions, the human capital theory schematic becomes more concrete:

YEARS OF SCHOOLING $\rightarrow$ KNOWLEDGE $\rightarrow$ HOURLY WAGE LOGGED

Say we estimate an OLS simple regression equation such as the following:

$$Y_{WAGE} = a + b_{YEARS}X_{YEARS}$$

If human capital theory works as its proponents claim, a positive coefficient for YEARS OF SCHOOLING (X_{YEARS}) should be substantially diminished when KNOWLEDGE (X_{KNOW}) is introduced into the regression equation:

$$Y_{WAGE} = a + b_{YEARS}X_{YEARS} + b_{KNOW}X_{KNOW}$$

Consistent with this, when all 3009 cases are used in the analysis, the simple and multiple OLS regression results are as follows:

$$Y_{WAGE} = 5.742 + 0.043X_{YEARS}$$
$$Y_{WAGE} = 5.454 + 0.017X_{YEARS} + 0.018X_{KNOW}$$

The unstandardized regression coefficient for X_{YEARS} remains statistically significant, but its numerical value becomes much smaller when our productivity proxy is introduced. This is precisely what human capital theory implies.

What we do not see, however, is that when the data set is divided into nine geographical regions, the regression results vary substantially from place to place. When we regress Y_{WAGE} on X_{YEARS}, the coefficient for X_{YEARS} varies from a statistically nonsignificant ($p > .05$) 0.017 to a statistically significant ($p < .001$) 0.053. After our productivity proxy has been introduced, the same coefficient varies from a statistically nonsignificant ($p > .05$) −0.003 to a statistically significant ($p < .001$) 0.021.

Similarly, with X_{YEARS} in the equation, from region to region the coefficient for X_{KNOW} varies from a statistically significant ($p < .05$) 0.011 to a statistically significant ($p < .001$) 0.023. As we would expect, moreover, when the residuals for the multiple regression equation with all 3009 cases are used as the dependent variable in a one-way analysis of variance with region as the independent variable, the F value is statistically significant ($p < .001$).

This degree of variability in regression slopes makes a strong case for paying attention to nesting. Inasmuch as the earnings attainment processes intrinsic to human capital theory vary from place to place, they merit investigation with multilevel analysis. This would give us added confidence in our coefficient estimates and inferential tests, and we may even be able to explain *why* coefficients vary.

2.2   NESTING ILLUSTRATED: SCHOOL ACHIEVEMENT AND NEIGHBORHOOD QUALITY

The nature of nesting and corresponding contextual effects are easy to illustrate further. Research concerning neighborhood effects on school achievement provides an instructive example. Imagine a cohort of 331 beginning kindergarten students in 12 randomly selected elementary schools located in two contiguous counties in Appalachian West Virginia (Bickel, Smith, & Eagle, 2002). The children, with few exceptions, are from impoverished rural families living in impoverished rural neighborhoods.

In spite of shared poverty, however, the neighborhoods vary with respect to measured quality (cf. Furstenburg, Cook, Eccles, Elder, & Samerhoff, 1990). If a sense of stability, safety, social cohesion, and shared world view pervades a neighborhood, students bring this with them to school. In the aggregate, this yields a foundation for development of an in-school neighborhood—a school-level context in which individual students are nested—that provides a secure and hopeful environment. Children are not socially isolated, culturally adrift, and precociously fatalistic, as pervasive typifications of poor rural areas would have it (Inkeles & Smith, 1974). Instead, this kind of Appalachian neighborhood—this kind of context—provides the social and cultural wherewithal for learning to occur (see also Bickel & Maynard, 2004).

It is useful to recognize, however, that neighborhood quality, in spite of its nesting-intensive sound, need not be construed only as a contextual variable. It can also be treated as a characteristic of individuals simply by assigning neighborhood quality values to each individual in a data set. One of the virtues of multilevel regression is that it enables us to treat a variable such as neighborhood quality as **both** a characteristic of individuals **and** a contextual variable in the **same** analysis. We can clarify this with our 12-school West Virginia data set.

Figures 2.1 through 2.3 below illustrate three different kinds of relationships between neighborhood quality and a standardized measure of vocabulary achievement, the Woodcock–Johnson 22 (Woodcock & Johnson, 1990; Bickel & McDonough, 1998). In spite of the contextual-sounding nature of neighborhood quality as a concept, only one relationship, displayed in Figure 2.3, was estimated with explicit conceptual and statistical acknowledgment of nesting.

Table 2.1 and Figure 2.1 depict the relationship between individual students' vocabulary achievement at the beginning of kindergarten and neighborhood quality measured

TABLE 2.1. Reading Achievement for West Virginia Kindergarten Students: Individual-Level Analysis with OLS

$$Y = 10.233 + 0.325X_{INCOME1} + 0.208X_{EDUCATION1} + 0.330X_{HEADSTART1} - 0.586X_{ETHNIC1} + 0.093X_{NEIGHBOR1}$$
$$(0.228)\ (0.113) \qquad (0.154) \qquad\qquad (0.537) \qquad\qquad (0.812) \qquad\qquad (0.034)$$

$$R^2 = 10.4\%$$
$$N = 308$$

at the student level. Controls are included for the influence of family income, parents' education, ethnicity, and Head Start participation. Variable name subscripts make it clear that we are analyzing individual-level data.

We have found an interesting relationship that merits further investigation. However, since neighborhood quality is construed exclusively as a characteristic of *individuals*, this is *not* an analysis that acknowledges nesting. With nearly 22% of the variability in reading achievement occurring between schools (intraclass correlation coefficient = 0.216), it certainly should be, but it's not.

Given a comparable set of control variables, this time measured as characteristics of schools, Table 2.2 and Figure 2.2 illustrate the relationship between *school mean* vocabulary achievement and neighborhood quality measured at the *school level*. Variable name subscripts indicate that we are analyzing level-two data. This relationship too may prompt further empirical inquiry. However, since all variables are measured at the school level and all are construed as characteristics of schools, this is another analysis that does *not* involve nesting.

Interestingly, while Figures 2.1 and 2.2 both report regressions of vocabulary achievement on neighborhood quality, they have very different slopes. Both are positive, but the slope estimated with individual-level data in Figure 2.1 is 0.093; the slope esti-

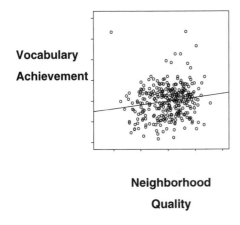

FIGURE 2.1. Individual vocabulary achievement by neighborhood quality at student level.

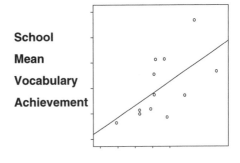

FIGURE 2.2. School mean vocabulary achievement by neighborhood quality at school level.

TABLE 2.2. Reading Achievement for West Virginia Kindergarten Students: School-Level Analysis with OLS

$$Y = 10.222 - 0.682X_{INCOME2} - 2.536X_{EDUCATION2} + 2.214X_{HEADSTART2} - 8.014X_{ETHNIC2} + 0.932X_{NEIGHBOR2}$$
$$(0.744)\ (1.644)\qquad (2.474)\qquad\quad (5.520)\qquad\quad (8.642)\qquad\quad (0.515)$$

$$R^2 = 65.7\%$$
$$N = 12$$

mated with school-level data in Figure 2.2 is more than nine times as large, 0.932, though with so few cases it is not statistically significant.

Differences of this magnitude, sometimes involving different signs, are common-place when comparing analyses of aggregated and nonaggregated data (Kreft & De Leeuw, 1998; Snijders & Bosker, 1999). Moreover, Robinson's (1950) well-known cautionary observations concerning ecological inference still apply with undiminished force. Specifically, making inferences about individuals from grouped data often generates misleading results.

Finally, with controls in place, Table 2.3 and Figure 2.3 display the relationship between individual students' vocabulary achievement and neighborhood quality measured at the level of the student, as in Table 2.1. In this instance, however, the individual students are treated as **nested** within schools. This means that the intercept and the neighborhood quality slope for individuals are permitted to **vary** from school to school. Furthermore, school-to-school variability in the intercept and the neighborhood quality slope are treated as functions of neighborhood quality at the school level. This means that a school-level or contextual measure of neighborhood quality is used as another independent variable, also contributing to explaining variability in the vocabulary achievement dependent variable.

Table 2.3 and Figure 2.3 thus illustrate an analysis that explicitly recognizes nesting. In this instance students are nested within schools. Variable name subscripts indicate that we are using variables measured at the individual level **and** variables measured at the school level. As with Table 1.6 in our annual family income example, we also see a multiplicative interaction term, $X_{\text{NEIGHBOR2}} * X_{\text{NEIGHBOR1}}$, created by using an independent variable measured at two levels—in this case, the individual and the school.

Unfamiliar measures such as R_1^2, the reporting of two sample sizes, and the nature of alternative estimators used in this analysis will be fully explained as we proceed. Moreover, there is additional interpretable output, concerning characteristics of the random coefficients; this output is routinely provided with multilevel regression, but it is new to users of OLS regression. We will introduce this gradually as we learn more about this procedure.

TABLE 2.3. Reading Achievement for West Virginia Kindergarten Students: Multilevel Analysis with Alternative Estimators

$Y = 0.755 + 0.210X_{\text{INCOME1}} + 0.296X_{\text{EDUCATION1}} + 0.301X_{\text{HEADSTART1}} - 0.012X_{\text{ETHNIC1}}$
  (6.494) (0.109)   (0.149)   (0.524)   (0.842)

  $+ 0.074X_{\text{NEIGHBOR1}} + 0.275X_{\text{NEIGHBOR2}} + 0.004X_{\text{NEIGHBOR2}} * X_{\text{NEIGHBOR1}}$
   (0.037)   (0.186)   (0.003)

$$R_1^2 = 14.1\%$$
$$N_1 = 308$$
$$N_2 = 12$$

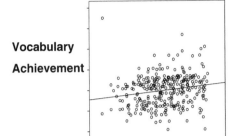

Vocabulary

Achievement

Neighborhood

Quality

FIGURE 2.3. Individual vocabulary
achievement by neighborhood quality,
multilevel results.

For now we may say simply that R_1^2 is a
multilevel regression analogue of the usual R^2
statistic used with OLS regression. Two sample
sizes refer to the students (N_1) nested in
schools (N_2). The alternative estimators are
called *restricted maximum likelihood* (REML).
They are well suited to analyzing data in which
nesting gives rise to group-to-group variability
in intercepts and slopes, meaning that it is useful to estimate intercepts and slopes while permitting them to take on different values from
one school to another.

SPSS Routine 2.1 is the routine for estimating this multilevel equation. Much of the output will be new to readers who have not
worked with multilevel analysis, and application of the routine is optional. As noted for

---

SPSS Routine 2.1. Multilevel Analysis of Vocabulary Achievement

1. Open the SPSS data file and click on ANALYZE.
2. Go to MIXED MODELS and click on LINEAR.
3. Since the school is the level-two grouping variable in which individuals are nested, insert the school identifier into the SUBJECTS box.
4. Click on CONTINUE; insert vocabulary achievement as the dependent variable into the DEPENDENT VARIABLE box; and insert the independent variables $X_{INCOME1}$, $X_{EDUCATION1}$, $X_{HEADSTART1}$, $X_{ETHNIC1}$, $X_{NEIGHBOR1}$, and $X_{NEIGHBOR2}$, and the cross-level interaction term $X_{NEIGHBOR2} * X_{NEIGHBOR1}$, into the COVARIATE(S) box.
5. Click on FIXED at the bottom of the screen. In the small box in the middle of the screen, change FACTORIAL to MAIN EFFECTS. Move the independent variables and cross-level interaction terms from the FACTORS AND COVARIATES box to the MODEL box.
6. Click on CONTINUE.
7. Click on the RANDOM key at the bottom of the screen. The school identifier is already in the SUBJECTS box, and now we also insert it into the COMBINATIONS box.
8. In the small box in the middle of the screen, change FACTORIAL to MAIN EFFECTS.
9. Near the top of the screen, click on INCLUDE INTERCEPT, and move the independent variable $X_{NEIGHBOR1}$ into the MODEL box.
10. Just above INCLUDE INTERCEPT and to the right of COVARIANCE TYPE, select UNSTRUCTURED.
11. Click on CONTINUE, and then click on the STATISTICS button.
12. On the left, under MODEL STATISTICS, select PARAMETER ESTIMATES and TESTS FOR COVARIANCE PARAMETERS.
13. Click on CONTINUE and click on OK.

SPSS Routine 1.1, the primary benefit of actually running the analysis at this stage is gaining confidence in and familiarity with the mechanics of the MIXED MODELS procedure, which makes multilevel regression possible with SPSS. Either SPSS Routine 1.1 or 2.1 can be used as a step-by-step guide for using SPSS with the Windows interface to do conventional multilevel analyses.

The unstandardized slope for individual-level neighborhood quality in Table 2.3, based on a multilevel regression analysis of nested data, is 0.074, not too different from the OLS slope for individual-level data in Table 2.1. If we estimate an OLS regression equation that includes both individual and school-level measures of neighborhood quality, as in Table 2.4, the OLS coefficient for individual-level neighborhood quality and the multilevel coefficient become still more similar. With OLS, of course, slopes and the intercept cannot vary from group to group, so nesting is only simulated. Contextual variables and cross-level interaction terms are tacked on in a jerry-rigged way.

As we move through our discussion, we will learn how to use *both* individual-level *and* group-level variables as explanatory factors in the *same* multilevel regression equation explaining variability in the same individual-level dependent variable, as we have done in Table 2.3. The same equation will include the effects of individual characteristics and the effects of contextual characteristics. In other words, we will learn how to do methodologically creditable, substantively useful analyses of *nested* data without resorting to conceptually crude (even if numerically close) OLS approximations, as in Table 2.4.

As an aside, critics of the research that has found no effects for Head Start often attribute disappointing findings, such as those reported in Table 2.4, to regression model misspecification. Among other objections, the absence of a prior achievement control variable is cited as a serious deficiency (Bickel & McDonough, 1998). If we respecify the equation in Table 2.4 so that the dependent variable is reading achievement at the *end* of kindergarten, with the beginning-of-kindergarten measure as a control, we get the OLS results in Table 2.5.

Addition of a pretest control still leaves us with no Head Start effects. In Chapter 11 we will address the question of Head Start effects, making further regression model specification improvements. Specifically, we will use a multilevel growth model in an effort to give Head Start its due.

TABLE 2.4. Reading Achievement for West Virginia Kindergarten Students: Simulating Multilevel Analysis with OLS

$$Y = -0.755 + 0.277X_{INCOME1} + 0.175X_{EDUCATION1} + 0.377X_{HEADSTART1} - 0.377X_{ETHNIC1}$$
$$(6.494)\ (0.112) \qquad (0.152) \qquad\qquad (0.529) \qquad\qquad (0.800)$$

$$-\ 0.082X_{NEIGHBOR1} + 0.314X_{NEIGHBOR2} + 0.005X_{NEIGHBOR2} * X_{NEIGHBOR1}$$
$$(0.034) \qquad\qquad (0.094) \qquad\qquad (0.004)$$

$$R^2 = 14.0\%$$
$$N = 308$$

TABLE 2.5. Reading Achievement for West Virginia Kindergarten Students: Simulating Multilevel Analysis with OLS; Pretest Included

$$Y = 4.106 + 0.018X_{INCOME1} + 0.055X_{EDUCATION1} - 0.162X_{HEADSTART1} + 0.410X_{ETHNIC1}$$
$$(1.103)\ (0.091) \qquad (0.122) \qquad\qquad (0.428) \qquad\qquad (0.642)$$

$$+\ 0.000X_{NEIGHBOR1} + 0.074X_{NEIGHBOR2} + 0.006X_{NEIGHBOR2} * X_{NEIGHBOR1}$$
$$(0.029) \qquad\qquad (0.080) \qquad\qquad (0.010)$$

$$R^2 = 55.7\%$$
$$N = 308$$

2.3   NESTING ILLUSTRATED: COMPARING PUBLIC AND PRIVATE SCHOOLS

Other examples of nesting and associated contextual effects are numerous. During the 1980s, for example, education research and policy journals shared a near-obsession with comparisons of the effectiveness and equity of public and private schools (Berliner & Biddle, 1995). Arguments offered by proponents of private schooling held that private schools were superior to their public counterparts because they enjoyed a more favorable disciplinary climate, made stronger academic demands on all students, were administratively streamlined, and were better able to promote parental involvement and a sense of community (see, e.g., Coleman & Hoffer, 1987; Chubb & Moe, 1992; see also the more recent work by Benveniste, Carnoy, & Rothstein, 2003). Individual students, as a result, were presumed to be nested in differing educational contexts, depending on whether they attended a public or private school.

The information reported in Figure 2.4 concerns standardized math achievement test scores for 3642 public school students and 3543 private school students. The information is taken from a widely used subset of the High School and Beyond data set (cf. Singer, 1998; Raudenbush & Bryk, 2002).

Descriptive summaries such as this have often been used to illustrate—and sometimes to substantiate!—the claim that private schools are more effective in promoting measured achievement than public schools. Pertinent examples include the very influential report by Coleman, Hoffer, and Kilgore (1982) and the frequently cited account by Chubb and Moe (1992).

If the educational contexts represented by public and private schools did in fact differ in learning-related ways, they would give rise to contextual or group effects. Students nested in differing contexts, as a result, might

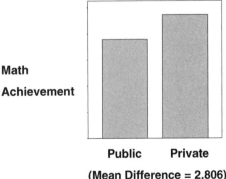

FIGURE 2.4. Public–private school math achievement.

experience enhanced or diminished achievement. These contextual effects typically would manifest the more favorable educational environments provided by private schools. It would be conceptual mistake, therefore, to treat attendance at a public or private school solely as a characteristic of individual students, as has often been done (see, e.g., Coleman et al. 1982). To do so means failing to acknowledge nesting when it is obviously present. The public–private variable, in this instance, should be treated as a gauge or indicator of a group or contextual phenomenon occurring at the school level, rather than a measure made on individual students.

Let us suppose, however, that we erroneously treat the public–private school variable solely as a characteristic of individuals, ignoring the fact that this organizational factor is best understood as a contextual variable. Compounding this error, we treat other independent variables, such as student socioeconomic status (SES), in the same way: We rightly acknowledge SES as a characteristic of individual students, *but* we do not also treat SES as an aggregated contextual factor, a characteristic of schools in which individual students are nested. If we again use the often-cited subset of the High School and Beyond data containing 160 schools and 7185 students, what is the substantive meaning of this misspecification of our regression model?

With math achievement as the dependent variable, Table 2.6 reports the value of the public–private coefficient for an OLS regression equation with the public–private variable and SES both treated as characteristics of individual students, but with no variables representing contextual factors. In addition, using the same dependent variable, Table 2.6 reports the value of the public–private coefficient for an alternative multilevel regression model estimated with REML estimators. REML estimators are the alternatives to OLS used in producing the results reported in Table 2.3. (Standard errors in Table 2.6 are in parentheses.)

Simply using alternative estimators such as REML, of course, does not mean that we are doing multilevel analysis. As we have noted and as we shall further explain, however, REML estimators are better suited to multilevel regression analysis than OLS. Fortunately for all of us, the unstandardized regression coefficients for REML and OLS are interpreted in the same way.

Furthermore, in our regression equation using REML estimators, SES has been treated as a characteristic of individual students *and* as an aggregated contextual characteristic of schools, with the school mean for SES used as the contextual variable. The public–private variable has been treated as a characteristic of schools only. For both the OLS and multilevel REML analyses, a positive coefficient represents an advantage for private high schools.

TABLE 2.6. Public–Private Coefficients

Public–private coefficient without contextual effects = 2.806 (0.155)
Public–private coefficient with SES contextual effect = 1.210 (0.308)

The substantial difference in the size of the unstandardized regression coefficients for the public–private variable is due to differences in regression model specification. With OLS estimators used in the absence of contextual variables, the private school advantage is more than twice as large as when the public–private variable is construed as a contextual factor in a multilevel model.

The difficulties posed by failure to include variables representing contextual effects are further clarified when we inquire about the effect of SES, in aggregated form, at the school level. We learn that an important school-level contextual variable is completely overlooked in the conventional OLS analysis, in which contextual variables have not been included. If we fail to include a variable representing SES aggregated to the school level, the coefficient for the SES contextual variable is constrained to equal zero in the OLS equation. The consequences of this manifestation of regression model misspecification are conspicuously evident in Table 2.7.

We have just seen in Table 2.6 that failure to include SES aggregated to the school level constitutes a troublesome specification error because it results in inflation of the coefficient for the public–private contextual variable. Beyond that, Table 2.7 makes clear that the same kind of specification error prompted us to completely overlook a substantial group-level SES effect. Furthermore, as still another adverse consequence of the same mistake, Table 2.8 suggests that the unstandardized regression coefficient for SES at the individual level may have been slightly overestimated.

Figures 2.5 and 2.6 illustrate the point that the multilevel regression model with contextual effects and REML estimators is more effective than the OLS model in accounting for math achievement differences between public and private school students. Since the multilevel model corrects for particular forms of specification error in the OLS model, this is exactly what we would expect: A correctly specified model does a better job of explaining variability in a dependent variable than a poorly specified model (Gujarati, 2006).

We closed our neighborhood quality illustration of nesting with the promise that eventually we would learn how to use both individual-level and group-level variables as

TABLE 2.7. School-Level SES Coefficients

SES contextual variable excluded: Unstandardized coefficient = 0.000 (N/A)
SES contextual variable included: Unstandardized coefficient = 5.509 (0.376)

TABLE 2.8. Individual-Level SES Coefficients

SES individual-level coefficient with contextual variables excluded = 2.191 (0.117)
SES individual-level coefficient with contextual variable included = 2.133 (0.121)

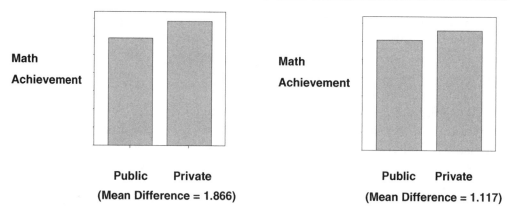

FIGURE 2.5. Public–private school math achievement: OLS adjustment.

FIGURE 2.6. Public–private school math achievement: Multilevel adjustment.

explanatory factors in the same multilevel regression equation. While we have not gotten to the execution stage yet, it is worth emphasizing that the second set of results in Tables 2.6, 2.7, and 2.8 are in fact coefficients taken from one multilevel regression equation, with students nested in schools. The same equation includes both individual-level variables and group-level or contextual variables: it is a multilevel regression equation.

We have already seen such equations for our family income example in Table 1.6 and our reading achievement example in Table 2.3. Though we have not yet worked through specification of the multilevel regression model or estimation of coefficients, standard errors, and summary statistics, it seems useful to continue to jump the gun, looking at the equations that give rise to the results we are discussing. In the process we may compare these results with OLS estimates.

Beginning with a conventional OLS multiple regression equation in which both the public–private variable and SES are treated exclusively as characteristics of individuals, we get the results in Table 2.9. This is the equation that gave us the first set of numbers in Tables 2.6, 2.7, and 2.8.

The multilevel regression equation that gave us the second set of numbers in Tables 2.6, 2.7, and 2.8 is presented in Table 2.10. These estimates have been corrected for the effects of nesting-engendered intraclass correlation, with the intercept and the slope for

TABLE 2.9. Public and Private School Math Achievement: Individual-Level Analysis with OLS Estimators

$$Y = 11.377 + 2.191X_{SES1} + 2.806X_{PRIVATE1}$$
$$\quad (0.109)\ (0.117) \qquad (0.155)$$

$$R^2 = 8.6\%$$
$$N = 7185$$

TABLE 2.10. Public and Private School Math Achievement: Multilevel Analysis with Alternative Estimators

$Y = 12.751 + 2.133X_{SES1} + 5.509X_{SES2} + 1.210X_{PRIVATE2} + 1.035X_{SES2} * X_{SES1} - 1.639X_{PRIVATE2} * X_{SES1}$
  (0.143) (0.121)   (0.376)   (0.308)   (0.299)   (0.240)

$$R_1^2 = 12.6\%$$
$$N_1 = 7185$$
$$N_2 = 160$$

X_{SES1} permitted to vary from school to school. X_{SES2} and $X_{PRIVATE2}$ are contextual variables that help explain variability in student math achievement and contribute to accounting for variability in the random intercept and random slope.

The cross-level interaction terms $X_{SES2} * X_{SES1}$ and $X_{PRIVATE2} * X_{SES1}$ permit us to address two interesting questions raised by the substantive literature comparing public and private schools: Does the relationship between math achievement and individual student SES vary with the SES composition of the school? And does the relationship between math achievement and individual student SES vary with school type, public or private? (see Huang, 2000).

The only difference between SPSS Routine 2.2 and the two already presented is inclusion of a contextual variable. Like SPSS Routines 1.1 and 2.1, SPSS Routine 2.2 can be used as a step-by-step guide for doing conventional multilevel analyses with SPSS.

The estimated coefficients measure the contextual effect of the public–private variable (1.210), the contextual SES effect (5.509), and the individual-level SES effect (2.133). The interaction term $X_{SES2} * X_{SES1}$ tells us that individual-level SES pays off even more handsomely as the average SES of the context provided by a school increases. The interaction term $X_{PRIVATE2} * X_{SES1}$ suggests that individual-level SES advantages and disadvantages are diminished in private schools.

As with Table 2.3, the multilevel regression results in Table 2.10 include some unfamiliar statistics that we briefly defined above. Again, moreover, we acknowledge that there is additional essential output concerning characteristics of the random coefficients, which we will gradually introduce as we proceed.

As we have already explained, moreover, it is useful to bear in mind that differences between coefficients estimated with OLS and with multilevel procedures are often surprisingly small. This holds in spite of the fact that OLS regression analyses are inherently single-level and do not permit intercepts and slopes to vary from group to group. As a case in point, when the contextual variables and cross-level interaction terms from the multilevel model in Table 2.10 are added to the OLS equation in our public–private example, the multilevel coefficients and the OLS coefficients are almost the same, as we see in Table 2.11.

Figure 2.7, moreover, much more closely approximates Figure 2.6: OLS and multilevel adjustments for math achievement give almost exactly the same results when the same individual-level and contextual independent variables and cross-level interaction

---

SPSS Routine 2.2. Multilevel Regression Analysis with Type of School and SES as Contextual Variables

1. Open the SPSS data file and click on ANALYZE.
2. Go to MIXED MODELS and click on LINEAR.
3. Since the school is the level-two grouping variable in which students are nested, insert the school identifier into the SUBJECTS box. This means that individual students are grouped in schools.
4. Click on CONTINUE; insert math achievement as the dependent variable into the DEPENDENT VARIABLE box; and insert the independent variables X_{SES1}, X_{SES2}, and $X_{PRIVATE2}$, and the cross-level interaction terms $X_{SES2} * X_{SES1}$ and $X_{PRIVATE2} * X_{SES1}$, into the COVARIATE(S) box.
5. Click on FIXED at the bottom of the screen. In the small box in the middle of the screen, change FACTORIAL to MAIN EFFECTS. Move the independent variables and cross-level interaction terms from the FACTORS AND COVARIATES box to the MODEL box.
6. Click on CONTINUE.
7. Click on the RANDOM button at the bottom of the screen. The school identifier is already in the SUBJECTS box, and now we also insert it into the COMBINATIONS box.
8. In the small box in the middle of the screen, change FACTORIAL to MAIN EFFECTS.
9. Near the top of the screen, click on INCLUDE INTERCEPT, and move the independent variable X_{SES1} into the MODEL box.
10. Just above INCLUDE INTERCEPT and to the right of COVARIANCE TYPE, select UNSTRUCTURED.
11. Click on CONTINUE, and click on the STATISTICS button.
12. On the left, under MODEL STATISTICS, select PARAMETER ESTIMATES and TESTS FOR COVARIANCE PARAMETERS.
13. Click on CONTINUE and click on OK.

TABLE 2.11. Public and Private School Math Achievement: Simulating Multilevel Analysis with OLS

$$Y = 12.766 + 2.132X_{SES1} + 5.170X_{SES2} + 1.271X_{PRIVATE2} + 1.044X_{SES2} * X_{SES1}$$
$$(0.074)\ (0.112) \qquad (0.191) \qquad (0.158) \qquad\qquad (0.300)$$

$$- 1.642X_{PRIVATE2} * X_{SES1}$$
$$(0.240)$$

$$R_1^2 = 12.6\%$$
$$N_1 = 7185$$
$$N_2 = 160$$

terms are included in both equations. On average, nevertheless, the standard errors in the multilevel regression equation are larger, as we would expect.

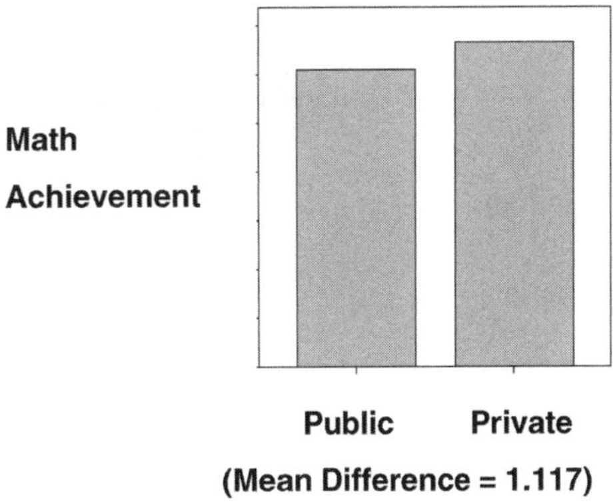

Math Achievement

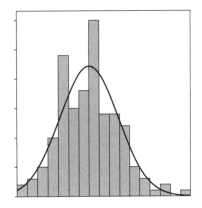

Public   Private
(Mean Difference = 1.117)

2.4 CAUTIONARY COMMENT ON RESIDUALS IN MULTILEVEL ANALYSIS

While comparison of Figures 2.5, 2.6, and 2.7 makes an important point with regard to the effects of proper specification of a regression model, it also sets the stage for a brief cautionary comment regarding the more

FIGURE 2.7. Simulated multilevel adjustment with OLS.

complex nature of residuals in multilevel regression (Diez-Roux, 2002). Figures 2.5, 2.6, and 2.7 were constructed with residuals from OLS and multilevel regression analyses. This works well enough with OLS estimators and with level-one residuals in multilevel analyses (Hilden-Minton, 1995).

Odd as it may seem to long-time users of OLS multiple regression, however, a multilevel model has more than one set of residuals. If a multilevel model has more than two levels, residuals can be estimated for each. One of the limitations of SPSS versions 11.5 through 14.0 is that higher-level residuals cannot be saved in straightforward fashion with a simple command statement. With some extra work, however, they are not too difficult to obtain.

The conceptual basis for higher-level residuals is not hard to understand. For example, if an intercept is permitted to vary from one second-level group to another, the location of the regression line for each group may vary with respect to the reported overall or average regression line. Similarly, if one or more slopes are permitted to vary from group to group, this may be another source of variability for each group's regression line. Random intercepts and random slopes are thus sources of error for estimated values of the dependent variable when it is aggregated to second and higher levels.

Testable assumptions of multilevel regression analysis include normality of level-one residuals and multivariate normality of higher-level residuals. In addition, residuals at different levels are assumed to be uncorrelated and to have uniform variance. Figure 2.8 displays the near-normal distribution of estimated level-two or school-level residuals for the analysis reported in Table 2.10. Figure 2.9 makes

FIGURE 2.8. Estimated school-level residuals.

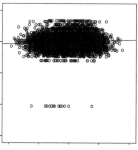

School-Level

Residuals

Individual-Level

Residuals

FIGURE 2.9. School-level residuals regressed on individual-level residuals.

clear that the school-level and individual-level residuals are, as a practical matter, uncorrelated ($r = 0.07$).

Higher-level residuals have gotten a good deal of recent attention because they are sometimes used in research on school effectiveness (Goldstein, Huiqi, Rath, & Hill, 2000; Betebenner, 2004; Leyland, 2004; Thum, 2004). This kind of research tends to be driven by narrowly quantitative gauges of human capital theoretic concepts, such as measures of "value added" to students' standardized test scores.

The usual argument is that some schools do better or worse than we might reasonably expect from their student composition and other factors that can be statistically controlled. Examination of school-level residuals enables us to identify high-performing and low-performing schools, using information such as that presented in Figure 2.10 for the High School and Beyond subsample (Hershberg, Simon, & Lea-Kruger, 2004). (Confidence intervals for level-two residuals are usually part of such a layout, but they are not available with SPSS versions 11.5 through 14.0.)

Analyses of approximately this kind were often done with OLS residuals long before multilevel regression was introduced. As with multilevel regression, the operating assumption was that once extraneous factors such as SES, ethnicity, prior achievement, and gender were statistically controlled, comparison of residuals would tell us which schools were doing better or worse than expected after student characteristics were taken into consideration.

Some authors have suggested, however, that a fair assessment of the substantive value of analyses of higher-order residuals requires the admonition that we not be too quick to embrace this procedure for policy-making purposes (Tanner, Jones, & Treadway, 2000; McCaffery, Lockwood, Koertz, & Hamilton, 2004; Watson, 2004; Brasington & Haurin, 2005; see also Goldstein, 1998). This holds in spite of the enthusiasm of seminal figures in the development of multilevel modeling for immediate use of school effectiveness research of precisely this sort (see, e.g., Goldstein et al., 2000).

Bear in mind what we are doing when we use residuals to compare schools. We have controlled for a more or less readily identifiable, easy-to-measure set of independent variables, and whatever variability is left is attributed to differences in school effectiveness, with effectiveness conceptualized in very narrow terms, and with reasons for school-to-school differences based fundamentally on speculation.

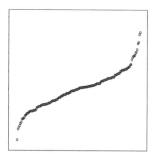

FIGURE 2.10. Ranked school-level residuals.

Furthermore, school-level residuals estimated via multilevel regression analysis are subject to shrinkage. This means that REML (or maximum livelihood) estimation of the random coefficients in a multilevel regression model gives greater weight to large groups, such as large schools or large classrooms, than to small groups (Tate, 2004). The effect on school-level residuals is to make them, too, functions of school size. As a result, very high-performing schools that also happen to be very small will be comparatively devalued relative to larger schools.

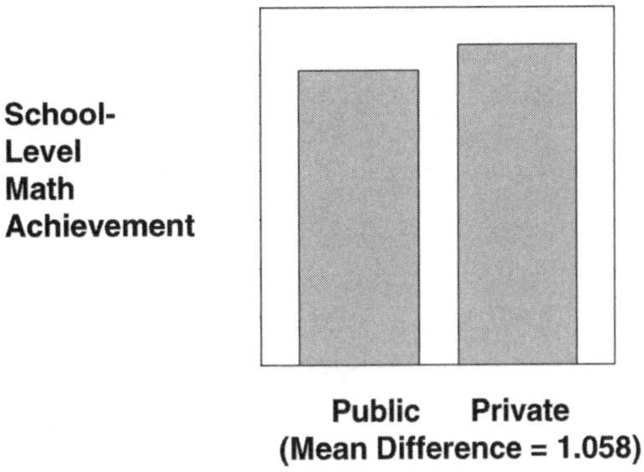

FIGURE 2.11. OLS adjustment at the school level.

For some observers, it is difficult to see that any substantive explanatory power is gained by what they take to be an aridly empirical exercise in which the role of shrinkage is not suitably acknowledged. Instead, it seems like an invitation to treat differences in school quality as manifestations of whatever reform, innovation, or bundle of ostensibly best practices happens to be under discussion (cf. Thrupp, 1999; Alicias, 2005). Nevertheless, use of higher-level residuals in organizational performance studies has occasioned sophisticated, ongoing research among students of multilevel regression analysis and school effectiveness (Rumberger & Palardy, 2004). Use of higher-level residuals in studying organizational effectiveness, however, is not a topic that we will discuss further here.

It is worth noting, finally, that when adjusted for SES differences at the *school level*, the private school advantage in terms of *mean* math achievement is reduced to 1.058 test score points, as illustrated in Figure 2.11. We see that if the school rather than the individual student is treated as the unit of analysis, differences between public and private schools in terms of measured achievement become still smaller.

This provides another illustration of the often-made observation that most of the variability in student achievement occurs *within* schools rather than *between* schools (Jencks et al., 1972). However, the fact that we can usefully speak of achievement in these terms—*within schools* and *between schools*—again demonstrates the conceptual and statistical importance of multilevel regression.

2.5   NESTING AND CORRELATED RESIDUALS

We have now seen that nesting brings analytical opportunities in the form of contextual variables as potentially interesting explanatory factors. The estimators that we use as alternatives to OLS permit intercepts and slopes to vary from group to group, providing estimates of standard errors that are not inflated due to nesting-engendered intraclass correlation. Contextual variables and cross-level interaction terms contribute to explaining variability in the dependent variable in the usual way. And they also contribute to explaining variability in random intercepts and random slopes.

Nesting, however, also assures that there are additional methodological admonitions that need to be heeded. With regard to level-one residuals specifically, when observations are not independent, the residuals produced by a regression equation will not be independent (Beck, 2003). Instead, they will manifest *autocorrelation*—a term that is ubiquitous in the literature on regression analysis. In accounts of multilevel analysis, however, nesting-engendered dependence among residuals is rarely if ever characterized as an instance of autocorrelation, though that is certainly what it is (Kennedy, 2003).

It is well known among users of OLS regression analysis that if residuals are correlated, the standard errors of regression coefficients are inaccurate, and tests of significance will be misleading (Bowerman & O'Connell, 1993). Since intraclass correlation is almost always positive, its effects are almost always comparable to those of positive autocorrelation: artificially deflated standard errors, an increased probability of erroneously rejecting null hypotheses, and specious inflation of R^2 values (Singer, 1987; Fox, 1997).

For example, a Kentucky data set contains California Basic Educational Skills Test math achievement scores for nearly 50,000 eighth-grade students in 347 schools in 2001 (National Evaluation Systems, 2002; Johnson, 2005). We estimate an OLS multiple regression equation by using just two individual-level independent variables, gender and ethnicity; no contextual variables are included. The OLS results are reported in Table 2.12.

However, when the residuals from this regression analysis are used as the dependent variable in a one-way analysis of variance (ANOVA) in which the school is the independent variable, we get the results reported in Table 2.13: Grouping within schools produces residual values that are correlated.

In an effort to compensate for correlated residuals, we again use REML estimators. The regression results obtained using this procedure with the Kentucky data are included in Table 2.14. Since we have introduced no contextual variables, the example in Table 2.14 is a random coefficient regression equation, but not a multilevel regression analysis. With the REML estimators, however, we may permit estimates of the intercept and slopes to vary from school to school, across the groups in which students are nested. The information reported makes this random coefficient equation look very much like a conventional OLS regression output.

TABLE 2.12. Eighth-Grade Math Achievement in Kentucky: OLS Estimates of Gender and Ethnicity Coefficients

$$Y_{\text{MATH}} = 49.22 - 1.28X_{\text{GENDER1}} - 11.58X_{\text{ETHNIC1}}$$
$$(0.10) \quad (0.20) \qquad\qquad (0.32)$$

$$R^2 = 2.7\%$$
$$N = 49{,}616$$

TABLE 2.13. ANOVA of OLS Residuals

	Sums of squares	df	Mean square	F	Sig. level
Between	1,482,251	346	4284	13.31	.000
Within	15,515,236	48,193	322		
Total	169,977,487	48,539			

$$\omega^2 = 0.081$$

TABLE 2.14. Random Coefficients with REML Estimators Compensating for Correlated Residuals

$$Y_{MATH} = 45.11 - 1.14X_{GENDER1} - 10.18X_{ETHNIC1}$$
$$\phantom{Y_{MATH} = 45.11} (0.50) \quad (0.21) \phantom{X_{GENDER1}} (0.55)$$

$$R_1^2 = 2.5\%$$
$$N_1 = 49,616$$
$$N_2 = 347$$

We can further clarify the meaning of random coefficient regression by paraphrasing Singer and Willett (2003, p. 54). Imagine a population of regression coefficients. For each school we randomly select from the population an intercept and a slope for each independent variable. Intercepts and slopes are thus random variables, and random coefficient regression analysis acquires its name in this way.

All three standard errors reported in Table 2.14 are larger than the same standard errors reported in Table 2.12. With 347 schools, the differences in standard error estimates have no effect on decisions about statistical significance. Nevertheless, it is clear that downward bias in standard errors due to correlated residuals increases the probability of erroneously rejecting the null hypothesis with the OLS results.

In Table 2.15, moreover, we see that with REML estimators permitting use of a random intercept and random slope, the correlation among individual-level residuals has diminished almost to zero. This is because random coefficient regression does not simply combine the individual school samples into one, and then estimate an overall regression equation while ignoring school differences. Instead, random coefficient regression

TABLE 2.15. ANOVA of REML Residuals

	Sums of squares	df	Mean square	F	Sig. level
Between	29,418	346	85	0.274	1.000
Within	15,086,614	48,193	313		
Total	15,116,032	48,539			

$$\omega^2 = 0.006$$

uses its capacity to permit coefficients to vary across groups to compute a weighted average, which then takes the form of the overall intercept and slopes. It is this random coefficient regression equation that yields uncorrelated residuals.

It is instructive to examine this process more closely. If we plot the OLS residuals from Table 2.12 against the REML residuals from Table 2.14, as shown in Figure 2.12, we see that they are closely associated ($r = 0.94$). This suggests that the really conspicuous virtue of the random coefficient regression equation is not that it does a better job of explaining variability in math achievement, but that it eliminates positive correlation among the residuals, thereby helping to avoid inflated standard errors.

To illustrate this more clearly, imagine that we are studying county-level voting behavior in five very different states: Arkansas, California, Michigan, Nebraska, and New York. We begin by estimating OLS simple regression equations individually for each of the five states. County-level percentage of people voting for George W. Bush in the 2004 U.S. presidential election (Y_{BUSH}) is the dependent variable, and county-level median family income in units of $1000 ($X_{INCOME}$) is the independent variable. We get the state-by-state results reported in Table 2.16.

The five OLS regression equations are very different, exhibiting dramatic variability with respect to intercepts and slopes. If we ignore these differences and combine the 369 counties from the five states, the overall OLS regression results are as in Table 2.17. Combining information from the five states and estimating an overall OLS regression equation gives us interpretable results, but the intercepts and slopes in each state are badly misrepresented by the intercept and slope in the overall regression. In truth, given the variability in intercepts and slopes reported in Table 2.16, it is hard to imagine how it could be otherwise.

If we use the combined five-state data set with REML estimators and permit the intercept and slopes to vary across the five states, we get the results reported in Table 2.18. The REML coefficients in the random coefficient equation are a bit different from the OLS coefficients, and the REML standard errors are larger, just as we would expect.

Still, except for the differences in standard errors, there is no basis for making the case that either procedure does a substantially better job of representing the variability in the state-by-state regression analyses.

However, if we save the residuals from the OLS regression analysis and from the random coefficient regression analysis, we can put together the correlation matrix in Table 2.19. (The five states are represented by dummy variables with conventional abbreviations. OLS and REML residuals are in the columns as labeled.) All bivariate correlations of county-level OLS residuals with

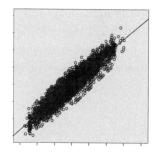

OLS

Residuals

Level-One REML Residuals

FIGURE 2.12. OLS residuals by level-one REML residuals.

TABLE 2.16. OLS Simple Regression: County-Level Voting Behavior in Five States

Arkansas

$$Y_{BUSH} = 29.468 + 0.689X_{INCOME}$$
$$(6.771)\ (0.192)$$

$$R^2 = 15.0\%$$
$$N = 75$$

California

$$Y_{BUSH} = 87.495 - 0.718X_{INCOME}$$
$$(6.334)\ (0.124)$$

$$R^2 = 37.6\%$$
$$N = 58$$

Michigan

$$Y_{BUSH} = 55.868 - 0.033X_{INCOME}$$
$$(3.818)\ (0.082)$$

$$R^2 = 0.0\%$$
$$N = 83$$

Nebraska

$$Y_{BUSH} = 123.824 - 1.261X_{INCOME}$$
$$(7.810)\ (0.193)$$

$$R^2 = 1.5\%$$
$$N = 93$$

New York

$$Y_{BUSH} = 56.257 - 0.110X_{INCOME}$$
$$(5.783)\ (0.116)$$

$$R^2 = 0.2\%$$
$$N = 60$$

TABLE 2.17. OLS Simple Regression: County-Level Voting Behavior, States Combined

$$Y_{BUSH} = 78.297 - 0.469X_{INCOME}$$
$$(3.022)\ (0.068)$$

$$R^2 = 11.4\%$$
$$N = 369$$

TABLE 2.18. Random Coefficient Regression: County-Level Voting Behavior, States Combined

$$Y_{BUSH} = 56.861 - 0.297X_{INCOME}$$
$$(4.217) \quad (0.322)$$

$$R_1^2 = 5.3\%$$
$$N_1 = 286$$
$$N_2 = 5$$

TABLE 2.19. Bivariate Correlations: Residuals by State Dummy Variables

	OLS	REML
REML	*0.727*	
AR	–0.312	–0.002
CA	0.102	–0.004
MI	–0.102	–0.002
NE	0.602	0.012
NY	–0.152	–0.005

the states they represent are numerically **much** larger than the corresponding random coefficient residuals. Furthermore, all five (boldfaced and italicized) correlation coefficients for OLS residuals are statistically significant, while none of the random coefficient residuals correlates significantly with its state. This is because each state's OLS county-level residuals tend to be similar to each other—they are correlated—and different from residuals for other states. The random coefficient residuals, by contrast, do not exhibit this pattern of within-state homogeneity.

We see this contrast between OLS and random coefficient regression residuals again in Table 2.20, which reports descriptive statistics for **differences** between the county-level residuals computed using individual **state-by-state** OLS regression analyses, as in Table 2.16, and residuals for the overall OLS regression analysis and the overall random coefficient regression analysis. Differences between the state-by-state regressions and the overall OLS regression are consistently much larger than differences between the state-by-state and overall random coefficient regression analysis. When SPSS reports bivariate correlations between state-by-state residuals and overall residuals from random coefficient regression analyses, they range in value from 0.999 to 1.000!

Again, this is because random coefficient regression does not simply combine the individual state samples into one, and then estimate an overall regression equation while ignoring state differences. Instead, random coefficient regression uses its capacity to per-

TABLE 2.20. State-by-State Residuals Minus OLS and REML Overall Residuals

	OLS				REML			
	Min.	Max.	Mean	Standard deviation	Min.	Max.	Mean	Standard deviation
AR	−7.6	18.9	8.3	5.5	−1.3	0.9	0.0	0.5
CA	−0.7	13.0	3.2	3.2	−0.0	0.4	0.1	0.1
MI	−10.5	8.0	2.5	3.9	−0.2	0.1	−0.0	0.1
NE	−23.5	1.8	−13.9	4.9	−0.8	0.8	−0.2	0.3
NY	−7.5	11.0	4.6	4.0	−0.1	0.2	0.1	0.1

mit coefficients to vary across groups to compute a weighted average, which takes the form of the overall regression equation. This enables us to effectively address the joint problems of dependent observations and correlated residuals.

Just as a matter of curiosity, we might want to see the Y_{BUSH}-by-X_{INCOME} relationship for all 49 states in the data set. (Voting data for Alaska were not available when this data set was assembled.) It might also be interesting to see what a multilevel regression equation using the same variables, though with median family income now measured at both the county and state levels, would look like. Both the random coefficient equation and the multilevel equation are reported in Table 2.21.

TABLE 2.21. Y_{BUSH}-by-X_{INCOME} Relationship

Random coefficient regression

$Y_{BUSH} = 57.974 - 0.032X_{INCOME}$
    (1.286) (0.088)

$$R_1^2 = 0.0\%$$
$$N_1 = 3140$$
$$N_2 = 49$$

Multilevel regression

$Y_{BUSH} = 58.996 - 0.023X_{INCOME1} - 0.648X_{INCOME2} - 0.023X_{INCOME2} * X_{INCOME1}$
    (1.147) (0.087)   (0.170)   (0.013)

$$R_1^2 = 9.0\%$$
$$N_1 = 3140$$
$$N_2 = 49$$

Simulating multilevel regression with OLS

$Y_{BUSH} = 60.329 - 0.026X_{INCOME1} - 0.537X_{INCOME2} - 0.026X_{INCOME2} * X_{INCOME1}$
    (0.235) (0.045)   (0.029)   (0.005)

$$R^2 = 5.3\%$$
$$N = 3140$$

SPSS Routines 1.1 through 2.1–2.3 differ from each other only with regard to very concrete and obvious details. With a little practice in using SPSS Mixed Models and the Windows interface, the SPSS routines are easy to follow.

We will discuss county-level voting behavior in the 2004 presidential election much more thoroughly in Chapter 6, "Giving OLS Regression Its Due." For now, notice that Y_{BUSH} is unrelated to county-level median family income in each equation reported in Table 2.21. However, the aggregated state-level contextual variable $X_{INCOME2}$ has a statistically significant slope: In the multilevel regression equation, each $1000 increase in state-level median family income corresponds, on average, to a 0.648-point decrease in the percentage of people voting for Bush.

SPSS Routine 2.3. Random Coefficient Regression or Multilevel Regression?

1. Open the SPSS data file and click on ANALYZE.
2. Go to MIXED MODELS and click on LINEAR
3. Since the state is the level-two grouping variable in which counties are nested, insert the state identifier into the SUBJECTS box.
4. Click on CONTINUE; insert the percentage voting for Bush as the dependent variable into the DEPENDENT VARIABLE box; and insert the independent variables $X_{INCOME1}$ and $X_{INCOME2}$, and the cross-level interaction term $X_{INCOME2}$ * $X_{INCOME1}$, into the COVARIATE(S) box.
5. Click on FIXED at the bottom of the screen. In the small box in the middle of the screen, change FACTORIAL to MAIN EFFECTS. *For a random coefficient regression model* with $X_{INCOME1}$ as the only independent variable, move $X_{INCOME1}$ from the FACTORS AND COVARIATES box to the MODEL box. *For a multilevel regression model,* move the independent variables $X_{INCOME1}$ and $X_{INCOME2}$, and the cross-level interaction term $X_{INCOME2}$ * $X_{INCOME1}$, from the FACTORS AND COVARIATES box to the MODEL box.
6. Click on CONTINUE.
7. Click on the RANDOM button in the middle of the screen. The state identifier is already in the SUBJECTS box, and now we also insert it into the COMBINATIONS box.
8. In the small box in the middle of the screen, change FACTORIAL to MAIN EFFECTS.
9. Near the top of the screen, click on INCLUDE INTERCEPT, and move the independent variable $X_{INCOME1}$ into the model box. *This applies for both random coefficient regression and multilevel regression models. Both have a random intercept and one random slope.*
10. Just above INCLUDE INTERCEPT and to the right of COVARIANCE TYPE, select UNSTRUCTURED.
11. Click on CONTINUE and click on the STATISTICS button.
12. On the left, under MODEL STATISTICS, select PARAMETER ESTIMATES and TESTS FOR COVARIANCE PARAMETERS.
13. Click on CONTINUE and click on OK.

Table 2.21 also shows us that our conclusions might have been a bit different had we sought to mimic a multilevel regression model with OLS multiple regression. The example-after-example consistency in comparisons of OLS results with those for random coefficient and multilevel regression is striking: similar coefficient values, but larger standard errors when REML estimators are used with random coefficient regression to permit level-one coefficients to vary from group to group.

In this instance, moreover, the difference is substantively consequential. Had we relied on the OLS simulation of multilevel regression, we would have concluded that the cross-level interaction term, $X_{INCOME2} * X_{INCOME1}$, is statistically significant. However, the actual multilevel regression results show us that this is not correct, again illustrating the inferential difficulties posed for OLS by nested data.

2.6   NESTING AND EFFECTIVE SAMPLE SIZE

Nesting and efforts to deal with it by using multilevel regression make determination of effective sample size more difficult than is the case with OLS regression (Bland, 2000). Among other difficulties, each level in a multilevel analysis has a sample size that is different from the sizes for the other levels. After all, if we have 49,616 students nested in 347 schools, the nominal sample sizes at the student level and school level are as given: 49,616 and 347. In addition, each school has a sample size of its own, and these are rarely the same from one school to another.

Perhaps we can use familiar material taken from discussion of OLS regression to introduce the complex topic of suitable sample size in multilevel regression. Much of the material in the next few pages may be well known to many readers, and it is not difficult to look up in textbooks on survey sampling and regression analysis. (See, e.g., the recent work on statistical power with categorical moderator variables by Aguinis, 2004.)

Computing the standard error of an unstandardized regression coefficient with OLS is straightforward. For an independent variable X_i, the formula for the standard error S_b is presented in Table 2.22. S_R^2 is the variance of the OLS residuals; SS_{Xi} is the sum of the squared deviations for X_i with respect to its arithmetic mean; and VIF is the Variance Inflation Factor, computed by dividing 1 by $1 - R_j^2$. (R_j^2 for the coefficient corresponding to any one independent variable is calculated by regressing that variable on all the other independent variables.) The smaller the standard error, the greater the statistical power—the likelihood that we will detect a relationship if one exists in the population from which the sample was selected.

TABLE 2.22. Standard Error of an OLS Slope

$$S_b = (((S_R^2)/SS_{Xi}) * VIF)^{1/2}$$

We can illustrate application of the formula in Table 2.22 by using all 4359 observations in our income and occupation data set. Hourly wage (X_{WAGE}) is the dependent variable. (For this example, hourly wage is not logged.) The independent variables are level of educational attainment in years completed ($X_{EDUCATION}$), years of work experience (X_{YEARS}), race (X_{BLACK}), and union membership (X_{UNION}). Results of the OLS multiple regression analysis are reported in Table 2.23.

Continuing the illustration, we will focus specifically on the relationship between Y_{WAGE} and $X_{EDUCATION}$. The unstandardized regression coefficient for $X_{EDUCATION}$ is 0.647, making it 23.96 times as large as its standard error and statistically significant by any reasonable standard. The standard error itself is 0.027. This value is determined in straightforward fashion by using the formula for S_b (see Table 2.24).

Using the just-reported value for the standard error, a 95% confidence interval for the unstandardized regression coefficient is similarly easy to compute. We see this for the $X_{EDUCATION}$ coefficient in Table 2.25.

Given such a large sample, we may understandably judge that the complexity of our analysis need not be constrained by concern for statistical power. Even if added complexity produces comparatively strong correlations among independent variables, we may surmise that inflated standard errors due to multicollinearity will not pose problems for estimation and inference simply because we have so many cases; micronumerosity is not a problem here (cf. Goldberger, 1991)!

In response to the analytical opportunities promised by large sample size, we may introduce additional explanatory factors: X_{MARRY}, coded 1 if married and 0 otherwise; $X_{BLACKED}$, a multiplicative interaction term created with X_{BLACK} and $X_{EDUCATE}$; $X_{BLACKYRS}$, a

TABLE 2.23. Rudimentary Earnings Function

$$Y_{WAGE} = -3.789 + 0.647X_{EDUCATION} + 0.303X_{YEARS} - 0.862X_{BLACK} + 0.928X_{UNION}$$
$$(0.376) \quad (0.027) \quad\quad (0.017) \quad\quad (0.141) \quad\quad (0.105)$$

$$R^2 = 15.3\%$$
$$N = 4359$$

TABLE 2.24. Computing the Standard Error of an OLS Slope

$$S_b = (((S_R^2)/SS_{Xi}) * VIF)^{1/2}$$
$$0.027 = ((8.696/13286.310) * 1.130)^{1/2}$$

TABLE 2.25. Confidence Interval Construction for an OLS Slope

$$b_{EDUCATION} - t_{.05}S_{bEDUCATION} \text{ to } b_{EDUCATION} + t_{.05}S_{bEDUCATION}$$
$$0.647 - 1.960(0.027) \text{ to } 0.647 + 1.960(0.027)$$
$$0.594 \text{ to } 0.700$$

multiplicative interaction term created with X_{BLACK} and X_{YEARS}; and $X_{BLACKUN}$, a multiplicative interaction term created using X_{BLACK} and X_{UNION}. Results for the respecified OLS multiple regression equation are reported in Table 2.26.

Even with more than 4000 observations, however, we may *eventually* behave with a bit more statistical prudence, acknowledging that multiplicative interaction terms are *very* closely associated with one or both of the variables used to create them. As a safeguard against multicollinearity, we may decide to center the main-effect independent variables with respect to their means, and then create interaction terms using the mean-centered variables. As a result, usual measures of multicollinearity have satisfactory values: All Variance Inflation Factors are small, ranging from 1.021 to 1.254, and the value of the Condition Index is only 1.669.

Results of the OLS multiple regression analysis are easy to interpret. Given the large sample, it is no surprise that all coefficients save two—those corresponding to the interaction terms $X_{BLACKYRS}$ and $X_{BLACKUN}$—are statistically significant. Everything seems to be in order. But *is* everything in order? Or should we treat each observation as if it were *nested* within one of nine occupational groups, and incorporate *nesting* into determination of effective sample size? Perhaps so, but what place has nesting in a discussion of effective sample size?

Treating observations as nested is another way of saying that the observations may be *clustered* into sampling units (Goldstein, 1999). Whether or not nesting or clustering occurs as a result of explicitly made decisions in sample design, it may introduce intraclass correlation; this means that observations are not independent and that as a result of the absence of independence, we have less information than we thought.

Given a large sample with observations clustered into groups, nesting almost certainly will manifest itself in a *design effect*. This means that our *effective* sample size— the sample size that should be used in determining degrees of freedom, calculating standard errors, and running tests of significance—will be smaller than we had expected. The approximate design effect for determining loss of information due to dependence among nested observations can be computed easily using the formula in Table 2.27, where n is the average number of observations per group or cluster (Kalton, 1983). In this instance, the value of the intraclass correlation with X_{WAGE} as the dependent variable is 0.117, and n is 484. The design effect due to nesting of observations within occupational categories is calculated in Table 2.28.

TABLE 2.26. A More Complex Earnings Function

$$Y_{WAGE} = 5.922 + 0.542X_{EDUCATION} + 0.246X_{YEARS} - 0.571X_{BLACK} + 1.106X_{UNION} + 0.495X_{MARRY}$$
$$\quad (0.046)\ (0.030) \qquad\qquad (0.018) \qquad (0.149) \qquad (0.110) \qquad (0.099)$$

$$+\ 0.283X_{BLACKED} - 0.010X_{BLACKYRS} + 0.008X_{BLACKUN}$$
$$\quad (0.108) \qquad\quad (0.055) \qquad\qquad (0.310)$$

$$R^2 = 17.7\%$$
$$N = 4359$$

TABLE 2.27. Sample Design Effect

Design effect = $1 + (n - 1)$ * intraclass correlation

TABLE 2.28. Computimg a Sample Design Effect

$57.51 = 1 + (484 - 1) * 0.117$

Now that we have acknowledged cluster-engendered dependence among observations, we see in Table 2.29 that the *effective* sample size—the sample size that determines the power of inferential procedures—is **much** smaller than the nominal sample size of 4359 (Kish, 1989). Quite a shock! Throughout the analyses reported in Tables 2.23 through 2.26, we have been tacitly proceeding as if we were working with a simple random sample. When we recognize that we are working with a cluster sample in which individuals are nested in occupational groups, however, the OLS standard errors, tests of significance, and confidence intervals become suspect.

Table 2.30 reproduces the OLS regression results from Table 2.26 **but** with standard errors adjusted to reflect a discouragingly small effective sample size of about 76, rather than the nominal sample size of 4359. According to the OLS results in Table 2.26, all the unstandardized coefficients except those for the interaction terms $X_{BLACKYRS}$ and $X_{BLACKUN}$ were statistically significant. In Table 2.30, however, only the intercept and the slopes for $X_{EDUCATION}$ and $X_{EXPERIENCE}$ are statistically significant. The standard error for $X_{EDUCATION}$, moreover, is more than five times as large as in Table 2.26, and the standard error for X_{YEARS} is more than six times as large.

With an intraclass correlation of only 0.117, loss of this much information due to clustering may seem to be a gross exaggeration. When we have a relatively small number

TABLE 2.29. Effective Sample Size

Effective sample size = N/design effect

$75.80 = 4359/57.51$

TABLE 2.30. Earnings Function Corrected for Unconditional Intraclass Correlation

$Y_{WAGE} = 5.922 + 0.542X_{EDUCATION} + 0.246X_{YEARS} - 0.571X_{BLACK} + 1.106X_{UNION}$
$\quad\quad\;\; (0.256)\;(0.141)\quad\quad\quad\;\;(0.104)\quad\quad(0.820)\quad\quad\;\;(0.656)$

$\quad\quad + 0.495X_{MARRY} + 0.283X_{BLACKED} - 0.010X_{BLACKYRS} + 0.008X_{BLACKUN}$
$\quad\quad\quad\;\;(0.562)\quad\quad\;\;(0.552)\quad\quad\quad\;(0.536)\quad\quad\quad\;\;(2.107)$

$R^2 = 17.7\%$
Effective N = 76

of clusters with a comparatively large number of cases in each, however, this is *exactly* the kind of outcome we should expect. It is odd indeed to think of a large number of within-cluster observations as diminishing rather than enhancing statistical power for the overall sample. In the case of the average number of observations for each sampling cluster or group, however, an outcome of this troublesome sort is predictable. The more observations that are nested in each group, the greater the cost in terms of effective sample size (Snijders & Bosker, 1999).

By way of clarifying this contrary-to-commonsense phenomenon, imagine a hypothetical sample of 1000 students. If they are nested in 100 schools, they have 100 school-based sources of contextual diversity. If they are nested in only 10 schools, however, they have only 10 school-based sources of contextual diversity. In the latter instance, similarity among observations due to grouping costs us a great deal more information. This is why researchers who design cluster and multistage samples place a premium on obtaining a large number of clusters or groups for any total sample size (Kish, 1965/1995; Mok, 1995).

With a multilevel regression framework and unstandardized coefficients that are permitted to vary across second-level groups, clustering is automatically taken into consideration in determining the effective sample size and number of degrees of freedom for use in inferential tests. Furthermore, when we discuss the distinction between *unconditional* and *conditional* intraclass correlation, we will see that the effective sample size for the occupation and income analysis, as it is specified in Table 2.30, is actually about 428 cases (Mok, 1995).

This more comfortable number occurs because, with a full complement of independent variables in the equation for hourly wage, the conditional or effective intraclass correlation is reduced to 0.019, much smaller than the original estimate of 0.117. This is because one or more independent variables have explained or accounted for a substantial portion of the variability between groups.

Inserting the *conditional* intraclass correlation into the design effect formula in Table 2.28 yields a value of 10.18., rather than the originally reported design effect of 57.51. The resulting effective sample size computed with the formula in Table 2.29 is about 428 cases. This is still only a fraction of the original 4359, but much more useful than the previous estimate of 76, as is manifest in the results reported in Table 2.31. With smaller standard errors, now X_{UNION} is statistically significant, along with $X_{\text{EDUCATION}}$

TABLE 2.31. Earnings Function Corrected for Conditional Intraclass Correlation

$$Y_{\text{WAGE}} = 5.922 + 0.542X_{\text{EDUCATION}} + 0.246X_{\text{YEARS}} - 0.571X_{\text{BLACK}} + 1.106X_{\text{UNION}} + 0.495X_{\text{MARRY}}$$
$$(0.157)\ (0.100) \qquad\quad (0.065) \qquad\quad (0.539) \qquad\quad (0.391) \qquad\quad (0.327)$$

$$+\ 0.283X_{\text{BLACKED}} - 0.010X_{\text{BLACKYRS}} + 0.008X_{\text{BLACKUN}}$$
$$(0.382) \qquad\qquad (0.213) \qquad\qquad (1.199)$$

$$R^2 = 17.7\%$$
$$\textit{Effective N} = 428$$

and X_{YEARS}. It may seem odd indeed to acknowledge that effective sample size depends, at least on part, on how a regression model is specified. With nested data, however, this is how things work.

As we have already suggested, the number of individual-level cases is only one of the sample sizes of concern when we move from OLS to multilevel regression. **What about the second-level sample size?** In the present example, with only 9 occupational categories, the second-level or group-level sample size is only 9! Since there is no third level, this number is not subject to change due to intraclass correlation and resulting design effects. Nevertheless, we should ask ourselves just what sorts of limitations this unusually small number of cases imposes.

For example, we might aggregate education to the occupation level, using it as a level-two explanatory factor in accounting for variability in income. The effective sample size used in testing the resulting regression coefficient for statistical significance or constructing a confidence interval, however, is only 9. How much confidence can we have in regression-based inferential statistics estimated from only nine cases?

Continuing with the same example, we might use alternative estimators such as REML in place of OLS, enabling us to permit the level-one intercept and one or more level-one slopes to vary across occupation groups. This is certainly how we would proceed if we were planning a multilevel regression analysis. Again, since there are only nine groups with respect to which the intercept and coefficients might vary, sample size for the random coefficients is only 9. And the same small sample size would hold for cross-level interaction terms created from a variable with a random slope.

The effective sample size in Table 2.32 is only 9, the number of occupational groups. Nevertheless, all coefficients are statistically significant! Y_{WAGE} increases with educational attainment at the individual level **and** at the group level. In addition, the cross-level interaction term ($X_{EDUCATION2} * X_{EDUCATION1}$) tells us that the positive effect of individual-level education ($X_{EDUCATION1}$) is further increased as group-level education ($X_{EDUCATION2}$) increases.

How do we get statistically significant coefficients for all terms with this absurdly small sample? The relationships are strong; the main-effect variables have been centered with respect to their overall means, rendering them orthogonal to the cross-level interaction term; and there are no other independent variables with which our explanatory factors might be confounded.

Nevertheless, as we are beginning to discern, multilevel regression has nasty surprises of its own. Table 2.33 illustrates this. The last three entries, each with an effective

TABLE 2.32. Miltilevel Regression Earnings Function

$Y_{WAGE} = 5.740 + 0.406X_{EDUCATION1} + 1.238X_{EDUCATION2} + 0.179X_{EDUCATION2} * X_{EDUCATION1}$
(0.230) (0.035)   (0.320)   (0.051)

$R_1^2 = 12.1\%$
Effective $N = N_2 = 9$

TABLE 2.33. What Is the Sample Size?

Nominal effective sample size for OLS regression

$N = 3459$

Effective sample size for OLS corrected for intraclass correlation

$N = 76$

Effective sample size for OLS corrected for conditional intraclass correlation

$N = 428$

Effective sample size for occupation-level contextual variables

$N = 9$

Effective sample size for random regression coefficients

$N = 9$

Effective sample size for cross-level interaction terms

$N = 9$

sample size of 9, would be the same even if we counted all 3459 individual-level observations without regard for the (unconditional or conditional) intraclass correlation. No matter how we look at it, there are only nine observations—nine occupational categories—at level two in which the level-one observations are nested.

As we continue with our discussion of multilevel regression (especially in Chapter 10, "Determining Sample Sizes for Multilevel Regression"), we will learn that the best sample design for analyses of nested data is one that maximizes the number of level-two observations, thereby distributing the level-one observations across a comparatively large set of level-two categories. Referring back to the formula in Table 2.28, we see that this approach, for any nominal sample size, results in the largest effective sample size.

Determination of suitable sample sizes at each level of a multilevel regression model is a complex and underresearched issue (Mok, 1995; Maas & Hox, 2004). For now, it is useful to repeat that clustering or nesting provides both analytical opportunities and methodological concerns. Determination of effective sample size for nested data is one of those concerns. Use of contextual variables and cross-level interaction terms as explanatory factors is one of those opportunities.

2.7   SUMMING UP

The social and behavioral sciences are heavily laden with questions that are never answered once and for all. In part, this is due to differences in conceptual frameworks and world views that separate practitioners into competing groups; in part, it is due to methodological limitations. Over the past couple of decades, however, progress has been made in resolving at least a few seemingly intractable issues. This includes uncertainty with regard to the meaning of neighborhood effects.

The fact that neighborhoods vary in quality is undeniable. The fact that participation in neighborhoods of different quality affects school achievement, children's social skills, and related factors may be a bit less certain. Still, few critics of neighborhood research have been so stubborn as to deny that differences in neighborhood quality have measurable consequences.

Researchers have differed, however, as to whether neighborhood differences and neighborhood effects are due mainly to differences in neighborhood SES. According to those for whom neighborhood effects are merely SES effects in disguise, people with similar levels of income, similar occupational statuses, similar educational levels, and similar tastes and consumption patterns tend to group together (see, e.g., Mayer & Jencks, 1989; Solon, Page, & Duncan, 2000). This applies not only to friendship groups and families but to larger units—in this case, neighborhoods. As a result, some children are nested in neighborhoods that are affluent, prestigious, and attractive, showcases for desirable social practices and cultural emblems. Less fortunate children are nested in less favorable circumstances (Lareau, 2003).

Other researchers, however, have argued that neighborhood quality cannot be reduced to indicators of SES. Instead, social support, useful cultural resources, the means for acquiring essential interpersonal skills, and safety and social stability vary substantially from one neighborhood to another, independent of SES composition (Varanian & Gleason, 1999; Bickel et al., 2002). While no one denies that neighborhood quality is confounded with SES, ethnicity, and other commonplace predictors, the independent-neighborhood-effects view has prevailed.

One reason why the neighborhood quality issue has recently approximated resolution is the development of analytical techniques that are better suited to handling nesting. Neighborhood quality, as we have seen, can be measured and analyzed at the individual level, at the group level, or at both levels simultaneously. In addition, relationships between individual-level outcomes (such as school achievement) and individual-level predictors (such as SES and ethnicity) can be treated as varying with group-level measures of neighborhood quality. We are no longer limited to choosing between modeling neighborhood effects at one level, individual or group. Instead, we can acknowledge nesting and model neighborhood effects simultaneously at more than one level.

The same methodological advances that have contributed to an approximate consensus with regard to neighborhoods and their outcomes have not, however, brought resolution to more thoroughly politicized issues. After more than two decades of high-profile research, for example, the often acrimonious debate over the comparative effectiveness of public and private schools continues (Greene & Mellow, 1998; Rothstein, Carnoy, & Benveniste, 1999; Lubienski & Lubienski, 2005).

Nevertheless, when we examine research from the early 1980s—the decade when public–private school research was the hottest of hot topics—it is clear that substantial conceptual and methodological progress has been made. In Coleman et al.'s (1982) still frequently cited book *High School Achievement*, for example, values on the type-of-school variable were treated as characteristics of students. At the time, however, others argued that the proper unit of analysis for public–private comparisons and other forms of school effectiveness was the school in which students were nested (cf. Bickel, 1987). The methodological tools for working with more than one level of analysis in the same equation were not yet widely known.

Subsequently, however, with the development and dissemination of the knowledge and software needed to do multilevel analyses, school type has been treated as a contextual factor, used primarily to explain relationships among individual-level outcomes (such as achievement) and individual-level predictors (such as gender, race, and SES). Furthermore, the same individual-level predictors can be aggregated to the school level and also used as characteristics of schools.

Debates as contentious and ideologically infused as that involving comparisons of public and private schools are not settled by methodological advances. Nevertheless, the application of tools designed to deal with the analytical problems and opportunities posed by nesting has introduced a level of conceptual clarity and methodological rigor that was previously missing (see, e.g., Bryk & Thum, 1989).

It remains true that analyses of this kind have been usefully approximated with OLS regression. OLS methods, however, do not enable us to address nesting-related issues such as relationships that differ from one context to another. By permitting coefficients to vary from group to group, however, alternative estimators used with random coefficient regression and multilevel regression deal with this problem quite effectively. As a result, when the existence of a statistically significant intraclass correlation makes clear that nesting is consequential, we have readily available analytical options that can be effectively invoked.

It can be especially interesting to estimate the unconditional intraclass correlation coefficient with no predictors in the equation, and then estimate the conditional intraclass correlation coefficient following introduction of one or more contextual variables. Reduction in the value of this measure of within-group homogeneity tells us that we are explaining in concrete terms just *why* a nonzero intraclass correlation exists. This is certainly an interesting objective for statistical work.

2.8   USEFUL RESOURCES

Blau, P. (1994) *Structural Contexts of Opportunity.* Chicago: University of Chicago Press.

I have made frequent references to the thinness of the theoretical and substantive literature in the social and behavioral sciences. This, as I see it, poses serious specification problems for productive use of multilevel regression. Nevertheless, an occasional theoretical or substantive source may make an unusually strong case for multilevel modeling. Such is true of the theoretical statement by sociologist Peter Blau in *Structural Contexts of Opportunity.* In his discussion of the effect on individual behavior of belonging to a multiplicity of collectivities, Blau posits the following:

Population structures entail not only multiple forms of differentiation, but multiple levels of structure, as well. For example, a nation is composed of provinces, which consist of counties, whose subunits are cities and towns, which contain neighborhoods. Similarly, the labor force can be divided into manual and non-manual workers, who, in turn, are divisible into major occupational groups, whose subunits are detailed occupations, which are composed of increasingly narrow specialties. (1994, p. 5)

Consistent with his earlier work (see, e.g., Blau, 1960, 1964), this unambiguous acknowledgment of the contextually occasioned nature of human behavior establishes the importance of nesting. Though methodologically astute, Blau does not acknowledge the existence of multilevel regression. Nevertheless, it seems abundantly clear from the foregoing quotation that he saw the need for statistical tools that permit modeling of nesting and its consequences. This stands in sharp contrast to the work of equally influential sociologists, such as Homans (1974) and Coleman (1986), who addressed some of the same issues while embracing a form of methodological individualism that ignored contextual factors entirely or relegated them to inconsequential status.

Farkas, G. (1996) *Human Capital or Cultural Capital?* New York: Aldine de Gruyter.

Arrow, K., Bowles, S., & Durlauf, S. (Eds.) (2000) *Meritocracy and Economic Inequality.* Princeton, NJ: Princeton University.

Poston, D. (2002) The Effects of Human Capital and Cultural Characteristics on the Economic Attainment Patterns of Male and Female Asian-Born Immigrants in the United States: A Multilevel Analysis. *Asian and Pacific Migration Journal, 11,* 197–220.

On the other hand, the fact that nesting and appreciation of its consequences are either ignored or unrecognized in recent empirical research that purports to evaluate programs and rigorously compare theoretical perspectives has been noted by Singer and Willett (2003) and others. In Farkas's widely read monograph, for example, he estimates a large number of OLS regression equations with a variety of data sets in an effort to account for the influence of cultural capital on student achievement. One of Farkas's data sets consists of measures on 486 students enrolled in the seventh or eighth grades in 22 middle schools in Dallas. It is not clear from Farkas's account how many classrooms are represented, but if there is more than one per school, the consequences of nesting could be quite consequential, especially since teacher characteristics are used as explanatory variables.

If data were collected from one classroom in each school, there would be only 22 second-level observations—by most standards, an unduly small number (Maas & Hox, 2005). Nevertheless, given the nature of the data and the objectives of Farkas's research, failure at least to acknowledge the possibility that group effects may exist at the school or classroom level seems an odd oversight. The likelihood that differences in aggregated levels of cultural capital characterize collections of schools and classrooms seems to provide opportunities that are too attractive to avoid.

Similarly, the methodologically sophisticated research reported in the volume edited by Arrow, Bowles, and Durlauf repeatedly and skillfully, with large data sets, carefully selected controls, and meticulously specified functional forms, examines the relationship in the United States between income and cognitive ability. In addition to educational level, some of the explanatory factors used to complement intelligence are closely related to cultural capital, as Farkas uses that concept.

As intended, the chapters of *Meritocracy and Economic Inequality* correct many of the conceptual, methodological, and interpretative errors in Herrnstein and Murray's (1994) well-known polemic *The Bell Curve*. Nevertheless, none of the specifications acknowledges the possibility that the relationship between income and cognitive ability may vary consequentially from one place to another.

In contrast both to Farkas and to Arrow et al., Poston was able to analyze the connection between income and individual-level variables such as education, while taking into consideration variability in that relationship from one group of immigrants to another. Recent groups of immigrants to the United States were categorized by nation of origin, and two group-level measures of cultural capital were used to account for variability in the income-by-education relationship. Though he had only 27 groups, Poston explicitly and profitably acknowledged nesting as a methodological issue and a source of analytical opportunities. To his credit, moreover, Poston used multilevel analysis in a way that is best suited to its specification demands: He framed a very specific question in multilevel terms and then estimated a suitably parsimonious multilevel regression equation.

3

Contextual Variables

3.1 CHAPTER INTRODUCTION

This is a long chapter that covers more conceptual territory than the straightforward title "Contextual Variables" suggests. Nevertheless, inclusion of a broad range of topics under this obvious-sounding title makes sense. We can use an empirical example to clarify this claim. Unfamiliar concepts introduced with the example will be thoroughly explained as we work through the chapter.

Suppose that we are using the High School and Beyond subsample introduced in Chapter 2. We know that it includes 7185 students nested in 160 schools. As is often the case, we are interested in investigating the association between student achievement and family SES. We start off simply, with scores from a standardized test of math achievement (Y_{MATH1}) as the dependent variable and a composite measure of family SES (X_{SES1}) as the only predictor.

With students grouped in 160 schools, we are obliged to investigate the possibility that nesting is consequential. We compute the unconditional intraclass correlation and find that it is statistically significant ($p < .000$) with a value of 0.153. This means that 15.3% of the variability in math achievement occurs between schools, with the other 84.7% occurring within schools.

Given this result, we decide to run our preliminary analysis with both the intercept and the slope for SES (centered with respect to its grand mean) permitted to vary across schools. We also permit the random intercept and random slope to be correlated. In other words, we estimate a simple random coefficient regression model without putting any constraints on the random terms. Results from this analysis yield a statistically significant ($p < .000$) and positive intercept, with a fixed component value of 12.649, and statistically significant ($p < .000$) and positive slope for SES, with a fixed component value of 2.193.

The results in Table 3.1 are easy to interpret: For each 1-unit increment in X_{SES1}, individual student math achievement increases, on average, by 2.193 points. Since the intercept is 12.649 and X_{SES1} has been centered with respect to its mean, if X_{SES1} were set equal to its mean, our best estimate of Y_{MATH1} would be 12.649. This is just the sort of interpretation we would offer if we were working with OLS regression.

As we have noted several times, however, with random coefficient regression or multilevel regression, there is additional *essential* output. These are the random component estimates in Table 3.2. Interpretation of random components is not difficult. The statistically significant residual variance is simply a measure of variability for the level-one or individual-level residuals. The statistically significant random intercept variance tells us that the intercept really does vary from school to school. The random slope variance tells us that the slope too really does vary from school to school. Finally, the statistically nonsignificant intercept-by-slope covariance makes clear that the random components for the slope and intercept are not correlated; they do not vary together.

At this juncture it makes sense to transform the random coefficient regression model into a multilevel model by introducing one or more *contextual variables*. In view of our statistically significant findings regarding random components, we use the contextual variables primarily *to account for school-to-school variability in the random intercept and the random slope for SES*. Since we are trying to explain variability in a slope, each contextual variable will correspond to an implied cross-level interaction term.

TABLE 3.1. Math Achievement by SES: Fixed Component Estimates

$$Y_{MATH1} = 12.649 - 2.193X_{SES1}$$
$$(0.245) \quad (0.128)$$

$$R_1^2 = 3.6\%$$
$$N_1 = 7185$$
$$N_2 = 160$$

TABLE 3.2. Math Achievement by SES: Random Component Estimates

Parameter	Estimate	Std. error	Wald Z^a	Sig. level
Residual variance	36.700	0.626	58.650	.000
Random intercept variance	8.682	1.080	8.041	.000
Intercept-by-slope covariance	0.051	0.406	0.129	.901
Random slope variance	0.694	0.281	2.472	.013

Note. As we shall see below, SPSS printouts refer to random component estimates as "estimates of covariance parameters."
[a]Wald Z tests for the statistical significance of random components are asymptotically valid, meaning that the larger the sample, the more suitable the test. Most specialized multilevel software packages use a χ^2-based alternative.

Still keeping things simple, we use one school-level variable, percentage of students enrolled in an academic curriculum (X_{ACAD2}), as our sole contextual variable. The implied cross-level interaction term ($X_{ACAD2} * X_{SES1}$) is created simply by multiplying the student-level SES measure by the school-level contextual variable percentage of academic enrollment.

When we estimate our multilevel regression equation, we find in Table 3.3 that the fixed component for the intercept is still statistically significant ($p < .000$), and its value has changed very little, now equal to 12.802. Since both independent variables have been centered with respect to their grand means, if X_{SES1} and X_{ACAD2} were set equal to their means, out best estimate of Y_{MATH1} would be 12.802. The fixed component for the student-level SES coefficient also remains statistically significant ($p < .000$), and its numerical value, 2.181, is almost exactly the same as in our random coefficient equation. The fixed component for the slope for the percentage academic contextual variable is statistically significant as well ($p < .000$), with a value of 8.238. In addition, the fixed component for the cross-level interaction term is statistically significant ($p < .008$), with a value of 1.345.

Like the random coefficient regression results in Table 3.1, the multilevel regression results in Table 3.3 are easy to interpret, just as if they were OLS coefficients. For every 1-unit increment in X_{SES1}, individual student math achievement increases, on average, by 2.181 points. For every 1-unit increment in the X_{ACAD2} contextual variable, individual student math achievement increases, on average, by 8.238 points. Clearly, if the contextual factor had not been included, we would have missed an important predictor of math achievement. Finally, for every 1-unit increment in the percentage of academic enrollment contextual variable, the relationship between individual student math achievement and individual student SES is diminished by 1.345 test score points.

We can see that the contextual variable and the cross-level interaction term contribute to determining estimated values of the dependent variable. Our primary aim in introducing these factors, however, was to account for variability in the statistically significant random components for the intercept and the slope for X_{SES1}. In other words, we wanted to explain why they vary. Have we succeeded?

We can easily calculate a conditional intraclass correlation coefficient value of 0.098, substantially less than the unconditional intraclass correlation of 0.153. The contextual variable and cross-level interaction term have accounted for 35.9% of the school-to-school variability in math achievement.

TABLE 3.3. Math Achievement by SES, Respecified: Fixed Component Estimates

$$Y_{MATH1} = 12.802 - 2.181X_{SES1} + 8.238X_{ACAD2} - 1.345X_{ACAD2} * X_{SES1}$$
$$\quad\quad (0.181)\ (0.126)\quad\quad (0.709)\quad\quad\quad (0.504)$$

$$R_1^2 = 13.6\%$$
$$N_1 = 7185$$
$$N_2 = 160$$

TABLE 3.4. Math Achievement by SES, Respecified: Random Component Estimates

Parameter	Estimate	Std. error	Wald Z	Sig. level
Residual variance	36.689	0.625	58.668	.000
Random intercept variance	4.316	0.585	7.376	.000
Intercept-by-slope covariance	0.751	0.293	2.565	.010
Random slope variance	0.599	0.269	2.225	.026

Furthermore, in Table 3.4 we see that while the variance of the random component for the intercept remains statistically significant ($p < .000$), its magnitude has been substantially diminished, from 8.682 to 4.317. Clearly, a large part of the school-to-school variability in the intercept has been accounted for by our contextual variable. The variance of the random component for the SES slope has also remained statistically significant ($p = .026$). However, while its magnitude has diminished from 0.694 to 0.599, it remains largely unexplained. Our contextual variable and cross-level interaction term have accounted for only a little of the variability in the random component of the SES slope.

Finally, the covariance between the random components of the intercept and slope has actually become much larger, reaching a statistically significant value, with introduction of the contextual variable and cross-level interaction term. This association was suppressed in the simple random regression equation. Now, however, we see that when controlling for percentage of students enrolled in an academic curriculum, as school mean achievement increases, the slope for X_{SES1} increases as well. In other words, with X_{ACAD2} held constant, higher-achieving schools yield greater payoffs for SES advantages than lower-achieving schools.

This example may seem an odd vehicle for providing a chapter overview. As we promised, however, it has enabled us to invoke a large number of seemingly disparate concepts and illustrate their links to contextual variables and to multilevel regression analysis. Some of the concepts have already been explained, and some have not. After we have finished this chapter, we will understand all the concepts just employed and appreciate the relationships among them.

3.2 CONTEXTUAL VARIABLES AND ANALYTICAL OPPORTUNITIES

For a variety of substantive and methodological reasons, nesting has to be explicitly acknowledged and systematically incorporated into any analysis that includes grouped data. Failure to do so renders the results of such an analysis suspect.

It is important to emphasize, however, that nesting is not simply a source of methodological problems to be solved with multilevel regression. Nesting can also be construed as a source of analytical opportunities, notably in the form of contextual variables and cross-level interaction terms.

To provide additional substantive examples of nesting and the need for contextual variables, we will again use county-level data for all 3140 U.S. counties in the year 2000. County-level differences in median income for two-parent families and families headed by a single mother are often enormous (Boggess & Roulet, 2001; Shields & Snyder, 2005) and quite consequential for the well-being of families and individuals (Rubin, 1994; Kennedy, Kawachi, Glass, & Prothro-Stith, 1998). Median income for two-parent families is $49,135, while median income for families headed by a single mother is $17,753. The income difference varies dramatically, from $3182 to $74,461, in a distribution that closely approximates normality (Annie E. Casey Foundation, 2004). How might we explain county-to-county variability in the *difference* in median family income for two-parent families and single-mother families (see Figure 3.1)?

Independent variables in a preliminary analysis of county-level differences in family income would include obvious factors such as ethnic composition, median income per capita, and rural–urban location (Economic Research Service [ERS], 2004a). In this instance, ethnic composition is simplified and represented by the percentage of a county population that is Black and the percentage of a county population that is Hispanic. Median per capita income is available for the immediately previous year, 1999; these values are used as proxies for the 2000 values.

In addition, the ERS of the U.S. Department of Agriculture assigns each county an urban–rural continuum score ranging from 1 to 9, with higher scores representing more rural areas (ERS, 2004b). The irregular distribution of urban–rural scores for the 3140 counties in this U.S. Bureau of the Census data set is displayed in Figure 3.2. The same information aggregated to the state level appears in Figure 3.3.

The process of aggregation has yielded a much more varied and irregular distribution at the state level than at the county level. In large part, this is due to the fact that

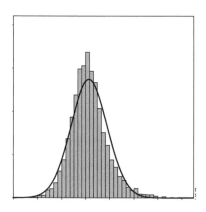

MEAN = 47139.99
STANDARD DEVIATION = 9871.88

FIGURE 3.1. Difference in median family income.

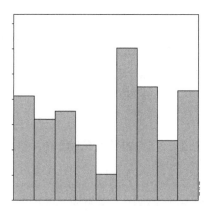

MEAN = 5.157
STANDARD DEVIATION = 2.680

FIGURE 3.2. County-level urban–rural continuum.

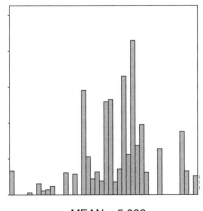

MEAN = 5.083
STANDARD DEVIATION = 3.139

FIGURE 3.3. State-level urban–rural continuum.

each county has an integer score ranging from 1 to 9. For each state, however, counties with different scores are combined, yielding a state-level urban–rural score that is an average of county values. Since none of the states is perfectly homogeneous with regard to this variable, decimals are included, assuring a much larger number of values. The same measure—in this instance, the urban–rural continuum score—yields very different variables at the county and state levels.

Table 3.5 reports the OLS unstandardized regression coefficient for the urban–rural continuum variable for an equation with percentage of Black residents, percentage of Hispanic residents, median per capita income, and urban–rural continuum score treated as characteristics of individual counties, with no contextual variables. Using the same family income difference dependent variable, Table 3.5 also reports the value of the urban–rural coefficient for a multilevel regression model using REML estimators, permitting the urban–rural coefficient to vary from state to state. In the multilevel model, the urban–rural variable is treated as a characteristic of individual counties *and* as an aggregated characteristic of states or a contextual variable.

For simplicity, in the multilevel equation percentage of Black residents, percentage of Hispanic residents, and median family income are treated as characteristics of individual counties only, without aggregated contextual variables. Each of the three, moreover, has been assigned a fixed coefficient rather than a random one, meaning that their slopes do not vary from context to context. REML estimators are still used, but in this example only the intercept and one of four slopes are random.

As we shall explain in Chapter 5, when a contextual variable is introduced to account for variability in a random slope, a cross-level interaction term is *implied*. This is something we have seen in several previous examples. In this case, the county-level variable X_{RURAL1} has been assigned a random slope, and the state-level variable X_{RURAL2} has been given the task of explaining the variability in that random slope. This implies the cross-level interaction term $X_{RURAL2} * X_{RURAL1}$.

TABLE 3.5. County-Level Urban–Rural Coefficients

Urban–rural coefficient without contextual variable = −289.39
(33.09)

Urban–rural coefficient with contextual variable = −236.49
(67.35)

There is no reason, however, why the contextual variable has to be the same level-one variable aggregated to level two. If we had theoretical, substantive, or commonsense reasons to do so, we might have assigned the task of explaining variability in the random slope for X_{RURAL1} to any other contextual variable, say, X_{BLACK2}, the proportion of state residents who are Black. This would have implied the cross-level interaction term X_{BLACK2} * X_{RURAL1}.

Furthermore, variability in a random slope (or a random intercept) may be treated as a function of more than one contextual variable. If variability in the slope for X_{RURAL1} were treated as a function of both X_{RURAL2} and X_{BLACK2}, this would imply inclusion of both X_{RURAL2} * X_{RURAL1} and X_{BLACK2} * X_{RURAL1} in the multilevel equation.

In Table 3.5, the urban–rural contextual variable and one cross-level interaction term are included in the multilevel equations that yielded the coefficients being compared. (The numbers in parentheses are standard errors.) We have seen examples like this before. In this instance both coefficients are negative, meaning that the county-level median income difference between intact and single-mother families declines as counties become more rural.

In the absence of a contextual variable and a cross-level interaction term, however, the absolute value of the urban–rural coefficient is 52.90 larger than when the additional terms are included. While this is not a huge difference, we may still be correct in judging that misspecification of the OLS regression model due to failure to acknowledge contextual factors and cross-level interaction terms has yielded a biased estimate of the county-level regression coefficient. (A formal test for model fit, the deviance difference, would be applicable here and is introduced in Section 3.6.)

If the OLS model is misspecified, this may also produce misleading results for the fixed slopes corresponding to the remaining independent variables. We investigate this in Table 3.6. Much as with previous comparisons of OLS and multilevel regression coef-

TABLE 3.6. County-Level Percent Black, Percent Hispanic, and Family Income Coefficients

Percent Black coefficient without contextual variable = 132.31
(5.52)
Percent Black coefficient with urban–rural contextual variable = 158.30
(6.97)
Percent Hispanic coefficient without contextual variable = –28.18
(6.39)
Percent Hispanic coefficient with urban–rural contextual variable = –28.36
(7.95)
Median family income coefficient without contextual variable = 609.37
(9.07)
Median family income coefficient with urban–rural contextual variable = 634.97
(9.98)

ficients, we see that differences due to alternative specification—in this case, exclusion or inclusion of a contextual variable and a cross-level interaction term—range from modest to minuscule. As we have come to take for granted, moreover, the multilevel standard errors are larger than the corresponding OLS standard errors. However, none of the coefficient or standard error differences is sufficiently large to change the substantive import of the analysis or to affect decision making with inferential tests.

Perhaps more consequential differences will be evident when we look at the coefficient for the contextual variable representing the urban–rural continuum. As with SES in the public–private school example in Chapter 2, the coefficient for the state-level contextual variable, consisting of aggregated values of the urban–rural continuum, is constrained to equal zero in the OLS equation. The meaning of this choice is evident in Table 3.7. The slope for the urban–rural contextual variable is *not* statistically significant. Furthermore, we see in Table 3.8 that the same is true of the implied cross-level interaction term. Since including these factors when obtaining the estimates in Tables 3.5 and 3.6 has little effect on the level-one coefficients, we may begin to suspect that omitting the contextual variable and cross-level interaction term would have been the right choice after all.

As we have done in previous examples, we can illustrate what is going on here via several different analytical strategies. Each table from Tables 3.9 through 3.12 represents an approach that might be used with a limited set of plausible explanatory variables. Each variable may be used at the county level, at the state level, or as a constituent of a cross-level interaction term.

The OLS multiple regression equation in Table 3.9 gives us the coefficients reported in Tables 3.5 and 3.6, estimated with contextual variables and cross-level interaction terms not included. (The dependent variable, difference in median family income for two-parent families and single-mother families, is here expressed in units of $1000.)

Table 3.10 is an alternative specification of the OLS regression model, this one including a contextual variable, X_{RURAL2}, and a cross-level interaction term, X_{RURAL2} *

TABLE 3.7. State-Level Urban–Rural Coefficients

Urban–rural contextual variable excluded: Unstandardized coefficient = 0.000
(N/A)

Urban–rural contextual variable included: Unstandardized coefficient = −163.70
(135.33)

TABLE 3.8. Cross-Level Interaction Terms

Cross-level interaction term excluded: Unstandardized coefficient = 0.000
(N/A)

Cross-level interaction term included: Unstandardized coefficient = −30.050
(43.743)

TABLE 3.9. OLS Regression: Family Income Difference

$$X_{\text{\$DIFFER}} = 31.383 + 0.132X_{\text{BLACK1}} - 0.028X_{\text{HISPANIC1}} + 0.609X_{\text{INCOME1}} - 0.289X_{\text{RURAL1}}$$
$$\quad\quad (0.70) \quad (0.005) \quad\quad (0.006) \quad\quad\quad (0.009) \quad\quad\quad (0.033)$$

$$R^2 = 73.5\%$$
$$N = 3140$$

TABLE 3.10. OLS Simulation of Multilevel Regression: Family Income Difference

$$Y_{\text{\$DIFFER}} = 31.385 + 0.127X_{\text{BLACK1}} + 0.030X_{\text{HISPANIC1}} - 0.592X_{\text{INCOME1}} - 0.267X_{\text{RURAL1}}$$
$$\quad\quad (0.080) \quad (0.006) \quad\quad (0.006) \quad\quad\quad (0.011) \quad\quad\quad (0.036)$$

$$- 0.179X_{\text{RURAL2}} - 0.043X_{\text{RURAL2}} * X_{\text{RURAL1}}$$
$$\quad (0.068) \quad\quad\quad (0.021)$$

$$R^2 = 73.7\%$$
$$N = 3140$$

X_{RURAL1}. Since OLS regression is inherently a single-level procedure, however, the contextual variable and interaction term have the tacked-on, jerry-rigged status we mentioned earlier.

Still another specification of this income difference function (Table 3.11) takes the form of a random coefficient regression model with REML estimators. In this instance, the intercept and the slope for X_{RURAL1} are permitted to vary from state to state. No effort is made, however, to explain this state-to-state variability.

In the fourth specification (Table 3.12), we have a random intercept and a random slope for X_{RURAL1}; REML estimators are used for all coefficients, whether random or fixed; and we include a contextual variable and a cross-level interaction term. The contextual variable and cross-level interaction term, moreover, are not merely tacked on, but are manifestations of the inherently two-level nature of the multilevel regression model.

We again see that different analytical strategies give us similar coefficient values. Notice, however, that the OLS simulation of multilevel regression in Table 3.11 gives us statistically significant slopes for the aggregated contextual variable (X_{RURAL2}) and for the cross-level interaction term ($X_{\text{RURAL2}} * X_{\text{RURAL1}}$). By contrast, in Table 3.12 the multilevel regression equation with a random intercept and a random slope finds a statistically

TABLE 3.11. Random Coefficient Regression: Family Income Difference

$$X_{\text{\$DIFFER}} = 31.714 + 0.159X_{\text{BLACK1}} - 0.028X_{\text{HISPANIC1}} + 0.635X_{\text{INCOME1}} - 0.249X_{\text{RURAL1}}$$
$$\quad\quad (0.199) \quad (0.007) \quad\quad (0.009) \quad\quad\quad (0.016) \quad\quad\quad (0.062)$$

$$R_1^2 = 77.2\%$$
$$N_1 = 3140$$
$$N_2 = 49$$

TABLE 3.12. Multilevel Regression: Family Income Difference

$$Y_{\$DIFFER} = 31.670 + 0.158X_{BLACK1} - 0.028X_{HISPANIC1} - 0.635X_{INCOME1} - 0.236X_{RURAL1}$$
$$\quad\quad\quad (0.205)\ (0.007) \quad\quad\ (0.008) \quad\quad\quad\quad (0.017) \quad\quad\quad\ (0.063)$$

$$\quad - 0.164X_{RURAL2} - 0.030X_{RURAL2} * X_{RURAL1}$$
$$\quad (0.160) \quad\quad\quad\ (0.043)$$

$$R_1^2 = 77.4\%$$
$$N_1 = 3140$$
$$N_2 = 49$$

significant coefficient for *neither* of the additional terms. In this instance, getting the correct results for tests of significance offers a strong argument for multilevel analysis.

3.3   CONTEXTUAL VARIABLES AND INDEPENDENT OBSERVATIONS

We have repeatedly reported that OLS and multilevel regression equations that include the same independent variables, including contextual factors, typically give similar coefficient values. This reminds us that multilevel modeling is just regression under a specific set of circumstances. We expect, however, that consequential differences may appear in standard error estimates.

Nevertheless, multilevel regression is not always a superior alternative to OLS regression. How do we decide when random coefficients, which imply the need for contextual variables and cross-level interaction terms, should be used? A simpler way of asking the same question goes like this: Are observations dependent? A good way to find out is to calculate the *intraclass correlation coefficient*.

In the multilevel analysis reproduced in Table 3.13, the intercept and the slope for X_{RURAL1} are random, meaning that they are permitted to vary across 49 of the 50 states. The fact that these coefficients are random explains the presence of the contextual variable, X_{RURAL2}, as well as the cross-level interaction term, $X_{RURAL2} * X_{RURAL1}$.

As we expected, the standard errors in the multilevel equation are larger than the downwardly biased standard errors in the OLS simulation. Even with similar coefficient values, this virtue of multilevel analysis makes for a predictable contrast: The contextual variable and the cross-level interaction term have statistically significant coefficients in the OLS equation, but *neither* is significant in the multilevel equation. If there are public policy implications or theoretically pertinent inferences to be drawn from analyses of family income differences, the meanings of these two equations are very different.

Including contextual effects in conventional OLS multiple regression equations ignores the fact that observations of residents nested in the same neighborhood, or students nested in the same school, or counties nested in the same state—observations nested within the same group!—are likely to be experientially and demographically sim-

TABLE 3.13. Family Income Difference Equations Compared

TABLE 3.12, Reproduced. Multilevel Regression: Family Income Difference

$$Y_{\$DIFFER} = 31.670 + 0.158X_{BLACK1} - 0.028X_{HISPANIC1} - 0.635X_{INCOME1} - 0.236X_{RURAL1}$$
$$\quad (0.205)\ (0.007) \qquad (0.008) \qquad\qquad (0.017) \qquad\qquad (0.063)$$

$$\quad - 0.164X_{RURAL2} - 0.030X_{RURAL2} * X_{RURAL1}$$
$$\quad (0.160) \qquad\qquad (0.043)$$

$$R_1^2 = 77.4\%$$
$$N_1 = 3140$$
$$N_2 = 49$$

TABLE 3.10, Reproduced. OLS Simulation of Multilevel Regression: Family Income Difference

$$Y_{\$DIFFER} = 31.385 + 0.127X_{BLACK1} + 0.030X_{HISPANIC1} - 0.592X_{INCOME1} - 0.267X_{RURAL1}$$
$$\quad (0.080)\ (0.006) \qquad (0.006) \qquad\qquad (0.011) \qquad\qquad (0.036)$$

$$\quad - 0.179X_{RURAL2} - 0.043X_{RURAL2} * X_{RURAL1}$$
$$\quad (0.068) \qquad\qquad (0.021)$$

$$R^2 = 73.7\%$$
$$N = 3140$$

ilar to each other, but different from observations in other groups. In other words, observations within groups may be dependent, a nesting-engendered phenomenon measured by the intraclass correlation.

Without within-group dependence, there is no need to permit coefficients to vary. Multilevel regression, with random coefficient variability explained by contextual variables and cross-level interaction terms, has no purpose. Perhaps our family income difference analyses illustrate just such a set of circumstances.

If this were the case, we would expect the intraclass correlation with family income difference as the dependent variable to be close to zero. As it turns out, however, the intraclass correlation coefficient value is large ($r = 0.371$). This tells us that about 37.1% of the variability in family income difference occurs between states, with the remaining 62.9% occurring within states. By most standards, this represents a high level of dependence. As a result, random coefficients, contextual variables, and cross-level interaction terms certainly have a role to play.

The intraclass correlation coefficient is easy to compute. To do so, however, we must use some of the additional essential information we get with multilevel regression analysis. Referring to our income difference data, in Table 3.14 we see a measure of residual variance (Residual) and a measure of the degree to which the random intercept varies from state to state (INTERCEPT1). Residual is just a measure of within-state variability in the dependent variability, while INTERCEPT1 is a measure of variability between states. These estimates are calculated with just a random intercept and no independent variables in the multilevel regression equation.

TABLE 3.14. Random Component Estimates for Family Income Difference

Parameter	Estimate	Std. error	Wald Z	Sig. level
Residual	43.620	1.110	39.282	.000
INTERCEPT1	25.764	5.915	4.356	.000

The intraclass correlation coefficient is comparable to the measure of association η^2, sometimes used with one-way ANOVA: between-group variability divided by total variability. Borrowing information from Table 3.14, we get the following:

$$r = \text{Between-group variability}/(\text{between-group variability} + \text{within-group variability})$$
$$= \text{INTERCEPT1}/(\text{INTERCEPT1} + \text{Residual})$$
$$= 25.764/(25.764 + 43.620) = 0.371$$

This is the *unconditional* intraclass correlation, meaning that there are no explanatory variables in the equation.

Getting information such as that reported in Table 3.14 is not at all difficult with SPSS. SPSS Routine 3.1 is just another routine using the Mixed Models procedure with the Windows interface. At the bottom of the SPSS output, values for random component variances for RESIDUAL and INTERCEPT are reported in the ESTIMATE column of the box labeled ESTIMATES OF COVARIANCE PARAMETERS. The RESIDUAL (within-group variability) and INTERCEPT (between-group variability) values are inserted into the formula for the intraclass correlation.

If the multilevel regression equation in Table 3.13 works as intended, introduction of contextual factors and cross-level interaction terms will diminish the intraclass corre-

---

SPSS Routine 3.1. Computing the Unconditional Intraclass Correlation

1. Open the SPSS data file and click on ANALYZE.
2. Go to MIXED MODELS and click on LINEAR.
3. Since the state is the level-two grouping variable, insert the state identifier into the SUBJECTS box.
4. Click on CONTINUE and insert income difference as a dependent variable into the DEPENDENT VARIABLE box.
5. Click on the RANDOM button at the bottom of the screen.
6. The state identifier is already in the SUBJECTS box; now also insert it into the COMBINATIONS box.
7. Near the top of the screen, click on INCLUDE INTERCEPT.
8. Click on CONTINUE, and then click on the STATISTICS button.
9. On the left, under MODEL STATISTICS, select PARAMETER ESTIMATES and TESTS FOR COVARIANCE PARAMETERS.
10. Click on CONTINUE and click on OK.

lation. In principle, it is possible for a properly specified model to account for all between-group variability, reducing the intraclass correlation to zero.

In this instance, we actually had a good deal of success in accounting for between-group variability in the analysis reported in Table 3.13. The information in Table 3.15 is of the same kind as that reported in Table 3.14; for ease of reference, a reproduction of Table 3.14 is appended to the bottom of the table. The new estimates of the variance components—the residual variance and the variance of INTERCEPT1—are calculated *after* we have included a contextual factor, X_{RURAL2}, and a cross-level interaction term, $X_{RURAL2} * X_{RURAL1}$. (The four level-one independent variables, X_{BLACK}, $X_{HISPANIC1}$, $X_{INCOME1}$, X_{RURAL1}, have not yet been introduced into the equation.)

We calculate the intraclass correlation in the same way as above, but now we are calculating the *conditional* intraclass correlation. We introduced the distinction between the unconditional and conditional intraclass correlation in Section 2.6 of Chapter 2, "Nesting and Effective Sample Size." The term *conditional* means simply that the coefficient value we calculate depends on—is conditioned by—the presence of explanatory variables in the equation.

The conditional intraclass correlation is calculated in the same way as the unconditional intraclass correlation, which we estimated as $r = 0.371$. Referring to Table 3.15, we again divide our estimate of variability between groups, INTERCEPT1, by our estimate of total variability, INTERCEPT1 plus Residual:

$$r = 10.522/(10.522 + 42.535) = 0.194$$

Including the contextual variable and cross-level interaction term in the multilevel regression equation has produced a substantial reduction in the proportion of variability that occurs between groups. We can see this even without computing the intraclass correlation coefficient simply by noting that the variance of INTERCEPT1 has been reduced from 25.764 to 10.522, while the residual variance is almost unchanged. Since one of our objectives in multilevel analysis is use of contextual factors and cross-level interac-

TABLE 3.15. Random Component Estimates for Family Income Difference; Contextual Variables and Cross-Level Interaction Terms Included

Parameter	Estimate	Std. error	Wald Z	Sig. level
Residual	42.535	1.108	39.283	.000
INTERCEPT1	10.522	2.573	4.089	.000

TABLE 3.14, Reproduced. Random Component Estimates for Family Income Difference; Contextual Variables and Cross-Level Interaction Terms Not Included

Parameter	Estimate	Std. error	Wald Z	Sig. level
Residual	43.620	1.110	39.282	.000
INTERCEPT1	25.764	5.915	4.356	.000

tion terms to explain why random components vary from context to context, it seems clear that including X_{RURAL2} and $X_{RURAL2} * X_{RURAL1}$ has paid off.

It may be, however, that X_{RURAL2} is not the most efficacious contextual variable, and the cross-level interaction term $X_{RURAL2} * X_{RURAL1}$ may be of less explanatory value than others. Nevertheless, we are on the right track methodologically, even if our substantive choices have not been the best ones.

At this point, then, we are faced with a substantive problem rather than a statistical one: There is a wide variety of possible responses. We may, for example, decide to use income aggregated to the state level, $X_{INCOME2}$, as an additional contextual variable to account for variability in the random slope for X_{RURAL1}. This implies the cross-level interaction term $X_{INCOME2} * X_{RURAL1}$. If we compute the conditional intraclass correlation with X_{RURAL2}, $X_{INCOME2}$, $X_{RURAL2} * X_{RURAL1}$, and $X_{INCOME2} * X_{RURAL1}$ in the equation, we get the information in Table 3.16.

The resulting conditional intraclass correlation has been diminished a good deal more. The two contextual factors and the two cross-level interaction terms are doing a very effective job of explaining the nesting-engendered intraclass correlation.

$$r = 1.790/(1.790 + 43.500) = 0.040$$

At the same time, these explanatory factors have reduced the residual variance, the amount of variability occurring within groups, by very little. However, this set of findings is not troubling. The primary purpose of contextual variables and cross-level interaction terms is to explain between-group variability (Hox & Maas, 2002). Within-group variability is a function of the level-one explanatory variables.

In Table 3.17, we have reported the residual variance and the intercept variance for the multilevel regression equation specified as in Table 3.18. Now that the level-one explanatory variables (X_{RURAL1}, $X_{INCOME1}$, X_{BLACK1}, and $X_{HISPANIC1}$) have been included, the residual variance has been sharply reduced, while INTERCEPT1 has been diminished

TABLE 3.16. Random Component Estimates for Family Income Difference, Respecified

Parameter	Estimate	Std. error	Wald Z	Sig. level
Residual	43.500	1.106	39.321	.000
INTERCEPT1	1.790	0.570	3.139	.002

TABLE 3.17. Random Component Estimates for Family Income Difference; All Independent Variables Included

Parameter	Estimate	Std. error	Wald Z	Sig. level
Residual	13.536	0.349	38.754	.000
INTERCEPT1	1.333	0.370	3.594	.000

TABLE 3.18. Multilevel Regression: Family Income Difference, Respecified

$$Y_{\$DIFFER} = 31.593 + 0.153X_{BLACK1} - 0.020X_{HISPANIC1} - 0.607X_{INCOME1} - 0.278X_{RURAL1} - 0.133X_{RURAL2}$$
$$\quad\;(0.194)\;(0.006)\qquad\quad(0.008)\qquad\qquad(0.010)\qquad\qquad(0.063)\qquad\qquad(0.169)$$

$$\quad - 0.043X_{RURAL2} * X_{RURAL1} + 0.046X_{INCOME2} - 0.002X_{INCOME2} * X_{RURAL1}$$
$$\quad\;(0.051)\qquad\qquad\qquad\quad(0.037)\qquad\qquad(0.011)$$

$$R_1^2 = 77.4\%$$
$$N_1 = 3140$$
$$N_2 = 49$$

only a little more. It is worth noting, however, that the results reported in Table 3.16 have left us with very little between-group variability to explain.

Notice, by the way, that if we were to compute the conditional intraclass correlation using the information in Table 3.17, its value would be 0.090. This is greater than the value calculated for Table 3.16. This illustrates the fact that the conditional intraclass correlation should be computed with contextual factors and cross-level interaction terms as independent variables, but *without* level-one explanatory variables. If we include the level-one predictors, the denominator in the formula for the conditional intraclass correlation coefficient varies accordingly, and coefficients cease to be comparable. The conditional coefficient no longer enables us to determine the comparative efficacy of specific sets of contextual variables and cross-level interaction terms in accounting for between-group variability from one specification to another.

We have now seen that contextual variables and cross-level interaction terms explain most of the variability in the dependent variable that occurs between groups. In addition, level-one independent variables explain most of the variability that occurs within groups. We have yet to acknowledge properly, however, that between-group variability is not manifest *only* in the random intercept, but *also* occurs in random slopes, permitting them to vary from group to group. Explanation of this variability, too, may be of substantive interest.

This is a good place to emphasize a crucial distinction: *A random regression coefficient has two components, fixed and random.* We will explain this more fully in Chapter 4. For now, we will note simply that the fixed component is a weighted average across groups, with larger groups contributing more to the overall average than smaller groups. The random component, by contrast, measures group-dependent deviations from this average (Snijders & Bosker, 1999, pp. 67–98).

So far, we have given most of our attention to fixed components, such as those reported in the multilevel equations in Tables 3.12, 3.13, and 3.18. Beginning with Tables 3.2 and 3.4 in our introductory example, however, we have also begun to discuss random components, often referred to as random effects. The random components include the intercept variance and the variances of random slopes.

In the preliminary stages of an analysis, it may be useful to estimate the random components *without* including contextual variables and cross-level interaction terms. In the absence of well-developed theory or informative substantive literature, this can help us decide *which* level-one coefficients, if any, should be permitted to vary across groups. The intraclass correlation provides an answer to the question "Should any coefficients be permitted to vary across higher-level groups?" Estimating level-one random components can help answer a more specific question: "*Which* coefficients should be permitted to vary across higher-level groups?"

Continuing with the family income difference analysis, we assign X_{INCOME1}, county-level median family income, a random slope rather than a fixed slope. We then estimate random components for INTERCEPT1, X_{RURAL1}, and X_{INCOME1}, as reported in Table 3.19.

Notice that the Table 3.19 caption includes the phrase "Estimates of Covariance Parameters" rather than "Random Component Estimates." "Estimates of Covariance Parameters" is the label that appears on SPSS printouts, acknowledging that when there is more than one random component, they may be *correlated*. They may vary together in substantively interpretable ways. Since we are permitting the intercept and the two slopes to vary from state to state, we have three random components. As a result, the random intercept may be correlated with one or more random slopes, and the random slopes may be correlated with each other.

Furthermore, just as contextual variables and cross-level interaction terms are used to account for variability in random components, they are also used to explain covariances. We will discuss this more fully in Section 3.7, "Contextual Variables and Covariance Structure."

In Table 3.19 we see estimates of covariance parameters corresponding to the multilevel regression equation in Table 3.18 but *without* the contextual variables and cross-level interaction terms. Table 3.20 reports estimates for the same parameters, but *with* the contextual variables and cross-level interaction terms included. When we introduce the contextual variables and cross-level interaction terms, all but one of the random component variance and covariance estimates in Table 3.20 is diminished, much as we would expect. It is true, however, that we are still not explaining much of the variability in the random component variance for the X_{RURAL1} slope, but it is clear that the decision to make the slope for X_{RURAL1} random is consistent with our data.

TABLE 3.19. Multilevel Regression: Family Income Difference, Respecified; Contextual Variables and Cross-Level Interactions Not Included; Estimates of Covariance Parameters

Parameter	Estimate	Std. error	Wald Z	Sig. level
Residual	15.215	0.394	38.639	.000
INTERCEPT1	2.446	0.720	3.400	.001
INTERCEPT1 by X_{INCOME1}	−0.096	0.442	−2.163	.006
X_{INCOME1}	0.012	0.004	2.742	.000
INTERCEPT1 by X_{RURAL1}	−0.261	0.152	−1.722	.085
X_{INCOME1} by X_{RURAL1}	0.018	0.012	1.337	.181
X_{RURAL1}	0.133	0.058	2.293	.022

TABLE 3.20. Multilevel Regression: Family Income Difference, Respecified; Contextual Variables and Cross-Level Interaction Terms Included; Estimates of Covariance Parameters

Parameter	Estimate	Std. error	Wald Z	Sig. level
Residual	15.199	0.393	38.659	.000
INTERCEPT1	1.784	0.542	3.289	.001
INTERCEPT1 by $X_{INCOME1}$	−0.076	0.038	−1.988	.047
$X_{INCOME1}$	0.008	0.003	2.535	.011
INTERCEPT1 by X_{RURAL1}	−0.201	0.131	−1.535	.125
$X_{INCOME1}$ by X_{RURAL1}	0.017	0.012	1.421	.155
X_{RURAL1}	0.118	0.058	2.003	.027

3.4   CONTEXTUAL VARIABLES AND INDEPENDENT OBSERVATIONS: A NINE-CATEGORY DUMMY VARIABLE

We have already used the national probability sample that includes annual income and occupation in nine categories for 4359 observations on adult males. A one-way ANOVA with income as the dependent variable and occupation as the independent variable yields the results reported in Table 3.21.

There is nothing surprising here: Occupation and income are associated, as is immediately evident in Table 3.22 and Figure 3.4. It is useful to reemphasize, however,

TABLE 3.21. ANOVA of Income by Occupation

	Sums of squares	df	Mean square	F	Sig. level
Between	70.16	8	8.77	32.71	.000
Within	1166.17	4350	0.27		
Total	1236.3	4358			

TABLE 3.22. OLS Regression of Hourly Income on Occupational Category

$Y = 3.708 + 3.469X_{OCCUPY1} + 3.203X_{OCCUPY2} + 3.514X_{OCCUPY3} + 1.888X_{OCCUPY4} + 2.396X_{OCCUPY5}$
   (0.388) (0.414)   (0.417)   (0.448)   (0.412)   (0.401)

   $+ 1.925X_{OCCUPY6} + 1.459X_{OCCUPY7} + 1.057X_{OCCUPY9}$
   (0.401)   (0.417)   (0.411)

$$R^2 = 6.4\%$$
$$N = 4359$$

Note. The occupation with the lowest mean hourly income, $X_{OCCUPY8}$, is the suppressed reference category.

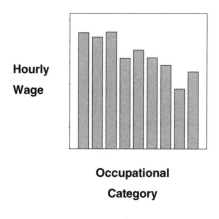

Hourly Wage

Occupational Category

FIGURE 3.4. Hourly wage by nine nominal categories of occupation.

that the statistically significant F value also means that individual-level observations are not independent. Instead, they may be construed as nested within socially constructed occupational categories (Kennedy, 2003, p. 150). If so, the OLS regression coefficients estimated using this data will have standard errors that are biased downward.

Using the simple procedure introduced above and the within-group and between-group variance component estimates provided in Table 3.23, it is easy to determine the magnitude of the unconditional intraclass correlation coefficient:

$$r = 1.283/(1.283 + 9.613) = 0.117$$

As we learned from our discussion of effective sample size, with a large number of cases and a small number of groups, this is a substantial intraclass correlation. It threatens to compromise the validity of tests of significance and the accuracy of confidence intervals.

With data nested in this fashion, contextual variables measured at the level of the occupation rather than the individual merit investigation. As a simple illustration, we may suspect that education-intensive occupations pay more than other occupations for each additional year of school completed. In Table 3.24 we suspend judgment about effective sample size, and we report the individual-level results of three analyses.

In the first analysis, the regression coefficient measuring the individual-level relationship between hourly wage and education is estimated using OLS estimators without contextual variables. In the second and third analyses, we see the same relationship estimated using REML estimators in a multilevel framework, along with a contextual variable for mean years of educational attainment at the occupation level. The only difference between the two multilevel analyses is that random components are permitted to vary together in one but not the other. The numbers in parentheses in Table 3.24 are standard errors.

Table 3.24 shows us that if we use OLS estimators and fail to include the contextual variable, we may underestimate the value of the unstandardized regression coefficient

TABLE 3.23. Random Component Estimates for Annual Income; No Independent Variables Included

Parameter	Estimate	Std. error	Wald Z	Sig. level
Residual	9.613	0.206	46.635	.000
INTERCEPT1	1.283	0.646	1.985	.048

TABLE 3.24. Hourly Wage and Education:
Individual-Level Coefficients

<u>OLS</u>

Hourly wage and education without contextual variables = 0.414
(0.029)

<u>Multilevel with correlated random components</u>

Hourly wage and education with contextual variables = 0.406
(0.035)

<u>Multilevel with independent random components</u>

Hourly wage and education with contextual variables = 0.423
(0.036)

for individual-level education. In this instance the difference is quite small. As we have come to expect, moreover, OLS underestimates the value of the standard error. Table 3.24 also shows us that with a multilevel regression model, permitting random components to be correlated or constraining them to be independent makes little or no difference. This is generally the case, though exceptions occur.

We see in Table 3.25, however, that if we do not include education aggregated to the occupation level, we will completely miss a substantial contextual effect of education on hourly wage. The same is true of the cross-level interaction term reported in Table 3.26. Again, however, the decision as to whether or not to permit random components to be correlated makes little difference for estimation of substantively interesting coefficients.

The equations that produced the regression coefficients and standard errors compared in Tables 3.24 through 3.26 are reported in Table 3.27. In each of the six equations, individual-level educational attainment ($X_{\text{EDUCATION1}}$) is positively related to hourly

TABLE 3.25. Hourly Wage and Education:
Contextual Coefficients

<u>OLS</u>

Education contextual coefficient = 0.000
(N/A)

<u>Multilevel with correlated random components</u>

Education contextual coefficient = 1.238
(0.319)

<u>Multilevel with independent random components</u>

Education contextual coefficient = 1.239
(0.318)

TABLE 3.26. Hourly Wage and Education:
Cross-Level Interaction Effects

OLS

Cross-level interaction = 0.000
(N/A)

Multilevel with correlated random components

Cross-level interaction = 0.178
(0.051)

Multilevel with independent random components

Cross-level interaction = 0.157
(0.052)

TABLE 3.27. OLS, REML/Random Coefficient, and REML/Multilevel Analyses
of Hourly Wage

OLS without contextual variables or cross-level interaction terms

$Y = 5.920 + 0.414X_{EDUCATION1}$
   (0.047) (0.029)

OLS simulation of multilevel analysis

$Y = 5.923 + 0.420X_{EDUCATION1} + 0.900X_{EDUCATION2} + 0.149 X_{EDUCATION1} * X_{EDUCATION2}$
   (0.047) (0.029)   (0.070)   (0.043)

REML/random coefficient regression; random components permitted to covary

$Y = 5.833 + 0.414X_{EDUCATION1}$
   (0.383) (0.060)

REML/random coefficient regression; random components constrained to be independent

$Y = 5.827 + 0.440X_{EDUCATION1}$
   (0.384) (0.054)

REML/multilevel; random components permitted to covary

$Y = 5.740 + 0.406X_{EDUCATION1} + 1.238X_{EDUCATION2} + 0.178X_{EDUCATION1} * X_{EDUCATION2}$
   (0.230) (0.035)   (0.320)   (0.051)

REML/multilevel; random components constrained to be independent

$Y = 5.738 + 0.423X_{EDUCATION1} + 1.238X_{EDUCATION2} + 0.157X_{EDUCATION1} * X_{EDUCATION2}$
   (0.229) (0.036)   (0.319)   (0.052)

wage. The size of the coefficient for this level-one variable varies little from one equation to another.

In each of the three equations that include the occupation-level contextual variable $X_{EDUCATION2}$, this group-level aggregate is positively related to hourly wage. The size of the coefficient for this level-two variable, however, is substantially smaller in the OLS simulation of multilevel regression than in the two multilevel equations.

In each of the three equations that include the cross-level interaction term, $X_{EDUCATION2} * X_{EDUCATION1}$, the coefficient is positive. This means that individual-level investments in education pay off best in occupations where the average level of educational attainment is comparatively high. This coefficient shows the greatest amount of variability from equation to equation, with the coefficient for the OLS simulation again smaller than either of the multilevel coefficients.

The OLS standard errors are consistently smaller. In this instance, however, that has no bearing on decisions as to statistical significance: All coefficients are statistically significant.

Table 3.27 makes clear that proper specification of a regression model inevitably entails more decisions than we may commonly acknowledge. Do we use OLS or alternative estimators such as REML? Is one level enough, or does a credible analysis require explicit inclusion of more than one level? Should all coefficients be fixed, or should one or more be random, permitted to vary from group to group? If random coefficients are used, which explanatory variables should be assigned random coefficients, and which should remain fixed? If random coefficients are used, which second-level variables and cross-level interaction terms should be used to explain why they vary? If more than one random coefficient is used, should they be permitted to vary together, or should they be constrained to be independent?

This is a long and difficult list of specification decisions! Moreover, they must all be made on top of the usual regression analysis decisions, especially selection of independent variables and identification of proper functional form. In this example, the added intellectual labor has yielded coefficient estimates that differ little from each other. Moreover, with alpha set at .05 or .01, decisions about statistical significance are the same from one equation to another.

Suppose we could get rid of all disclaimers and hedging, and make the unqualified assertion that OLS regression and multilevel regression coefficients will be nearly the same *whenever* individual-level and contextual variables are included in the same analysis. Even with effective correctives for standard errors and degrees of freedom, would that be sufficient to prompt abandonment of the difficult literature, specialized software, and overstated claims that come with multilevel regression? Not if we have information adequate to the task of specifying a suitable multilevel model, enabling us to get the best estimates we can get.

There is nothing new about this point of view. Beginning in Chapter 1 with the application of EGLS in Figures 1.1 though 1.3, our examples suggest that most correctives for violations of OLS assumptions yield only small coefficient differences and occasional changes in inferential judgments.

As conventional correctives do, multilevel regression explicitly takes into consideration more information in the specification, estimation, and testing of regression models than OLS. The additional information takes the form of variances and covariances of random terms. With the hourly-wage-by-education examples, if we permit the intercept and the coefficient for $X_{EDUCATION1}$ to vary across occupational groups, we get the additional measures reported in Tables 3.28 through 3.31. Again, the specific values reported depend on how the random coefficient model or multilevel regression model is specified.

Contextual factors and cross-level interaction terms are included in the equations that yielded the random component values in Tables 3.30 and 3.31, but not in Tables 3.28 and 3.29. This explains why the variances in Table 3.31 are smaller than those in Table 3.29, and why the variances and covariances in Table 3.30 are smaller than those in Table 3.28: Contextual effects and cross-level interaction terms are *intended* to account for variability in random components.

TABLE 3.28. Estimates of Covariance Parameters for Hourly Wage: Random Coefficient Regression; Random Components Permitted to Covary

Parameter	Estimate	Std. error	Wald Z	Sig. level
Residual	9.135	0.196	46.597	.000
INTERCEPT1	1.289	0.677	1.904	.057
INTERCEPT1 by $X_{EDUCATION1}$	0.170	0.100	1.693	.091
$X_{EDUCATION1}$	0.024	0.018	1.138	.188

TABLE 3.29. Estimates of Covariance Parameters for Hourly Wage: Random Coefficient Regression; Random Components Constrained to Be Independent

Parameter	Estimate	Std. error	Wald Z	Sig. level
Residual	9.138	0.196	46.582	.000
INTERCEPT1	1.291	0.679	1.901	.057
INTERCEPT1 by $X_{EDUCATION1}$	N/A	N/A	N/A	N/A
$X_{EDUCATION1}$	0.017	0.014	1.196	.232

TABLE 3.30. Estimates of Covariance Parameters for Hourly Wage: Multilevel Regression; Random Components Permitted to Covary

Parameter	Estimate	Std. error	Wald Z	Sig. level
Residual	9.137	0.196	46.581	.000
INTERCEPT1	0.436	0.256	1.703	.089
INTERCEPT1 by $X_{EDUCATION1}$	0.037	0.033	1.148	.251
$X_{EDUCATION1}$	0.004	0.008	0.491	.623

TABLE 3.31. Estimates of Covariance Parameters for Hourly Wage: Multilevel Regression; Random Components Constrained to Be Independent

Parameter	Estimate	Std. error	Wald Z	Sig. level
Residual	9.138	0.196	46.580	.000
INTERCEPT1	0.432	0.254	1.700	.089
INTERCEPT1 by $X_{\text{EDUCATION1}}$	N/A	N/A	N/A	N/A
$X_{\text{EDUCATION1}}$	0.004	0.007	0.507	.612

3.5 CONTEXTUAL VARIABLES, INTRACLASS CORRELATION, AND MISSPECIFICATION

At this point, we will reemphasize the judgment that multilevel regression is best understood as one of many correctives that enable us to use regression analysis even when well-known OLS assumptions have been violated. In a variety of ways, authors such as Heckman (1979), Kennedy (1998), Wooldridge (2002), Gujarati (2003, 2006), and Hayes and Cai (2005) have effectively argued that the assumption most frequently violated is *proper specification*.[1] Often, in this view, what appear to be violations such as nonrandom sampling, heteroscedasticity, nonadditivity, serial correlation, and nonlinearity can best be treated as manifestations of specification error.

This raises an interesting question: If we select the correct independent variables and use proper functional forms, can OLS approximations to a perfectly specified regression model rid us of dependence among observations, diminishing the intraclass correlation coefficient to an inconsequential value? After all, it is gradually becoming evident from our examples that the more closely an OLS specification approximates a suitable multilevel model, the better the OLS estimates.

Many of us who use applied statistics are accustomed to explaining away correlations by introducing judiciously selected control variables. This is intrinsic to the process of using statistics to understand why variables are correlated (see, e.g., the classic statement by Rosenberg, 1968) and fundamental to the development of manifest variable path analysis and structural equation modeling (Kenny, 1979; Davis, 1985). The distinction between unconditional and conditional intraclass correlation clearly implies that introducing a suitable set of explanatory factors can go a long way toward accounting for within-group homogeneity (Mok, 1995). Why not get rid of intraclass correlation in just this way?

For example, with the 12-school West Virginia data set introduced earlier, we use Woodcock–Johnson 22 reading test scores (Woodcock & Johnson, 1990) at the beginning of kindergarten as the dependent variable in a one-way ANOVA. Each of the schools represents a category of a nominal-level independent variable. This yields the

---

[1]The meaning of *proper specification* is not perfectly consistent from one source to another. In Section 3.2 we have used this expression to mean use of the correct set of independent variables and functional forms.

results reported in Table 3.32. No surprises: Schools differ with respect to mean student achievement.

In response, we might estimate an OLS multiple regression equation aimed at explaining student-to-student differences in reading achievement at the beginning of kindergarten. If we assume that differences among students and their social backgrounds account for the mean school differences, we could introduce a small but plausible complement of independent variables such as family income ($X_{INCOME1}$), respondent parent's educational level (X_{ED1}), race (X_{BLACK1}), and neighborhood quality (X_{HOOD1}), all measured at the individual level. (Independent variables are measured only at the individual level, because contextual effects by their nature take time to emerge, and the students in this analysis are just beginning kindergarten.)

If we save the residuals from the OLS regression analysis in Table 3.33 and use them as the dependent variable in another one-way ANOVA with each of the 12 schools representing a category of a dummy independent variable, we get the results reported in Table 3.34. The residuals are the Woodcock–Johnson 22 scores' net variability due to $X_{INCOME1}$, X_{ED1}, X_{BLACK1}, and X_{HOOD1}. The ω^2 values for Tables 3.32 and 3.34 indicate that the associ-

TABLE 3.32. ANOVA of Reading Achievement

	Sums of squares	df	Mean square	F	Sig. level
Between	1057.27	11	96.12	6.50	.000
Within	4391.95	297	14.79		
Total	5449.22	308			

$$\omega^2 = 0.16$$

TABLE 3.33. OLS Analysis of Reading Achievement at Start of Kindergarten

$$Y_{READ} = 10.233 + 0.298X_{INCOME1} + 0.201X_{ED1} - 0.578X_{BLACK1} + 0.101X_{HOOD1}$$
$$(0.228)\ (0.104) \qquad\quad (0.154) \qquad\quad (0.841) \qquad\quad (0.034)$$

$$R^2 = 10.3\%$$
$$N = 309$$

TABLE 3.34. ANOVA of Reading Achievement Residuals

	Sums of squares	df	Mean square	F	Sig. level
Between	1066.05	11	96.91	7.12	.000
Within	4045.69	297	13.62		
Total	5111.74	308			

$$\omega^2 = 0.18$$

ation between reading test scores and the school variable is almost exactly the same, actually increasing just a bit with introduction of the independent variables.

As an exercise with an entirely predictable but instructive outcome, we could reestimate the OLS regression analysis from Table 3.33 after adding 11 school dummy variables representing the 12 West Virginia elementary schools, with the highest-scoring school as the suppressed category (Kerlinger & Pedhazuer, 1973). We again save the residuals as new values for reading achievement scores' net variability due to $X_{INCOME1}$, X_{ED1}, X_{BLACK1}, and X_{HOOD1}, as well as variability due to unspecified differences among schools. The results are reported in Table 3.35.

If we do a one-way ANOVA with this set of residuals as the dependent variable and school as the independent variable, we get the results reported in Table 3.36. What could be more obvious? If we purge a dependent variable of variability due to a specific independent variable, such as school attended, that explanatory factor will no longer be related to the outcome measure.

But let's think about it. What is it that accounts for incoming kindergarten students' having higher or lower average reading scores at one elementary school than at another school? Since school effects have not had time to become manifest in student performance, it is reasonable to conclude that reading score differences are due to student characteristics that we have failed to control—characteristics other than $X_{INCOME1}$, X_{ED1}, X_{BLACK1}, and X_{HOOD1}. *If* we could identify and measure *all* such characteristics and incorporate them as independent variables, beginning school-to-school achievement differ-

TABLE 3.35. OLS Analysis of Reading Achievement at Start of Kindergarten, Respecified

Y_{READ} = 11.944 + 0.253$X_{INCOME1}$ + 0.344 X_{ED1} − 0.034 X_{BLACK1} + 0.058X_{HOOD1} − 3.583X_{SCHL1}
    (0.715) (0.101)   (0.149)   (0.851)   (0.033)   (1.058)

    − 3.327$_{SCHL2}$ − 2.608X_{SCHL3} − 0.223X_{SCHL4} − 2.563X_{SCHL5} − 1.189X_{SCHL6} − 2.237X_{SCHL7}
    (1.066) (0.887)   (1.152)   (0.917)   (1.227)   (1.099)

    − 2.939X_{SCHL8} − 0.131X_{SCHL9} + 2.548X_{SCHL11} − 0.321X_{SCHL12}
    (1.006)   (1.283)   (1.074)   (1.803)

$$R^2 = 21.1\%$$
$$N = 309$$

TABLE 3.36. ANOVA of Reading Achievement Net Association with School

	Sums of squares	df	Mean square	F	Sig. level
Between	00.00	11	0.00	0.00	1.000
Within	4731.33	297	15.93		
Total	4731.33	308			
			$\omega^2 = 0.00$		

ences would disappear. There would no longer be an association between reading achievement and the school variable. *The intraclass correlation due to students' being nested in schools would be zero.*

The possibility of producing the complete absence of an association between achievement and school in this example might be taken to suggest that a suitably specified OLS multiple regression equation would be free of the adverse consequences of dependent observations. With the correct set of independent variables and with each relationship expressed in the proper functional form, statistical dependence among observations might be completely eliminated. We would have been correct in suspecting that intraclass correlation was due to specification error. Methodological difficulties due to nesting would be gone.

There are, however, serious practical, methodological, and substantive problems associated with construing dependence among observations as a consequence of misspecification. To begin with, a perfectly specified regression model is never in the offing (Retherford & Choe, 1993; Hayes & Cai, 2005). Acknowledging the existence of contextual or grouping variables further emphasizes this judgment by forcing us to recognize that the consequences of grouping are never completely understood (Goldstein, 2003).

Furthermore, with 309 observations and only 12 school categories, introduction of 11 school dummies uses a comparatively small number of degrees of freedom. If, however, a second-level variable were constituted of a very large number of categories, representing these with dummy variables not only would be enormously clumsy but would use up a needlessly large number of degrees of freedom and might give rise to problems with multicollinearity.

In addition, creating dummy independent variables to represent schools in an OLS regression equation implies that we are treating this variable as a characteristic of individuals rather than as a second-level or contextual variable in which individuals are nested. In some instances this is the correct call (Tabachnick, 2005). Nevertheless, routine use of dummy variables as just described removes this decision from the realm of substantively informed judgment.

For now, we will use Tables 3.37 through 3.40 below to illustrate results that follow from deciding to use schools to create individual-level dummy variables, *or* deciding to treat school as a second-level variable in which individuals are nested. In each instance, we will again use X_{ED1}, $X_{INCOME1}$, X_{BLACK1}, and X_{HOOD1} as independent variables. In addition, to make clear that we are giving the effects of contextual variables time to develop, we will use the Woodcock–Johnson 22 reading achievement test score at the *beginning* of kindergarten as another *independent variable*, with the same test administered at the *end* of kindergarten providing values for the *dependent variable*.

When school membership is treated as a category of individual students, we will use OLS estimators and no contextual variables or cross-level interaction terms. This yields the equation with 11 dummy variables representing 12 schools. In the multilevel analysis, on the other hand, the intercept and the slope for $X_{ACHIEVE1}$ will be permitted to vary from school to school. The only contextual variable in the multilevel analysis will be the beginning-of-kindergarten achievement test score aggregated to the school level, $X_{ACHIEVE2}$. An implied cross-level interaction term, $X_{ACHIEVE2} * X_{ACHIEVE1}$, created with reading achievement measured at the individual and school levels, will be used as an additional explanatory factor.

Table 3.37 shows that with the exception of ethnicity and achievement, differences between the OLS coefficients and multilevel coefficients are extremely small. In the case of ethnicity, while the difference between coefficients is comparatively large, it is of no consequence since neither coefficient is statistically significant. In fact, the achievement coefficients are the only ones at the student level in either equation that are significant.

Recall, moreover, that the achievement coefficient in the multilevel equation is random, meaning that it corresponds to a sample size of 12 schools. The OLS coefficient, by contrast, corresponds to a sample size of 309 students. As expected, moreover, the standard error for the random coefficient is larger than the OLS coefficient.

The differences between standard errors produced by the two approaches would be larger if the OLS coefficients were not inflated due to multicollinearity. Eleven school dummies gives us 16 independent variables in the OLS equation. Variance inflation factors range from 1.169 to 10.467, with 6 of the 16 greater than the usual cutoff of 4.00 (Fox, 1997). Use of a large set of dummy variables in the OLS equation has made multicollinearity troublesome (Montgomery, Peck, & Vining, 2001).

TABLE 3.37. Analytical Status of Schools: Level-Two Grouping Variable or Level-One Dummy Variables?

Income coefficient with school at level one = 0.036 (0.084)
Income coefficient with school at level two = 0.042 (0.083)
Education coefficient with school at level one = 0.161 (0.125)
Education coefficient with school at level two = 0.160 (0.124)
Ethnicity coefficient with school at level one = 0.227 (0.706)
Ethnicity coefficient with school at level two = 0.143 (0.289)
Neighborhood coefficient with school at level one = –0.001 (0.028)
Neighborhood coefficient with school at level two = 0.001 (0.027)
Achievement coefficient with school at level one = 0.757 (0.048)
Achievement coefficient with school at level two = 0.845 (0.063)

Table 3.38 emphasizes again that in the absence of second-level contextual variables, their regression coefficients are constrained to be zero. In this instance, we see that when the second-level aggregated achievement variable is included in the multilevel regression model, it has a nonzero coefficient that turns out to be statistically significant. In the absence of this school-level variable, a substantial contextual effect would again have been overlooked.

As we know by now, failure to include one or more school-level variables would also mean that implied cross-level interactions were excluded. In this instance, the cross-level interaction term created using achievement at the individual and school levels is statistically significant, as we see in Table 3.39: For every 1-unit increment in $X_{ACHIEVE2}$, the relationship between student-level reading achievement at the end of kindergarten and student-level reading achievement at the beginning of kindergarten is increased by 0.041 points.

Notice how the role of the school variable differs from the OLS regression equation to the multilevel regression equation. In the OLS analysis, 12 school categories are used to create 11 dummy variables that are treated as characteristics of individuals. In the multilevel analysis, however, school is not explicitly introduced into the regression equation. Instead, the intercept and the slope for student-level beginning achievement are permitted to vary across the 12 school categories. In this example, moreover, variability in the intercept and in each slope is treated as a function of the aggregated school-level beginning achievement variable, as well as a cross-level interaction term. The contrast between the simplicity of the multilevel regression equation for reading achievement in Table 3.40 and the cluttered complexity of the OLS regression equation in Table 3.41 is striking.

As we are reminded again by Tables 3.42 and 3.43, second-level and cross-level explanatory factors are intended to account for school-to-school variability in random component estimates. In Table 3.42, the variance of the random component for the

TABLE 3.38. Analytical Status of Schools: School-Level Family Income Coefficients

Achievement contextual variable excluded: Unstandardized coefficient = 0.000	(N/A)
Achievement contextual variable included: Unstandardized coefficient = 1.097	(0.127)

TABLE 3.39. Analytical Status of Schools: Cross-Level Interaction Term

Cross-level interaction term excluded: Unstandardized coefficient = 0.000	(N/A)
Cross-level interaction term included: Unstandardized coefficient = 0.041	(0.018)

TABLE 3.40. Multilevel Analysis of Reading Achievement at End of Kindergarten

$$Y = 16.631 + 0.042X_{INCOME1} + 0.160X_{ED1} + 0.143X_{BLACK1} + 0.001X_{HOOD1} + 0.845X_{ACHIEVE1}$$
$$\quad (1.340) \ (0.083) \qquad (0.124) \qquad (0.268) \qquad (0.027) \qquad (0.063)$$

$$+ \ 1.097X_{ACHIEVE2} + 0.041X_{ACHIEVE2} \ ^* \ X_{ACHIEVE1}$$
$$\quad (0.127) \qquad\quad (0.018)$$

$$R^2 = 57.3\%$$
$$N_1 = 309$$
$$N_2 = 12$$

TABLE 3.41. OLS Analysis of Reading Achievement at End of Kindergarten

$$Y_{READ} = 14.965 + 0.036X_{INCOME1} + 0.161X_{ED1} + 0.227X_{BLACK1} - 0.001X_{HOOD1} + 0.757X_{ACHIEVE1}$$
$$\quad (2.219) \ (0.084) \qquad (0.125) \qquad (0.706) \qquad (0.028) \qquad (0.048)$$

$$- \ 2.952X_{SCHL1} - 2.633 \ X_{SCHL2} - 1.906 \ X_{SCHL3} - 1.532X_{SCHL4} - 0.951X_{SCHL5} - 0.104X_{SCHL6}$$
$$\quad (0.867) \qquad\quad (1.362) \qquad\quad (1.165) \qquad\quad (1.170) \qquad\quad (1.234) \qquad\quad (1.962)$$

$$- \ 3.031X_{SCHL7} - 2.743X_{SCHL8} + 0.967X_{SCHL9} + 5.880X_{SCHL11} + 0.426X_{SCHL12}$$
$$\quad (0.937) \qquad\quad (0.972) \qquad\quad (1.061) \qquad\quad (1.907) \qquad\quad (1.524)$$

$$R^2 = 59.4\%$$
$$N = 309$$

TABLE 3.42. Multilevel Analysis of West Virginia Reading Achievement: Contextual Variable and Cross-Level Interaction Term Not Included; Estimates of Covariance Parameters

Parameter	Estimate	Std. error	Wald Z	Sig. level
Residual	8.944	0.712	12.554	.000
INTERCEPT1	5.432	2.443	2.223	.026
INTERCEPT1 by $X_{ACHIEVE1}$	0.181	0.088	2.061	.039
$X_{ACHIEVE1}$	0.001	0.012	0.086	.931

TABLE 3.43. Multilevel Analysis of West Virginia Reading Achievement: Contextual Variable and Cross-Level Interaction Term Included; Estimates of Covariance Parameters

Parameter	Estimate	Std. error	Wald Z	Sig. level
Residual	9.305	0.773	12.033	.000
INTERCEPT1	0.281	0.322	0.872	.383
INTERCEPT1 by $X_{ACHIEVE1}$	−0.186	0.096	−0.195	.846
$X_{ACHIEVE1}$	0.001	0.000	—	—

Note. A dash (—) indicates a value too small to measure.

intercept, INTERCEPT1, is statistically significant, as is the covariance for INTERCEPT1 and the random component of the slope $X_{ACHIEVE1}$. In Table 3.43, however, after the contextual variable, $X_{ACHIEVE2}$, and the cross-level interaction term, $X_{ACHIEVE2} * X_{ACHIEVE1}$, have been added to the equation, INTERCEPT1 and the INTERCEPT1-by-$X_{ACHIEVE1}$ covariance are statistically *non*significant. They have been accounted for by the contextual variable and the cross-level interaction term.

We have gone a long way to make the point that within-group homogeneity as measured by the intraclass correlation can rarely be treated exclusively as a consequence of regression model misspecification. Nevertheless, since this approach at first blush is an intriguing possibility, it is best dispensed with once and for all (B. Andersen, 2004). A perfectly specified model is not a practically tenable way to explain away intraclass correlation and get rid of the adverse statistical consequences of grouping.

3.6   CONTEXTUAL VARIABLES AND VARYING PARAMETER ESTIMATES

As we know, use of OLS estimators entails the assumption of additivity, meaning that relationships between an independent and a dependent variable do not vary across categories of one or more other variables (Gujarati, 2006). The intercept and slopes for each equation are assumed to be the same for all groups, whether they be schools, districts, or some other units. All coefficients, in other words, are fixed.

The standard response to violation of the assumption of nonvarying slopes and intercepts is explicit acknowledgment of this variability through use of a limited set of interaction terms (Jaccard, Turrisi, & Wan, 1990). If relationships vary across a large number of unordered categories, however, other ways must be found to incorporate this variability into the analysis, such as use of random coefficient regression or multilevel regression, which will allow slopes and intercepts to vary from group to group (Kennedy, 1998).

For example, using our data set with nine occupational categories, we will again suspend judgment as to effective sample size and run separate regression equations for the relationship between hourly wage and level of educational attainment for each of the nine occupational groups. This gives us a slope and intercept for each category and permits comparison of occupation-specific coefficients with results for the entire sample. Table 3.44 reports intercepts and slopes for the nine occupational categories. Estimates that are boldfaced and italicized are significantly different from the overall intercept and slope.

It comes as no surprise that there is a good deal of variability with regard to the intercept. We also see, however, that the slope estimates vary from one nominal-level category of occupation to another, with some significantly greater and others significantly less than the overall or average slope. This is clearly an instance in which the assumption of nonvarying parameter estimates, meaning both the intercept and the slope, has been violated: Payoffs for investments in education vary from occupation to occupation (see, e.g., Sousza-Poza, 1998).

TABLE 3.44. Income and Occupation: Varying Intercept and Slope Estimates

Occupation	Intercept	Slope	Standard error	Sig. level
All N = 4359	0.215	0.497	0.038	.000
One n = 453	0.379	0.525	0.098	.000
Two n = 399	−2.895	0.785	0.148	.000
Three n = 233	−0.828	0.646	0.283	.023
Four n = 486	0.150	0.459	0.085	.000
Five n = 934	2.140	0.357	0.055	.000
Six n = 881	1.427	0.378	0.064	.000
Seven n = 401	1.038	0.378	0.074	.000
Eight n = 64	1.477	0.200	0.078	.005
Nine n = 508	1.625	0.270	0.066	.000

If we proceeded in conventional fashion, inserting interaction terms to correct for nonadditivity, with nine nominal-level occupational categories we would need nine same-level interaction terms just to deal with education. What if we found the same sort of group-to-group variability for years of experience, knowledge of the world of work, and still other independent variables? The number of interaction terms would quickly become unwieldy.

Failure to acknowledge that intercepts and slopes vary from context to context is yet another form of specification error, though one that is often left unacknowledged. Just as omission of an independent variable from a multiple regression equation tacitly constrains its slope to be zero, failure to permit intercepts and slopes to vary tacitly constrains them to be uniform across groups (Teachman, Duncan, Young, & Levy, 2001). If intercepts and slopes do in fact vary, the regression model will be misspecified.

In an analysis such as this, use of a random coefficient or multilevel regression model in which the intercept and slopes are permitted to vary from one occupational category to another seems essential. In addition, we may now include second-level variables as contextual factors that may be related to the first-level dependent variable, and that may account for variability in the random intercept. When one or more contextual variables are introduced and we begin thinking about two or more levels of analysis, we can also expect to see implied cross-level interaction terms as additional explanatory factors, which may account for variability in random slopes.

We can clarify all this further with a data set that contains 11th-grade composite achievement test scores from the Iowa Tests of Basic Skills (Hoover, Dunbar, & Frisbie, 2001). The sample consists of 298 Georgia secondary schools in 1996 (Bickel & Howley, 2000). The school is the unit of analysis, with schools nested in 155 districts. The number of schools per district ranges from 1 to 18. Level-one variables are measures on schools, and level-two contextual variables are measures on districts.

We begin by computing the intraclass correlation coefficient, using the information in Table 3.45:

$$r = 66.687/(66.687 + 188.858) = 0.261$$

In this instance, with 26.1% of the variability due to differences between districts, we know that the nesting of schools within districts has resulted in dependent observations. As a result, one or more coefficients may vary from group to group. Now, however, instead of just nine occupational categories, we have 155 school districts!

We can keep the example instructively simple by using just two independent variables at the school level: percentage of students sufficiently poor to be eligible for free/reduced cost lunch (POOR1) and percentage of students who are Black (BLACK1). Rather than immediately proceeding with the analysis, we may begin by asking which coefficients do in fact vary across second-level groups.

Ideally, questions such as this are addressed through reference to well-developed theory or richly informative substantive literature. Resources for answering questions as to how schools work, however, are thin and subject to contestation (see, e.g., Gerwitz, 1997; Thrupp, 1999; Gorard, 2000; Howley & Howley, 2004; Lee, 2004). As a result, we will answer the question in a nakedly empirical fashion, using covariance parameter estimates provided by SPSS.

Table 3.46 reports the residual variance, as well as measures of the degree to which the intercept and the slopes for POOR1 and BLACK1 vary from district to district. We also see the standard errors of these estimates of variability and their significance levels. Table 3.46 also gives estimates of the covariances of the random components. What can we learn from all this?

TABLE 3.45. Mean Composite Achievement in Georgia Secondary Schools: Residual Variance and Random Intercept Variance

Parameter	Estimate	Std. error	Wald Z	Sig. level
Residual	188.858	18.909	9.988	.000
INTERCEPT1	66.687	18.863	3.535	.000

TABLE 3.46. Mean Composite Achievement in Georgia Secondary Schools: Estimates of Covariance Parameters

Parameter	Estimate	Std. error	Wald Z	Sig. level
Residual	86.264	10.593	8.144	.000
INTERCEPT1	209.092	51.381	4.069	.000
X_{POOR1}	0.251	0.100	2.508	.012
INTERCEPT1 by X_{POOR1}	6.623	2.216	3.116	.002
X_{BLACK1}	0.130	0.046	2.820	.005
INTERCEPT1 by X_{BLACK1}	−1.231	1.308	−0.941	.347
X_{POOR1} by X_{BLACK1}	−0.054	0.056	−0.815	.415

When interpreting the random component variance estimates, we must bear in mind that a variance cannot be negative. As a result, tests of significance for the random components should be one-tailed tests. For a large sample, the critical value of the Wald Z statistic becomes 1.645 rather than 1.960.

Table 3.46 makes clear that estimates of variability for the intercept and both slopes are statistically significant. This tells us that the school-level intercept and the school-level slopes do in fact vary across the 155 districts included in the data set. Furthermore, we see that one of the covariances, INTERCEPT1 by X_{POOR1}, is statistically significant. This tells us that if we constrained the random components to be statistically independent, we would be making a specification error.

With this additional information, we can see that it is essential to estimate a multilevel regression model with a random intercept and with random slopes for both first-level independent variables. Beyond that, the random components should be permitted to covary.

Having made these empirically informed judgments, we have created two contextual variables to account for variability in the random components and to explain the INTERCEPT1-by-X_{POOR1} covariance. Specifically, we aggregated the school-level variable X_{POOR1} to the district level, creating the contextual variable X_{POOR2}. And we aggregated the school-level variable X_{BLACK1} to the district level, creating the contextual variable X_{BLACK2}. School-level and district-level variables were then used to create two implied cross-level interaction terms, X_{POOR2} * X_{POOR1} and X_{BLACK2} * X_{BLACK1}.

Estimates for the level-one intercept and slopes, along with their standard errors, are reported in Table 3.47, where they are compared with OLS estimates from a regression equation that included no district-level contextual variables or cross-level interaction terms. Standard errors are in parentheses.

The OLS and random coefficient/multilevel estimates differ because the OLS regression equation is misspecified, treating the intercepts and slopes as nonvarying or fixed from district to district, and not including aggregated district-level contextual variables and cross-level interaction terms. As expected, moreover, with the exception of the intercept, the multilevel estimates have larger standard errors.

TABLE 3.47. OLS and Random/Multilevel Intercepts and Slopes: School-Level Achievement in Georgia Secondary Schools

$$OLS\ intercept = 63.102$$
$$(1.370)$$
$$Multilevel\ intercept = 60.250$$
$$(1.247)$$

$$X_{POOR1}\ OLS\ slope = -0.295$$
$$(0.068)$$
$$X_{POOR1}\ multilevel\ slope = -0.278$$
$$(0.078)$$

$$X_{BLACK1}\ OLS\ slope = -0.286$$
$$(0.033)$$
$$X_{BLACK1}\ multilevel\ slope = -0.378$$
$$(0.072)$$

District-level contextual variables are entirely missing from the inherently single-level OLS regression equation. The consequences of this omission are starkly evident in Table 3.48. Both the percentage of poor students and the percentage of Black students as aggregated district-level variables have statistically significant and negative regression coefficients. In the OLS equation without contextual variables, however, these coefficients are erroneously constrained to equal zero.

As with contextual factors, in Table 3.49 we see that failure to include cross-level interaction terms in the inherently single-level OLS equation has adverse consequences. In this instance, we have a statistically significant coefficient for $X_{BLACK2}* X_{BLACK1}$ in the multilevel equation, which is missing from the OLS equation.

In the interest of closure, the equations that yielded the values compared in Tables 3.47 through 3.49 are reported in Table 3.50. For purposes of comparison, results of an OLS simulation of the multilevel regression equation are also included.

When parameter estimates vary over a large number of categories, such as the school districts in a state, OLS regression can no longer provide a properly specified model. Multilevel regression, permitting coefficients to vary across categories, should be used instead.

TABLE 3.48. District-Level Coefficients: School-Level Achievement in Georgia Secondary Schools

X_{POOR2} contextual variable excluded: Unstandardized slope = 0.000
(N/A)

X_{POOR2} contextual variable included: Unstandardized slope = -0.448
(0.062)

X_{BLACK2} contextual variable excluded: Unstandardized slope = 0.000
(N/A)

X_{BLACK2} contextual variable included: Unstandardized slope = -0.140
(0.041)

TABLE 3.49. Cross-Level Interaction Term Coefficients:
School-Level Achievement in Georgia Secondary Schools

$X_{POOR2} * X_{POOR1}$ cross-level interaction term excluded: Fixed slope = 0.000	(N/A)
$X_{POOR2} * X_{POOR1}$ cross-level interaction term included: Fixed slope = –0.006	(0.004)
$X_{BLACK2} * X_{BLACK1}$ cross-level interaction term excluded: Fixed slope = 0.000	(N/A)
$X_{BLACK2} * X_{BLACK1}$ cross-level interaction term included: Fixed slope = –0.004	(0.001)

TABLE 3.50. OLS and Multilevel Analyses of School-Level Composite Achievement

OLS regression equation as reported

$$Y_{ACHIEVE} = 63.102 - 0.0.295X_{POOR1} - 0.286X_{BLACK1}$$
$$\quad\quad (1.370)\ (0.068) \quad\quad (0.033)$$

$$R^2 = 26.5\%$$
$$N = 298$$

OLS simulation of multilevel regression

$$Y_{ACHIEVE} = 59.965 - 0.311\ X_{POOR1} - 0.353X_{BLACK1} - 0.439X_{POOR2} - 0.145X_{BLACK2} - 0.164X_{POOR2}$$
$$\quad\quad (0.979)\ (0.052) \quad\quad (0.039) \quad\quad (0.050) \quad\quad (0.036) \quad\quad (0.160)$$

$$\quad\quad * X_{POOR1} - 0.030X_{BLACK2} * X_{BLACKL1}$$
$$\quad\quad\quad (0.038)$$

$$R^2 = 68.8\%$$
$$N = 298$$

Multilevel regression equation

$$Y_{ACHIEVE} = 60.250 - 0.278\ X_{POOR1} - 0.378X_{BLACK1} - 0.448X_{POOR2} - 0.140X_{BLACK2} - 0.006X_{POOR2}$$
$$\quad\quad (1.246)\ (0.078) \quad\quad (0.072) \quad\quad (0.062) \quad\quad (0.041) \quad\quad (0.004)$$

$$\quad\quad * X_{POOR1} - 0.004X_{BLACK2} * X_{BLACKL1}$$
$$\quad\quad\quad (0.001)$$

$$R^2 = 66.3\%$$
$$N_1 = 298$$
$$N_2 = 155$$

3.7   CONTEXTUAL VARIABLES AND COVARIANCE STRUCTURE

When we find that one or more random components vary across categories such as districts, we want to be able to explain that variability. We also want to know if random components vary together. If they do, we want to be able to explain their covariance.

In addressing these issues with regard to Georgia schools and school districts, we compare Table 3.51 (Table 3.46 reproduced) with Table 3.52. The random component

TABLE 3.51. (TABLE 3.46, Reproduced). Mean Composite Achievement in Georgia Secondary Schools: Contextual Variable and Cross-Level Interaction Term Not Included; Estimates of Covariance Parameters

Parameter	Estimate	Std. error	Wald Z	Sig. level
Residual	86.264	10.593	8.144	.000
INTERCEPT1	209.092	51.381	4.069	.000
X_{POOR1}	0.251	0.100	2.508	.012
INTERCEPT1 by X_{POOR1}	6.623	2.216	3.116	.002
X_{BLACK1}	0.130	0.046	2.820	.005
INTERCEPT1 by X_{BLACK1}	−1.231	1.308	−0.941	.347
X_{POOR1} by X_{BLACK1}	−0.054	0.056	−0.815	.415

TABLE 3.52. Mean Composite Achievement in Georgia Secondary Schools: Contextual Variable and Cross-Level Interaction Term Included; Estimates of Covariance Parameters

Parameter	Estimate	Std. error	Wald Z	Sig. level
Residual	86.113	10.617	8.111	.000
INTERCEPT1	11.666	18.903	0.607	.537
X_{POOR1}	0.082	0.000	—	—
INTERCEPT1 by X_{POOR1}	0.941	0.615	1.528	.126
X_{BLACK1}	0.094	0.000	—	—
INTERCEPT1 by X_{BLACK1}	−0.773	0.704	−1.098	.272
X_{POOR1} by X_{BLACK1}	−0.047	0.000	—	—

Note. A dash (—) indicates a value too small to measure.

variances and covariances in Table 3.51 were computed without contextual factors or cross-level interaction terms included in the multilevel regression equation. When the results reported in Table 3.52 were computed, however, these additional factors were incorporated into the analysis.

Comparing the two tables, we see that the random component variance estimates for INTERCEPT1, X_{POOR1}, and X_{BLACK1} have been substantially diminished by introduction of the contextual variables and cross-level interaction terms. The same is true of the values for INTERCEPT1 by X_{POOR1}, INTERCEPT1 by X_{BLACK1}, and X_{POOR1} by X_{BLACK1}. In fact, all six terms have been reduced to statistical nonsignificance, and three are so small that SPSS was unable to estimate Wald Z values and significance levels.

In this example, we were able to explain the variability in our random components. In addition, we were able to explain random component covariances. Both explanations were accomplished through use of contextual variables and cross-level interaction terms.

To further illustrate why we should be sensitive to the fact that random coefficients may vary together, we turn again to our large Kentucky data set (see Table 3.53). We use

TABLE 3.53. Eighth-Grade Reading Achievement in Kentucky: Estimates of Covariance Parameters; Information for Computing Unconditional Intraclass Correlation

Parameter	Estimate	Std. error	Wald Z	Sig. level
Residual	337.685	2.147	157.295	.000
INTERCEPT1	45.359	4.463	10.163	.000

reading achievement as the dependent variable and a student-level dummy variable called $X_{NONWHITE1}$ as the only independent variable. $X_{NONWHITE1}$ was created by coding White students as 0 and members of all other ethnic groups as 1. $X_{NONWHITE1}$ differs from the $X_{ETHNIC1}$ variable used in previous analyses, in that $X_{ETHNIC1}$ was created after selecting out all students who were located in a category other than White or Black. This resulted in a loss of 0.41% of all cases.

$$r = 45.359/(45.359 + 337.865) = 0.120$$

With an intraclass correlation coefficient of 0.120, we know that a properly specified regression model will have one or more random coefficients. If there is more than one random component, they may vary together.

For purely illustrative purposes, we use randomly selected school identification numbers and take a small subsample of 55 schools. We then estimate an OLS intercept and slope for each school. Intercept estimates vary from 30.09 to 64.58, with a mean of 48.55. Slope estimates vary from −26.12 to 23.50, with a mean of −4.09. When intercept and slope estimates are correlated, we get an r value of −0.33. The negative relationship between intercepts and slopes for the 55 randomly selected schools is displayed in Figure 3.5.

Before offering a tentative substantive interpretation of this negative slope-by-intercept covariance, we should emphasize that the coefficient estimates used in Figure 3.5 were generated by using OLS regression. As such, they exhibit greater variability than the group-specific estimates that would be used to compute the weighted averages that yield REML estimates for a random intercept and a random slope. This is due to a phenomenon called shrinkage.

When we invoke the concept *shrinkage*, we are acknowledging that group-specific estimates in multilevel analysis are pulled or shrunk toward an overall average (Hox, 2002). The degree of shrinkage is a function of the

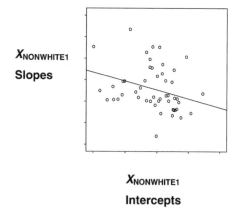

FIGURE 3.5. Slopes by intercepts: Reading achievement by $X_{NONWHITE1}$.

number of cases in a group. The fewer the number of cases, the greater the shrinkage (Tate, 2004). In other words, the groups with a smaller number of cases will weigh less heavily in estimating the value of the overall or average slope than will groups with a larger number. For present purposes, the overall effect of primary interest is diminished variability in random coefficient estimates.

Furthermore, covariances among random components are sensitive to the way variables have been centered. In their classic paper on centering, Kreft, De Leeuw, and Aiken (1995) demonstrate that when compared to raw scores, grand-mean centering results in a substantial reduction in random component covariances. Group-mean centering, moreover, may diminish the covariance still further. In the absence of a stricture that centering will always be used and will always be done in the same way, this can generate a good deal of confusion. We can see this in Table 3.54.

We immediately see that the INTERCEPT1-by-$X_{NONWHITE1}$ covariance (see the bold-faced, italicized entries in Table 3.54) has a smaller absolute value with group-mean centering than with grand-mean centering, and that the absence of centering yields the largest covariance. Moreover, the covariance obtained by using group-mean centering is not statistically significant. If we compute Pearson's r for the correlation between INTERCEPT1 and the $X_{NONWHITE1}$ slope after using grand-mean centering, $r = -0.30$. However, when the same information is obtained by using group-mean centering, $r = -0.21$. Without centering, $r = -0.54$.

TABLE 3.54. Eighth-Grade Reading Achievement in Kentucky: Estimates of Covariance Parameters

Parameter	Estimate	Std. error	Wald Z	Sig. level
Group-mean centered				
Residual	328.968	2.120	155.180	.000
INTERCEPT1	46.360	4.553	10.182	.000
INTERCEPT1 by $X_{NONWHITE1}$	*−6.619*	*3.529*	*−1.876*	*.061*
$X_{NONWHITE1}$	21.353	4.450	4.796	.000
Grand-mean centered				
Residual	329.057	2.121	155.162	.000
INTERCEPT1	42.969	4.321	9.944	.000
INTERCEPT1 by $X_{NONWHITE1}$	*−8.413*	*3.250*	*−2.588*	*.010*
$X_{NONWHITE1}$	18.788	4.020	4.664	.000
Raw scores				
Residual	422.806	2.777	152.822	.000
INTERCEPT1	27.825	3.799	7.323	.000
INTERCEPT1 by $X_{NONWHITE1}$	*−15.993*	*4.728*	*−3.383*	*.001*
$X_{NONWHITE1}$	31.729	8.437	3.761	.000

Having made these cautionary comments, how might we account for the negative association between OLS estimates of intercepts and slopes for the 55 analyses in our illustration? In search of an answer, we may consider the possibility that as schools get larger, mean achievement levels increase, but the achievement-related costs associated with not being White increase as well (Howley & Howley, 2005).

In this small sample, school size varies from 60 to 519 students, with a mean of 179. In Figure 3.6, we see the slopes-by-intercepts relationship *net* the influence of school size. Clearly, the slope of the OLS regression line that summarizes the slope-by-intercept relationship is much less steep than in Figure 3.5.

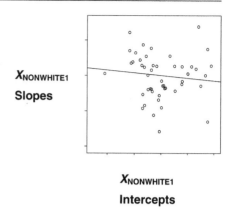

$X_{\text{NONWHITE1}}$
Slopes

$X_{\text{NONWHITE1}}$
Intercepts

FIGURE 3.6. Slopes by intercepts: Reading achievement by $X_{\text{NONWHITE1}}$, net school size.

With suggestive evidence from this small subsample indicating that school-specific intercepts and slopes are correlated, we estimate a random coefficient regression equation in which the intercept and the slope for $X_{\text{NONWHITE1}}$ are permitted to vary across schools. Results of the analysis are reported in Tables 3.55 and 3.56. (No contextual variables are included in this preliminary example.) The parameter estimates in Table 3.56 make clear that the intercept and slope do in fact vary from school to school, *and* that the random components for INTERCEPT1 and $X_{\text{NONWHITE1}}$ have a negative covariance.

TABLE 3.55. Eighth-Grade Reading Achievement in Kentucky: Random Coefficient Regression

$$Y = 48.381 - 6.743X_{\text{NONWHITE1}}$$
$$(0.392) \quad (0.453)$$

$$R_1^2 = 2.0\%$$
$$N_1 = 49,616$$
$$N_2 = 347$$

TABLE 3.56. Eighth-Grade Reading Achievement in Kentucky: Random Coefficient Regression; Estimates of Covariance Parameters

Parameter	Estimate	Std. error	Wald Z	Sig. level
Residual	329.057	2.121	155.162	.000
INTERCEPT1	42.969	4.321	9.944	.000
INTERCEPT1 by $X_{\text{NONWHITE1}}$	−8.413	3.250	−2.588	.010
$X_{\text{NONWHITE1}}$	18.788	4.020	4.664	.000

As we saw with reference to the second section of Table 3.54, Pearson's $r = -0.30$. This is little different from the small-sample estimate of -0.33 that we calculated with the OLS information used to construct Figure 3.5. Similarly, the negative and statistically significant coefficient for INTERCEPT1 * $X_{NONWHITE1}$ is consistent with the information provided by Figures 3.5 and 3.6. Had we chosen to constrain covariances among random components to equal zero, we would have completely missed this substantively interesting relationship.

If we take Figures 3.5 and 3.6 seriously and introduce school size (X_{SIZE2}) and the implied cross-level interaction term (X_{SIZE2} * $X_{NONWHITE1}$) into the analysis, we get the results reported in Tables 3.57 and 3.58. The INTERCEPT1-by-$X_{NONWHITE1}$ covariance has been substantially reduced, corresponding to a diminished Pearson's $r = -0.22$.

Clearly, when we are working with a multilevel regression model, one important aspect of proper specification is deciding which coefficients should be fixed and which should be random. Another important part of proper specification is deciding on a suitable *covariance structure* when there is more than one random term. Still another step in proper specification is identification of contextual variables and cross-level interaction terms that may contribute to explaining both the variances *and* the covariances that come with use of random coefficients.

A specific covariance structure tells us the nature of the relationships that are permitted to exist among random components (SPSS, 2003; see also Wolfinger, 1993; Abdulnabi, 1999). For example, the default option with SPSS is called *variance components*. If we select variance components as the covariance structure, we are permitting the variances of random components to vary, *but* we are specifying that they do *not* vary *together*.

TABLE 3.57. Eighth-Grade Reading Achievement in Kentucky: Multilevel Regression; Unstructured

$$Y = 51.731 - 5.572X_{NONWHITE1} + 1.312X_{SIZE2} - 1.512X_{SIZE2} * X_{NONWHITE2}$$
$$(0.336)\ (0.613)\qquad\qquad (0.393)\qquad\quad (1.512)$$

$$R_1^2 = 2.2\%$$
$$N_1 = 49{,}616$$
$$N_2 = 347$$

TABLE 3.58. Eighth-Grade Reading Achievement in Kentucky: Multilevel Regression; Unstructured; Estimates of Covariance Parameters

Parameter	Estimate	Std. error	Wald Z	Sig. level
Residual	331.446	2.172	152.572	.000
INTERCEPT1	19.572	2.056	9.518	.000
INTERCEPT1 by $X_{NONWHITE1}$	−4.503	2.156	−2.088	.037
$X_{NONWHITE1}$	21.485	4.956	4.3335	.000

Variance components covariance structure is sometimes referred to as the traditional choice (SAS Institute, 1999). In the social and behavioral sciences, however, random intercepts and random slopes are usually modeled to permit correlations among them. Snijders and Bosker (1999) offer the unambiguous admonition that a random intercept should *always* be permitted to vary with random slopes—a judgment they illustrate with interesting examples. Singer (1998) has also noted that an unstructured approach to covariance structure is the one most frequently used in the social and behavioral sciences. Similarly, all of the multilevel models used by Kreft and De Leeuw (1998) in their introductory text permit random components to vary together. Raudenbush and Bryk (2002), as another example, routinely permit random components to covary.

If we specify an unstructured approach to covariance structure, using SPSS or any other software, we impose no constraints on relationships among random components. We are not only permitting the random intercept and all random slopes to vary together; we are also acknowledging that the variances and covariances of random components may differ from level to level of the independent variables used in the analysis. The unstructured option, in effect, covers all the bases, providing a measure of assurance that we have not missed anything important.

On the other hand, the unstructured option requires more parameters to estimate a model. This uses up degrees of freedom, and may yield misleading information about model fit when we apply the deviance difference statistic (Hox, 2002, pp. 50–51).

It is true that the variance components option and the unstructured option are not our only choices. For example, if we were willing to stipulate that our random components were not only uncorrelated but had the same variance for each level of each independent variable, we could use the scaled identity option. Furthermore, there are numerous other covariance structures that permit intermediate levels of complexity with regard to variances of random components and relationships among them (see, e.g., Abdulnabi, 1999; Singer & Willett, 2003). Moreover, SPSS, SAS, and other versatile software packages permit us to specify a different covariance structure for each random component.

Typically, however, we have little or no theoretical or substantive information that would prompt us to choose one covariance structure over another. What do we do? All told, there is good reason to use the unstructured option routinely, permitting the random components to vary together. We shall adhere to this stricture. It is instructive, nevertheless, to illustrate the consequences of this decision.

Returning to the model estimated in Tables 3.57 and 3.58, we run the analysis using the variance components option, meaning that the intercept and slopes are *not* permitted to vary together. Results are reported in Tables 3.59 and 3.60.

In general, choice of covariance structure has little effect on fixed component estimates, but may yield more accurate estimates of their standard errors (SAS Institute, 1999). It is no surprise, therefore, that when comparing the results reported in Tables 3.57 and 3.59, we find only very small differences in estimates for the intercept and slopes. In this instance, moreover, the same applies to differences in standard errors. In

TABLE 3.59. Eighth-Grade Reading Achievement in Kentucky:
Multilevel Regression; Variance Components

$$Y = 51.733 - 5.587X_{NONWHITE1} + 1.357X_{SIZE2} - 1.561X_{SIZE2} * X_{NONWHITE2}$$
$$\quad (0.336)\ (0.623) \qquad\qquad (0.377) \qquad\ (0.436)$$

$$R_1^2 = 2.2\%$$
$$N_1 = 49,616$$
$$N_2 = 347$$

TABLE 3.60. Eighth-Grade Reading Achievement in Kentucky: Multilevel Regression;
Variance Components; Estimates of Covariance Parameters

Parameter	Estimate	Std. error	Wald Z	Sig. level
Residual	331.451	2.173	152.562	.000
INTERCEPT1	19.848	2.080	9.541	.000
$X_{NONWHITE1}$	21.757	5.047	4.311	.000

addition, comparing Tables 3.58 and 3.60 shows us that the random component variances and their standard errors are almost exactly the same. Is there any reason to believe that either model provides a better fit? How do we make a judgment?

One applicable set of decision-making tools that we have not used so far in comparisons of multilevel regression models estimated in different ways consists of the *deviance difference* and *information criteria*. Routinely, SPSS reports the deviance, here referred to as the *−2 log likelihood*, and four information criteria, as we see in Table 3.61. When we get to Chapter 9, we will learn more about information criteria. For now we will simply note that each measure has a *smaller-is-better* interpretation, meaning that the model with the smaller value is the one with the better overall fit (SAS Institute, 1999; Burnham & Anderson, 2002; Kuha, 2004; Cavanaugh, 2005).

The information criteria differ because each has its own formula to punish analysts for using additional parameters in estimating coefficients (Luke, 2004). The −2 log likelihood statistic includes no disincentives for using additional parameters. Differences

TABLE 3.61. Information Criteria for Tables 3.58 and 3.60

Criterion	Variance components	Unstructured
−2 log likelihood	406542.1	*406537.8*
Akaike's Information Criterion	406556.1	*406553.8*
Hurvich and Tsai's Criterion	406556.1	*406553.8*
Bozdogan's Criterion	*406624.4*	406631.8
Schwarz's Bayesian Criterion	*406617.4*	406623.8

between the basic –2 log likelihood statistic and the other measures, therefore, are analogous to the difference between R^2 and adjusted R^2 in OLS regression.

When we are comparing alternative multilevel model specifications using the difference between two deviance values or the information criteria, all measures are estimated using maximum likelihood (ML) rather than REML. Estimating coefficients with REML and then estimating information criteria for the same model with ML is very easy to do, as we shall explain in Chapter 4.

With the information in Table 3.61, we can calculate the deviance difference in this instance as follows:

$$\text{Deviance difference} = 406542.1 - 406537.8 = 4.3$$
$$df = 8 - 7 = 1$$

For each measure in Table 3.61, the smaller value has been boldfaced and italicized. Comparison of the five different decision-making measures yields conflicting results.

The deviance (–2 log likelihood) is sometimes construed as a measure of lack of fit: The larger the deviance, the less well the model fits the data. The deviance becomes interpretable when we use deviances from competing models to compute the deviance difference.

The deviance difference is distributed approximately as χ^2, with degrees of freedom equal to the difference between the numbers of parameters used in estimating competing models. The model reported in Tables 3.57 and 3.58 uses eight parameter estimates: one for the intercept, one for each of the three slopes, and one for each of the four random terms. The model reported in Tables 3.59 and 3.60 uses seven parameter estimates: one for the intercept, one for each of the three slopes, and one for each of the three parameter estimates. The critical value of χ^2 with one degree of freedom and the alpha level set at .05 is 3.841, which we have exceeded. This indicates that the model with an unstructured approach to covariance structure provides a better fit.

The information criteria, however, provide conflicting results. The most commonly used criteria are Akaike's Information Criterion and Schwarz's Bayesian Criterion (Abdulnabi, 1999). In this instance, Akaike's Information Criterion indicates that the unstructured model is the better-fitting one, while Schwarz's Bayesian Criterion indicates that the variance components model provides the better fit. If we referred to the less commonly used information criteria, we would be faced with the same sort of ambiguity.

What do we make of this? Again we see that choice of covariance structure has made very little difference in the multilevel models that we have used for examples.

We continue with this example, still trying to account for random component variances and covariances, in Table 3.62. Starting with the model in Tables 3.57 and 3.59, we add the contextual variables $X_{\text{NONWHITE2}}$ (non-White status aggregated to the school level) and X_{GENDER2} (gender aggregated to the school level) as additional predictors of variability in the random component of the intercept and the random component of the slope for $X_{\text{NONWHITE1}}$.

TABLE 3.62. Eighth-Grade Reading Achievement in Kentucky: Multilevel Regression, Respecified; Unstructured

$$Y = 50.890 - 6.189X_{\text{NONWHITE1}} + 7.981X_{\text{GENDER1}} + 1.069X_{\text{SIZE2}} + 3.456X_{\text{NONWHITE2}} + 26.206X_{\text{GENDER2}}$$
$$\quad (0.417) \; (0.483) \qquad\qquad (0.372) \qquad\qquad (0.450) \qquad\quad (2.214) \qquad\qquad (6.604)$$

$$\quad - 1.096X_{\text{SIZE2}} * X_{\text{NONWHITE1}} - 0.673X_{\text{SIZE2}} * X_{\text{GENDER1}} - 17.814X_{\text{NONWHITE2}} * X_{\text{NONWHITE1}}$$
$$\quad\;\; (0.759) \qquad\qquad\qquad (0.365) \qquad\qquad\qquad (2.771)$$

$$\quad - 6.434X_{\text{NONWHITE2}} * X_{\text{GENDER1}} + 1.719X_{\text{GENDER2}} * X_{\text{GENDER1}} + 11.010X_{\text{GENDER2}} * X_{\text{NONWHITE1}}$$
$$\quad\;\; (1.408) \qquad\qquad\qquad (4.907) \qquad\qquad\qquad (10.267)$$

$$R_1^2 = 12.5\%$$
$$N_1 = 49{,}616$$
$$N_2 = 347$$

In addition, X_{GENDER1} is introduced as an additional level-one predictor with a random slope. Variability in the slope for X_{GENDER1} is also treated as a function of X_{SIZE2}, $X_{\text{NONWHITE2}}$, and X_{GENDER2}. This gives us five more implied cross-level interaction terms: $X_{\text{NONWHITE2}} * X_{\text{NONWHITE1}}$, $X_{\text{NONWHITE2}} * X_{\text{GENDER1}}$, $X_{\text{GENDER2}} * X_{\text{GENDER1}}$, $X_{\text{GENDER2}} * X_{\text{NONWHITE1}}$, and $X_{\text{SIZE2}} * X_{\text{GENDER1}}$.

The additional cross-level interaction terms enable us to determine if the relationship between $X_{\text{NONWHITE1}}$ and reading achievement varies from level to level of $X_{\text{NONWHITE2}}$ ($X_{\text{NONWHITE2}} * X_{\text{NONWHITE1}}$); if the relationship between X_{GENDER1} and reading achievement varies from level to level of $X_{\text{NONWHITE2}}$ ($X_{\text{NONWHITE2}} * X_{\text{GENDER1}}$); if the relationship between X_{GENDER1} and reading achievement varies from level to level of X_{GENDER2} ($X_{\text{GENDER2}} * X_{\text{GENDER1}}$); if the relationship between $X_{\text{NONWHITE1}}$ and reading achievement varies from level to level of X_{GENDER2} ($X_{\text{GENDER2}} * X_{\text{NONWHITE1}}$); and if the relationship between X_{GENDER1} and reading achievement varies from level to level of X_{SIZE2} ($X_{\text{SIZE2}} * X_{\text{GENDER1}}$).

Substantively, the most interesting results in Table 3.62 concern the cross-level interaction terms $X_{\text{NONWHITE2}} * X_{\text{NONWHITE1}}$ and $X_{\text{NONWHITE2}} * X_{\text{GENDER1}}$. Their statistically significant and negative coefficients tell us that as the proportion of a school's students who are non-White increases, average reading achievement levels of individual non-White students and individual female students diminishes.

To some readers, these substantively interesting results may seem statistically dubious because the multilevel regression model is becoming quite complex, and complex models may be unstable (Kreft & De Leeuw, 1998). Furthermore, the inferential properties of cross-level interaction terms are not well understood (Mok, 1995; Hox, 2002).

It is known, however, that coefficient estimates for cross-level interaction terms are most stable and their tests of significance are most reliable when a large number of observations at level one is nested in a large number of observations at level two (Kreft & De Leeuw, 1998; also see Maas & Hox, 2005). In this instance we have an unusually large number of observations at both the student level and the school level, and the t values for both coefficients are large by any conventional standard. Furthermore, in an OLS multiple regression equation with the same variables, all variance inflation factors are below 2.00, and the condition index is only 2.618, meaning that multicollinearity is not a problem.

All this lends credibility to the statistical and substantive value of these interesting results. This holds even though there was only a very small increase in the R_1^2 summary statistic.

Note in Table 3.63 that the random intercept is in fact correlated with both random slopes. These correlations, moreover, remain statistically significant even with level-two contextual variables and cross-level interaction terms in the equation. What would have happened if we had used variance components instead of the unstructured option? In other words, *what would have happened if we had gotten it wrong?*

By now it comes as no surprise that the multilevel regression coefficients and standard errors reported in Table 3.64 are very similar to those in Table 3.62. Use of variance components rather than the unstructured option does not change the substantive import of our fixed components; nor does it have any effect on their tests of significance. Comparing random component variances in Tables 3.63 and 3.65 also shows little difference

TABLE 3.63. Reading Achievement by Non-White Status among Kentucky Eighth Graders: Multilevel Regression, Respecified; Unstructured; Estimates of Covariance Parameters

Parameter	Estimate	Std. error	Wald Z	Sig. level
Residual	316.447	2.082	151.983	.000
INTERCEPT1	18.042	1.906	9.465	.000
$X_{\text{NONWHITE1}}$	14.777	3.603	4.099	.000
INTERCEPT1 by $X_{\text{NONWHITE1}}$	−5.411	1.987	−2.852	.004
X_{GENDER1}	2.084	0.755	2.759	.006
INTERCEPT1 by X_{GENDER1}	−2.477	0.873	−2.838	.005
$X_{\text{NONWHITE1}}$ by X_{GENDER1}	0.247	1.198	0.206	.837

TABLE 3.64. Eighth-Grade Reading Achievement in Kentucky: Multilevel Regression, Respecified; Variance Components

$Y = 51.880 - 6.298X_{\text{NONWHITE1}} + 8.111X_{\text{GENDER1}} + 1.068X_{\text{SIZE2}} + 3.555X_{\text{NONWHITE2}} + 25.886X_{\text{GENDER2}}$
   (0.421) (0.494)   (0.372)   (0.454)   (2.229)   (6.656)

$- 1.279X_{\text{SIZE2}} * X_{\text{NONWHITE1}} - 0.833X_{\text{SIZE2}} * X_{\text{GENDER1}} - 17.185X_{\text{NONWHITE2}} * X_{\text{NONWHITE1}}$
   (0.789)   (0.366)   (2.845)

$- 6.329X_{\text{NONWHITE2}} * X_{\text{GENDER1}} + 1.185X_{\text{GENDER2}} * X_{\text{GENDER1}} + 8.042X_{\text{GENDER2}} * X_{\text{NONWHITE1}}$
   (1.407)   (4.914)   (10.073)

$$R_1^2 = 12.5\%$$
$$N_1 = 49{,}616$$
$$N_2 = 347$$

between the two sets of estimates. If any obvious gains come with use of the unstructured option, they will have to be manifest in the random component covariances.

Because differences between results for the analyses in Tables 3.62 and 3.64 and in
Tables 3.63 and 3.65 are not large, we might suspect that simply sticking with variance
components is a parsimonious and otherwise reasonable choice. It may seem that little
or nothing of value was gained by estimating 19 parameters for the unstructured option
rather than 16 parameters for variance components. (Each coefficient estimate, each
variance component estimate, and each covariance estimate represents an additional
parameter. The additional parameters estimated with the unstructured configuration are
the covariances among random components.)

Use of the unstructured option seems the correct call, however, if we bear in mind
that one purpose of contextual variables and cross-level interaction terms in multilevel
analysis is to account for variability in random components *and* to explain why
covariances among random terms differ from zero. If we go back to Tables 3.54 and 3.58,
we see that we had substantial success in explaining the random component covariance
INTERCEPT1 by $X_{NONWHITE1}$ as a function of school size. Introduction of additional contextual factors and cross-level interaction terms, however, did not contribute to further
diminution of this covariance.

Still, it is certainly worth knowing that school size increases are related to increases
in average reading achievement levels, and that school size increases undercut achievement for non-White and female students. It is also worth acknowledging that school size
was the only contextual factor that was chosen in an informed way. $X_{GENDER2}$ and
$X_{NONWHITE2}$ were selected simply because they were available.

With the information in Table 3.66, we can calculate the deviance difference in this
instance as follows:

$$\text{Deviance difference} = 402698.2 - 402680.2 = 18.0$$
$$df = 19 - 16 = 3$$

Though the unstructured option still seems the better choice, comparisons of the deviance difference and the information criteria yield conflicting results. This is still further
evidence that choice of covariance structure has made very little difference in the multilevel models that we have used for examples.

TABLE 3.65. Reading Achievement by Non-White Status among Kentucky Eighth Graders:
Multilevel Regression, Respecified; Variance Components; Estimates of Covariance Parameters

Parameter	Estimate	Std. error	Wald Z	Sig. level
Residual	316.457	2.082	151.965	.000
INTERCEPT1	18.347	1.935	9.483	.000
$X_{NONWHITE1}$	15.719	3.860	4.073	.000
$X_{GENDER1}$	2.019	0.746	2.706	.007

TABLE 3.66. Information Criteria for Tables 3.62 and 3.64

Criterion	Variance components	Unstructured
−2 log likelihood	402698.2	402680.2
Akaike's Information Criterion	402730.2	402718.2
Hurvich and Tsai's Criterion	402730.2	402718.2
Bozdogan's Criterion	402886.3	402903.5
Schwarz's Bayesian Criterion	402870.3	402884.5

This certainly is a long discussion to illustrate consequences of our decision to use the option for unstructured covariance structure routinely. The illustrations, however, lend credibility to our decision. Covariances among random components may be instructive, and permitting random components to covary usually has little effect on parameter estimates. As a result, we adhere to the convention prevailing in the social and behavioral sciences and routinely use the unstructured option.

3.8   CONTEXTUAL VARIABLES AND DEGREES OF FREEDOM

Finally, we use a data set that includes 281 kindergarten students from 12 randomly selected elementary schools located in two contiguous counties in western West Virginia (Bickel et al., 2002). We run an OLS regression equation with a measure of individual students' social skills taken at the end of the school year as the dependent variable (Gresham & Elliott, 1990). We then try to account for variability in social skills with one individual-level predictor, a student-level measure of neighborhood quality, along with an aggregated school-level contextual variable for neighborhood quality (Furstenberg et al., 1990). Our results are reported in Table 3.67.

In this equation, all independent variables—whether at the individual level or the school level—correspond to the same number of degrees of freedom, sample size minus the number of parameters estimated. Since we are estimating three parameters (the intercept and two slopes), we have 278 degrees of freedom for tests of significance with each regression coefficient. However, it seems odd indeed to use the same number of degrees of freedom for both $X_{NEIGHBOR1}$ and $X_{NEIGHBOR2}$. After all, while there are 281 students, there are only 12 schools, and $X_{NEIGHBOR2}$ is a contextual variable—neighborhood quality aggregated to the school level.

TABLE 3.67. OLS Analysis of Student Social Skills

$$Y = 24.838 - 0.182\,X_{NEIGHBOR1} + 0.341 X_{NEIGHBOR2}$$
$$(0.265)\ (0.0239)\qquad\qquad (0.097)$$

$$R^2 = 10.5\%$$
$$N = 281$$

If we run the same regression equation using REML estimators in a random coefficient model in which we permit the intercept to vary across schools, SPSS applies the correct number of degrees of freedom at both the individual level and the school level. The individual-level degrees of freedom remain the same (278), but number of degrees of freedom at the school level is equal to $N_2 - k - 1$, where N_2 is the number of groups and k is the number of independent variables at level two (Snijders & Bosker, 1999, pp. 86–87). With 12 schools, this gives us 10 degrees of freedom for testing $X_{NEIGHBOR2}$ rather than 278 (Snijders & Bosker, 1999, p. 86). This is an enormous difference with potentially profound implications for tests of significance for regression coefficients. The random coefficient regression results with a random intercept appear in Tables 3.68 and 3.69.

By now we are accustomed to seeing larger standard errors with random coefficient regression equations than with OLS equations that contain the same variables. If we compute a t value for the OLS estimate of the $X_{NEIGHBOR2}$ coefficient, we get 3.515, quite a bit larger than the t value of 2.480 for the corresponding random coefficient. In either case, however, with the alpha level set at the usual .05, we reject the null hypothesis.

However, with 10 degrees of freedom and a t value of 2.480, the p value at or above which the $X_{NEIGHBOR2}$ coefficient is statistically significant is .023. If we had used 278 degrees of freedom as with OLS, the p value would have been approximately .014 (Levin & Fox, 2002, pp. 446–447). Not only does OLS yield a deflated standard error for level-two variables; it also applies an incorrect number of degrees of freedom. Here that error would be inconsequential, but eventually it catches up with us (Bickel & McDonough, 1998).

Recall, moreover, that if the level-one regression coefficient for the $X_{NEIGHBOR1}$ had been random rather than fixed—if the level-one slope had been permitted to vary across

TABLE 3.68. Random Coefficient Analysis of Student Social Skills

$$Y = 24.961 + 0.183X_{NEIGHBOR1} + 0.305X_{NEIGHBOR2}$$
$$(0.361)\ (0.038) \qquad\qquad (0.123)$$

$$R_1^2 = 12.8\%$$
$$N_1 = 281$$
$$N_2 = 12$$

TABLE 3.69. Random Coefficient Analysis of Student Social Skills; Estimates of Covariance Parameters

Parameter	Estimate	Std. error	Wald Z	Sig. level
Residual	14.045	0.804	17.474	.000
INTERCEPT1	2.591	1.274	2.033	.041
INTERCEPT1 by $X_{NEIGHBOR1}$	–0.003	0.068	–0.041	.967
$X_{NEIGHBOR1}$	0.007	0.006	1.163	.245

schools—the number of degrees of freedom available for testing it would have been determined by the number of second-level groups (in this case, the 12 schools), rather than the number of level-one observations. With a random intercept and one random slope, the number of degrees of freedom used in t tests for the regression coefficients would have been the same as the number of degrees of freedom for a single contextual variable at the school level: $N_2 - k - 1$. We will clarify this further when we get to our discussion of suitable sample sizes for multilevel regression models.

In Table 3.69 the cross-level interaction term $X_{NEIGHBOR2}$ * $X_{NEIGHBOR1}$ has been inserted into our multilevel regression equation. This term is implied by our use of a random slope with $X_{NEIGHBOR1}$ and use of $X_{NEIGHBOR2}$ to account for variability in that random slope. Even with a multiplicative interaction term, collinearity diagnostics are about as good as they get. Variance inflation factors range from 1.001 to 1.079, and the condition index is 1.322.

Though multicollinearity is virtually nonexistent, when we compare Tables 3.70 and 3.71 we see that with assignment of a random slope to $X_{NEIGHBOR1}$, the standard error of its regression coefficient has substantially increased. With a t value of 3.327, the corresponding p value would be approximately .001 if we were computing degrees of freedom from all 281 cases. Once we make the $X_{NEIGHBOR1}$ slope random, however, the number of available degrees of freedom shrinks to 10, and SPSS computes a p value of .010. Since we have set our alpha level at .05, we make the same decision about statistical significance. Nevertheless, it is clear that this will not always be the case.

The t value for the coefficient corresponding to the cross-level interaction term, $X_{NEIGHBOR2}$ * $X_{NEIGHBOR1}$, is 1.211, smaller than any conventionally used critical value. It is

TABLE 3.70. Multilevel Analysis of Student Social Skills

$$Y = 24.969 + 0.183X_{NEIGHBOR1} + 0.298X_{NEIGHBOR2} + 0.023X_{NEIGHBOR2} * X_{NEIGHBOR1}$$
$$\quad (0.364)\ (0.055) \qquad\quad (0.124) \qquad\qquad (0.019)$$

$$R_1^2 = 13.3\%$$
$$N_1 = 281$$
$$N_2 = 12$$

Note. Random coefficients are boldfaced and italicized.

TABLE 3.71. Multilevel Analysis of Student Social Skills; Estimates of Covariance Parameters

Parameter	Estimate	Std. error	Wald Z	Sig. level
Residual	14.033	0.803	17.484	.000
INTERCEPT1	2.590	1.271	2.033	.042
INTERCEPT1 by $X_{NEIGHBOR1}$	–0.004	0.067	–0.061	.951
$X_{NEIGHBOR1}$	0.007	0.006	1.070	.306

worth noting, however, that the number of degrees of freedom assigned to the fixed slope for a cross-level interaction term is also $N_2 - k - 1$, the same number of degrees of freedom assigned to the random slope used in creating this multiplicative term. Occasionally a cross-level interaction term may be created by using level-one and level-two predictors that both have fixed slopes. In cases such as this, the number of degrees of freedom for the cross-level interaction terms is $N_1 - k - 1$.

When SPSS is used, degrees of freedom for fixed components of random coefficients is actually calculated by using a procedure called *Satterthwaite's approximation* (Satterthwaite, 1946; Dallal, 2005; SPSS, 2005b). The number of degrees of freedom in use will thus be a bit different from those resulting from direct application of the simple formulas presented here. In practice, this difference is seldom consequential. Nevertheless, seeing degrees of freedom expressed with decimals rather than whole numbers on an SPSS printout does seem odd.

3.9   SUMMING UP

We have subsumed a great deal under the straightforward chapter title "Contextual Variables," because this obliges us to invoke a broad range of issues in multilevel regression analysis. We have seen, for example, that use of contextual variables is not limited to multilevel models. Instead, these group-level explanatory factors have been used in OLS regression models for at least three decades. The same is true for discretionary employment of cross-level interaction terms with OLS regression, though their use is implied in multilevel models with one or more random slopes.

The meaning of these group-level explanatory factors, however, differs from OLS regression to multilevel regression. In OLS regression, contextual variables and attendant cross-level interaction terms are used exclusively as predictors of a level-one dependent variable. Furthermore, even though we refer to contextual variables as being located at the group level, OLS regression is an inherently single-level procedure.

In multilevel regression, contextual variables and implied cross-level interaction terms are used as predictors, as in OLS, but their primary function is to account for variability in random components. As we shall see in Chapter 5, moreover, multilevel regression models really are explicitly specified to operate at different levels. When we are working with two levels, for example, there are two sets of equations that are eventually combined into one. Contextual variables are located at level two.

Our discussion of contextual variables has also shown us that without nesting-engendered homogeneity, the distinction between OLS regression and multilevel regression would be at most a mathematical oddity. Nevertheless, even though nesting is pervasive and consequential, we need not simply assume that it exists. We can compute the unconditional intraclass correlation coefficient and be sure. This enables us to determine the amount of variability in a dependent variable that exists between groups rather than within them. It also enables us to avoid making an analysis unduly complex in situations where OLS regression will do just fine.

After introducing one or more contextual variables and implied cross-level interaction terms, moreover, we can compute the conditional intraclass correlation coefficient. This enables us to determine how much of the between-group variability has been explained.

In addition, introduction of judiciously selected contextual variables and cross-level interaction terms may enable us to account for variability in the random components of the intercept and one or more slopes. Success in this effort, meaning substantial reduction in the variability of random components, may be of real substantive importance.

Much the same may be true of covariances among random components, whether they are an intercept and a slope or two slopes. If our choice of covariance structure permits random components to vary together, and if a nonzero covariance occurs, contextual factors may be used in an effort to explain this covariance. Success in our efforts to account for random component covariances may provide useful information. We have seen, moreover, that measures such as Akaike's Information Criterion and Schwarz's Bayesian Criterion can be useful in evaluating multilevel regression model fit in terms of different covariance structures.

Again, the straightforward concept *contextual variable* may helpfully be used to subsume a diverse but interrelated set of ideas pertinent to discussion of multilevel modeling. With nested data, contextual variables and all that their proper understanding entails will soon follow.

3.10 USEFUL RESOURCES

Barr, R., & Dreeben, R. (1983) *How Schools Work*. Chicago: University of Chicago Press.

Even after a quarter century of methodological advances, Barr and Dreeben's monograph merits reading, especially for the clear and uncomplicated way in which they used contextual variables. The authors' thesis was that school organization—social context—was too little studied as a source of achievement differences among students. For too long, they held, pride of place had been given to characteristics of individuals.

As a remedy, Barr and Dreeben began with a fairly conventional model of reading achievement. In a departure from conventional practice, they measured one of their explanatory factors, student aptitude, at both the individual and reading group levels. Aptitude aggregated to the level of the reading group was a contextual variable. Group mean aptitude, in the authors' analysis, exerted a substantial influence on reading achievement, exceeding the influence of individual aptitude. Contextual factors, they concluded, were consequential and underappreciated sources of achievement variability among elementary school students.

Barr and Dreeben's research has more than its share of methodological difficulties. Nevertheless, their acknowledgment of the importance of contextual variables is, in its own way, exemplary. This is exactly the sort of conceptual and methodological sensitivity one might expect from sociologists, but at least until recently, it has been difficult to find.

Even beyond that, Barr and Dreeben specified a very plausible mechanism for their use of group mean aptitude as a contextual variable: Pace of instruction is a function of group mean aptitude, and measured achievement is a function of pace of instruction. Once stated, this sounds perfectly obvious. Barr and Dreeben's work, however, had the virtue of formulating a retrospectively obvious assertion in terms of testable relationships involving a contextual variable.

Boyd, L., & Iversen, G. (1979) *Contextual Analysis: Concepts and Statistical Techniques.* Belmont, CA: Wadsworth.

Iversen, G. (1991) *Contextual Analysis.* Newbury Park, CA: Sage.

Bickel, R., Smith, C., & Eagle, T. (2002) Poor Rural Neighborhoods and Early School Achievement. *Journal of Poverty, 6,* 89–108.

Bickel, R., & Howley, C. (2000) The Influence of Scale on School Performance: A Multi-Level Extension of the Matthew Principle. *Education Policy Analysis Archives, 8.* Retrieved from http://epaa.asu.edu/epaa/v8n22

Bickel, R., & McDonough, M. (1998) No Effects to Fade: Head Start in Two West Virginia Counties. *Educational Foundations, 12,* 68–89.

Barr and Dreeben do not acknowledge the path-breaking work on contextual analysis done by Boyd and Iversen, but they seem clearly to be working in that tradition. Texts written in this tradition may still be read with profit. Boyd and Iversen anticipate and effectively address many of the issues that demand the attention of contemporary students of multilevel regression analysis.

In their textbook accounts, however, Boyd and Iversen rely exclusively on OLS estimators. While they acknowledge the importance of nesting and group-to-group variability in intercepts and slopes, by limiting themselves to OLS regression they cannot incorporate random coefficients into their models. Contextual variables with OLS regression, moreover, fit the tacked-on, jerry-rigged characterization we have already introduced. Nevertheless, these authors' work represents an effort to accomplish what good social scientists have always wanted to do: to take context seriously in their statistical models, thereby getting away from undue reliance on measures taken at the level of the individual. Work done using concepts and procedures explained in Boyd and Iversen's textbooks is still being produced. The three articles by Bickel and associates used OLS-based contextual analysis rather than multilevel regression.

Oberwittler, D. (2004) A Multilevel Analysis of Neighbourhood Contextual Effects on Serious Juvenile Offending. *European Journal of Criminology, 1,* 201–235.

Lochman, J. (2004) Contextual Factors in Risk and Prevention Research. *Merrill–Palmer Quarterly, 50,* 311–325.

Today, however, most applications of contextual variables as explanatory factors use multilevel regression analysis with alternative estimators. An accessible analysis that uses contextual variables in the analysis of neighborhood characteristics and criminal behavior is provided by Oberwittler. Oberwittler's choice of contextual variables in analyzing data collected in Germany is rooted in perspectives that explain delinquent behavior in terms of social disorganization and subcultural influences. As a result, his work constitutes an interesting effort to evaluate the cross-national explanatory power of established, even if rudimentary, theoretical frameworks that have been used by American social scientists for decades.

Lochman's review article on the role of a broad range of contextual factors in child development is especially interesting. The following quotation is straightforward and instructive:

Efforts to understand the development of childhood psychopathology have placed a growing emphasis on contextual factors that influence children's development. . . . A child's developmental course is set within the child's social ecology, and an ecological framework is needed to understand these effects. . . . Children not only have important interactions in their microsystems of . . . child–family, child–peer, and teacher–student interactions, but these fields also relate to each other in important ways. . . . The influence of neighborhood context on individuals, and on school and family contextual factors, can also be pivotal. (Lochman, 2004, pp. 311–312)

Thinking of contextual factors and their role in understanding of nested data in the ecological terms used by Lochman makes perfect sense. This is suggestive of the broad applicability of multilevel regression.

4

From OLS to Random Coefficient to Multilevel Regression

4.1   CHAPTER INTRODUCTION

Multilevel regression analysis is a specific application of random coefficient regression models. Without a mathematical foundation in random coefficient regression, multilevel regression would not be feasible. This is because multilevel analysis begins with acknowledgment that nesting is substantively and methodologically consequential. By permitting coefficients to vary from group to group, random coefficient regression acknowledges that nesting-engendered homogeneity may give rise to varying intercepts and slopes. Furthermore, when contextual variables are added—transforming random coefficient regression models into multilevel regression models—we have a means of providing substantively interesting *explanations* of group-to-group variability in intercepts and slopes.

We decide if random coefficient regression is needed by computing the unconditional intraclass correlation coefficient. If this measure has a statistically significant value, we know that within-group homogeneity is sufficiently consequential to inflate standard errors estimated for the usual fixed OLS coefficients. Alternative estimators, such as maximum likelihood (ML) and restricted maximum likelihood (REML), can be used to compute coefficients that have both fixed *and* random components, permitting variability from one context to another. In this way, the intraclass correlation is acknowledged. When contextual factors are added, the intraclass correlation may be explained.

In general, the fixed components are of greatest substantive interest for most analysts. Fortunately for all of us, the alternative estimators provide fixed component values that are interpreted in the same way as OLS regression coefficients.

The random component values, moreover, are also easy to interpret. In fact, we can use random components, for either the intercept or one or more slopes, to construct intervals for the fixed components. These intervals are not the same as the usual confidence intervals, which gauge the consequences of random sampling error. Instead, the intervals constructed for fixed components with random components enable us to estimate how much intercepts and slopes vary across a set of groups due to nesting-engendered homogeneity.

Beyond that, we may introduce contextual variables in an effort to explain random coefficient variability and narrow the intervals that span coefficient values across groups. When the contextual factors and associated cross-level interaction terms have been added, our random coefficient model becomes a multilevel model.

As we have seen, once we acknowledge random component variability, we may also wish to acknowledge that random components may vary together. Our choice of covariance structure determines if random components are permitted to vary and covary. As a result, random coefficient regression presents us with another specification decision for which we may or may not have adequate information. As explained in Chapter 3, we have decided to use the unstructured option as a matter of routine.

With random coefficient regression, moreover, we have a more complex error term than with OLS regression. Furthermore, as we shall see, each time we add another random component, the error term becomes still more complex. The added complexity of the error term takes predictable forms, but unless this is clearly spelled out, it is difficult to discern.

For better or worse, random coefficient regression models, and the multilevel models they permit, employ notational conventions that are a bit different from the familiar OLS conventions. There is nothing esoteric or unduly complicated about this alternative set of conventions, but it is something else that must be learned as part of the process of mastering multilevel regression analysis. Random coefficient regression and multilevel regression also have their own peculiar set of summary measures and model-fit decision-making tools. Although these are additional things to learn, again, they are not particularly difficult.

Throughout the rest of our discussion, the objective will be to make random coefficient and multilevel regression models easier to actually construct. We will finally get to *execution*! We do so by emphasizing again that random coefficient regression and multilevel regression can be usefully construed as regression analysis modified to be more informative and more accurate in specific circumstances. When the power and versatility of OLS multiple regression are exhausted by their encounter with nested data, multilevel analysis enables regression analysts to continue. This judgment becomes especially persuasive when we develop our long presidential election example in Chapters 6 and 7.

We will begin our work by using a simple OLS regression equation as a point of departure. As we proceed through the remaining examples, we will actually construct and evaluate increasingly complex and informative regression models. After we have more adequately introduced the random coefficient models that enable us to use varying intercepts and varying slopes, we will apply what we have learned to rigorously specified multilevel regression models.

It is useful, however, to keep in mind the OLS regression → random coefficient regression → multilevel regression sequence, because it helps us see how multilevel regression emerged. For our purposes, the only difference between random coefficient regression and multilevel regression is that the latter employs contextual factors and cross-level interaction terms to explain variability in random components, while the former does not. Some social scientists, in fact, refer to multilevel models as random coefficient models.

4.2   SIMPLE REGRESSION EQUATION

We shall begin simply and diagnostically. Most people who do applied research know the form of a simple regression equation, as presented in Table 4.1. The dependent variable is Y, the independent variable is X, and the random error term is designated e. The parameter estimate of primary interest in most circumstances is b, the unstandardized regression coefficient or slope. The numerical value of the slope tells us, on average, how much of an increase or decrease in Y corresponds to a 1-unit increase or decrease in X. The intercept tells us the value of Y when X is equal to zero. When we do OLS regression analysis, we find parameter estimates that, with the data set at hand, minimize the sum of the squared deviations between observed and predicted values on the dependent variable Y.

In conventional OLS regression models, the intercept and slope are fixed, meaning that we assume they do not vary with respect to groups such as classrooms, schools, occupational positions, or states. The error term, however, is random: Its values differ from one observation to another and are assumed to be independently distributed with uniform variance. This means that residuals are not correlated and exhibit homoscedasticity. The same assumptions hold for level-one residuals in random coefficient and multilevel regression models.

A crucial difference between OLS regression and multilevel regression with random coefficients is that in the latter kind of analysis, the intercept and slopes need not be fixed. Instead, either or both may vary across groups or contexts, such as classrooms, schools, or neighborhoods.

4.3   SIMPLE REGRESSION WITH AN INDIVIDUAL-LEVEL VARIABLE

Table 4.2 presents a simple OLS regression equation estimated using the large Kentucky data set that enabled us to put together some of our previous examples. With nearly 50,000 eighth-grade students in 347 schools in 135 districts in 2001, this is a large data set by any standard.

TABLE 4.1. OLS Simple Regression Model

$$Y = a + bX + e$$

TABLE 4.2. OLS Regression of Reading Achievement on Gender

$$Y = 51.830 + 7.391X_{GENDER1}$$
$$(0.085)\ (0.172)$$

$$R^2 = 3.7\%$$
$$N = 49,616$$

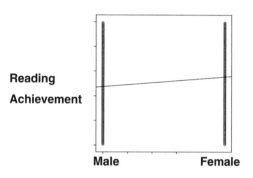

FIGURE 4.1. Reading achievement by student gender.

The dependent variable, Y, is a score on the California Basic Educational Skills Test, a state-mandated standardized test of reading achievement (National Evaluation Systems, 2002). The independent variable, X, is individual student gender, a dummy or categorical variable coded 0 for males and 1 for females. For the sake of simplicity, there is no group or contextual effect in this preliminary analysis. This is just a concrete example of the abstract equation from Table 4.1. By dividing the intercept and slope by their standard errors (in parentheses), we get t values of 641.63 and 43.41—values that are statistically significant at alpha levels far smaller than those conventionally prescribed, such as .05, .01, or .001.

As we see in Figure 4.1, since $X_{GENDER1}$ is a dichotomy or dummy variable, we are using the term *slope* a bit loosely, but the usage is conventional (Hardy, 1993). The unstandardized regression coefficient in the simple regression equation tells us that female students in Kentucky score, on average, 7.391 points higher than male students on this test of eighth-grade reading achievement (cf. Gujarati, 2006, p. 297).

4.4   MULTIPLE REGRESSION: ADDING A CONTEXTUAL VARIABLE

In the abstract, a multiple regression equation can be represented as in Table 4.3. The equation in Table 4.1 is just a special case in which $K = 1$. The ellipsis indicates that—constrained by satisfaction of the usual assumptions, as well as by theoretical and substantive knowledge and data set limitations—a multiple regression equation can have an indefinitely large number of independent variables. Otherwise, the form of the equation and the meaning of its terms are the same as in simple regression.

If we estimate a multiple regression equation with two independent variables (gender at the individual level and gender composition at the school level), and again use individual eighth-grade reading achievement as the dependent variable, we get the results reported in Table 4.4. This is an example of an OLS regression equation that includes both individual-level and group-level independent variables.

TABLE 4.3. OLS Multiple Regression Model

$$Y = a + b_1X_1 + b_2X_2 + \ldots + b_KX_K + e$$

TABLE 4.4. OLS Regression of Reading Achievement on Gender and Gender Composition

$$Y = 51.362 + 7.391X_{GENDER1} + 31.305X_{GENDER2}$$
$$(0.084)\ (0.169)(1.280)$$

$$R^2 = 4.8\%$$
$$N = 49,616$$

As we know, however, given the inherently single-level nature of OLS multiple regression analysis, both $X_{GENDER1}$ and $X_{GENDER2}$ are treated as if they were characteristics of individual students. Yes, we characterize $X_{GENDER2}$ as a contextual variable, and we have measured it at the group level. Analytically, however, it occupies the same level of analysis and has the same number of degrees of freedom as $X_{GENDER1}$.

As with the simple regression equation, dividing the intercept and slopes by their standard errors makes clear that each is statistically significant at any alpha level we might realistically choose. Gender therefore has both individual-level and contextual or school-level effects on reading achievement: Female students, on average, score 7.391 points higher than males, *and* for every 1% increase in the number of female students in a school, individual students of both genders score, on average, 31.305 points higher. (One reason the numerical value of the coefficient for the contextual variable is so large is naturally limited variability in gender composition from school to school. The coefficient of variability for $X_{GENDER2}$ is only 4.2%.)

Comparing Figures 4.1 and 4.2 makes clear that individual-level gender and gender aggregated to the school level are very different variables. The numerical values of the slopes and their graphic representations, moreover, show us that the two variables are related to reading achievement in different ways.

4.5 NESTING (AGAIN!) WITH A CONTEXTUAL VARIABLE

Before we go further, it is useful to emphasize another easy-to-overlook but crucial difference between the individual-level and

Reading Achievement

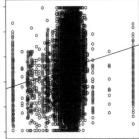

Gender Composition

FIGURE 4.2. Reading achievement by gender aggregated to the school level.

school-level variables. Within the same school and across all schools, students are coded 0 or 1 on the individual-level variable $X_{GENDER1}$, depending on whether they are males or females. However, *within* the same school, *all* students will be assigned the *same* value on $X_{GENDER2}$, and that value will be the *mean* value of $X_{GENDER1}$ for that school.

For example, if half of all students in a school with an enrollment of 500 were male and half were female, we would find 250 students coded 1 on $X_{GENDER1}$ and 250 students coded 0 on $X_{GENDER1}$. All students in that school, however, would have the same value on $X_{GENDER2}$, 0.50, which is the school-level mean for $X_{GENDER1}$.

What we are really talking about, of course, is nesting. This example also makes clear that the contextual variable, $X_{GENDER2}$, is a characteristic of the grouping variable (in this case, schools) rather than of individuals. Students are grouped or nested within schools.

Given the nature of the independent variables—gender at the individual level and at the group level—it is not surprising that they are correlated. In this case, however, the correlation is modest ($r = 0.129$), inflating the standard error of the regression coefficient for each variable by less than 2%. For now at least, this puts to rest concerns as to possibly adverse consequences of multicollinearity involving the specific individual-level and group-level measures we have taken from the Kentucky data set (Chatterjee, Hadi, & Price, 2000).

4.6   IS THERE A PROBLEM WITH DEGREES OF FREEDOM?

Though multicollinearity is not cause for concern with regard to the analysis reported in Table 4.4, we do have other problems inherent in the multilevel nature of our analysis. As is clear from our discussion of basic issues, we are certainly using too many degrees of freedom, based on the number of students rather than the number of schools, in testing the statistical significance of the coefficient for our group-level contextual variable, $X_{GENDER2}$.

The Kentucky data set includes 49,616 students and 347 schools. The correct number of degrees of freedom used in testing the regression coefficient for $X_{GENDER1}$ is 49,613. However, the correct number of degrees of freedom for the coefficient corresponding to $X_{GENDER2}$ is only 344. If we erroneously used individual-level degrees of freedom in evaluating a school-level regression coefficient, the desirable inferential properties of regression analysis would be compromised by inflating the probability of erroneously rejecting the null hypothesis.

With reference to Tables 2.22 through 2.33 in Chapter 2, we have already mentioned the possible presence of design effects due to nesting and illustrated the consequences for effective sample size and degrees of freedom. We will develop these issues further below. For now we will simply emphasize the obvious but ironically easy-to-overlook fact that sample size and degrees of freedom vary from level to level of a multilevel regression analysis.

4.7   IS THERE A PROBLEM WITH DEPENDENT OBSERVATIONS?

There may be still other reasons why OLS estimators with fixed coefficients are unsuitable for the analysis in Table 4.4. After all, we have students nested within schools, meaning that we may have violated three already discussed assumptions intrinsic to usual applications of OLS regression analysis: independent observations, nonvarying slopes and intercepts, and uncorrelated residuals. To find out if we have a problem requiring use of alternatives to OLS regression that permit intercepts and slopes to vary, we may begin by computing the intraclass correlation coefficient to determine if student achievement varies between schools as well as within schools; we use the information in Table 4.5 for this purpose. As in Chapter 3, INTERCEPT1 is the variance of the random component of the intercept in a two-level model with no predictors at level one or level two. Residual is just the level-one residual variance.

$$r = 20.653/(20.653 + 340.156) = 0.056$$

An intraclass correlation of 0.056 may not seem large, but with an average of 143 students per school, even a small intraclass correlation can give very misleading results. In the present instance, a nominal alpha level of .05 would be equal, in practice, to an actual alpha level of very roughly .50 (Singer, 1987).

The intraclass correlation coefficient tells us that our observations are not independent. Some of the variability in the dependent variable is accounted for simply by virtue of the fact that students are grouped within different schools. This implies, furthermore, that residuals from OLS regression analyses will be positively correlated. Finally, intercepts and slopes are likely to vary from group to group.

When residuals are temporally correlated, there are well-known correctives for positive or negative autocorrelation. These have been developed as part of the ongoing process of finding ways to use regression analysis even when one or more assumptions have been violated. The Cochrane–Orcutt and Prais–Winsten procedures, for example, have long and effective histories (Gujarati, 2003).

When the correlation among residuals is not temporally patterned, however, but is occasioned by a nominal-level variable such as group membership, these familiar procedures that are so useful with time series data cannot be applied (Chatfield, 2003). While positive autocorrelation and positive intraclass correlation have comparably adverse consequences, they require different remedies.

TABLE 4.5. Reading Achievement in Kentucky: The Intraclass Correlation Coefficient; Estimates of Covariance Parameters

Parameter	Estimate	Std. error	Wald Z	Sig. level
Residual	340.156	2.199	154.688	.000
INTERCEPT1	20.653	2.111	9.782	.000

An effective method for dealing with intraclass correlation begins with estimation of a random coefficient or multilevel regression model using estimators more suitable than OLS (Angeles & Mroz, 2001). One of the most widely used alternatives to OLS is ML (Kleinbaum, 1996). A closely related method of estimation is REML, which we have used throughout our discussion of basic issues.

4.8   ALTERNATIVES TO OLS ESTIMATORS

By way of introducing our account of alternative estimators, we may ask a by-now-familiar question: "What would the OLS regression equation in Table 4.2 look like if we used REML estimators and permitted the intercept and level-one slope to vary from school to school?"

Table 4.6 compares results of a random coefficient regression equation with REML estimators and random intercept and random slope with the OLS results from Table 4.2. As we have become accustomed to seeing, there is very little difference between the OLS intercept and slope and the random coefficient regression intercept and slope. Standard errors for the random coefficient estimates, however, are larger than the OLS standard errors.

The reproduction of Table 4.2 appended to Table 4.6 gives us the basic information we need to report OLS regression results for the relationship between reading achievement and student-level gender. As we know, however, the process of measuring the same relationship using random coefficient regression with REML estimators is incomplete without the additional information reported in Table 4.7.

As we saw with our jumping-the-gun example in Chapter 1, estimating a random coefficient regression equation with REML (or ML) is not difficult with SPSS. Just look at the computer screen and follow the instructions in SPSS Routine 4.1. To add a contex-

TABLE 4.6. Random Coefficient Regression of Reading Achievement on Gender; Unstructured

$$Y = 51.294 + 7.522X_{GENDER1}$$
$$(0.314)\ (0.212)$$

$$R_1^2 = 3.8\%$$
$$N_1 = 49,616$$
$$N_2 = 347$$

TABLE 4.2, Reproduced. OLS Regression of Reading Achievement on Gender

$$Y = 51.830 + 7.391X_{GENDER1}$$
$$(0.085)\ (0.172)$$

$$R^2 = 3.7\%$$
$$N = 49,616$$

TABLE 4.7. Random Coefficient Regression of Reading Achievement on Gender; No Contextual Variables in Model; Unstructured; Estimates of Covariance Parameters

Parameter	Estimate	Std. error	Wald Z	Sig. level
Residual	325.169	2.112	153.962	.000
INTERCEPT1	20.702	2.109	9.815	.000
INTERCEPT1 by $X_{GENDER1}$	–2.378	0.976	–2.437	.015
$X_{GENDER1}$	3.338	0.904	3.692	.000

SPSS Routine 4.1. Estimating a Random Coefficient Regression Equation with REML

1. Open the SPSS data file and click on ANALYZE.
2. Go to MIXED MODELS and click on LINEAR.
3. Since school is the level-two or grouping variable, insert the school identifier into the SUBJECTS box.
4. Click on CONTINUE, insert reading achievement as the dependent variable into the DEPENDENT VARIABLE box, and insert student-level gender into the COVARIATE(S) box.
5. Click on FIXED. In the small box in the middle of the screen, change FACTORIAL to MAIN EFFECTS. Move the student-level gender variable from the FACTORS AND COVARIATES box to the MODEL box. Click on CONTINUE.
6. Click on the RANDOM button at the bottom of the screen. The school identifier is already in the SUBJECTS box, and now we also insert it into the COMBINATIONS box. Move the student-level gender variable from the FACTORS AND COVARIATES box to the MODEL box.
7. In the small box in the middle of the screen, change FACTORIAL to MAIN EFFECTS.
8. Near the top of the screen, click on INCLUDE INTERCEPT, and insert student-level gender into the MODEL box.
9. Just above INCLUDE INTERCEPT and to the right of COVARIANCE TYPE, select UNSTRUCTURED.
10. Click on CONTINUE, and then click on the STATISTICS button.
11. On the left, under MODEL STATISTICS, select PARAMETER ESTIMATES and TESTS FOR COVARIANCE PARAMETERS.
12. Click on CONTINUE and click on OK.
13. Near the bottom of the SPSS output, values for the INTERCEPT and SLOPE, along with their standard errors, appear in the ESTIMATE and STD. ERROR columns of the box labeled ESTIMATES OF FIXED EFFECTS.
14. Just below the ESTIMATES OF FIXED EFFECTS box, values for the variances and covariances of random components appear in the ESTIMATE column of the box labeled ESTIMATES OF COVARIANCE PARAMETERS.

TABLE 4.8. Random Coefficient Regression of Reading Achievement on Gender; School-Level Gender Included as a Contextual Variable; Unstructured

$$Y = 51.239 + 7.519X_{GENDER1} + 27.940X_{GENDER2}$$
$$(0.304)\ (0.211)\qquad\qquad (6.609)$$

$$R_1^2 = 4.2\%$$
$$N_1 = 49{,}616$$
$$N_2 = 347$$

TABLE 4.9. Random Coefficient Regression of Reading Achievement on Gender; School-Level Gender Included as a Contextual Variable; Unstructured; Estimates of Covariance Parameters

Parameter	Estimate	Std. error	Wald Z	Sig. level
Residual	325.165	2.112	153.964	.000
INTERCEPT1	19.237	1.976	9.737	.000
INTERCEPT1 by $X_{GENDER1}$	−2.397	0.946	−2.535	.011
$X_{GENDER1}$	3.314	0.904	3.669	.000

tual variable, as in Table 4.4, we need only minor modifications to this routine. Specifically, in item 4, insert school-level gender into the COVARIATE(S) box along with student-level gender. And in item 5, move the school-level gender variable from the FACTORS AND COVARIATES box to the MODEL box along with the student-level gender variable. We than get the results in Tables 4.8 and 4.9.

In Table 4.8, we see that, as with OLS, there is a substantial relationship between reading achievement and the school-level contextual variable, $X_{GENDER2}$. It is clear from comparing Tables 4.7 and 4.9, however, that the contextual variable accounts for very little of the variability in the random terms.

While our respecifications of Tables 4.2 and 4.4 used REML estimators, the conceptual basis of the most commonly used alternatives to OLS is easier to understand if we begin with ML. This leads directly to REML.

4.9   THE CONCEPTUAL BASIS OF ML ESTIMATORS

ML estimators are designed to find hypothesized population parameters that make our observed sample data most likely (Wonnacott & Wonnacott, 1990; Gujarati, 2003). The job of ML estimators is to find parameter values that do the best job of making this case. In other words, given the observed data, what parameter values would we expect to find (Vogt, 1999)?

For a simple but instructive example, we follow Kmenta (1997, pp. 175–183) and refer back to the social skills data used in generating the information in Tables 3.70 and

3.71. Suppose that for illustrative purposes we have 70 cases, each measured on the social skills variable. The distribution of social skills for this sample of 70 cases is shown in Figure 4.3.

We know that these 70 cases are a simple random sample taken from an unidentified population, but we do not know which one. As it turns out, we have three data sets, and all have the same number of cases and the same social skills measure. We treat each data set as if it were an entire population. We generate histograms for the social skills variable for each of the three data sets. Using intuition and common-sense, we try to select the data set that maximizes the likelihood that it generated the sample data yielding the histogram in Figure 4.3.

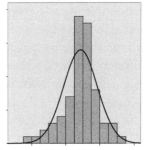

Mean = 24.338
Standard Deviation = 4.997

FIGURE 4.3. Simple random sample: Social skills.

Since all three candidate data sets are approximately normally distributed, we know that they differ only with respect to central tendency and variability. As a result, our choice is easy: Since the mean and standard deviation in Figure 4.3 are very similar to the same measures in Data Set Candidate 2 (Figure 4.5), but different from Data Set Candidates 1 (Figure 4.4) and 3 (Figure 4.6), we choose Data Set Candidate 2. Our choice may be the wrong one, but it seems clear that we have maximized the likelihood that we are right.

When we get past simple statistics such as the mean and standard deviation, the choices become more mathematically complex, but the same basic principle applies. In the case of multiple regression analysis, ML estimators provide values for the intercept and slopes that have the greatest likelihood of giving rise to the observed data—the values actually appearing in our data set (Nunnally & Bernstein, 1994).

For example, suppose we have a national probability sample of 1588 families. For each family, we have annual income as well as educational level and race of the self-reported family head in the year 2000. We use ML to estimate the intercept and slopes in

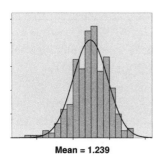

Mean = 1.239
Standard Deviation = 0.238

FIGURE 4.4. Data Set Candidate 1: Social skills.

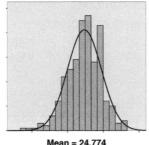

Mean = 24.774
Standard Deviation = 4.751

FIGURE 4.5. Data Set Candidate 2: Social skills.

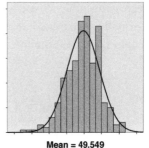

Mean = 49.549
Standard Deviation = 9.501

FIGURE 4.6. Data Set Candidate 3: Social skills.

a multiple regression equation in which annual family income is the dependent variable and educational level and race are independent variables. Given specific distributions for all variables, what parameter values maximize the probability of the observed values for the dependent variable and the independent variables (Wonnacott & Wonnacott, 1984)?

Using data taken from the Child Development Supplement of the Panel Study of Income Dynamics (Institute for Social Research, 2003) along with ML estimation for the intercept and slopes, we get the results shown in Table 4.10 for individual-level variables with no contextual factors. Thus, for a family whose head is Black and has 16 years of education, the predicted value on family income is $108,413.37. For a family whose head is White and has 12 years of education, the predicted value for family income is $77,085.10. Given the nature of ML estimation, the intercept and slope values are those that maximize the joint probability of these two and the remaining 1586 sets of values for Y_{INCOME}, X_{BLACK}, and $X_{EDUCATION}$ (Wooldridge, 2002).

Notice that in Figure 4.7, however, this straightforward, easy-to-interpret analysis presents us with a difficulty in the form of a non-normal distribution of residuals. This is commonplace with income analyses, because income distributions are usually skewed to the right. However, as we have illustrated in Figures 4.4 through 4.6, the assumption of normality is essential to ML estimation because it makes possible straightforward comparison of statistics such as means, standard deviations, and more complex measures.

An often effective response to a sharp rightward skew in a residual plot is use of natural logarithms of the dependent variable, as in Table 4.11. Interpretation of the coefficients changes after logging of the dependent variable. In Table 4.11, for example, we see that each one-level increase in $X_{EDUCATION}$ corresponds, on average, to a 12.8% increase in annual family income. In addition, families headed by someone who is Black experience, on average, a 9.1% decrease in annual income.

Having acknowledged changes in interpretation prompted by logging the dependent variable, we see in Figure 4.8 that the residuals for the regression analysis with ML estimators are now normally distributed, consistent with the requirements of ML estimation.

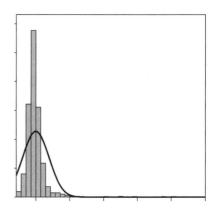

FIGURE 4.7. Residual plot for total family income.

TABLE 4.10. An Earnings Function with ML Estimators

$$Y_{INCOME} = -31448.970 - 4849.716X_{BLACK} + 9044.843X_{EDUCATION}$$
$$(11293.813) \quad (1740.209) \qquad (762.604)$$

$$N = 1588$$

TABLE 4.11. Earnings Logged: ML Estimators

$$Y_{\text{LNINCOME}} = 9.279 - 0.091 X_{\text{BLACK}} + 0.128 X_{\text{EDUCATION}}$$
$$(0.096)\ (0.011)\qquad\ (0.018)$$

$$N = 1588$$

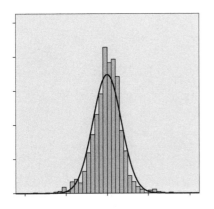

FIGURE 4.8. Residual plot for total family income, logged.

ML is a computationally intensive, iterative process that was known but impractical to employ before the development of high-speed computers. It is more restrictive than OLS, in that it assumes a normally distributed error term even for large samples. In addition, even with a normally distributed error term, regression coefficients estimated with small samples may be biased, because ML does not take into consideration the number of parameters used in model estimation (Nunnally & Bernstein, 1994).

4.10 DESIRABLE PROPERTIES OF REML ESTIMATORS

SPSS and most other statistical software packages that permit estimation and testing of random coefficient and multilevel regression models offer ML as one method of estimation. However, in most applications, the closely related REML procedure is more likely to be used (Kreft & De Leeuw, 1998). We have used REML estimators in the examples of random coefficient and multilevel regression models already presented.

The advantage of REML over ML estimators is diminished bias in estimates of the random components of random regression coefficients for small samples. This occurs because REML, in contrast to ML, takes into consideration the number of parameters used in model estimation. The difference between the ML and REML estimators, however, becomes quite small as the number of group-level observations becomes large (Luke, 2004).

To compare illustrative results of application of ML and REML, Table 4.12 reports three random coefficient regression equations. In each, the dependent variable is math achievement as measured by the California Basic Educational Skills Test. There are two level-one independent variables, which we have used in previously reported analyses with the Kentucky data set: $X_{\text{NONWHITE1}}$ and X_{GENDER1}. The intercept and the slope for $X_{\text{NONWHITE1}}$ are random, while the slope for X_{GENDER1} is fixed. There are no contextual variables.

In comparing the results of ML and REML methods of estimation, we begin with the entire sample of nearly 50,000 students and 347 schools. Then we report the same analy-

TABLE 4.12. Comparing ML and REML Estimators: Random Coefficient Analyses of Math Achievement

ML: Full sample

$$Y_{MATH} = \textbf{\textit{49.068}} - \textbf{\textit{8.705}}X_{NONWHITE1} - 1.154X_{GENDER1}$$
$$(0.430)\ (0.607) \qquad\qquad (0.186)$$

$$R^2 = 3.6\%$$
$$N_1 = 49,616$$
$$N_2 = 347$$

REML: Full sample

$$Y_{MATH} = \textbf{\textit{49.068}} - \textbf{\textit{8.705}}X_{NONWHITE1} - 1.154X_{GENDER1}$$
$$(0.430)\ (0.607) \qquad\qquad (0.186)$$

$$R^2 = 3.6\%$$
$$N_1 = 49,616$$
$$N_2 = 347$$

ML: 10% simple random sample

$$Y_{MATH} = \textbf{\textit{49.060}} - \textbf{\textit{11.057}}X_{NONWHITE1} + 0.163X_{GENDER1}$$
$$(0.565)\ \ (1.006) \qquad\qquad (0.595)$$

$$R^2 = 3.9\%$$
$$N_1 = 4964$$
$$N_2 = 57$$

REML: 10% simple random sample

$$Y_{MATH} = \textbf{\textit{49.065}} - \textbf{\textit{11.465}}X_{NONWHITE1} + 0.167X_{GENDER1}$$
$$(0.567)\ \ (1.018) \qquad\qquad (0.596)$$

$$R^2 = 3.3\%$$
$$N_1 = 4964$$
$$N_2 = 57$$

ML: 5% random sample

$$Y_{MATH} = \textbf{\textit{48.900}} - \textbf{\textit{12.639}}X_{NONWHITE1} - 1.084X_{GENDER1}$$
$$(0.612)\ \ (1.365) \qquad\qquad (0.854)$$

$$R^2 = 3.1\%$$
$$N_1 = 2508$$
$$N_2 = 46$$

REML: 5% simple random sample

$$Y_{MATH} = \textbf{\textit{49.899}} - \textbf{\textit{12.648}}X_{NONWHITE1} - 1.076X_{GENDER1}$$
$$(0.611)\ \ (1.356) \qquad\qquad (0.856)$$

$$R^2 = 2.9\%$$
$$N_1 = 2508$$
$$N_2 = 46$$

Note. Random coefficients are boldfaced and italicized.

ses for a 10% simple random sample and a 5% simple random sample. Notice that the samples are being selected on students. While we will have 10% and 5% simple random samples of Kentucky eighth graders, the school percentages will be different from these.

A useful summary of the information in Table 4.12 might go like this: Differences in sample size assure substantial differences in intercepts, slopes, and standard errors. *For any sample size*, however, differences between ML and REML estimates are small, though they do get a bit larger as sample sizes get smaller.

The summary statement we have just made with regard to Table 4.12 applies almost as neatly to Table 4.13: Differences in sample size assure substantial differences in the estimates of random component variances and covariances. *For any sample size*, however, differences between ML and REML estimates are small, though they do get a bit larger as sample sizes get smaller.

None of our samples, however, including the 5% simple random sample, is all that small by most standards. This applies to the number of students, the number of schools, and the average number of students within schools. Perhaps differences between ML and REML estimators would be become a lot clearer if we pared down sample sizes a good deal more. In addition, while we have varied sample size, we have not varied the number of parameters estimated in our comparisons of ML and REML estimates. In general, as the number of parameters estimated increases, the difference between ML and REML estimates becomes larger (SAS Institute, 1999).

Again, this discussion of alternative estimators is prompted by the fact that in some instances, OLS estimates cannot be effectively corrected to deal with violation of specific assumptions. When this happens—as in the cases of varying parameter estimates, nonindependence of observations, and nonindependence of residuals—useful alternatives are sometimes available. ML is one such alternative, and REML is another.

4.11 APPLYING REML ESTIMATORS WITH RANDOM COEFFICIENT REGRESSION MODELS

By way of illustrating application of REML estimators, recall the simple OLS regression equation from Table 4.1: $Y = a + bX + e$. We have already estimated OLS coefficients for this equation in Table 4.2, and we compared these with random coefficient estimates for the same equation in Table 4.6. *In Table 4.14 we are merely expressing the same equation with notation that has become conventional with random coefficient and multilevel regression models.* Yes, for the first time we are also making the structure of the more complex error term explicit, but beyond that *it's just notation!*

Other textbooks introduce these notational conventions *much* earlier, and this does help in construction of random coefficient and multilevel models. However, consistent with our "It's just regression!" theme, we have delayed introduction of material that might make multilevel regression seem fundamentally different from OLS regression.

The random intercept is represented by β_{0J}, the random slope is represented by β_{1J}, and the independent variable corresponding to the random slope is represented as

TABLE 4.13. Comparing ML and REML Estimators: Random Coefficient Analyses of Math Achievement; Estimates of Covariance Parameters

Parameter	Estimate	Std. error	Wald Z	Sig. level
ML: Full sample				
Residual	400.448	2.631	152.200	.000
INTERCEPT	39.567	3.961	9.989	.000
INTERCEPT by $X_{\text{NONWHITE1}}$	–13.191	3.791	–3.480	.001
$X_{\text{NONWHITE1}}$	36.993	7.270	5.088	.000
REML: Full sample				
Residual	400.455	2.631	152.198	.000
INTERCEPT	39.750	3.987	9.970	.000
INTERCEPT by $X_{\text{NONWHITE1}}$	–13.238	3.824	–3.462	.001
$X_{\text{NONWHITE1}}$	37.438	7.351	5.093	.000
ML: 10% simple random sample				
Residual	395.642	8.533	46.365	.000
INTERCEPT	47.356	6.585	7.191	.000
INTERCEPT by $X_{\text{NONWHITE1}}$	–13.259	7.405	–1.791	.073
$X_{\text{NONWHITE1}}$	16.024	16.767	0.956	.339
REML: 10% simple random sample				
Residual	395.624	8.533	46.364	.000
INTERCEPT	47.024	6.533	7.198	.000
INTERCEPT by $X_{\text{NONWHITE1}}$	–13.387	7.261	–1.844	.065
$X_{\text{NONWHITE1}}$	14.251	16.317	0.873	.382
ML: 5% simple random sample				
Residual	403.801	12.356	32.680	.000
INTERCEPT	41.086	7.965	5.158	.000
INTERCEPT by $X_{\text{NONWHITE1}}$	–0.758	11.937	–0.064	.949
$X_{\text{NONWHITE1}}$	13.194	25.481	0.518	.605
REML: 5% simple random sample				
Residual	403.953	12.366	32.666	.000
INTERCEPT	41.482	8.033	5.164	.000
INTERCEPT by $X_{\text{NONWHITE1}}$	–0.714	12.087	–0.059	.953
$X_{\text{NONWHITE1}}$	15.174	26.089	0.582	.561

TABLE 4.14. Simple Regression with Random Coefficients

$$Y = \beta_{0J} + \beta_{1J}\text{GENDER1} + (u_{0J} + u_{1J} * \text{GENDER1} + e_{IJ})$$

GENDER1. Beta coefficients such as these are routinely used to represent random intercepts, unstandardized random slopes, and unstandardized fixed slopes in random coefficient and multilevel regression models. As such, they are *just conventions*—more or less convenient ways to distinguish random coefficient and multilevel regression models from OLS regression models. We will discuss subscript conventions for beta coefficients in Section 4.14.

The added complexity of the error term (in parentheses) stems from the fact that it captures residual variance, as in OLS regression, *as well as* group-to-group variability in the random intercept relative to the overall intercept, *and* group-to-group variability in the random slope relative to the overall slope. As with OLS regression, the error term or residual, e_{ij}, varies randomly about the fitted or predicted value of Y. In addition, u_{0j} varies with respect to the random intercept, β_{0j}; and u_{1j} varies with respect to the random slope, β_{1j} (Kennedy, 1998). We assume, moreover, that level-one residuals vary independently of each other and independently of the level-two error terms, u_{0j} and u_{1j} (Snijders & Bosker, 1999).

The random intercept, therefore, may be expressed in the form $\beta_{0j} + u_{0j}$: a fixed value for the intercept plus a measure of the variability of the intercept from group to group. The random slope is expressed as $\beta_{1j} + u_{1j}$: a fixed value for the slope plus a measure of the variability of the slope from group to group. When we express the random intercept and random slope in this way, we add the u_{0j} and u_{1j} * GENDER1 components to the error term. For the slope specifically, it is important to note the following: $(\beta_{1j} + u_{1j})$ * GENDER1 gives us β_{1j}GENDER1 + u_{1j} * GENDER1.

For the sake of clarity, we will illustrate construction of the more complex error term that comes with random coefficient regression with additional examples. In earlier examples, we introduced a data set that enabled us to examine relationships between hourly wage and a variety of explanatory factors within nine categories of occupation. The individual worker is the unit of analysis, and workers are nested within occupational groups. No contextual factors will be introduced.

The first random coefficient regression model, with level of educational attainment in years (YEARS1) as the only independent variable, is presented in Table 4.15. Both the intercept and the slope for YEARS1 have been permitted to vary across occupational categories. (In the interest of realism, REML estimates of coefficients are reported below the specified models.) Error terms in Tables 4.15 through 4.18 are boldfaced and italicized.

In Tables 4.16 and 4.17 the model becomes increasingly complex, as first union membership (UNION1, coded 1 if member of a labor union and 0 otherwise) and then race (BLACK1, coded 1 if Black and 0 otherwise) are added as additional independent variables. Again, the intercept and slopes in each model have been permitted to vary

TABLE 4.15. Error Term with One Random Slope

$$Y = \beta_{0j} + \beta_{1j}\text{YEARS1} + (u_{0j} + u_{1j} * \textbf{\textit{YEARS1}} + \textbf{\textit{e}}_{\textbf{\textit{ij}}})$$

$$Y = 5.833 + 0.414\text{YEARS1}$$

TABLE 4.16. Error Term with Two Random Slopes

$$Y = \beta_{0J} + \beta_{1J}YEARS1 + \beta_{2J}UNION1 + (u_{0J} + u_{1J} * YEARS1 + u_{2J} * UNION1 + e_{IJ})$$

$$Y = 5.837 + 0.402YEARS1 + 1.058UNION1$$

TABLE 4.17. Error Term with Three Random Slopes

$$Y = \beta_{0J} + \beta_{1J}YEARS1 + \beta_{2J}UNION1 + \beta_{3J}BLACK1 + (u_{0J} + u_{1J} * YEARS1 + u_{2J} * UNION1$$
$$+ u_{3J} * BLACK1 + e_{IJ})$$

$$Y = 5.832 + 0.395YEARS1 + 1.111UNION1 - 0.565BLACK1$$

across districts. In Table 4.16, we see that by adding the independent variable UNION1 and permitting its slope to vary across occupational groups, we have necessarily added another component, $u_{2J} * UNION1$, to the error term. In Table 4.17, with addition of BLACK1 as another independent variable that has been assigned a random coefficient, the error term becomes more complex still.

The random slopes follow the same form as that given with reference to Table 4.14: $(\beta_{1J} + u_{1J}) * YEARS1$; $(\beta_{2J} + u_{2J}) * UNION1$; and $(\beta_{3J} + u_{3J}) * BLACK1$. The random intercept has the form $\beta_{0J} + u_{0J}$. In this way, each additional random component adds to the complexity of the error term. This is a very complex error term indeed. Four random components in one multilevel regression model is more than we will usually encounter.

Adding fixed components to a multilevel regression equation, however, leaves the error term unchanged. In Table 4.18 an additional independent variable, marital status (X_{MARRY1}, coded 1 if married and 0 otherwise), has been added to the equation from Table 4.17. This additional explanatory factor, however, has been assigned a fixed slope. As a result, the concrete regression results in Table 4.18 are different from those in Table 4.17, but the error term specification remains the same.

If we want estimates of the random component variances used in Table 4.18, we know where to look: estimates of covariance parameters. In Table 4.19 we find estimates of the variances of random components: u_{0J}, u_{1J}, u_{2J}, u_{3J}. Since variances cannot be negative, we know that they will be tested for significance with one-tailed tests.

As we will discuss further in the next section, random component estimates can be informative—sometimes alarmingly so!—in a way we have not yet acknowledged. For

TABLE 4.18. Error Term with Three Random Slopes and One Fixed Slope

$$Y = \beta_{0J} + \beta_{1J}YEARS1 + \beta_{2J}UNION1 + \beta_{3J}BLACK1 + \beta_{40}X_{MARRY1} + (u_{0J} + u_{1J} * YEARS1$$
$$+ u_{2J} * UNION1 + u_{3J} * BLACK1 + e_{IJ})$$

$$Y = 5.839 + 0.377YEARS1 + 1.026UNION1 - 0.393BLACK1 + 0.885X_{MARRY1}$$

TABLE 4.19. Random Coefficient Analyses of Hourly Wage; REML Estimators; Unstructured; Estimates of Covariance Parameters

Parameter	Estimate	Std. error	Wald Z	Sig. level
Residual (e_{ij}^2)	8.619	0.186	46.453	.000
INTERCEPT (u_{0j}^2)	1.294	0.676	1.913	.056
INTERCEPT by YEARS1	0.157	0.093	1.679	.093
YEARS1 (u_{1j}^2)	0.021	0.016	1.290	.197
INTERCEPT by BLACK1	−0.377	0.389	−0.968	.333
YEARS1 by BLACK1	−0.064	0.058	−1.106	.269
BLACK1 (u_{2j}^2)	0.361	0.266	1.358	.175
INTERCEPT by UNION1	−0.412	0.452	−0.912	.362
YEARS1 by UNION1	−0.048	0.064	−0.753	.452
BLACK1 by UNION1	0.008	0.268	0.028	.977
UNION1 (u_{3j}^2)	0.458	0.499	0.920	.357

example, the intercept variance in the hourly-wage-by-occupation illustration is statistically significant with a value of 1.294. In Table 4.18 we reported an estimated value for the intercept itself of 5.839. Since all independent variables have been centered with respect to their grand means, 5.839 is our best estimate of the value of the dependent variable if all independent variables were set equal to their means.

As we saw with Table 2.25 in our Chapter 2 discussion of effective sample size, a conventional 95% confidence interval for an intercept or slope is easy to compute. All we need is an intercept or slope value, a t value, and a standard error. Then we are justified in asserting that 95% of the time in the long run the population parameter will be included in an interval constructed in this way (Snedecor & Cochran, 1989).

Suppose, however, that we frame the issue a bit differently: *Given that the intercepts and slopes summarized in random regression coefficients vary from group to group, what range do they cover?* Since the random component variance for the intercept is normally distributed (Hox, 2002), we know that 95% of the distribution is included in an interval that includes the range 1.960 standard deviations above and below the mean. If we use the intercept value of 5.839 and the square root of the intercept variance ($1.294^{1/2} = 1.138$) as the standard deviation, we get the results reported in Table 4.20.

TABLE 4.20. Variability with Respect to a Random Intercept for a Random Coefficient Model

$a_{\text{INTERCEPT}} - t_{.05}S_{a\text{INTERCEPT}}$ to $a_{\text{INTERCEPT}} + t_{.05}S_{a\text{INTERCEPT}}$

$5.839 - 1.960(1.138)$ to $5.839 + 1.960(1.138)$

3.660 to 8.069

This means that 95% of the intercepts for our occupational groups will fall within an uncomfortably wide interval from 3.660 to 8.069. At least the interval does not contain both positive and negative values, which is sometimes the disconcerting case for both intercepts and slopes, making interpretation of results much more difficult (Tabachnick, 2005).

Is there anything we can do to narrow the interval, making us more comfortable with the overall or average slope estimate? Yes, we can try to account for the variability in the random components by introducing one or more level-two contextual variables and implied cross-level interaction terms into the random coefficient regression equation that gave us the information in Tables 4.18 through 4.20. We now have a multilevel regression model, as in Table 4.21. In this case, years of educational attainment has been aggregated to the occupational level, giving us the contextual variable X_{YEARS2}. This aggregated variable enables us to determine if income varies with the average educational level of the occupational group.

The implied cross-level interaction terms enable us to address the following questions: Does the relationship between an individual worker's income level and his or her level of educational attainment vary with the average educational level of the occupational group (X_{YEARS2} * YEARS1)? Does the relationship between individual workers' income level and union membership status vary with the average educational level of the occupational group (X_{YEARS2} * UNION1)? Does the relationship between individual workers' income level and race vary with the average educational level of the occupational group (X_{YEARS2} * BLACK1)?

When we examine Table 4.22, the estimates of random component variances make clear that the contextual variable (X_{YEARS2}) and the three cross-level interaction terms (X_{YEARS2} * YEARS1, X_{YEARS2} * UNION1, X_{YEARS2} * BLACK1) have accounted for a substantial amount of the variability in these variances. In addition, we see that the values of the covariances among random components have also been diminished, much as we would expect.

Ignoring the issue of statistical significance for this calculation, if we take the new estimate of the intercept variance and recalculate the interval from Table 4.20, we get the results reported in Table 4.23. The interval that includes 95% of the intercepts across occupational categories is now quite a bit narrower. As a result, the use of an average or overall intercept makes a lot more sense.

TABLE 4.21. Table 4.18 with Contextual Variables and Cross-Level Interaction Terms

$$Y = 5.742 + 0.382\text{YEARS1} + 1.001\text{UNION1} - 0.403\text{BLACK1} + 0.883X_{MARRY1} + 1.267X_{YEARS2}$$
$$\quad (0.254) \ (0.028) \qquad\quad (0.211) \qquad\quad (0.253) \qquad\quad (0.092) \qquad\qquad (0.292)$$

$$\quad + 0.162X_{YEARS2} * \text{YEARS1} - 0.598X_{YEARS2} * \text{UNION1} - 0.594X_{YEARS2} * \text{BLACK1}$$
$$\quad\quad (0.041) \qquad\qquad\qquad (0.300) \qquad\qquad\qquad (0.441)$$

$$R_1^2 = 8.7\%$$
$$N_1 = 4395$$
$$N_2 = 9$$

TABLE 4.22. Multilevel Regression Analysis of Hourly Wage; REML Estimators; Unstructured Estimates of Covariance Parameters

Parameter	Estimate	Std. error	Wald Z	Sig. level
Residual (e_{IJ}^2)	8.616	0.205	42.089	.000
INTERCEPT (u_{0J})	0.610	0.403	1.514	.192
INTERCEPT by YEARS1	0.028	0.448	0.063	.950
YEARS1 (u_{1J}^2)	0.003	0.000	—	—
INTERCEPT by BLACK1	–0.321	0.283	–0.968	.333
YEARS1 by BLACK1	–0.064	0.058	–1.106	.269
BLACK1 (u_{2J}^2)	0.609	1.116	0.546	.585
INTERCEPT by UNION1	0.063	.309	0.204	.838
YEARS1 by UNION1	0.015	.740	0.020	.984
BLACK1 by UNION1	–0.111	1.485	–0.075	.941
UNION1 (u_{3J}^2)	0.229	1.078	0.212	.832

Note. A dash (—) indicates a value too small to measure.

TABLE 4.23. Variability with Respect to a Random Intercept for a Multilevel Model

$$a_{\text{INTERCEPT}} - t_{.05}S_{a\text{INTERCEPT}} \text{ to } a_{\text{INTERCEPT}} + t_{.05}S_{a\text{INTERCEPT}}$$

$$5.839 - 1.960(0.610) \text{ to } 5.839 + 1.960(0.610)$$

$$4.644 \text{ to } 7.034$$

4.12 FIXED COMPONENTS AND RANDOM COMPONENTS

Another instructive way to clarify the meaning of the more complex error term is by emphasizing the fact that the random intercept and a random slope each consist of two components. In the simple example of a random coefficient model we began developing in Table 4.14, β_{0J} is the fixed component of the random intercept, and u_{0J} is the random component of the random intercept. In the same way, β_{1J} is the fixed component of the random slope, and u_{1J} is the random component of the slope. Again, the random component captures group-to-group variability in the slope, while the fixed component is a weighted average for the slope across all groups.

The distinction between random components and fixed components is a new one for users of OLS regression. Intercepts and slopes in OLS regression equations are *fixed* and do not vary from group to group. If a regression coefficient is estimated for students within schools, for example, we judge that it is the same for all schools.

However, as we now know, there are many instances in which coefficients do in fact vary across schools and other groups. For example, the relationship between family income and measured achievement may differ markedly from one school to another in a data set that contains information on hundreds of schools. In circumstances such as this, we use alternatives to OLS estimators, such as ML or REML, and we permit the coefficients to vary across schools. *Intercepts* and *slopes* in regression equations such as this are commonly referred to as *random*.

Throughout our discussion, we will refer to regression coefficients that are *not* permitted to vary across higher-level groups as *fixed regression coefficients*. We will refer to regression coefficients that *are* permitted to vary as *random regression coefficients*.

Fixed regression coefficients are fixed. That's it. But random regression coefficients have *two components*: *fixed and random*. The fixed component is interpreted in the same way as an OLS unstandardized regression coefficient. The random component is an estimate of the *variance* of the random regression coefficient as it varies from group to group.

We can illustrate this by again estimating a rudimentary earnings function with the Child Development Supplement of the Panel Study of Income Dynamics data set (Institute for Social Research, 2003). Annual family income is logged, and we employ a very limited set of independent variables: race of household head (coded 1 if Black and 0 otherwise); years of educational attainment of the household head; and the character of the place of residence as measured by the nine-level urban–rural continuum.

OLS regression coefficients and standard errors are presented in Table 4.24. Interpretations of the coefficients are straightforward: If the household head is Black, annual income is reduced, on average, by 48.8% relative to that of households headed by non-Blacks; for every 1-year increment in level of educational attainment, family income is increased, on average, by 12.7%; for every 1-unit increase in the rural character of place of residence, annual income is decreased, on average, by 3.4%. Since all three independent variables are centered with respect to their grand means, the intercept tells us the predicted value of the dependent variable for a family head with average values for X_{BLACK}, $X_{EDUCATION}$, and $X_{URBANRURAL}$.

However, if we suspect that one or more of the relationships reported in Table 4.24 varies from state to state, we may use the state as a grouping variable, with a random intercept and one or more random slopes. We then run the same analysis using a random coefficient regression equation with a random intercept and one, two, or three random slopes. In this example we will be gratuitously extravagant and use three random slopes.

Assignment of random slopes to all three independent variables is, by most standards, excessive. In addition, our decision is based on little more than suspicion. We have not referred to a well-developed theoretical perspective on income attainment in making this judgment. The status attainment research that figured so conspicuously in

TABLE 4.24. Another OLS Multiple Regression Earnings Function

$Y_{LNINCOME} = 4.002 - 0.488X_{BLACK1} + 0.127X_{EDUCATION1} - 0.034X_{URBANRURAL1}$
    (0.020) (0.080)   (0.006)   (0.008)

$R^2 = 28.3\%$
$N = 1291$

the sociological literature during the late 1960s and 1970s is suggestive with regard to each of these variables, but hardly compelling with respect to the decision at hand—assignment of fixed or random status to the slopes for X_{BLACK1}, $X_{EDUCATION1}$, and $X_{URBANRURAL1}$ (see, e.g., the broad-ranging collection edited by Grusky, 2001).

This is hardly the best way to proceed when specifying a random coefficient regression model, but for the purposes of the present exercise, we will continue. We will see in Table 4.26, moreover, that our decisions are consistent with our sample data, since the random component variances of all coefficients are statistically significant.

The intercept and slopes reported in Table 4.25 are the *fixed components*. They are overall estimates or averages that summarize intercepts and slopes as they vary from one state to another. The coefficients reported in Table 4.25 are interpreted in the same way as OLS coefficients, such as those in Table 4.24. As usual, the numerical values of the fixed OLS coefficients and the random regression coefficients are very similar, and the standard errors for random coefficient estimates are larger than the standard errors for the OLS estimates.

In Table 4.26 we see estimates of the *random components*—measures of the degree to which the random intercept and random slopes vary across the grouping variable (in

TABLE 4.25. Fixed Components for Random Coefficient Earnings Function

$$Y_{LNINCOME} = 4.02 - 0.384BLACK1 + 0.142EDUCATION1 - 0.028URBANRURAL1$$
$$\quad\quad\quad (0.038)(0.133) \quad\quad\quad (0.013) \quad\quad\quad\quad\quad (0.013)$$

$$R_1^2 = 20.4$$
$$N_1 = 1291$$
$$N_2 = 50$$

TABLE 4.26. Random Components for Random Coefficient Earnings Function; Unstructured; Estimates of Covariance Parameters

Parameter	Estimate	Std. error	Wald Z	Sig. level
Residual	0.389	0.002	24.797	.000
INTERCEPT1	0.098	0.027	3.664	.000
INTERCEPT1 by EDUCATION1	−0.005	0.006	−0.994	.320
EDUCATION1	0.042	0.010	4.321	.000
INTERCEPT1 by BLACK1	−0.007	0.068	−0.111	.912
EDUCATION1 by BLACK1	0.009	0.022	0.491	.623
BLACK1	0.498	0.194	2.567	.012
INTERCEPT1 by URBANRURAL1	−0.009	0.006	−1.438	.150
EDUCATION1 by URBANRURAL1	0.002	0.002	1.151	.250
BLACK1 by URBANRURAL1	0.025	0.014	1.773	.108
URBANRURAL1	0.005	0.002	2.270	.023

this example, the state). We see that all variances are statistically significant. This means that the intercepts and slopes do indeed vary across states. None of the covariances, however, is statistically significant, meaning that none of the random components vary together.

4.13 INTERPRETING RANDOM COEFFICIENTS: DEVELOPING A CAUTIONARY COMMENT

Throughout our discussion we will continue to emphasize that the fixed components of random regression coefficients are interpreted in the same way as OLS coefficients. After all, it's just regression! Significance testing and confidence interval construction, moreover, are also done in exactly the same way.

Nevertheless, we should continue to bear in mind that random regression coefficients do in fact vary from group to group. As a result, an intercept or slope may be very different from one second-level category to another, sometimes making interpretation thoroughly problematic (Tabachnick, 2005). The coefficient that we actually interpret—the fixed component of a random coefficient—is a weighted average over all second-level categories. The random component tells us how much the fixed component varies, and it may vary a great deal (Hox, 2002).

In our previous illustration of this idea, we used the fixed component of a random intercept. This time we will take the fixed component of a random slope from Table 4.25. It is easy to modify the procedure specified in Table 4.23 for random intercepts to accommodate random slopes. Moreover, now that we have clarified the distinction between fixed components and random components, we can spell out the procedure in a way that is a bit more instructive. We simply take the fixed component of the coefficient of interest and add and subtract the product of a specified t value and the square root (standard deviation) of the random component. In this case, we will use the fixed component of the random coefficient for BLACK1 from Table 4.25 and the random component for the same independent variable from Table 4.26. The result is reported in Table 4.27.

There is little comfort in saying that 95% of the 50 slopes will be included in this interval. A slope corresponding to the lower level of the interval would indicate that if the head of a household is Black, annual family income is *decreased* by 176.7% when

TABLE 4.27. Variability with Respect to a Random Slope for a Random Coefficient Model

$$b_{\text{FIXED}} - t_{.05}(b_{\text{RANDOM}})^{1/2} \text{ to } b_{\text{FIXED}} + t_{.05}b_{\text{RANDOM}}^{1/2}$$

$$-0.384 - 1.960(0.498)^{1/2} \text{ to } -0.384 + 1.960(0.498)^{1/2}$$

$$-1.767 \text{ to } 0.999$$

compared with that of households headed by a non-Black. A slope corresponding to the upper limit of the interval would mean that if the head of a household is Black, annual family income is *increased* by 99.9% when compared with that of households headed by a non-Black. The difference in the magnitude and substantive import of the two slopes is enormous.

Emphatically, this finding makes the relationship between the annual income and BLACK1 very difficult to interpret. This example forcefully reminds us that the fixed slope is in fact a weighted *average*, and the random component has an important role to play in its interpretation.

The obvious question at this point is one we have asked before: At this stage of the analysis, can anything be done to narrow the interval? In response, we again acknowledge that variability in the random components can be reduced through introduction of contextual factors and cross-level interaction terms. Accordingly, we transform our random coefficient regression equation into a multilevel regression equation.

Table 4.28 reports the results of a multilevel regression analysis in which the aggregated state-level contextual variable ($X_{URBANRURAL2}$), along with three cross-level interaction terms ($X_{URBANRURAL2}$ * BLACK1, $X_{URBANRURAL2}$ * EDUCATION1 and $X_{URBANRURAL2}$ * URBANRURAL1), have been introduced as additional explanatory factors. The cross-level interaction terms are implied by our choice of $X_{URBANRURAL2}$ as a contextual variable.

Table 4.29 reports the random component variances and covariances. The variance of the random component for BLACK1 is now statistically nonsignificant. As a result, we conclude that the population value of the variance of BLACK1 is not different from zero. If we recalculate the interval in Table 4.27, using this additional information, we get the result reported in Table 4.30.

The statistically significant fixed component for BLACK1, taken from the multilevel regression model, has gotten smaller. Moreover, by accounting for variability in its random component, we have eliminated the enormous uncertainty as to its meaning. Clearly, multilevel regression analysis can be much more informative than random coef-

TABLE 4.28. Table 4.25 with Contextual Variable and Cross-Level Interaction Terms

$$Y = 11.008 + 0.136EDUCATION1 - 0.462BLACK1 - 0.051URBANRURAL1$$
$$\quad (0.053)\ (0.017) \qquad\qquad (0.139) \qquad\qquad (0.016)$$

$$\quad - 0.056X_{URBANRURAL2} + 0.041X_{URBANRURAL2} * BLACK1$$
$$\quad (0.032) \qquad\qquad (0.087)$$

$$\quad - 0.018X_{URBANRURAL2} * EDUCATION1 + 0.013X_{URBANRURAL2} * URBANRURAL1$$
$$\quad (0.010) \qquad\qquad\qquad (0.009)$$

$$R_1^2 = 21.5\%$$
$$N_1 = 1291$$
$$N_2 = 50$$

TABLE 4.29. Table 4.26 with Contextual Variable and Cross-Level Interaction Terms

Parameter	Estimate	Std. error	Wald Z	Sig. level
Residual	0.388	0.016	24.816	.000
INTERCEPT1	0.092	0.026	3.495	.000
INTERCEPT1 by EDUCATION1	−0.009	0.006	−1.511	.131
EDUCATION1	0.007	0.002	2.606	.009
INTERCEPT1 by EDUCATION1	0.006	0.100	0.063	.950
EDUCATION1 by BLACK1	−0.064	0.058	−1.106	.269
EDUCATION1 by BLACK1	0.009	0.022	0.415	.678
BLACK1	0.224	0.161	1.397	.162
INTERCEPT1 by URBANRURAL1	−0.009	0.006	−1.438	.150
EDUCATION1 by URBANRURAL1	0.002	0.002	1.151	.250
BLACK1 by URBANRURAL1	0.025	0.014	1.773	.076
URBANRURAL1	0.003	0.002	1.571	.114

TABLE 4.30. Variability with Respect to a Random Slope for a Random Coefficient Model, Recalculated

$$[b_{\text{FIXED}} - t_{.05}(b_{\text{RANDOM}})]^{1/2} \text{ to } [b_{\text{FIXED}} + t_{.05}(b_{\text{RANDOM}})]^{1/2}$$

$$[-0.462 - 1.960 * (0.000)^{1/2}] \text{ to } [-0.462 + 1.960*(0.000)^{1/2}]$$

$$-0.462 \text{ to } -0.462$$

ficient regression. Just as clearly, it would be difficult to overstate the importance of a properly specified multilevel model in all its complexity.

4.14   SUBSCRIPT CONVENTIONS

The subscript conventions used with random coefficient regression and multilevel regression are not hard to learn, though they receive little attention in currently available accounts. The same conventions apply to full-fledged multilevel models, as we shall see, though in that context they get a bit more complicated.

The first subscript for a beta coefficient representing a random intercept is 0, distinguishing it from slopes. The second subscript for the intercept, J, indicates that the intercept is permitted to vary over J groups.

The first subscript for a beta coefficient representing a random slope is 1, 2, . . . , I, depending on how many independent variables are in the equation. The second subscript for the slope, J, indicates that the slope is permitted to vary over J groups.

We shall return to notational conventions as our models become more complex.

4.15 PERCENTAGE OF VARIANCE EXPLAINED FOR RANDOM COEFFICIENT AND MULTILEVEL MODELS

In Table 4.14, we presented a simple random coefficient regression equation that specified the relationship between reading achievement and gender for our Kentucky data set. It is a simple matter to specify a random coefficient regression model that uses student-level ethnicity in place of student-level gender (see Table 4.31). Except for the independent variable name, the models are identical.

Coefficient estimates for this model are reported in Tables 4.32 and 4.33. By now, most of the output from analyses of this kind is beginning to look familiar. However, we still have not explained the summary statistic R_1^2, as it appears in Table 4.32.

The familiar R^2 statistic, equal to the squared correlation of observed and predicted values of the dependent variable, is not used with models containing random coefficients. However, the alternative R_1^2 statistic is sufficiently like R^2 to make it intuitively appealing to regular users of OLS regression. In addition, it is easy to compute (Snijders & Bosker, 1999, pp. 99–105). We will give more attention to the meaning and computation of the R_1^2 summary statistic for multilevel models in Chapter 10. For now, the following brief account will do the job.

R_1^2 is conceptually similar to the conventional R^2. However, instead of reporting the amount of variability in the individual-level dependent variable explained by a random

TABLE 4.31. Simple Regression with Random Coefficients

$$Y = \beta_{0J} + \beta_{1J}\text{ETHNIC1} + (u_{0J} + u_{1J} * \text{ETHNIC} + e_{IJ})$$

TABLE 4.32. Random Coefficient Regression of Reading Achievement on Ethnicity; Fixed Components

$$Y = 51.268 - 6.994X_{\text{ETHNIC1}}$$
$$(0.316)\ (0.516)$$

$$R_1^2 = 2.0\%$$
$$N_1 = 49,616$$
$$N_2 = 347$$

TABLE 4.33. Random Coefficient Regression of Reading Achievement on Ethnicity; Estimates of Covariance Parameters

Parameter	Estimate	Std. error	Wald Z	Sig. level
Residual	331.429	2.172	152.578	.000
INTERCEPT1	20.894	2.145	9.741	.000
INTERCEPT1 by ETHNIC1	–2.482	2.248	–1.103	.270
ETHNIC1	22.748	5.031	4.521	.000

regression equation, it tells us the ***proportional reduction in errors of prediction*** when our model is compared with the unconditional or null model (Kreft & De Leeuw, 1998).

To calculate R_1^2 for the random coefficient model in Table 4.32, we begin by estimating the unconditional model, containing only a random intercept with no explanatory variables. The idea of an intercept-only model—one in which the random intercept is the only predictor—is an odd one for most of us for whom OLS multiple regression analysis is a staple statistical tool. The intercept gets a lot more attention in random coefficient regression and multilevel regression than in OLS regression.

For the example at hand, the random components for the null model—the random-intercept-only model—are reported in Table 4.34. The residual variance (Residual) measures the within-school variance in reading achievement for the 347 schools in our Kentucky data set. The intercept variance (INTERCEPT1) measures the between-school variance in reading achievement.

Earlier, we used these measures to estimate the intraclass correlation coefficient. After acknowledging that Residual plus INTERCEPT1 provides an estimate of the total variance in the level-one dependent variable, we simply divided this sum into INTERCEPT1, our estimate of between group variance. The resulting intraclass correlation coefficient value told us the proportion of variance between groups.

The rationale for R_1^2 is similar. Now, however, the sum of the residual variance and intercept variance is divided into the sum of the residual variance and intercept variance for a ***conditional model***—a random coefficient or multilevel regression model that has one or more independent variables. Table 4.35 provides this additional information.

It is important to acknowledge that Table 4.35 does not contain a variance estimate for the slope for ETHNIC1. This is because calculation of R_1^2 with general purpose software such as SPSS requires that ***all slopes be fixed***. So, while the intercept is random, ETHNIC1, which has a random slope in this example, is temporarily assigned a fixed slope when we are estimating R_1^2 (Snijders & Bosker, 1999).

TABLE 4.34. Unconditional (Null) Model for Reading Achievement; Random Coefficient Regression; Estimates of Covariance Parameters

Parameter	Estimate	Std. error	Wald Z	Sig. level
Residual (e_{ij}^2)	340.214	2.223	152.867	.000
INTERCEPT (u_{0j})	20.910	2.150	9.726	.000

TABLE 4.35. Conditional Model for Reading Achievement; Random Coefficient Regression; Estimates of Covariance Parameters

Parameter	Estimate	Std. error	Wald Z	Sig. level
Residual (e_{ij}^2)	333.315	2.180	156.865	.000
INTERCEPT1(u_{0j})	20.847	2.141	9.738	.000

The R_1^2 summary statistic is then calculated by dividing the sum of Residual and INTERCEPT1 for the conditional model by the sum of Residual and INTERCEPT1 for the null model, subtracting the result from one, and multiplying by 100:

$$R_1^2 = (1 - [(\text{RESIDUAL}_{\text{FIXED}} + \text{INTERCEPT1}_{\text{FIXED}})/(\text{RESIDUAL}_{\text{NULL}} + \text{INTERCEPT1}_{\text{NULL}})] * 100)$$

$$2.0\% = [1 - (333.315 + 20.847)/(340.214 + 20.910)] * 100$$

Including the independent variable, ETHNIC1, in our conditional random coefficient model reduces errors in predicting reading achievement by 2.0% when compared with the null model. As we shall see in Chapter 10, this simple procedure can easily be extended to include any number of independent variables and can be applied, in straightforward fashion, to models with more than two levels.

At this point it may be useful to briefly return to the information criteria summary statistics that we have used in several examples in Chapter 3. The information criteria do not have the intuitive appeal of R_1^2, but as we have already illustrated, they can be useful for decision-making purposes (Burnham & Anderson, 2002; Cavanaugh, 2005).

Suppose, for example, that we are not convinced that adding ETHNIC1 to the null model in Table 4.35 improved the fit of the model to the observed data. After all, the value of the R_1^2 statistic is quite small. Since the null model and the conditional model are nested, meaning that the only differences between them have to do with addition and deletion of parameter estimates, we can make this decision with the deviance difference statistic.

In contrast to the procedure for calculating R_1^2, when we are using the deviance difference and information criteria, random slopes remain random. It is important to remember, however, that the compared deviance values and the information criteria must be estimated with ML rather than REML.

As we have seen in Chapter 3, the deviance difference is calculated simply by subtracting the −2 log likelihood or deviance value for the conditional model from the same measure for the null model (Hox, in press). As already noted, the −2 log likelihood measure and the information criteria have smaller-is-better interpretations.

With the information in Table 4.36, the deviance difference in this instance is calculated as follows:

$$\text{Deviance difference} = 407632.3 - 406543.7 = 1088.6$$

$$df = 6 - 3 = 3$$

Degrees of freedom are determined by subtracting the number of parameters used in estimating the null model from the number used in estimating the conditional model. In this instance, the conditional model used three additional parameters: the fixed component of the random slope for ETHNIC1, the random component of the random slope for ETHNIC1, and the covariance of the random components for the random intercept and the random slope.

TABLE 4.36. Information Criteria for Reading Achievement by ETHNIC1

Criterion	Null model	Conditional model
–2 log likelihood	407632.3	*406543.7*
Akaike's Information Criterion	407636.3	*406551.7*
Hurvich and Tsai's Criterion	407636.3	*406551.7*
Bozdogan's Criterion	407655.8	*406590.7*
Schwarz's Bayesian Criterion	407653.8	*406586.7*

Note. The smaller value for each measure is boldfaced and italicized.

With the alpha level set at .05 and with three degrees of freedom, the critical value of χ^2 is 7.815 (Gujarati, 2003). Our computed deviance statistic easily exceeds this value. As a result, we reject the null hypothesis of no difference between the two models and conclude that the conditional model provides a better fit. With their smaller-is-better interpretations, we would reach the same conclusion if we used one or more of the information criteria.

The deviance difference and information criteria are used routinely when random coefficient regression and multilevel regression models are compared (R. Andersen, 2004). While they lack the intuitive appeal of R_1^2, they are easy to use as model-fit decision-making tools (Abdulnabi, 1999; Burnham & Anderson, 2002, 2004; Cavanaugh, 2005). Even with its intuitively appealing interpretation, R_1^2 is used inconsistently in published research.

4.16 GRAND-MEAN CENTERING

Grand-mean centering is a seemingly innocuous but quite consequential procedure that we have used in examples throughout our presentation. When employed with OLS regression, grand-mean centering clarifies interpretation of regression coefficients and permits use of multiplicative interaction terms without generating troublesome multi-collinearity (Preacher, 2003).

For example, if we refer back to the OLS regression model presented in Table 4.4, we may be interested in whether or not the relationship between reading achievement and the individual-level predictor $X_{GENDER1}$ varies from level to level of the contextual variable, $X_{GENDER2}$. In response to this question, we create the multiplicative interaction term $X_{GENDER2} * X_{GENDER1}$. When we run the analysis, we get the results reported in Table 4.37.

The OLS slopes for $X_{GENDER1}$ and $X_{GENDER2}$ in Table 4.37 are similar to those reported in Table 4.4, but the intercept is quite different. Furthermore, the standard errors are enormous, and none of the coefficients is statistically significant. With nearly 50,000 cases, this is astonishing!

TABLE 4.37. OLS Regression of Reading Achievement on Gender and Gender Composition; Multiplicative Interaction Term Added

$$Y = -1.503 + 8.023X_{GENDER1} + 28.532X_{GENDER2} - 0.422X_{GENDER2} * X_{GENDER1}$$
$$(10.102)\ (6.438)\qquad (16.750)\qquad\qquad (4.335)$$

$$R^2 = 4.8\%$$
$$N = 49{,}616$$

An examination of SPSS collinearity diagnostics for this OLS simulation of a multi-level model is instructive: The variance inflation factor for $X_{GENDER1}$ is 1424.801, and the same measure for $X_{GENDER2}$ is 1450.869. The condition index is 459.279. Rules of thumb for these measures vary from source to source, but our values are huge by any standard. They are strong evidence of badly inflated standard errors and imprecise coefficient estimates due to multicollinearity (Chatterjee et al., 2000; Gujarati, 2003).

In response, we center both $X_{GENDER1}$ and $X_{GENDER2}$ with respect to the grand mean for $X_{GENDER1}$, and then recalculate the interaction term using the centered variables. When we rerun the OLS multiple regression equation with grand-mean-centered independent variables, we get the results reported in Table 4.38.

The information in Table 4.38 is much more compatible with that in Table 4.4. The standard errors are no longer badly inflated, the intercept is consistent with what we would expect, and the OLS slopes for $X_{GENDER1}$ and $X_{GENDER2}$ are both statistically significant. The OLS coefficient for the interaction term is not statistically significant, but this is not cause for concern. Instead of being suspect as just another artifact of multicollinearity, this may be plausibly acknowledged as a legitimately interpretable result of our regression analysis. All three variance inflation factors are at or below 1.015, and the condition index is 1.148. Due to grand-mean centering, multicollinearity is no longer a problem.

In this OLS example, grand-mean centering enabled us to render the multiplicative interaction term approximately orthogonal to the main effect independent variables used to create it (Iversen, 1991). The use of centering for this and other purposes has become commonplace among users of OLS multiple regression analysis (Jaccard & Turrisi, 2003).

Furthermore, when we are working with random coefficient and multilevel regression models, it is best that *all* independent variables be centered—usually with respect

TABLE 4.38. OLS Regression of Reading Achievement on Gender and Gender Composition; Multiplicative Interaction Term Added; Independent Variables Centered

$$Y = 51.638 + 7.391X_{GENDER1} + 35.307X_{GENDER2} + 0.925X_{GENDER2} * X_{GENDER1}$$
$$(0.086)\ (0.172)\qquad (2.158)\qquad\qquad (4.371)$$

$$R^2 = 4.8\%$$
$$N = 49{,}616$$

to their grand means, as with the OLS examples just given (Snijders & Bosker, 1999; Hox, 2002). This simply means that independent variables at all levels are expressed as deviation scores, assuring that zero is an interpretable value. In the present example, the grand mean for gender is subtracted from each student's value for $X_{GENDER1}$, and the same grand mean is subtracted from each school's value for $X_{GENDER2}$.

It may seem odd to speak in terms of values, and especially of means, when we are working with dummy variables such as gender. However, recall that the male students in our Kentucky data set were assigned a score of 0 on $X_{GENDER1}$, and female students were given a score of 1. If there were 500 students in a school, and half were male and half were female, we would compute the $X_{GENDER1}$ mean for that school as in Table 4.39. Grand-mean centering of the independent variable $X_{GENDER1}$ for males and females in this school would be done as in Table 4.40.

Centering a group-level variable (in this case, $X_{GENDER2}$) at the school level is done in the same way (see Table 4.41). In practice, however, centering level-two independent variables may be a bit more tedious than Table 4.41 suggests. After all, each value for $X_{GENDER2}$ is a school mean, expressed as the proportion of students who are female. With SPSS 13.0 and 14.0, school means are easy to compute by using the AGGREGATE function. By default, the AGGREGATE function adds the school means to the existing data file. Each observation has a value, and each student in the same school has the same value. It is then easy to find the grand mean for $X_{GENDER1}$ and calculate deviation scores.

With SPSS 11.5 and 12.0, however, the process is a bit more tedious. One must first use the AGGREGATE function to create a separate data file containing school means. The original data file can then be merged with the new AGGREGATE file as described in SPSS Routine 4.2. Now each observation has the correct value on $X_{GENMEAN}$, which in this case is $X_{GENDER2}$, and centering can be done as above. For those of us who struggle with software, this procedure may take some practice. It is far easier, however, than inserting computed school means one at a time.

TABLE 4.39. Computing the Mean for a Level-One Dummy Variable

$X_{GENDER1}$ mean = $((250 * 0.000) + (250*1.000))/500 = 0.500$

TABLE 4.40. Centering a Level-One Dummy Variable with Respect to the Grand Mean

$X_{GENDER1}$ centered for males = $0.000 - 0.500 = -0.500$

$X_{GENDER1}$ centered for females = $1.000 - 0.500 = 0.500$

TABLE 4.41. Centering a Level-Two Variable with Respect to the Level-One Grand Mean

$X_{GENDER2}$ centered for schools = $X_{GENDER2} - 0.500$

SPSS Routine 4.2. Merging Data Files to Include Aggregated Variables

1. Open the aggregate data file.
2. Change the name of the aggregated variable so it can be distinguished from the original variable; for example, change $X_{GENDER1}$ to $X_{GENMEAN}$.
3. Click on DATA, MERGE FILES, and ADD VARIABLES.
4. Insert the original file name into the FILE NAME box and click on OPEN.
5. Click on MATCH CASES and WORKING DATA FILE.
6. Move the item in the EXCLUDED VARIABLES box to the KEY VARIABLES and click on OK.

Since same-level interaction terms serve the same role and are used as frequently with multilevel regression as with OLS regression, a primary reason for grand-mean centering is, as just described, to guard against multicollinearity. This is also an important reason for using grand-mean centering with a multilevel regression in which one or more cross-level interaction terms are employed.

Still another reason for using grand-mean centering is to minimize adverse effects that follow when random intercepts and random slopes are strongly correlated with each other (Kreft & De Leeuw, 1998; Wooldridge, 2004). We illustrated this in Table 3.54 in our discussion of covariance structures for multilevel models.

In brief, covariances among random slopes and between random slopes and random intercepts have consequences that are comparable to multicollinearity (Gill & King, 2003). When relationships among these various factors are strong, they interfere with efficient estimation of random regression coefficients (Murtazashvilli & Wooldridge, 2005). Grand-mean centering of all independent variables is a useful corrective (Kreft et al., 1995; Nezlek, 2001).

4.17 GRAND-MEAN CENTERING, GROUP-MEAN CENTERING, AND RAW SCORES COMPARED

So far, our presentation has offered grand-mean centering as if it were the only kind we need seriously consider. Actually, however, other forms of centering are available and are sometimes quite useful (Raudenbush & Bryk, 2002).

The most commonly discussed alternative with respect to random coefficient regression and multilevel regression is *group-mean centering*, also referred to as *context centering*. For example, if we are using our U.S. Bureau of the Census data set to study county-level variability in voting for George W. Bush in 2004, we might use a measure of family structure ($X_{FAMILY1}$) at the county level as an independent variable. $X_{FAMILY1}$ is the percentage of all county residents living in a traditional nuclear family, defined as having a husband, a wife, and at least one child under age 18. Table 4.42 depicts the centering options for this variable.

TABLE 4.42. Centering Options

Centering at level one with respect to the **grand** mean

$X_{FAMILY1}$ − grand mean = $X_{FAMILY1}$ grand-mean-centered
(This is done using just the overall or grand mean.)

Centering at level one with respect to **group** means

$X_{FAMILY1}$ − group mean = $X_{FAMILY1}$ group-mean-centered
(This is done for **each group**, using the mean for that group.)

Tables 4.43 and 4.44 below report results of three random coefficient regression analyses. In each instance, we have used percentage of county residents voting for Bush in the 2004 presidential election as the level-one dependent variable (Y_{BUSH}), and percentage of all county residents living in traditional nuclear families as the level-one independent variable ($X_{FAMILY1}$). The only differences in the way the three equations are specified pertain to centering.

In Table 4.43, notice the enormous difference between the value of the fixed component of the random intercept when $X_{FAMILY1}$ is expressed in raw scores, and the value of the same estimate with either grand-mean or group-mean centering. In general, the intercepts will be similar with grand-mean or group-mean centering, but the raw score intercept will be substantially different (Kreft et al., 1995).

In a random coefficient analysis that has only level-one independent variables with no contextual factors, grand-mean centering and use of raw scores will result in the same value for the fixed component of the random slope. Use of group-mean centering, however, will result in a slope estimate that differs from the other two, though the difference is often small (Kreft et al., 1995). We see this in Table 4.43, in which the slopes and standard errors estimated with grand-mean centering and raw scores are the same, but the fixed component and standard error for the slope estimated with group-mean centering are slightly larger.

TABLE 4.43. Centering Options and Use of Raw Scores
Illustrated for Y_{BUSH} as a Function of $X_{FAMILY1}$; Fixed Components

---

Independent variable **grand-mean**-centered

Y_{BUSH} = 58.787 + 1.995$X_{FAMILY1}$
(1.080) (0.157)

Independent variable **group-mean**-centered

Y_{BUSH} = 58.787 + 1.998$X_{FAMILY1}$
(1.328) (0.160)

Independent variable in **raw scores**

Y_{BUSH} = 23.855 + 1.995$X_{FAMILY1}$
(0.276) (0.157)

Our primary concern in Table 4.44 is with the intercept-by-slope covariances: Each type of centering yields a different value, though the covariances with grand-mean and group-mean centering are both statistically nonsignificant. The much larger and statistically significant value of the INTERCEPT1-by-X_{FAMILY1} covariance produced with raw scores is consistent with our earlier observation that one of the virtues of centering, whether with the grand mean or with group means, is that it improves estimates of coefficients by reducing potentially troublesome correlations among random components.

Some authors have taken the position that group-mean centering is more effective than grand-mean centering in diminishing correlations among random components, and that group-mean centering minimizes bias in estimating variances of random components (Raudenbush & Bryk, 2002). Others, however, have suggested that each of the two forms of centering is sufficiently effective that choices between them need not be made on this basis (Kreft et al., 1995). Either way, it is clear that centering, whether with grand means or with group means, should always be used in multilevel regression.

Given this, it is important to remember that different forms of centering alter the *interpretation* of multilevel models. Interpretation of the fixed coefficient of a random intercept is a prime example. If we avoid centering altogether and use scores raw for all variables, the following is true: The intercept is our best estimate of the value of the dependent variable when all independent variables are set equal to zero. With grand-mean centering, however, the intercept is our best estimate of the value of the dependent variable when all independent variables are set equal to their grand means. With group-mean centering, the intercept is our best estimate of the value of the dependent variable when all independent variables are set equal to their group means (Paccagnella, 2006).

TABLE 4.44. Centering Options and Use of Raw Scores Illustrated for Y_{BUSH} as a Function of X_{FAMILY1}; Estimates of Covariance Parameters

Parameter	Estimate	Std. error	Wald Z	Sig. level
Independent variable **grand-mean**-centered				
Residual	106.664	2.757	36.688	.000
INTERCEPT1	50.687	12.067	4.200	.000
INTERCEPT1 by X_{FAMILY1}	1.311	1.386	0.946	.344
X_{FAMILY1}	0.756	0.234	3.235	.001
Independent variable **group-mean**-centered				
Residual	106.061	2.762	38.665	.000
INTERCEPT1	80.069	19.586	4.088	.000
INTERCEPT1 by X_{FAMILY1}	−1.436	1.805	−0.796	.426
X_{FAMILY1}	0.772	0.235	3.285	.001
Independent variable in **raw scores**				
Residual	106.665	2.757	36.688	.000
INTERCEPT1	236.568	70.820	3.341	.001
INTERCEPT1 by X_{FAMILY1}	−11.925	3.822	−3.235	.002
X_{FAMILY1}	0.756	0.234	3.235	.001

Notice that with grand-mean centering we are merely rescaling the independent variables by taking deviation scores. We are not creating a new independent variable. Instead, an equation estimated with raw scores will be equivalent to the same equation estimated with grand-mean centering (Hox, 2002). Yes, some parameter estimates may differ, as with the intercept estimates in Table 4.43, but fitted values of the dependent variable will be the same (Paccagnella, 2006). It is in this sense that the models are equivalent.

With group-mean centering, however, we do create a new variable. Specifically, the means subtracted from independent variable raw scores *vary* from group to group. As a result, we are not merely rescaling predictors; we are rescaling them *differently* from one context to another. Consequently, group-mean centering will yield fitted values for the dependent variables that differ from those obtained using raw scores or grand-mean centering.

In general terms, what have we learned about centering from our discussion of the examples in Tables 4.43 and 4.44?

First, when working with multilevel models, center all independent variables.

Second, choose your method of centering based on how you want to interpret your results. In the absence of a good reason to prefer one form of centering over another, follow the recommendation offered by Snijders and Bosker (1999), Hox (2002), and Luke (2004): Use the simpler, more commonly employed form, grand-mean centering.

Third, use of grand-mean centering or group-mean centering will yield similar estimates for the fixed component of a random intercept. The intercept will, however, be interpreted in a different way. Use of raw scores usually yields a very different value, and it too has its own distinctive interpretation.

Fourth, use of grand-mean centering or raw scores will yield the same value for the fixed component of a level-one random slope. Use of group-mean centering, however, will yield a different value. Whether you are using raw scores, grand-mean centering, or group-mean centering, however, the *level-one* random slope will be interpreted in the same way.

Fifth, either form of centering effectively diminishes the magnitude of the intercept-by-slope covariance when compared with use of raw scores. In this way, centering contributes to controlling potentially troublesome correlations among random components.

These observations are affirmed when we introduce a contextual factor, as in Tables 4.45 and 4.46 below. For the level-one independent variable $X_{FAMILY1}$, the same centering options apply as before. However, in both of the first two equations, the contextual variable $X_{FAMILY2}$ is grand-mean-centered, while $X_{FAMILY2}$ is expressed in raw scores in the third equation.

When we compare fixed components of random intercepts and level-one random slopes in Table 4.45, things are much as they were in Table 4.43. The random intercept in the equation in which $X_{FAMILY1}$ is expressed in raw scores is a good deal smaller and is no longer statistically significant. This merely adds emphasis to a difference we had found in Table 4.43. Otherwise, fixed component estimates and standard errors have changed very little. The fixed component estimates of the random slopes are the same

TABLE 4.45. Centering Options and Use of Raw Scores Illustrated for Y_{BUSH} as a Function of $X_{FAMILY1}$ and $X_{FAMILY2}$; Contextual Variable Added; Fixed Components

Level-one independent variable *grand-mean*-centered

$$Y_{BUSH} = 58.879 + 1.948X_{FAMILY1} + 0.823X_{FAMILY2}$$
$$\quad\quad\;\;(1.113)\;\;(0.157)\quad\quad\;\;(0.475)$$

Level-one independent variable *group-mean*-centered

$$Y_{BUSH} = 57.763 + 1.932X_{FAMILY1} + 2.713X_{FAMILY2}$$
$$\quad\quad\;\;(1.007)\;\;\;(0.160)\quad\quad\;\;(0.416)$$

Level-one independent variable in *raw scores*

$$Y_{BUSH} = 10.333 + 1.948X_{FAMILY1} + 0.823X_{FAMILY2}$$
$$\quad\quad\;\;(8.413)\;\;(0.157)\quad\quad\;\;(1.745)$$

when we are using raw scores or grand-mean centering, but group-mean centering yields a slightly different value.

Notice, however that with group-mean centering, the slope for the contextual variable $X_{FAMILY2}$ is much larger than in the analyses in which $X_{FAMILY1}$ is grand-mean-centered or not centered. In fact, with a two-tailed t test, the $X_{FAMILY2}$ slope is statistically significant only when $X_{FAMILY1}$ is group-mean-centered. Since we expect $X_{FAMILY2}$ to be positively related to Y_{BUSH}, however, we will use one-tailed tests, making all three estimates of the slope for $X_{FAMILY2}$ statistically significant.

We are left, however, with a large difference between the $X_{FAMILY2}$ slope estimated with group-mean centering and the slopes estimated with raw scores and grand-mean centering. How do we interpret this? It is at this juncture that the choice between grand-mean and group-mean centering becomes crucial. Each presents us with a different way of separating individual-level effects from group-level effects.

In the example in Table 4.45, with grand-mean centering $X_{FAMILY2}$ has a statistically significant slope equal to 0.823. This is our best estimate of the relationship between the dependent variable and $X_{FAMILY2}$ after we control for $X_{FAMILY1}$. This is consistent with the way we have interpreted coefficients for contextual variables throughout this book. The contextual effect in this case is the expected difference in Y_{BUSH} for counties that have the same value on $X_{FAMILY1}$, but that are located in states differing by 1 unit on $X_{FAMILY2}$. In other words, *for every 1-unit increment in $X_{FAMILY2}$, Y_{BUSH}* increases by 0.823 points.

With group-mean centering, however, the $X_{FAMILY2}$ slope is much larger. This is because with group-mean centering the $X_{FAMILY2}$ slope has a different interpretation: It is the expected difference in the mean of Y_{BUSH} for states that differ by 1 unit on the mean for $X_{FAMILY2}$ (cf. Raudenbush & Bryk, 2002, p. 141). In other words, *for every 1-unit increment in the mean of $X_{FAMILY2}$, the mean of Y_{BUSH}* increases by 2.713 points.

As with Table 4.44, we see in Table 4.46 that both grand-mean centering and group-mean centering substantially reduce the random component covariance, when compared with raw scores.

TABLE 4.46. Centering Options and Use of Raw Scores Illustrated for Y_{BUSH} as a Function of $X_{FAMILY1}$ and $X_{FAMILY2}$; Contextual Variable Added; Estimates of Covariance Parameters

Parameter	Estimate	Std. error	Wald Z	Sig. level
Level-one independent variable *grand-mean*-centered				
Residual	106.604	2.754	36.706	.000
INTERCEPT1	53.766	13.019	4.130	.000
INTERCEPT1 by $X_{FAMILY1}$	2.136	1.479	1.444	.149
$X_{FAMILY1}$	0.752	0.232	3.253	.001
Level-one independent variable *group-mean*-centered				
Residual	106.568	2.752	38.722	.000
INTERCEPT1	44.587	10.678	4.176	.000
INTERCEPT1 by $X_{FAMILY1}$	1.145	1.263	0.906	.365
$X_{FAMILY1}$	0.794	0.241	3.295	.001
Level-one independent variable in *raw scores*				
Residual	106.605	2.754	38.706	.000
INTERCEPT1	209.640	64.377	3.256	.001
INTERCEPT1 by $X_{FAMILY1}$	−11.037	3.605	−3.061	.002
$X_{FAMILY1}$	0.752	0.231	3.253	.001

The best textbook discussion of the comparative consequences of using grand-mean centering or group-mean centering is provided by Raudenbush and Bryk (2002, pp. 134–148). They introduce other ways to think about and visualize the meaning of the coefficients that follow from centering decisions.

One interpretation that is commonly found in discussions of grand-mean and group-mean centering uses the distinction between **between-groups** and **within-groups** regressions. Our voting behavior illustration of this distinction closely parallels an example from Raudenbush and Bryk (2002), using the High School and Beyond subset to analyze math achievement.

A between-groups regression is done by aggregating variables of interest to the group level and running the analysis with the group rather than the individual observation as the unit of analysis. In the Y_{BUSH}-by-$X_{FAMILY1}$ example, this would mean regressing the state-level mean of Y_{BUSH} on the state-level mean of $X_{FAMILY1}$. By contrast, a within-groups regression is just a conventional individual-level regression analysis in which slopes are assumed to be uniform across groups. In this case, we would simply regress Y_{BUSH} on $X_{FAMILY1}$, using all 3091 counties.

What does this distinction have to do with our choice of centering methods? We begin by using the county-level voting behavior data with group-mean centering applied to the level-one predictor $X_{FAMILY1}$. $X_{FAMILY2}$ is a contextual variable. We then estimate a random coefficient equation in which only the intercept is random, and we get the results reported in Tables 4.47 and 4.48. With group-mean centering, the coefficient for

TABLE 4.47. Y_{BUSH} as a Function of $X_{FAMILY1}$ and $X_{FAMILY2}$; Level-One Independent Variable *Group-Mean*-Centered; Random Intercept; All Slopes Fixed

$$Y_{BUSH} = 12.868 + 1.806X_{FAMILY1} + 2.598X_{FAMILY2}$$
$$(1.113) \quad (0.157) \qquad (0.475)$$

TABLE 4.48. Y_{BUSH} as a Function of $X_{FAMILY1}$ and $X_{FAMILY2}$; Level-One Independent Variable *Group-Mean*-Centered; Random Intercept; All Slopes Fixed; Estimates of Covariance Parameters

Parameter	Estimate	Std. error	Wald Z	Sig. level
Residual	111.688	2.866	38.970	.000
INTERCEPT1	43.922	10.514	4.177	.001

$X_{FAMILY1}$ is equal to the slope for the within-group regression. The slope for $X_{FAMILY2}$ is equal to the slope for the between-group regression.

Now let's do the same analysis, using grand-mean centering. Our results are reported in Tables 4.49 and 4.50. Notice that the slope for $X_{FAMILY1}$ is the same as in Table 4.47; it is equal to the within-group regression. The slope for the group-level variable, however, is much smaller. We can see how to interpret this if we use the following increasingly concrete formulas:

Contextual effect = Between-groups effect – Within-groups effect

Contextual effect = State effect – County effect

0.792 = 2.598 – 1.806

Say we have two counties with the same value on $X_{FAMILY1}$, but the counties are located in states that differ on $X_{FAMILY2}$. *The contextual effect is the change in* Y_{BUSH} *for each 1-*

TABLE 4.49. Y_{BUSH} as a Function of $X_{FAMILY1}$ and $X_{FAMILY2}$; Level-One Independent Variable *Grand-Mean*-Centered; Random Intercept; All Slopes Fixed

$$Y_{BUSH} = 44.491 + 1.806X_{FAMILY1} + 0.792X_{FAMILY2}$$
$$(7.449) \quad (0.070) \qquad (0.424)$$

TABLE 4.50. Y_{BUSH} as a Function of $X_{FAMILY1}$ and $X_{FAMILY2}$; Level-One Independent Variable *Grand-Mean*-Centered; Random Intercept; All Slopes Fixed; Estimates of Covariance Parameters

Parameter	Estimate	Std. error	Wald Z	Sig. level
Residual	111.688	2.866	38.970	.000
INTERCEPT1	43.922	10.514	4.177	.001

unit increase in $X_{FAMILY2}$. Again, this is exactly the way in which we have treated contextual effects throughout our presentation.

We are faced, then, with still another question in multilevel regression model specification: Should we use grand-mean centering or group-mean centering? In large measure, the answer depends on how we want to interpret slopes for group-level variables.

Suppose a political scientist is interested in making a tentative but informed judgment about who would win a U.S. presidential election. Furthermore, suppose that the political scientist has a data set much like ours, with counties at level one and states at level two. In view of the winner-take-all way in which the Electoral College uses state-level votes, group-mean centering might very well be a better choice than grand-mean centering. Imagine, however, that another political scientist is a student of county government and county-level voting behavior. Given the same data set, it is pretty clear that grand-mean centering would be the better choice.

Throughout the rest of our discussion of multilevel models, we will be trying to account for variability in a level-one dependent variable, using independent variables at more than one level. The multilevel equations we construct for this purpose are best suited to use of grand-mean centering. If, however, our primary interest is in measuring relationships between group-level independent variables and group-level outcomes, we may decide that group-mean centering is a better choice.

We began our discussion of centering by focusing on its value in controlling multicollinearity when same-level or cross-level interaction terms are used. We also acknowledged that troublesome correlations may occur among random components, and centering is valuable in controlling this form of multicollinearity as well. We now see, in addition, that different forms of centering enable us to select different ways of interpreting the fixed component for a random intercept and the slope of a group-level variable. In most applications, grand-mean centering is the best choice. Group-mean centering may be used, however, if there is good theoretical or substantive reason for preferring it.

4.18 SUMMING UP

Just as it can be useful to provide a chapter overview through use of an example, we can do much the same with a chapter summary. Suppose that we use a Texas data set in which the high school is the unit of analysis (Bickel et al., 2001) in an effort to determine if there is a relationship between school mean scores on a high-stakes measure of 10th-grade reading achievement and the percentage of each school's students who are mobile. A mobile student is one who enrolls more than 6 weeks after the beginning of the current semester.

With 1001 schools nested in 713 districts, we know that most districts have only one high school. Including level-two units with only one case at level one is permissible, so long as this does not apply to all districts. This is due to a process that Snijders and Bosker (1999) refer to as *exchangeability*, and other authors refer to as *borrowing strength* (Raudenbush & Bryk, 2002). In other words, data from districts with a comparatively large number of schools will be used to inform estimates made for districts with a smaller number of schools.

One consequence of exchangeability is that larger districts will weigh more heavily in estimating average or overall coefficients than smaller districts. In effect, coefficients for smaller districts will be affected more by shrinkage than coefficients for larger districts will be.

When we calculate the intraclass correlation coefficient, we find that it is statistically significant, with a value of 0.220. The nesting of schools within districts gives rise to a consequential degree of district-level homogeneity among schools.

We immediately see that nesting is likely to inflate the standard errors of regression coefficients, so we decide to use random coefficient regression, with REML estimators serving as substitutes for OLS estimators. With school means for 10th-grade reading achievement as the dependent variable and school percentage of mobile students as the only predictor, we estimate a random coefficient regression equation. We permit the intercept and the slope to vary from district to district, and we select the unstructured option for our covariance parameter structure. The results are shown in Tables 4.51 and 4.52.

Our regression results are easy to summarize. The fixed component for the intercept is statistically significant ($p < .000$) and equal to 39.201. Since the independent variable has been grand-mean-centered, the intercept is the predicted value for reading achievement if percent mobile is set equal to its mean. In addition, the value of the random component for the intercept is statistically significant ($p < .000$) and equal to 1.108. This is the variance of the intercept as it varies across districts. Recalling that random compo-

TABLE 4.51. Reading Achievement and Percent Mobile; Random Coefficient Model

$$Y = 39.201 - 0.089\text{MOBILE1}$$
$$(0.074)\ (0.010)$$

$$R_1^2 = 10.8\%$$
$$N_1 = 1001$$
$$N_2 = 713$$

TABLE 4.52. Reading Achievement and Percent Mobile: Random Coefficient Model; Estimates of Covariance Parameters

Parameter	Estimate	Std. error	Wald Z	Sig. level
Residual	2.893	0.237	12.223	.000
INTERCEPT1	1.108	0.258	4.295	.000
INTERCEPT1 by MOBILE1	0.027	0.145	1.890	.059
MOBILE1	0.007	0.002	3.279	.001

nents are normally distributed, if we construct an interval to capture district-to-district variability in the intercept, we find that 95% of all intercept values fall within the range 37.13 to 41.265.

The fixed component for the percent mobile slope is statistically significant ($p < .000$), with a value of –0.089. This means that for each 1-point increase in percentage of mobile students, the value of the reading achievement outcome measure decreases, on average, by 0.089 points. In addition, the value of the random component for the percent mobile slope is 0.007. This is the variance of the random component for the slope. If we construct an interval to capture district-to-district variability in the slope, we find that 95% of all slope values fall within the range –0.103 to –0.075. The width of this interval, going from negative to positive, renders the slope difficult to interpret in substantive terms. We hope to find district-level contextual factors that will diminish slope variability, making the slope more readily interpretable.

The covariance of the random components for the intercept and the percent mobile slope is statistically significant ($p = .059$) with a value of 0.027. The value of Pearson's r for this relationship is 0.307. This means that the random components for the intercept and slope vary together, with one tending to increase as the other increases.

In an effort to explain variability in the random components of the intercept and the slope, and to account for their covariance, we introduce percent mobile aggregated to the district level as a contextual factor ($X_{MOBILE2}$). In addition, we recognize that a cross-level interaction term created with percent mobile at the school level and at the district level is implied by our specification decisions. The results are shown in Tables 4.53 and 4.54.

TABLE 4.53. Reading Achievement and Percent Mobile: Multilevel Regression Model

$Y = 39.088 - 0.177\text{MOBILE1} + 0.023X_{MOBILE2} + 0.002X_{MOBILE2} * \text{MOBILE1}$
$(0.080)\ (0.017)(0.017)(0.001)$

$R_1^2 = 14.0\%$
$N_1 = 1001$
$N_2 = 713$

TABLE 4.54. Reading Achievement and Percent Mobile: Multilevel Regression Model; Estimates of Covariance Parameters

Parameter	Estimate	Std. error	Wald Z	Sig. level
Residual	2.884	0.238	12.095	.000
INTERCEPT1	1.138	0.255	4.456	.000
INTERCEPT1 by MOBILE1	0.016	0.113	1.232	.245
MOBILE1	0.005	0.002	2.744	.006

We have transformed our simple random coefficient regression model into a multi-level regression model. The fixed component for the intercept is little different, now equal to 39.088. The random component for the intercept is now 1.138, a little larger than in the random coefficient equation. Clearly, the contextual factor has not contributed to explaining variability in the random intercept.

The fixed component for the slope has also increased a bit, now equal to –0.177. Evidently part of the relationship between reading achievement and MOBILE1 was suppressed before introduction of the contextual variable and cross-level interaction term. The random component for the slope, however, has diminished, as has the intercept-by-slope covariance. The contextual variable and cross-level interaction term have helped to account for variability in these terms. As a result, if we construct an interval to capture district-to-district variability in the slope, we find that 95% of all slope values fall within the range –0.230 to 0.016. The width of this interval is narrower than before we introduced the contextual variable and cross-level interaction term, but it still ranges from negative to positive, still rendering the slope difficult to interpret.

The fixed component for the contextual variable representing the percentage of each district's students who are mobile is not statistically significant ($p = .189$). Furthermore, since the contextual variable has not been permitted to vary from group to group of a higher-level factor, it has no random component.

The fixed component for the cross-level interaction term created with the percent mobile variable at the school and district levels is statistically significant ($p < .000$). This means that the relationship between the reading achievement dependent variable and school-level percent mobile variable varies from category to category of percent mobile at the district level. In this instance, each 1-point increase in the percent mobile contextual variable corresponds to a 0.002-point increase in the reading-achievement-by-MOBILE1 relationship.

The summary measure, R_1^2, has a value of 14.0%, and each of the smaller-is-better information criteria has a smaller value with the multilevel regression model than with the random coefficient regression model (see Table 4.55). In addition, the deviance statistic is statistically significant ($p < .049$) with a value of 6.200 with two degrees of freedom. Each of the summary measures is consistent with the judgment that the multilevel regression model provides a better fit than the random coefficient regression model.

$$\text{Deviance difference} = 4292.3 - 4286.1 = 6.2$$
$$df = 7 - 5 = 2$$

The concepts and procedures used in this simple example enable us to concretely summarize random coefficient regression models and their transformation into multi-level regression models. As we see, random coefficient regression provides the statistical foundation for multilevel models. For our purposes, the essential difference between the two types of models is that multilevel regression seeks to *explain* random component variances and covariances, while random coefficient regression stops with measuring them.

TABLE 4.55. Information Criteria for Tables 4.51 and 4.53

Criterion	Random coefficient regression	Multilevel regression
–2 log likelihood	4292.3	*4286.1*
Akaike's Information Criterion	4300.3	*4294.1*
Hurvich and Tsai's Criterion	4300.3	*4294.2*
Bozdogan's Criterion	4323.9	*4317.7*
Schwarz's Bayesian Criterion	4319.9	*4313.5*

Note. The smaller value for each measure is boldfaced and italicized.

4.19 USEFUL RESOURCES

Williams, L. (2002) The Prophecy of Place: A Labor Market Study of Young Women and Education. *American Journal of Sociology and Economics, 61*, 681–712.

Typically, the intimate connection between random coefficient regression and multilevel regression is taken for granted and glossed over in published research. This is as it should be, since the conceptual link between these analytical procedures has become well known among those who use multilevel regression.

For someone trying to acquire a basic knowledge of multilevel modeling, however, experienced practitioners' taken-for-granted notions may be a source of confusion, hiding distinctions that are by no means obvious to beginners. This is one reason why Williams's article is especially useful. Williams is writing for a journal that includes many economists among its readers. Though econometricians have done path-breaking work in the development of random coefficient regression, few economists are familiar with multilevel regression. Perhaps this is why Williams provides an unusually clear and detailed account of the place of random coefficient regression in her multilevel analyses.

Using individual-level data from the National Longitudinal Survey of Youth, along with group-level variables constructed with data taken from 95 labor market areas, Williams contextualizes young women's educational attainment processes. She finds that structurally determined factors, such as sector composition, affect females and males differently. In addition, she identifies contextual variables—such as women's representation in higher education and in the workforce—that condition the relationship between educational aspirations and educational attainment. Williams's presentation is strengthened because of the clarity she brings to her discussion of the place of different social organizational levels and relationships between them.

Chevalier, A., Harmon, C., & Walker, I. (2002) *Does Education Raise Productivity, or Just Reflect It?* Dublin: Policy Evaluation and Governance Programme, Institute for the Study of Social Change.

It is difficult to find recent research reports that use random coefficient regression without explicitly embedding such analyses in a multilevel framework. Nevertheless, in some instances, it remains true that the question "Do regression coefficients vary?" is important in and of itself, even without identifying contextual factors that account for that variability.

As part of their evaluation of human capital theoretic accounts relative to the screening hypothesis, Chevalier, Harmon, and Walker raise just such questions. Specifically, they want to know if payoffs for investments in education vary from person to person. Applications of random coefficient regression constitute a comparatively small part of their overall analysis. Nevertheless, it is instructive to see that interesting questions can be addressed by using uncomplicated applications of random coefficient regression, in which coefficients vary but their variability is not explained.

Wright, R., Dielman, T., & Nantell, T. (1977) *Analysis of Stock Repurchases with a Random Coefficient Regression Model* (Working Paper No. 149). Ann Arbor: Division of Research, Graduate School of Business Administration, University of Michigan.

Swamy, P. (1970) Efficient Inference in a Random Coefficient Regression Model. *Econometrica, 38,* 311–323.

The working paper by Wright, Dielman, and Nantell uses random coefficient regression analysis as developed in the pioneering work of Swamy. As a working paper, the Wright et al. manuscript has an unfinished appearance, but this clearly is an instance in which researchers were interested primarily in whether or not coefficients did in fact vary from one context to another. In this instance, the random components of interest correspond to the slope for rate of return on stocks repurchased by 40 firms.

While the authors are interested in the consequences for their 40 firms of operating in different economic contexts, this early work does not employ contextual variables to account for coefficient variability. In very straightforward fashion, however, the authors report the existence of a mean slope of 15.2% and a range of variability of 11.9% with respect to that mean.

Wright and colleagues take seriously the distributional assumptions that apply to random coefficients and to residuals. Furthermore, much as an analyst doing regression analysis of any sort might consider deleting unduly influential observations, they raise the possibility of deleting firms with the most discrepant slopes. For a variety of reasons, then, this three-decade-old exploration of the use of random coefficient regression is instructive, making parallels between random coefficient and conventional OLS regression quite clear.

The article by Swamy, like his book-length account of random coefficient regression (Swamy, 1971), is densely mathematical by any standard. Nevertheless, this is the material that provided the statistical tools for Wright et al.'s interesting paper. In spite of the demands that Swamy's work places on the reader, there are instructive sections that can be quoted with profit:

> . . . it is unlikely that interindividual differences observed in a cross section sample can be explained by a simple regression equation with a few independent variables. In such situations, the coefficient[s] . . . of a regression model can be treated as random to account for interindividual heterogeneity. (Swamy, 1970, p. 311)

And later, after a densely mathematical discussion of the properties of the random coefficient estimators developed by the author:

> In closing, we note that many, if not all, micro units are heterogeneous with regard to the regression [coefficients] in a model. If we proceed blithely with cross section analysis ignoring such heterogeneity, we may be led to erroneous inferences. (Swamy, 1970, p. 322)

5

Developing the Multilevel Regression Model

5.1 CHAPTER INTRODUCTION

We have discussed the random coefficient regression model and applied it in specification and estimation of multilevel regression models. In the process, we have seen that with the random coefficient model serving as the statistical basis for multilevel models, we can achieve improvements over OLS approximations to multilevel regression. Contextual variables and cross-level interaction terms need no longer be simply tacked onto inherently single-level models. Instead, we may specify regression models that are constructed by combining equations from two or more analytical levels.

Construction of multilevel models entails a procedure entirely foreign to OLS regression: using intercepts and slopes as *outcomes!* We acknowledge that intercepts and slopes may vary across groups, and we use contextual variables in an effort to explain that variability in substantively interesting ways.

The equations specified with an intercept or slope as a dependent variable are structurally just as simple as they sound: It really is just regression! Until we become accustomed to working with such equations, they may seem a lot more complicated than they really are. We have already seen several reasons for this.

First, with multilevel regression there are at least two levels and two models. As with OLS, the level-one dependent variable will be an outcome of substantive interest— a conventional measure such as individual students' reading achievement test scores. The independent variables in a level-one model are also substantively conventional. Along with the intercept, they include obvious level-one measures such as race, gender, and SES. One or more of these measures, however, may have a coefficient with a random component as well as a fixed component.

At level two, however, the dependent variables are random components of regression coefficients. Each random component, whether an intercept or a slope, has its own equation. Explanatory factors for random components are substantively conventional measures such as school mean SES or school size.

After the level-one and level-two models have been specified, they are combined by using a straightforward process of substitution. It is this combined or full equation for which we actually estimate coefficients and offer interpretations.

A second reason why the equations constituting a multilevel model may seem unduly confusing has to do with notation. The beta coefficients used to represent random terms at level one and the gamma coefficients used to represent fixed coefficients at level two are new to experienced users of OLS regression.

We can make all this concrete with a simple example. Suppose we have an individual-level measure of reading achievement (X_{RACH}). We wish to account for student-to-student variability in reading achievement with a level-one measure of family SES class background (X_{FSES}). With OLS this would be straightforward.

$$X_{RACH} = a + bX_{FSES} + r_{IJ}$$

We may, however, have good reason to suspect that both the intercept and the slope for X_{FSES} vary across a level-two grouping variable such as school. As a result, we decide to make the intercept and slope random coefficients. At that point, our straightforward and uncomplicated OLS regression equation will be modified as follows:

$$X_{RACH} = \beta_{0J} + \beta_{1J}FSES1 + (u_{0J} + u_{1J} * FSES1 + r_{IJ})$$

This is the level-one model, a random coefficient regression model. The random intercept is β_{0J}, the random slope is β_{1J}, and the greater complexity of the error term reflects the fact that in addition to the usual level-one residual, r_{IJ}, it now includes variability with respect to the random slope, u_{0J}, and the random intercept, $u_{1J} * FSES1$. By changing X_{FSES} to FSES1, we are merely indicating that the level-one independent variable now has a random slope.

Rather than stop with a random coefficient regression model, we suspect that variability in the random intercept and random slope are functions of the school-level variable, X_{FSES2}. This is just family SES aggregated to the school level. As a result, the level-two model takes the following form:

$$\beta_{0J} = \gamma_{00} + \gamma_{01}X_{FSES2} + u_{0J}$$
$$\beta_{1J} = \gamma_{10} + \gamma_{11}X_{FSES2} + u_{1J}$$

This is the level-two model. As we see, it has a separate equation for each random coefficient.

The next step is to substitute the level-two terms into the level-one equation:

$$X_{RACH} = \gamma_{00} + \gamma_{01}X_{FSES2} + \gamma_{10}FSES1 + \gamma_{11}X_{FSES2}*FSES1$$
$$+ (u_{1J} * FSES1 + u_{0J} + e_{IJ})$$

This is the final equation, the one for which we estimate values to insert for the gamma coefficients. Notice that the process of substituting the level-two model into the level-one model has created a cross-level interaction term. The cross-level interaction term is *implied* when the level-one and level-two models are combined to create the final model.

Clearly, the level-one and level-two models are *linked*. The cross-level interaction term makes this explicit, and the linking of different levels is manifest in the way the full model is created.

Unfamiliar structure and distinctive notation may indeed make multilevel models seem more complex than they really are. Fortunately, however, the coefficients for the full model are interpreted in exactly the same way as OLS regression coefficients. Yes, as we have already illustrated, the magnitude of these fixed components may vary sharply from group to group. As summary measures of intercept and slope values, however, their interpretation is familiar and straightforward.

As we add more random components to a multilevel model, it quickly becomes quite complex. It is easy to inadvertently make a multilevel model so complex that interpretations become problematic. Once again, we acknowledge that specification decisions in multilevel regression are numerous, difficult, and often based on very limited information. All this complicates the process of settling on a particular specification as the best.

5.2   FROM RANDOM COEFFICIENT REGRESSION TO MULTILEVEL REGRESSION

Let us use Table 5.1 to look once more at the random coefficient regression model discussed above. We first introduced this rudimentary model with a single level-one independent variable in Table 4.14, and subsequently added the contextual variable $X_{GENDER2}$. The model has a random intercept, a predictor with a random slope at level one, and a contextual variable with a fixed slope at level two. (The subscripts for the $X_{GENDER2}$ slope, β_{20}, indicate that the slope corresponds to the second predictor in the equation (2), but that the slope does not vary (0).

We have repeatedly referred to this as a random coefficient regression model, *but is it also a multilevel regression model*? After all, it does have predictors at two levels. Per-

TABLE 5.1. Is This a Multilevel Model?

$$Y = \beta_{0J} + \beta_{1J}GENDER1 + \beta_{20}X_{GENDER2} + (u_{0J} + u_{1J} * GENDER1 + e_{IJ})$$

haps the best answer is an unsatisfactorily equivocal "yes and no." Yes, it has both individual-level and contextual variables, and a suitably complex error term. However, treating the individual-level random intercept and the individual-level random slope as functions of the school-level variable, X_{GENDER2}, is done off-handedly—as an afterthought, with too little concern for the meaning of proper specification of a multilevel regression model.

In addition, we have not explicitly acknowledged the need to link together the individual level and the school level. We have referred to the linking of levels in previous examples, and have explained that linking is accomplished through use of contextual variables and cross-level interaction terms. For both substantive and methodological reasons, however, it is necessary to give more attention to the peculiar nature of multilevel regression models, which we shall now do.

5.3   EQUATIONS FOR A RANDOM INTERCEPT AND RANDOM SLOPE

We can begin by explicitly defining variability in the random intercept as a function of one or more second-level variables (in this case, one or more characteristics of schools) as in Table 5.2. In this instance, school-to-school variability in the random intercept is expressed as a function of X_{GENDER2}, gender aggregated to the school level.

In effect, the random intercept, β_{0J}, takes the position of a *dependent variable* in a simple regression equation. As with the beta coefficients, the gamma notation represents another set of conventions and takes a bit of getting accustomed to, but the equation in Table 5.2 is just a *simple regression equation* with all the usual terms, including an *intercept, γ_{00}, slope, γ_{01}, and error term, u_{0J}. The objective of the equation is to account for school-to-school variability in the random intercept, β_{0J}.*

The random slope is expressed in the same general way (see Table 5.3): just another *simple regression equation* with all the usual terms, but now the random slope, β_{1J}, is the dependent variable. *Intercepts and slopes*, in effect, are being expressed as *outcomes*, functions of higher-level variables.

TABLE 5.2. Level-Two Model: Equation for a Random Intercept

$$\beta_{0J} = \gamma_{00} + \gamma_{01}X_{\text{GENDER2}} + u_{0J}$$

TABLE 5.3. Level-Two Model: Equation for a Random Slope

$$\beta_{1J} = \gamma_{10} + \gamma_{11}X_{\text{GENDER2}} + u_{1J}$$

5.4   SUBSCRIPT CONVENTIONS FOR TWO-LEVEL MODELS: GAMMA COEFFICIENTS

Notice that the first subscript for the gamma coefficient used in estimating the intercept is a 0, while the first subscript for gamma coefficients used in estimating the slope is a 1. This is consistent with the subscript conventions presented in Chapter 4 for beta coefficients, wherein the first subscript for an intercept is always 0, and the first subscript for a slope is 1, 2, . . . , I, depending on how many independent variables there are in the equation. Here there is one independent variable in the equation for β_{0J}, $X_{GENDER2}$, and the same is true of the equation for β_{1J}.

The second subscript for gamma coefficient indicates that the random intercept, β_{0J}, is a function of the average intercept over all schools, γ_{00}, and school-to-school departures from same. Departures from the average intercept over all schools are represented by the γ_{0J} coefficient; the slope for the level-two independent variable $X_{GENDER2}$; and the error term, u_{0J}.

Similarly, the random slope, β_{1J}, is a function of the slope over all schools, γ_{10}, and school-to-school departures from same. Departures from the slope over all schools are represented by the γ_{11} coefficient; the slope for the level-two independent variable $X_{GENDER2}$; and the error term, u_{1J}.

Having said this, I still find that when working with gamma coefficients the subscripts are confusing, especially when we get to models with more than two levels, as we will in Chapter 8. To make sure we get the right subscripts for gamma coefficients in a two-level random coefficient model, the following additional explanation may be useful. It will also serve as a point of departure for understanding subscripts for three-level models.

The first subscript for a gamma coefficient in a two-level model tells us what we are trying to account for: variability in a random intercept, or variability in a random slope. For example, in the following equation for a random intercept, β_{0J}, we see that the first subscript for each of the gamma coefficients—the intercept, γ_{00}, and the slopes, γ_{01} and γ_{02}—is a zero: $\beta_{0J} = \gamma_{00} + \gamma_{01}X_1 + \gamma_{02}X_2$. When the first subscript of a gamma coefficient in a two-level model is a zero, we know that we are trying to account for variability in a random intercept. Notice that the second subscript in the example identifies the independent variable used in explaining variability in β_{0J}. As we see, γ_{01} corresponds to independent variable X_1, γ_{02} corresponds to independent variable X_2, and so on.

In other words, if we are trying to account for variability in the random intercept in a two-level model, γ_{00} is the common intercept across groups; γ_{01} and γ_{02} are the effects of the group-level predictors on group-specific intercepts.

If we are trying to account for variability in a random slope in a two-level model, the first subscript identifies the specific random slope we are trying to explain. For example, if we are trying to account for variability in two random slopes by using two second-level independent variables, we would have two equations: $\beta_{1J} = \gamma_{10} + \gamma_{11}X_1 + \gamma_{12}X_2$ and $\beta_{2J} = \gamma_{20} + \gamma_{21}X_1 + \gamma_{22}X_2$. Notice again that the second subscript in the example identifies the independent variable (in this example, either X_1 or X_2). Since the intercepts, γ_{10} and γ_{20}, do not correspond to an independent variable, each has a second subscript equal to zero.

In other words, if we are trying to account for variability in a random slope in a two-level model, γ_{10} and γ_{20} are the common slopes associated with individual-level predictors across groups; γ_{11} and γ_{12} are the effects of the group-level predictors on the group specific slopes.

5.5   THE FULL EQUATION

When we substitute the terms from Tables 5.2 and 5.3 into the now-familiar equation from Table 5.1, we can see what develops in Table 5.4. Now there is no need to equivocate: We definitely have a multilevel regression model!

If we want to trace the emergence of the final multilevel regression model more compactly, the process is outlined in Table 5.5. The level-one model expresses the dependent variable, Y, as a function of the level-one independent variables. The level-two model expresses the random intercept and random slope as functions of one or more level-two contextual variables. The final model is derived by combining the level-one and level-two models. Again, the final equation is the one we actually run with SPSS or other general purpose software, giving us substantively interesting values for the intercept and slopes.

TABLE 5.4. A Multilevel Regression Model

$$Y = \beta_{0J} + \beta_{1J}\text{GENDER1} + (u_{0J} + u_{1J} * \text{GENDER1} + e_{IJ})$$

$$Y = \gamma_{00} + \gamma_{01}X_{\text{GENDER2}} + u_{0J} + (\gamma_{10} + \gamma_{11}X_{\text{GENDER2}} + u_{1J}) * \text{GENDER1}$$

$$Y = \gamma_{00} + \gamma_{01}X_{\text{GENDER2}} + \gamma_{10}\text{GENDER1} + \gamma_{11}X_{\text{GENDER2}} * \text{GENDER1} + u_{0J} + u_{1J} * \text{GENDER1} + e_{IJ}$$

TABLE 5.5. Constructing a Final (Full, Complete) Multilevel Regression Model

Level-one model

$$Y = \beta_{0J} + \beta_{1J}\text{GENDER1} + e_{IJ}$$

Level-two model

$$\beta_{0J} = \gamma_{00} + \gamma_{01}X_{\text{GENDER2}} + u_{0J}$$

$$\beta_{1J} = \gamma_{10} + \gamma_{11}X_{\text{GENDER2}} + u_{1J}$$

Full model

$$Y = \gamma_{00} + \gamma_{01}X_{\text{GENDER2}} + \gamma_{10}\text{GENDER1} + \gamma_{11}X_{\text{GENDER2}} * \text{GENDER1} + u_{1J} * \text{GENDER1} + u_{0J} + e_{IJ}$$

5.6   AN *IMPLIED* CROSS-LEVEL INTERACTION TERM

In addition to the main effect independent variables GENDER1 and $X_{GENDER2}$, the full equation now has a cross-level interaction term, $X_{GENDER2}$ * GENDER1. We have seen cross-level interaction terms in many examples already presented. We have explained, moreover, that when a contextual variable is used to explain variability in a random slope, the level-one and level-two independent variables form a cross-level interaction term. In Table 5.5 we see how such terms emerge.

Yes, this is still regression analysis. However, the special circumstances addressed by multilevel models have now been fully acknowledged. In this instance, the process of substituting the random intercept and random slope to create the full equation shows us that the cross-level interaction term is *implied* by our choices of fixed and random coefficients.

5.7   ESTIMATING A MULTILEVEL MODEL: THE FULL EQUATION

The cross-level interaction term, $X_{GENDER2}$ * GENDER1, and the level-two independent variable, $X_{GENDER2}$, have fixed slopes. The level-one independent variable, GENDER1, has a random slope, and the level-one intercept is also random. When we estimate the equation (see Table 5.6) and divide each coefficient by its standard error, we see that the fixed component of the intercept, the random component of the slope corresponding to GENDER1, and the fixed slope corresponding to $X_{GENDER2}$ are statistically significant ($p < .000$). The fixed slope corresponding to the cross-level interaction term, however, is not statistically significant ($p = .421$).

Table 5.7 makes clear that the random intercept and the random slope for GENDER1 do in fact vary from school to school, and that the INTERCEPT1-by-GENDER1 covariance is statistically significant as well. If we estimate the same multilevel regression equation after deleting the contextual variable and the cross-level interaction term, we see by comparing Table 5.7 with Table 5.8 that the additional terms left most of the school-to-school variability in INTERCEPT1 and GENDER1 unexplained, and the same applies to the INTERCEPT1-by-GENDER1 covariance.

TABLE 5.6. Kentucky Reading Achievement and Gender: Fixed Component Estimates for a Multilevel Model

$$Y = 51.239 + 7.516 GENDER1 + 27.764 X_{GENDER2} - 0.965 X_{GENDER2} * GENDER1$$
$$\quad\;\; (0.304)\;(0.213) \qquad\qquad (6.678) \qquad\quad\; (5.211)$$

$$R_1^2 = 4.1\%$$
$$N_1 = 49,616$$
$$N_2 = 347$$

TABLE 5.7. Kentucky Reading Achievement and Gender: Contextual Variable and Cross-Level Interaction Term Included; Estimates of Covariance Parameters

Parameter	Estimate	Std. error	Wald Z	Sig. level
Residual	325.167	2.112	168.473	.000
INTERCEPT1	19.239	1.976	9.736	.000
INTERCEPT1 by GENDER1	−2.413	0.950	−2.540	.011
GENDER1	3.351	0.909	3.685	.000

TABLE 5.8. Kentucky Reading Achievement and Gender: Contextual Effect and Cross-Level Interaction Term Not Included; Estimates of Covariance Parameters

Parameter	Estimate	Std. error	Wald Z	Sig. level
Residual	325.169	2.112	153.962	.000
INTERCEPT1	20.702	2.109	9.815	.000
INTERCEPT1 by GENDER1	−2.378	0.976	−2.437	.015
GENDER1	3.318	0.904	3.670	.000

These results are very similar to those reported in Tables 4.8 and 4.9, when we were working with reading achievement as a function of GENDER1 and $X_{GENDER2}$ in a random coefficient regression model. Though the fixed and random components are nearly the same in this instance, the two analyses are conceptually different. Now, with explicit specification of a level-one model, a level-two model, a full model, and inclusion of an implied cross-level interaction term, we are working with a multilevel regression model—a more complex and potentially more informative analytical tool than the random coefficient model on which it is based.

In spite of the increasing conceptual sophistication of our model, however, we still have not managed to explain school-to-school variability in the random intercept and random slope, and the INTERCEPT1-by-GENDER1 negative covariance remains unaccounted for as well. Based on previous research, we may suspect that gender is confounded with SES in ways that cause the relationship between reading achievement and student gender to vary from one second-level group to another (Bickel & Howley, 2003; Bickel & Maynard, 2004). In response, we introduce a measure of SES aggregated to the school level, X_{POOR2}, as an additional explanatory factor—one that may contribute to accounting for variability in the random intercept and in the random slope for GENDER1. X_{POOR2} is just the percentage of each school's students who are eligible for free/reduced cost lunch. Though we are introducing no additional random components, explicitly specifying X_{POOR2} as a predictor of variability in the random slope for GENDER1 modifies our level-two and full models as indicated in Table 5.9.

Empirical results based on the full model are reported in Tables 5.10 and 5.11. The fixed component estimates in Table 5.10 show us that the contextual variable X_{POOR2} and the cross-level interaction term X_{POOR2} * GENDER1 both have statistically significant

TABLE 5.9. Constructing a Final Multilevel Regression Model: X_{POOR2} as an Additional Level-Two Predictor

Level-one model

$$Y = \beta_{0J} + \beta_{1J}GENDER1 + e_{IJ}$$

Level-two model

$$\beta_{0J} = \gamma_{00} + \gamma_{01}X_{GENDER2} + \gamma_{02}X_{POOR2} + u_{0J}$$

$$\beta_{1J} = \gamma_{10} + \gamma_{11}X_{GENDER2} + \gamma_{12}X_{POOR2} + u_{1J}$$

Full model

$$Y = \gamma_{00} + \gamma_{01}X_{GENDER2} + \gamma_{02}X_{POOR2} + \gamma_{10}GENDER1 + \gamma_{11}X_{GENDER2} * GENDER1$$
$$+ \gamma_{12}X_{POOR2} * GENDER1 + (u_{1J} * GENDER1 + u_{0J} + e_{IJ})$$

TABLE 5.10. Kentucky Reading Achievement and Gender: Fixed Component Estimates for a Multilevel Model; X_{POOR2} as an Additional Level-Two Predictor

$$Y = 49.016 + 8.033GENDER1 + 17.111X_{GENDER2} + 2.968X_{GENDER2} * GENDER1$$
$$\quad\;\;(0.258)\;\;\;(0.266)\qquad\qquad(4.86)\qquad\qquad\;\;(5.183)$$

$$\quad\; - 0.183X_{POOR2} + 0.389X_{POOR2} * GENDER1$$
$$\qquad(0.118)\qquad\quad\;\;(0.117)$$

$$R_1{}^2 = 7.2\%$$
$$N_1 = 49,616$$
$$N_2 = 347$$

coefficients. Individual reading achievement scores, on average, decline as the percentage of economically poor students in a school increases, but the female advantage relative to male students actually increases, on average, as X_{POOR2} increases.

In Table 5.11 we see that respecifying our regression model has substantially diminished the variance of the random component for INTERCEPT1, and has explained away the statistically significant and negative INTERCEPT1-by-GENDER1 covariance. This is because as the percentage of students who are economically poor increases, reading achievement scores, on average, diminish; *and* as the percentage of economically poor

TABLE 5.11. Kentucky Reading Achievement and Gender: Estimates of Covariance Parameters; X_{POOR2} as an Additional Level-Two Predictor

Parameter	Estimate	Std. error	Wald Z	Sig. level
Residual	325.156	2.112	153.973	.000
INTERCEPT1	8.405	0.967	8.693	.000
INTERCEPT1 by GENDER1	−0.171	0.648	−0.264	.792
GENDER1	2.949	0.862	3.418	.001

students increases, the reading achievement advantage of female students, on average, increases.

As we examine estimates of covariance parameters under a variety of different circumstances, we may also notice that the residual variance changes very little. This is because the gains that have come with regression model respecification have not made an appreciable contribution to accounting for within-school variance in the reading achievement dependent variable. This is also manifest, from model to model, in persistently small R_1^2 values. If we introduce additional pertinent level-one predictors, we will do better in this regard.

For example, if we introduce ethnicity (ETHNIC1, coded 1 if a student is Black and 0 otherwise) as a student-level independent variable with a random slope—along with the aggregated contextual variable ($X_{ETHNIC2}$) and a cross-level interaction term ($X_{ETHNIC2}$ * ETHNIC1)—into the multilevel regression analysis, we get the level-one model, level-two model, and full model described in Table 5.12.

This is not the only model that could have followed from adding ETHNIC1 and $X_{ETHNIC2}$ to the analysis. As things stand, we have specified $X_{ETHNIC2}$ as a predictor of variability in the random intercept and the random slope for ETHNIC1, but not as a predictor of variability in the random intercept for GENDER1. Had we done so, there would have been still one more factor included in the full model: the cross-level interaction term GENDER1 * $X_{ETHNIC2}$. We might also have included X_{POOR2} as a predictor of variability in the random slope for ETHNIC1. This would have led to inclusion of the cross-level interaction term ETHNIC1 * X_{POOR2}. Whether or not these or other modifications would have represented improved regression model specification, they certainly would have made the final equation more complicated.

The most interesting findings in Table 5.13 concern the cross-level interaction terms $X_{GENDER2}$ * GENDER1 and $X_{ETHNIC2}$ * ETHNIC1. $X_{GENDER2}$ * GENDER1 was

---

TABLE 5.12. Constructing a Final Multilevel Regression Model: ETHNIC1 as an Additional Level-One Predictor

Level-one model

$Y = \beta_{0J} + \beta_{1J}GENDER1 + \beta_{2J}ETHNIC1e_{IJ}$

Level-two model

$\beta_{0J} = \gamma_{00} + \gamma_{01}X_{GENDER2} + \gamma_{02}X_{POOR2} + \gamma_{03}X_{ETHNIC2} + u_{0J}$

$\beta_{1J} = \gamma_{10} + \gamma_{11}X_{GENDER2} + \gamma_{12}X_{POOR2} + u_{1J}$

$\beta_{2J} = \gamma_{20} + \gamma_{21}X_{GENDER2} + \gamma_{22}X_{ETHNIC2} + u_{1J}$

Full model

$Y = \gamma_{00} + \gamma_{01}X_{GENDER2} + \gamma_{02}X_{POOR2} + \gamma_{02}X_{ETHNIC2} + \gamma_{10}GENDER1 + \gamma_{20}ETHNIC1$
$\quad + \gamma_{11}X_{GENDER2} * GENDER1 + \gamma_{12}X_{POOR2} * GENDER1 + \gamma_{22}X_{ETHNIC2} * ETHNIC1$
$\quad + \gamma_{22}X_{GENDER2} * ETHNIC1 + (u_{1J} * GENDER1 + u_{2J} * ETHNIC1 + u_{0J} + e_{IJ})$

TABLE 5.13. Kentucky Reading Achievement and Gender: Fixed Component Estimates for a Multilevel Model; ETHNIC1 as an Additional Level-One Predictor

$Y = 48.868 + 8.033\text{GENDER1} - 8.033\text{ETHNIC1} + 16.533X_{\text{GENDER2}} - 5.465X_{\text{ETHNIC2}} - 0.183X_{\text{POOR2}}$
    (0.258) (0.263)   (0.501)   (4.768)   (1.458)   (0.012)

$+ 3.782X_{\text{GENDER2}} * \text{GENDER1} - 16.061\ X_{\text{ETHNIC2}} * \text{ETHNIC1} + 9.087X_{\text{GENDER2}} * \text{ETHNIC1}$
    (0.511)   (2.848)   (10.796)

$+ 0.382X_{\text{POOR2}} * \text{GENDER1}$
    (0.112)

$$R_1^2 = 9.4\%$$
$$N_1 = 49{,}616$$
$$N_2 = 347$$

included in Table 5.10, but its coefficient was statistically nonsignificant. Now that the model has been respecified, however, this term emerges as statistically significant at any reasonable alpha level. This tells us that as the percentage of a school's students who are female increases, individual female students, on average, have an increased advantage in reading achievement.

The $X_{\text{ETHNIC2}} * \text{ETHNIC1}$ term is new with this respecification. Its coefficient tells us that as the percentage of a school's students who are Black increases, individual Black students, on average, experience an increased disadvantage in reading achievement.

Our stated objective in this instance was to identify level-one predictors that would make a substantial contribution to explaining the residual variance, variability in the dependent variable occurring within schools. Comparing Tables 5.11 and 5.14 indicates that we have made some progress, with Residual being reduced from 325.156 to 316.426. Nevertheless, consistent with the still small R_1^2 summary statistic, our multilevel regression model is not particularly effective in this regard.

TABLE 5.14. Kentucky Reading Achievement and Gender: Estimates of Covariance Parameters; ETHNIC1 as an Additional Level-One Predictor

Parameter	Estimate	Std. error	Wald Z	Sig. level
Residual	316.426	2.082	151.979	.000
INTERCEPT1	7.981	0.935	8.540	.000
INTERCEPT1 by GENDER1	−1.042	0.663	−1.571	.116
GENDER1	2.273	0.836	3.268	.001
INTERCEPT1 by ETHNIC1	−1.959	1.349	−1.452	.146
GENDER1 by ETHNIC1	−0.676	1.424	−0.475	.635
ETHNIC1	17.127	3.949	4.342	.000

5.8   A MULTILEVEL MODEL WITH A RANDOM SLOPE AND FIXED SLOPES AT LEVEL ONE

Decisions as to which independent variables have random slopes and which have fixed slopes are best made through reference to substantive and theoretical knowledge, when this is available. As a result, the same multilevel regression equation commonly contains, at the same level, coefficients that are permitted to vary across higher-level groups along with coefficients that are not permitted to vary (Hausman, 1978).

For example, we have seen that data on individuals and the urban–rural character of the areas in which they live are available in the Child Development Supplement of the Panel Study of Income Dynamics data set (Institute for Social Research, 2003). In Tables 5.15 through 5.17 below, we have specified a multilevel regression model in which the natural logarithm of family income in units of $1000 is the dependent variable. The individual-level independent variables are family head's race (coded 1 if Black and 0 otherwise), family head's educational level in years, and a value on the urban–rural continuum variable.

We have, moreover, assigned the coefficients for race and educational level fixed slopes, while the intercept and the urban–rural slope at the individual level are permitted to vary across states. The random urban–rural slope reflects our suspicion that the relationship between family income and area of residence may vary with the urban–rural context provided by the state.

The level-one model is defined in Table 5.15, and the level-two model with its random intercept and random slope are defined in Table 5.16. After substituting terms and adding the individual-level variables to which we have assigned fixed slopes, we have the full equation as reported in Table 5.17. Concretely, the multilevel regression equa-

TABLE 5.15. Level-One Model
for an Earnings Function

$$Y_{\text{INCOME}} = \beta_{0J} + \beta_{1J}\text{URBANRURAL1} + e_{IJ}$$

TABLE 5.16. Level-Two Model
for an Earnings Function

$$\beta_{0J} = \gamma_{00} + \gamma_{01}X_{\text{URBANRURAL2}} + u_{0J}$$

$$\beta_{1J} = \gamma_{10} + \gamma_{11}X_{\text{URBANRURAL2}} + u_{1J}$$

TABLE 5.17. Multilevel Model for an Earnings Function

$$Y = \gamma_{00} + \gamma_{01}X_{\text{URBANRURAL2}} + \gamma_{10}\text{URBANRURAL1} + \gamma_{11}X_{\text{URBANRURAL2}} * \text{URBANRURAL1} + \gamma_{20}X_{\text{BLACK1}}$$

$$+ \gamma_{30}X_{\text{EDUCATE1}} + (u_{0J} + u_{1J} * \text{URBANRURAL1} + e_{IJ})$$

TABLE 5.18. Multilevel Regression Earnings Function; Fixed Component Estimates

$Y = 4.086 - 0.079X_{\text{URBANRURAL2}} + 0.018X_{\text{URBANRURAL2}} * \text{URBANRURAL1} - 0.059\text{URBANRURAL1}$
    $(0.045)\ (0.028)$ (0.009) (0.014)

  $- 0.491X_{\text{BLACK 1}} + 0.144X_{\text{EDUCATE1}}$
    (0.075) (0.008)

$$R_1^2 = 23.1\%$$
$$N_1 = 1541$$
$$N_2 = 50$$

tion with a random intercept, one random slope, and two fixed slopes appears in Table 5.18. Estimates of the random component variances and covariances are reported in Table 5.19 below.

In Table 5.18, we see that all regression coefficients are statistically significant. We learn that even when we control for X_{BLACK1} and X_{EDUCATE1}, as places of individual family residence become more rural, substantial income disadvantages are, on average, incurred. In addition, as states become more rural, additional family income disadvantages are, on average, incurred. The $X_{\text{URBANRURAL2}} * \text{URBANRURAL1}$ cross-level interaction term, however, indicates that the individual-level family income losses associated with living in more rural areas are diminished as states become more rural.

In addition, the coefficients for individual-level variables with fixed slopes, X_{BLACK1} and X_{EDUCATE1}, show us that annual income for families headed by someone who is Black are, on average, 49.1% lower than for other families, and each additional year of education completed by the family head yields, on average, a 14.4% increase in annual income.

Since the urban–rural variable plays a conspicuous role in this set of examples, we have included Figures 5.1 and 5.2 (Beale, 2004; Howe, 2005).

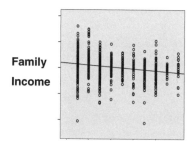

Urban–Rural Continuum

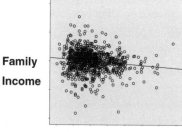

Urban–Rural Continuum

FIGURE 5.1. Family income by urban–rural continuum; no controls.

FIGURE 5.2. Family income by urban–rural continuum; controls in place as in Table 5.18.

TABLE 5.19. Multilevel Regression Earnings Function; Estimates of Covariance Parameters

Parameter	Estimate	Std. error	Wald Z	Sig. level
Residual	0.421	0.019	22.189	.000
INTERCEPT1	0.069	0.022	3.157	.002
INTERCEPT1 by URBANRURAL1	−0.009	0.006	−1.474	.141
URBANRURAL1	0.006	0.003	2.033	.042

In this application of multilevel regression, Table 5.19 makes clear that the random components for INTERCEPT1 and URBANRURAL1 are statistically significant. (Again, since variances cannot be negative, we are using one-tailed tests.) However, the INTERCEPT1-by-URBANRURAL1 covariance is not statistically significant, meaning that the two random components do not vary together.

5.9 COMPLEXITY AND CONFUSION: TOO MANY RANDOM COMPONENTS

One of the limitations of some instructional accounts of multilevel regression models is that they do not go beyond very simple examples. The typical thinness of the theoretical and substantive literature available to guide model specification decisions is, no doubt, one reason why multilevel regression models do not become more complex than they usually are (see, e.g., Klein & Kozlowski, 2000; Stemler, Sternberg, Grigorenko, Jarvin, & Macomber, 2003; Hofmann, 2005). Just as when we are working with OLS multiple regression analysis, complex exercises in arid empiricism involving unguided selection of too many explanatory variables may generate confusion.

The complexity of multilevel models is something we have referred to previously, but it is easier to appreciate now that we are writing out equations for the level-one, level-two, and full models. In truth, we have already completed some rather complex multilevel regression analyses, such as the Kentucky reading achievement example reported in Tables 5.13 and 5.14, using a random intercept and two random slopes. We may explicitly examine consequences of using more than one random slope, perhaps generating undue complexity, by using the model presented in Tables 5.15 through 5.19 as a point of departure.

Table 5.20 presents the level-one, level-two, and full models for a rather complex multilevel regression analysis in which the fixed coefficients assigned to X_{BLACK1} (now BLACK1) and $X_{EDUCATE1}$ (now EDUCATE1) have been made random. Since URBANRURAL1 was already assigned a random slope in Table 5.15, we now have a model with a random intercept and *three* random slopes.

You may recall that we illustrated a random coefficient regression model with three random slopes when we estimated an earnings function with a different data set in Tables 4.18 through 4.21. Now that we are explicitly specifying multilevel regression

TABLE 5.20. Augmented Multilevel Earnings Function

Level-one model

$$Y_{\text{INCOME}} = \beta_{0J} + \beta_{1J}\text{URBANRURAL1} + \beta_{2J}\text{BLACK1} + \beta_{3J}\text{EDUCATE1} + e_{IJ}$$

Level-two model

$$\beta_{0J} = \gamma_{00} + \gamma_{01}X_{\text{URBANRURAL2}} + u_{0J}$$
$$\beta_{1J} = \gamma_{10} + \gamma_{11}X_{\text{URBANRURAL2}} + u_{1J}$$
$$\beta_{2J} = \gamma_{20} + \gamma_{21}X_{\text{URBANRURAL2}} + u_{2J}$$
$$\beta_{3J} = \gamma_{30} + \gamma_{31}X_{\text{URBANRURAL2}} + u_{3J}$$

Multilevel model

$$Y = \gamma_{00} + \gamma_{01}X_{\text{URBANRURAL2}} + \gamma_{10}\text{URBANRURAL1} + \gamma_{20}\text{BLACK1} + \gamma_{30}\text{EDUCATE1}$$
$$+ \gamma_{11}X_{\text{URBANRURAL2}} * \text{URBANRURAL1} + \gamma_{21}X_{\text{URBANRURAL2}} * \text{BLACK1} + \gamma_{31}X_{\text{URBANRURAL2}}$$
$$* \text{EDUCATE1} + (u_{0J} + u_{1J} * \text{URBANRURAL1} + u_{2J} * \text{BLACK1} + u_{3J} * \text{EDUCATE1} + e_{IJ})$$

models, however, incorporating additional random coefficients becomes a more complex task. What level-two contextual variables, for example, should be used in an effort to account for variability in the random components?

In the simpler model that we are using as a point of departure, we used one contextual variable, $X_{\text{URBANRURAL2}}$, to account for variability in the random intercept and the random slope for URBANRURAL1. We made clear, however, that we had other choices. With more random components we are faced with even more decisions, making specification of our multilevel regression model complex indeed.

Suppose we decide in this example that variability in the intercept and all three random slopes is in fact a function of $X_{\text{URBANRURAL2}}$. This produces the multilevel regression model specified in Table 5.20. The top portion of Table 5.21 makes concrete the earnings function specified in Table 5.20. To facilitate comparison, the bottom portion contains results from the similar but less complex earnings function estimated in Table 5.18. Estimates of the random component variances and covariances are reported in Table 5.22.

Substantively, it is not at all clear that anything has been gained by making the model more complex. Since the models are nested, we may use the −2 log likelihood-based deviance statistic introduced in Chapter 3 to compare models with regard to goodness of fit, as we have done in Table 5.23.

Nine parameters (6 fixed components, 2 random components, and 1 covariance) were used in estimating the simple model in Table 5.18, while 19 parameters (8 fixed components, 4 random components, and 7 covariances) were used in estimating the more complex model in Table 5.21. With degrees of freedom equal to the difference in the number of parameters used in estimating the two models (in this case, 10), the critical value of χ^2 with alpha set at .05 is 18.307. The result of the deviance test tells us that the more complex model, whatever its interpretative merit, provides a better fit to the data:

TABLE 5.21. Comparing Multilevel Earnings Functions: Augmented Multilevel Regression Earnings Function; Fixed Component Estimates

$Y = 4.133 - 0.058X_{URBANRURAL2} + 0.010X_{URBANRURAL2}$ * URBANRURAL1
  (0.050) (0.031)   (0.011)

  $- 0.054URBANRURAL1 + 0.137EDUCATE1 - 0.294BLACK1$
  (0.018)   (0.017)   (0.172)

  $- 0.016X_{URBANRURAL2}$ * EDUCATE1 $+ 0.059X_{URBANRURAL2}$ * BLACK1
  (0.010)   (0.107)

$$R_1^2 = 22.0\%$$
$$N_1 = 1541$$
$$N_2 = 50$$

TABLE 5.18, Reproduced. Multilevel Regression Earnings Function; Fixed Component Estimates

$Y = 4.086 - 0.079X_{URBANRURAL2} + 0.018X_{URBANRURAL2}$ * URBANRURAL1
  (0.045) (0.028)   (0.009)

  $- 0.059URBANRURAL1 + 0.491X_{BLACK1} - 0.144X_{EDUCATE1}$
  (0.014)   (0.0075)   (0.008)

$$R_1^2 = 23.7\%$$
$$N_1 = 1541$$
$$N_2 = 50$$

TABLE 5.22. Augmented Earnings Function; Estimates of Covariance Parameters

Parameter	Estimate	Std. error	Wald Z	Sig. level
Residual	0.386	0.018	21.689	.000
INTERCEPT1	0.072	0.023	3.161	.002
INTERCEPT1 by URBANRURAL1	−0.010	0.006	−1.566	.117
URBANRURAL1	0.006	0.003	2.271	.023
INTERCEPT1 by EDUCATE1	−0.009	0.005	−1.689	.091
URBANRURAL1 by EDUCATE1	0.003	0.002	1.630	.103
EDUCATE1	0.006	0.002	2.448	.014
INTERCEPT by BLACK1	0.168	0.104	0.162	.871
URBANRURAL1 by BLACK1	0.036	0.019	1.848	.065
EDUCATE1 by BLACK1	0.004	0.021	0.165	.869
BLACK1	0.372	0.302	1.231	.218

TABLE 5.23. Information Criteria Summary for Tables 5.18 and 5.21

| Criterion | Earnings functions | |
	Simple	Complex
–2 log likelihood	2235.6	*2192.4*
Akaike's Information Criterion	2241.6	*2212.4*
Hurvich and Tsai's Criterion	2241.6	*2214.6*
Bozdogan's Criterion	*2259.5*	2280.0
Schwarz's Bayesian Criterion	*2256.5*	2269.0

Note. The smaller value for each measure is boldfaced and italicized.

$$\text{Deviance difference} = 2235.6 - 2192.4 = 43.2$$
$$df = 19 - 9 = 10$$

As we have seen in previous examples, however, when we refer to the information criteria (again estimated with ML), which punish analysts for using additional degrees of freedom, results are mixed. Two of the four smaller-is-better criteria are consistent with the deviance tests, and two are not.

At this point it may be best to invoke the distinction between results of goodness-of-fit measures and judgments about the practical meaning of the two sets of results. If we examine Table 5.21, we see that the two models discern similar relationships between annual family income and urban–rural residence and between annual family income and level of educational attainment. As place of residence at the individual level becomes more rural, annual family income, on average, decreases. As family heads become better educated, annual family income, on average, increases.

There are no other statistically significant coefficients in the more complex equation, but the simpler equation has statistically significant coefficients for the level-one variable X_{BLACK1}, the contextual variable $X_{\text{URBANRURAL2}}$, and the cross-level interaction term $X_{\text{URBANRURAL2}}$ * URBANRURAL1. Analysts accustomed to working with OLS regression might immediately suspect that differences between the two models may be due, at least in part, to multicollinearity.

However, variance inflation factors for the simpler model range from 1.039 to 1.209, and for the more complex model from 1.042 to 1.306. Condition indices for the two models are almost exactly the same, 1.637 and 1.803. Difference in degree of collinearity among independent variables seems clearly not to be a source of statistical and substantive differences between the simpler and more complex models.

Differences between the two models with regard to the statistical significance of household head's race may very well be due to the fact that this variable has a fixed coefficient in the simpler model, but a random coefficient in the more complex model. Recall that the sample size corresponding to a random coefficient for a level-one independent variable is equal to the number of second-level groups, not the number of level-one cases. As a result, the sample size corresponding to the fixed coefficient for X_{BLACK1} is 1541, while the sample size corresponding to the random coefficient BLACK1 is 50. This makes for a substantial difference in statistical power.

Rather than continue with this makeshift analysis of possible reasons as to why the two models yield different results, a better response may be simply to acknowledge that by adding random coefficients and cross-level interaction terms in the absence of good reason to do so, we made the model *more complex but less informative*. We would have been better served by sticking with the simpler model, or we should learn a lot more about the social processes involved in income determination (Arrow, Bowles, & Durlauf, 2000).

As we noted above, the same sort of confusion often follows if we make an OLS multiple regression model more complex than our knowledge warrants. *With multilevel regression, however, there are many more ways of making this same mistake.*

5.10 INTERPRETING MULTILEVEL REGRESSION EQUATIONS

It is clear from our efforts to compare differently specified earnings functions that we need a more systematic way of interpreting the results of multilevel regression analysis. We will begin with the data set containing information on nearly 50,000 Kentucky eighth graders. We have specified a variety of random coefficient regression and multilevel regression models building on the simple random coefficient model first presented in Table 4.14. We can augment this model in a variety of straightforward ways.

Ethnicity is rarely missing from analyses aimed at accounting for achievement differences among students. For this example, we have coded ethnicity 1 for Blacks and 0 for Whites. The dichotomous simplicity of the ethnicity variable reflects the descriptively uncomplicated nature of ethnic diversity in the Appalachian United States (Bickel & Howley, 2003). Due to limitations of the Kentucky data set, gender and ethnicity are the only student-level variables available.

Referring to the growing literature on school size, we decide to treat gender (GENDER1) and ethnicity (ETHNIC1) at the student level as predictors with random coefficients, and we also make the intercept random (see, e.g., Bickel, McDonough, & Williams, 1999; Bickel & Dufrene, 2001). We treat the two random slopes and the random intercept as functions of four school-level contextual variables: gender ($X_{GENDER2}$) and ethnicity ($X_{ETHNIC2}$) aggregated to the school level; the percentage of students who are eligible for free/reduced cost lunch (X_{POOR2}); and school size expressed in 100-student units (X_{SIZE2}).

Figures 5.3 and 5.4 illustrate the distributions of the individual-level and school-level ethnicity variables with respect to reading achievement. Since ethnicity is a dichotomy that is then aggregated to the school level, Figures 5.3 and 5.4 for ethnicity are similar to Figures 4.1 and 4.2 for gender. In both cases, we are reminded that we have very different variables involved in very different relationships at the individual level and school level. Configurations such as this, defining differences between explanatory vari-

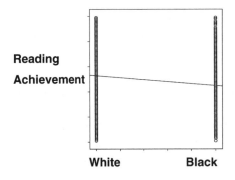

FIGURE 5.3. Reading achievement by student ethnicity.

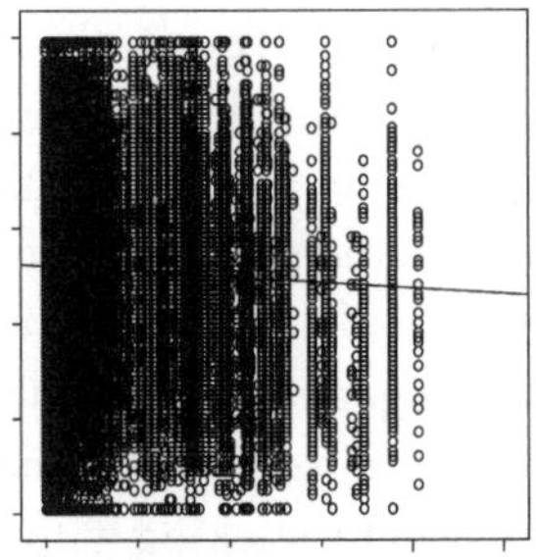

FIGURE 5.4. Reading achievement by ethnicity aggregated to school level.

ables at different levels of analysis, contribute to making multilevel regression interesting and useful.

With eighth-grade reading achievement as the dependent variable, our multilevel regression model is specified in Table 5.24. If we had lingering doubts about the importance of cautionary comments concerning the value of planned parsimony in multilevel regression models, Table 5.24 is sure to dispel them. Three random components and four contextual variables imply eight cross-level interaction terms. What may have seemed like a fairly simple model becomes quite complex.

TABLE 5.24. Reading Achievement: An Interpretable Multilevel Regression Model

Level-one model

$$Y = \beta_{0J} + \beta_{1J}\text{GENDER1} + \beta_{2J}\text{ETHNIC1} + (u_{0J} + u_{1J} * \text{GENDER1} + u_{2J} * \text{ETHNIC1} + e_{IJ})$$

Level-two model

$$\beta_{0J} = \gamma_{00} + \gamma_{01}X_{\text{GENDER2}} + \gamma_{02}X_{\text{ETHNIC2}} + \gamma_{03}X_{\text{POOR2}} + \gamma_{04}X_{\text{SIZE2}} + u_{0J}$$

$$\beta_{1J} = \gamma_{10} + \gamma_{11}X_{\text{GENDER2}} + \gamma_{12}X_{\text{ETHNIC2}} + \gamma_{13}X_{\text{POOR2}} + \gamma_{14}X_{\text{SIZE2}} + u_{1J}$$

$$\beta_{2J} = \gamma_{20} + \gamma_{21}X_{\text{GENDER2}} + \gamma_{22}X_{\text{ETHNIC2}} + \gamma_{23}X_{\text{POOR2}} + \gamma_{24}X_{\text{SIZE2}} + u_{2J}$$

Multilevel (full) model

$$Y = \gamma_{00} + \gamma_{01}X_{\text{GENDER2}} + \gamma_{02}X_{\text{ETHNIC2}} + \gamma_{03}X_{\text{POOR2}} + \gamma_{04}X_{\text{SIZE2}} + u_{0J} + (\gamma_{10} + \gamma_{11}X_{\text{GENDER2}}$$
$$+ \gamma_{12}X_{\text{ETHNIC2}} + \gamma_{13}X_{\text{POOR2}} + \gamma_{14}X_{\text{SIZE2}} + u_{1J}) * \text{GENDER1} + (\gamma_{20} + \gamma_{21}X_{\text{GENDER2}} + \gamma_{22}X_{\text{ETHNIC2}}$$
$$+ \gamma_{23}X_{\text{POOR2}} + \gamma_{24}X_{\text{SIZE2}} + u_{2J}) * \text{ETHNIC1}$$

$$Y = \gamma_{00} + \gamma_{01}X_{\text{GENDER2}} + \gamma_{02}X_{\text{ETHNIC2}} + \gamma_{03}X_{\text{POOR2}} + \gamma_{04}X_{\text{SIZE2}} + \gamma_{10}\text{GENDER1} + \gamma_{11}X_{\text{GENDER2}}$$
$$* \text{GENDER1} + \gamma_{12}X_{\text{ETHNIC2}} * \text{GENDER1} + \gamma_{13}X_{\text{POOR2}} * \text{GENDER1} + \gamma_{14}X_{\text{SIZE2}} * \text{GENDER1}$$
$$+ \gamma_{20}\text{ETHNIC1} + \gamma_{21}X_{\text{GENDER2}} * \text{ETHNIC1} + \gamma_{22}X_{\text{ETHNIC2}} * \text{ETHNIC1} + \gamma_{23}X_{\text{POOR2}} * \text{ETHNIC1}$$
$$+ \gamma_{24}X_{\text{SIZE2}}\text{ETHNIC1} + (u_{0J} + u_{1J} * \text{GENDER1} + u_{2J} * \text{ETHNIC1} + e_{IJ})$$

For all three random coefficients, other specifications are entirely possible, depending on substantive and theoretical knowledge and data limitations. Clearly, however, this is another illustration that depends more on commonsense, conventional wisdom, and instructional objectives than on insights derived from careful consideration of well-developed theory.

When we estimate coefficients and standard errors for the model in Table 5.24, we get the results reported in Table 5.25. Random component variances and covariances are reported in Table 5.26. Interpreting this complex set of results is straightforward. Referring to the fixed component estimates in Table 5.25, we see the following:

1. Each 1% increase in a school's students who are female ($X_{GENDER2}$) corresponds, on average, to a 16.745-point increase in measured reading achievement.
2. Each 1% increase in a school's students who are Black (X_{RACE2}) corresponds, on average, to a 4.093-point decrease in measured reading achievement.
3. Each 1% increase in a school's students who are eligible for free/reduced cost lunch (X_{POOR2}) corresponds, on average, to a 0.194-point decrease in measured reading achievement.

TABLE 5.25. Multilevel Reading Achievement Function; Fixed Component Estimates

$$Y = 49.249 + 16.745X_{GENDER2} - 4.093X_{ETHNIC2} - 0.194\ X_{POOR2} - 0.737\ X_{SIZE2} + 8.207GENDER1$$
$$(0.314)\quad (4.776)\qquad\qquad (1.489)\qquad\qquad (0.012)\qquad\qquad (0.353)\qquad\qquad (0.371)$$

$$-\ 4.647ETHNIC1 + 3.808X_{GENDER2} * GENDER1 + 13.688X_{GENDER2} * ETHNIC1$$
$$(0.872)\qquad\quad (4.887)\qquad\qquad\qquad\qquad (10.656)$$

$$-\ 17.526X_{ETHNIC2} * ETHNIC1 - 6.239\ X_{ETHNIC2} * GENDER1 - 0.388X_{SIZE2} * GENDER1$$
$$(2.872)\qquad\qquad\qquad (1.348)\qquad\qquad\qquad (0.393)$$

$$-\ 0.044X_{SIZE2} * ETHNIC1 + 0.032\ X_{POOR2} * GENDER1 + 0.097X_{POOR2} * ETHNIC1$$
$$(0.871)\qquad\qquad\qquad (0.012)\qquad\qquad\qquad (0.032)$$

$$R_1{}^2 = 9.7\%$$
$$N_1 = 49,616$$
$$N_2 = 347$$

TABLE 5.26. Multilevel Reading Achievement Function; Estimates of Covariance Parameters

Parameter	Estimate	Std. error	Wald Z	Sig. level
Residual	316.419	2.082	151.993	.000
INTERCEPT1	7.911	0.922	8.583	.000
INTERCEPT1 by GENDER1	−0.852	0.586	−1.455	.146
GENDER1	1.866	0.733	2.5465	.011
INTERCEPT1 by ETHNIC1	−1.458	1.295	−1.126	.260
GENDER1 by ETHNIC1	−0.456	1.186	−0.385	.701
ETHNIC1	14.560	3.707	3.938	.000

4. Each 100-student increase in school size (X_{SIZE2}) corresponds, on average, to a 0.737-point decrease in measured reading achievement.
5. Female students (GENDER1), on average, score 8.207-points higher than males.
6. Black students (ETHNIC1), on average, score 4.647 points lower than White students.
7. Each 1% increase in a school's students who are Black ($X_{ETHNIC2}$) increases the measured reading achievement disadvantage for individual Black students, on average, by 17.526 points.
8. Each 1% increase in a school's students who are Black ($X_{ETHNIC2}$) decreases the measured reading achievement advantage for individual female students, on average, by 6.239 points.
9. Each 1% increase in a school's students who are eligible for free/reduced cost lunch (X_{POOR2}) increases the measured reading achievement advantage for individual female students by 0.032 points.
10. Each 1% increase in a school's students who are eligible for free/reduced cost lunch (X_{POOR2}) decreases measured reading achievement disadvantage for individual Black students by 0.097 points.

These are exactly the kinds of interpretations we are accustomed to making with the unstandardized coefficients of a multiple regression equation estimated with OLS. In the present instance, however, we are interpreting the fixed components of regression coefficients in a multilevel regression model.

We have also explained, however, that random coefficients merit a bit more attention, because they do in fact take different values across categories of the level-two grouping variable. As we have already seen, this can yield unsettlingly broad ranges for coefficient estimates. With 347 schools in the Kentucky data set, we see the meaning of random coefficient variability for the estimated intercept and for the slopes for GENDER1 and ETHNIC1.

With normally distributed random components and a large sample, the intervals constructed in Table 5.27 contain 95% of the intercepts and 95% of the GENDER1 and ETHNIC1 slopes for the 347 schools in the Kentucky data set (Raudenbush & Bryk, 2002). The width of the interval for the random coefficient for ETHNIC1 covers an unusually broad range, including both positive and negative values. This renders its interpretation much more ambiguous than we may have thought. Yes, it remains true that the unstandardized regression coefficients in multilevel regression are interpreted in the same way as in OLS regression. OLS coefficients, however, are invariably fixed and cannot exhibit the kind of group-to-group variability we see in Table 5.27.

The negative coefficient for $X_{ETHNIC2}$ * ETHNIC1 indicates that the reading achievement disadvantage for individual Black students is exacerbated as the percentage of students in a school who are Black increases. The negative coefficient for $X_{ETHNIC2}$ * GENDER1 indicates that the reading achievement advantage for individual female students diminishes as the percentage of students in a school who are Black increases. The

TABLE 5.27. Multilevel Reading Achievement Function; Variability with Respect to Random Coefficients

$$a_{\text{INTERCEPT}} - t_{.05}S_{a\text{INTERCEPT}} \text{ to } a_{\text{INTERCEPT}} + t_{.05}S_{a\text{INTERCEPT}}$$

$$49.249 - 1.960(7.911)^{1/2} \text{ to } 49.249 + 1.960(7.911)^{1/2}$$

$$46.436 \text{ to } 52.062$$

$$b_{\text{GENDER1}} - t_{.05}S_{b\text{GENDER1}} \text{ to } b_{\text{GENDER1}} + t_{.05}S_{b\text{GENDER1}}$$

$$8.207 - 1.960(1.866)^{1/2} \text{ to } 8.207 + 1.960(1.866)^{1/2}$$

$$6.841 \text{ to } 10.885$$

$$b_{\text{ETHNIC1}} - t_{.05}S_{b\text{ETHNIC1}} \text{ to } b_{\text{ETHNIC1}} + t_{.05}S_{b\text{ETHNIC1}}$$

$$-4.647 - 1.960(14.560)^{1/2} \text{ to } 4.647 + 1.960(14.560)^{1/2}$$

$$-11.946 \text{ to } 2.832$$

positive coefficient for X_{POOR2} * GENDER1 indicates that the reading achievement advantage for individual female students increases as the percentage of students in a school who are eligible for free/reduced cost lunch increases. Finally, the positive coefficient for X_{POOR2} * ETHNIC1 indicates that the reading achievement disadvantage for individual Black students is diminished as the percentage of students in a school who are eligible for free/reduced cost lunch increases

We have illustrated each of the cross-level interaction terms below in Figures 5.5 through 5.16. In each instance, to facilitate illustration we have divided the school-level variable into consecutive thirds. The unstandardized slope for each analysis is reported beneath its figure. Some of the depicted slope differences are dramatically obvious, while others are barely discernible. Taken together with the slope values included beneath each figure, however, each makes its point.

Beginning with Figures 5.5 through 5.7, we see that the slope representing the relationship between reading achievement and ethnicity becomes more negative as the percentage of students who are Black increases. The X_{ETHNIC2} * ETHNIC1 interaction term provides the most visually arresting graphs because of the dramatic change in slope values from one analysis to another.

Figures 5.8 through 5.10 tell us that the slopes representing the relationship between reading achievement and gender become less positive as the percentage of students who are Black increases.

Figures 5.11 through 5.13 display the slopes representing the changing relationship between reading achievement and gender, as the slope becomes more positive with increases in the percentage of students who are eligible for free/reduced cost lunch.

Finally, in Figures 5.14 through 5.16 we see the different slopes representing the changing relationship between reading achievement and ethnicity, as the slope becomes less negative with increases in the percentage of students who are eligible for free/reduced cost lunch.

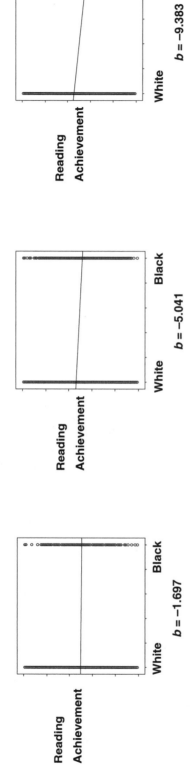

Reading
Achievement

White   Black

$b = -1.697$

FIGURE 5.5. X_{READING} by ETHNIC1, first third of X_{ETHNIC2}.

Reading
Achievement

White   Black

$b = -5.041$

FIGURE 5.6. X_{READING} by ETHNIC1, second third of X_{ETHNIC2}.

Reading
Achievement

White   Black

$b = -9.383$

FIGURE 5.7. X_{READING} by ETHNIC1, last third of X_{ETHNIC2}.

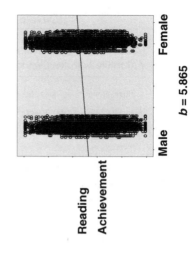

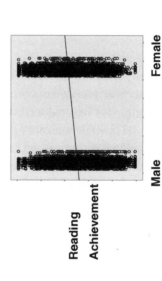

Reading
Achievement

Male   Female

$b = 8.534$

FIGURE 5.8. X_{READING} by GENDER1, first third of X_{ETHNIC2}.

Reading
Achievement

Male   Female

$b = 7.794$

FIGURE 5.9. X_{READING} by GENDER1, second third of X_{ETHNIC2}.

Reading
Achievement

Male   Female

$b = 5.865$

FIGURE 5.10. X_{READING} by GENDER1, last third of X_{ETHNIC2}.

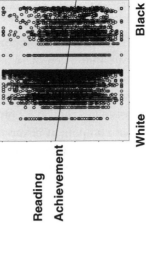

Reading
Achievement

Male   Female

$b = 6.687$

FIGURE 5.11. X_{READING} by GENDER1, first third of X_{POOR2}.

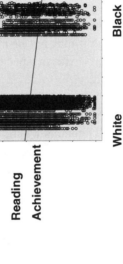

Reading
Achievement

Male   Female

$b = 7.310$

FIGURE 5.12. X_{READING} by GENDER1, second third of X_{POOR2}.

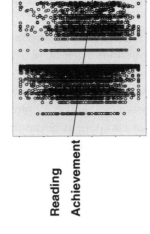

Reading
Achievement

Male   Female

$b = 8.145$

FIGURE 5.13. X_{READING} by GENDER1, last third of X_{POOR2}.

Reading
Achievement

White   Black

$b = -9.834$

FIGURE 5.14. X_{READING} by ETHNIC1, first third of X_{POOR2}.

Reading
Achievement

White   Black

$b = -8.853$

FIGURE 5.15. X_{READING} by ETHNIC1, second third of X_{POOR2}.

Reading
Achievement

White   Black

$b = -7.967$

FIGURE 5.16. X_{READING} by ETHNIC1, last third of X_{POOR2}.

Beyond all this, the random component variance and covariance estimates reported in Table 5.26 indicate that when these are compared with simpler specifications such as those presented in Tables 5.9 through 5.14, we are accounting for more of the variability in the random intercept and in the random slopes for GENDER1 and ETHNIC1. All random component estimates, however, remain statistically significant ($p < .000$), though none of the random component covariances is statistically significant.

Without contextual variables and cross-level interaction terms in the equation, two of the random component covariances (INTERCEPT1 by GENDER1 and GENDER1 by ETHNIC1) were statistically significant, as we see in Table 5.28. In our full multilevel model in Table 5.26, however, these have been explained.

5.11 COMPARING INTERPRETATIONS OF ALTERNATIVE SPECIFICATIONS

As we have acknowledged, there are many other plausible ways of specifying this multi-level model. Though it may not be manifest in the model in Table 5.24, we have learned that simplicity is a virtue in specifying multilevel regression models. Let's take this knowledge seriously.

Let's suppose that we decide to simplify the specification in Table 5.24 by assigning fixed slopes to GENDER1 (now $X_{GENDER1}$) and ETHNIC1 (now $X_{ETHNIC1}$). Only the intercept (INTERCEPT1) retains a random component, and it has the same predictors as before: $X_{GENDER2}$, $X_{ETHNIC2}$, X_{POOR2}, and X_{SIZE2}. In Table 5.29, we see that the primary consequences of this parsimonious respecification are elimination of the implied cross-level interaction terms and simplification of the error term.

Once again, a good part of the ease we felt in doing a pretty thorough simplification of this model stems from the absence of compelling theoretical or substantive reason for not doing so. Nevertheless, all the level-one and level-two explanatory variables included in Table 5.24 are still contained in our respecified multilevel regression model.

TABLE 5.28. Multilevel Reading Achievement Function; Contextual Factors and Cross-Level Interaction Terms Not Included; Unstructured; Estimates of Covariance Parameters

Parameter	Estimate	Std. error	Wald Z	Sig. level
Residual	316.459	2.083	151.943	.000
INTERCEPT1	20.923	2.140	9.776	.000
INTERCEPT1 by GENDER1	−2.448	0.968	−2.530	.011
GENDER1	3.051	0.865	3.528	.000
INTERCEPT1 by ETHNIC1	−2.659	2.258	−1.177	.239
GENDER1 by ETHNIC1	2.941	1.501	1.960	.005
ETHNIC1	23.022	4.948	4.653	.000

TABLE 5.29. Reading Achievement: An Interpretable Multilevel Regression Model, Simplified

Level-one model

$$Y = \beta_{0J} + (u_{0J} + e_{IJ})$$

Level-two model

$$\beta_{0J} = \gamma_{00} + \gamma_{01}X_{GENDER2} + \gamma_{02}X_{ETHNIC2} + \gamma_{03}X_{POOR2} + \gamma_{04}X_{SIZE2} + u_{0J}$$

Multilevel model

$$Y = \gamma_{00} + \gamma_{01}X_{GENDER1} + \gamma_{02}X_{ETHNIC1} + \gamma_{03}X_{GENDER2} + \gamma_{04}X_{ETHNIC2} + \gamma_{05}X_{POOR2} + \gamma_{06}X_{ETHNIC2} + (u_{0J} + e_{IJ})$$

Assigning fixed slopes rather than random ones (see Table 5.30), however, has eliminated all eight implied cross-level interaction terms, four of which we spent a great deal of time discussing and illustrating. *Since the deleted cross-level interaction terms were informative, we very well might have retained them, even though they are no longer implied.*

This is one of the few times we have seen a level-one model with just one random component, for the intercept. This accounts for the odd-looking level-one model, containing only the intercept and error term. Such models are commonplace in applications of multilevel regression (see, e.g., Goldstein et al., 1999).

In Table 5.31 we have retained the unstructured option for the variance components structure. However, with just one random component, the possibility of correlated random terms has been eliminated: There are no other random components with which

TABLE 5.30. Reading Achievement: An Interpretable Multilevel Regression Model, Simplified; Fixed Component Estimates

$$Y = 49.249 + 16.694X_{GENDER2} - 4.068X_{ETHNIC2} - 0.195X_{POOR2} - 0.737X_{SIZE2}$$
$$(0.311) \quad (4.725) \qquad (1.462) \qquad (0.012) \qquad (0.350)$$

$$+\ 7.418GENDER1 - 8.942ETHNIC1$$
$$(0.166) \qquad (0.279)$$

$$R_1^2 = 9.3\%$$
$$N_1 = 49,616$$
$$N_2 = 347$$

TABLE 5.31. Reading Achievement: An Interpretable Multilevel Regression Model, Simplified; Random Component Estimates

Parameter	Estimate	Std. error	Wald Z	Sig. level
Residual	318.946	2.091	152.560	.000
INTERCEPT1	7.672	2.890	8.623	.000

INTERCEPT1 might be correlated. Consequently, the results would be exactly the same if we had specified variance components as our covariance structure.

For the coefficients and standard errors that are common to Tables 5.25 and 5.31, there are only two substantial differences. First, the standard errors for GENDER1 and ETHNIC1 are much larger than the standard errors for $X_{GENDER1}$ and $X_{ETHNIC1}$. This is to be expected, since the random slopes for GENDER1 and ETHNIC1 correspond to the level-two sample size of 347, while the fixed slopes for $X_{GENDER1}$ and $X_{ETHNIC1}$ correspond to the level-one sample size of 49,616. Nevertheless, decisions as to statistical significance of the level-one gender and ethnicity variables are the same.

Of greater substantive interest, however, is the increase in absolute value, from –4.647 to –8.942, for the unstandardized slope of the ETHNIC1/$X_{ETHNIC1}$ independent variable. The sign and import of the coefficient are the same for both analyses: Black students, on average, do less well in reading achievement than White students. The magnitude of the relative difference between Blacks and Whites, however, is nearly twice as large when measured with a fixed slope rather than a random one. This is an especially interesting finding, since we have seen in Table 5.27 that the random coefficient for ETHNIC1 has a disturbingly broad range, including both positive and negative values. If its value were –8.942 instead of –4.647, the range would be a good deal narrower in comparison to the size of the coefficient.

Perhaps the most surprising result of comparing the two equations is the very small difference in the R_1^2. One might expect that deletion of eight cross-level interaction terms—four of them statistically significant and substantively interesting—would yield a greater decrease in the percentage reduction in errors of prediction than we have found, from 9.7% to 9.3%. Recall, however, that the primary function of cross-level interaction terms is explanation of variances for random components at level two, not explanation of the residual variance at level one.

At this point, when comparing the multilevel regression models in Tables 5.24 and 5.29, we might lean toward the simpler specification. Too little, it may understandably seem, has been gained by including the eight cross-level interaction terms. Recall, however, that when the additional contextual variables and cross-level interaction terms were not included, two of the random component covariances (INTERCEPT1 by GENDER1 and GENDER1 by ETHNIC1), were statistically significant. These same covariances had been accounted for when the contextual variables and cross-level interaction terms were in the equation. In addition, the random component variances, though still statistically significant, were a good deal smaller.

Of even greater substantive interest, we learned a great deal by including the cross-level interaction terms implied by our specification of random coefficients and contextual variables in Table 5.24, as we illustrated in Figures 5.5 through 5.16. Furthermore, the statistically significant slopes for cross-level interaction terms cannot be dismissed as substantively inconsequential artifacts of a large sample size. This is because creation of cross-level interaction terms makes the number of degrees of freedom used in testing a slope for statistical significance a function of sample size at level two—in this case, the 347 schools (SPSS, 2003).

TABLE 5.32. Information Criteria for Tables 5.24 and 5.30

Criterion	Simple model	Complex model
−2 log likelihood	402730.5	*402510.7*
Akaike's Information Criterion	402748.5	*402552.7*
Hurvich and Tsai's Criterion	402748.5	*402552.7*
Bozdogan's Criterion	402836.3	*402757.5*
Schwarz's Bayesian Criterion	402827.3	*402736.5*

Note. The smaller value for each measure is boldfaced and italicized.

Finally, adopting the more complex model specified in Table 5.24 is consistent with the deviance difference and information criteria values reported in Table 5.32. In this case, moreover, all information criteria are consistent with the deviance difference. Each of the smaller-is-better measures indicates that the more complex model provides the better fit. The model presented in Table 5.24 and the interpretation we have given it based on the results in Tables 5.25 and 5.26 hold for now.

$$\text{Deviance difference} = 402730.5 - 402510.7 = 219.8$$
$$df = 22 - 9 = 13$$

5.12   WHAT HAPPENED TO THE ERROR TERM?

As we have seen in numerous examples, when more random components are added to a multilevel model, the error term becomes more visually conspicuous. However, when we report our concrete estimates of the intercept and slopes in a multilevel regression equation, the error term disappears. We get estimates of random component variances and covariances, but that is all.

At first glance, this may be confusing. However, as with the less complex error term in OLS regression, none of the components of the error term is itself an intercept and none has a slope. In other words, it has no fixed components. As a result, there is nothing to report in the estimated final equation. So the error term exists explicitly as a component of a multilevel regression *model*, but, just as with OLS regression, we do not expect to see it as an estimated parameter in an *empirically derived equation*. It is of importance in evaluating the equation, however, as we have seen.

Understanding the composition of the error term is essential to understanding model specification. This is because each time we introduce an additional random term, we are specifying an additional *random component* of between-group variability. Each time we use the multilevel framework to introduce an additional random component, we do so with error. This additional error adds to the complexity of the error term.

By way of illustration, we compare two analyses of math achievement data from 12 randomly selected elementary schools in two contiguous counties in western West Virginia (Bickel & Howley, 2003). Three hundred thirty-one students were tested for their understanding of basic math concepts at the end of kindergarten. The data were analyzed using two different specifications of a multilevel regression model.

The first multilevel specification, presented in Table 5.33, uses math achievement at the end of kindergarten as measured by the Woodcock–Johnson 25 test of problem-solving skills as the dependent variable (Woodcock & Johnson, 1990). The only level-one independent variable is math achievement at the beginning of kindergarten, as measured by the same test. The intercept and the slope are permitted to vary from school to school. Variability in each random component is treated as a function of the aggregated school-level variable X_{HEAD2}, the proportion of students in each school who attended Head Start.

The second specification, presented in Table 5.34, uses the same math achievement dependent variable along with the same level-one independent variable and the same level-two contextual variable. However, only the intercept is treated as random, varying from school to school as a function of X_{HEAD2}. The individual-level slope remains fixed. With no random slopes, we have no cross-level interaction terms. The alternative multilevel regression models in Tables 5.33 and 5.34 illustrate the way in which the makeup of the error term varies with the number of random components.

TABLE 5.33. West Virginia Math Achievement with Random Intercept and One Random Slope

Level-one model

$$Y = \beta_{0J} + \beta_{1J}\text{PRETEST1} + e_{IJ}$$

Level-two model

$$\beta_{0J} = \gamma_{00} + \gamma_{01}X_{HEAD2} + u_{0J}$$

$$\beta_{1J} = \gamma_{10} + \gamma_{11}X_{HEAD2} + u_{1J}$$

Multilevel model

$$Y = \gamma_{00} + \gamma_{01}X_{HEAD2} + u_{0J} + (\gamma_{10} + \gamma_{11}X_{HEAD2} + u_{1J}) * \text{PRETEST1}$$

$$Y = \gamma_{00} + \gamma_{01}X_{HEAD2} + \gamma_{10}\text{PRETEST1} + \gamma_{11}X_{HEAD2} * \text{PRETEST1} + (u_{0J} + u_{1J} * \text{HEAD1} + e_{IJ})$$

TABLE 5.34. West Virginia Math Achievement with Random Intercept

Level-one model

$$Y = \beta_{0J} + \beta_{10}X_{PRETEST1} + e_{IJ}$$

Level-two model

$$\beta_{0J} = \gamma_{00} + \gamma_{01}X_{HEAD2} + u_{0J}$$

Multilevel model

$$Y = \gamma_{00} + \gamma_{01}X_{HEAD2} + \gamma_{10}X_{PRETEST1} + (u_{0J} + e_{IJ})$$

Suppose that we estimate the equation in Table 5.34 and get the concrete results reported in Tables 5.35 and 5.36. The only coefficient with a random component is the intercept. Its variance, however, is statistically nonsignificant whether or not the contextual variable is included in the equation.

As a result, we may decide to respecify again, formulating a model that has no random coefficients. Since there is no random component variability to explain, we also delete the contextual variable, X_{HEAD2}—though, again, we could have retained the contextual variable on substantive or theoretical grounds.

What would the resulting model look like? What would its error term look like? As we see in Table 5.37, we now have a conventional, inherently single-level OLS regression model. The error term is represented by level-one residuals. There are no other levels, so there are no higher-level residuals.

One of the lessons of this chapter, and of the entire book, is that theoretically thin disciplines fraught with conflict over proper interpretation of substantive findings may give multilevel regression analysts fits. Perhaps we have seen this clearly because we

TABLE 5.35. West Virginia Math Achievement: Fixed Component Estimates

$$Y = 17.981 + 0.582 X_{PRETEST1} - 2.120 X_{HEAD2}$$
$$\quad (0.435) \quad (0.040) \qquad (2.076)$$

$$R_1^2 = 42.4\%$$
$$N_1 = 331$$
$$N_2 = 12$$

TABLE 5.36. West Virginia Math Achievement: Estimates of Covariance Parameters

Parameter	Estimate	Std. error	Wald Z	Sig. level
Contextual variable included				
Residual	8.906	0.709	12.564	.000
INTERCEPT1	1.736	1.062	1.635	.122
Contextual variable not included				
Residual	8.926	0.711	12.542	.000
INTERCEPT1	2.082	1.268	1.641	.101

TABLE 5.37. West Virginia Math Achievement with No Random Components

$$Y_{IJ} = a + b_1 X_{PRETEST1} + (e_{IJ})$$

have made so many of our examples unduly complex, and have done so in an aridly empirical, even guesswork sort of way.

5.13 SUMMING UP

Throughout this presentation, we have made frequent use of the idea that multilevel modeling is but one of many correctives that constitute the voluminous literature on regression analysis. We can see this quite clearly if we think in terms of a hierarchy of procedures. We can begin with conventional OLS multiple regression analysis. This is a powerful statistical tool with one overriding virtue: Each independent variable serves as a control for all other independent variables.

Since so many questions of interest to researchers do not lend themselves to investigation through use of an experimental design, random assignment is not available to deal with confounding. With multiple regression, however, statistical control enables us to address confounding without random assignment. Our level of success is limited only by the quality of our data and by the substantive and theoretical knowledge available for regression model specification.

Regression analysis, however, brings with it a set of well-known assumptions— constraints that must be satisfied if multiple regression analysis is to work as advertised. One assumption too often overlooked is that of nonvarying coefficients. Nevertheless, if we are working with nested data, introducing within-group homogeneity, it is likely that intercepts and slopes will vary from group to group. In addition, standard errors will be deflated, and relationships among variables will be treated as if they are the same for all times and all places, when in fact they span a measurable, sometimes surprisingly substantial range of values.

Given this set of circumstances, random coefficient regression provides an obvious remedy. With alternative estimators that permit intercepts and slopes to vary from one group to another, we have a corrective for violation of the assumption of fixed coefficients.

Since random coefficient regression permits intercepts and slopes to vary, it is useful that it tells us how much they vary. By construing coefficients as having two components, fixed and random, we are provided with the tools to construct intervals that cover the context-to-context range of an intercept or slope. In addition, we may permit random components to vary together and measure their covariance.

While random coefficient regression is a useful corrective, it leaves random component variances and covariances unexplained. If we take another conceptual step and introduce contextual factors, however, we may find explanations for variability in random components and for covariances among random components. Contextual factors, moreover, may serve as moderator variables, explaining why associations among level-one variables sometimes vary from level to level of one or more group-level predictors.

Violation of the nonvarying coefficient assumption of OLS regression creates a need for random coefficient regression. Making best use of the additional information provided by random coefficient regression makes multilevel regression a valuable tool. The structured relationships among these closely related statistical procedures now seem almost obvious and certainly purposeful.

5.14 USEFUL RESOURCES

In spite of the difficulties presented by existing sources, those of us who would teach ourselves have to learn multilevel modeling somewhere. I encountered the texts below in the order in which they are listed. I doubt that a different ordering would have made learning this material any more or less frustrating.

Raudenbush, S., & Bryk, A. (2002) *Hierarchical Linear Models* (2nd ed.). Thousand Oaks, CA: Sage.
Snijders, T., & Bosker, R. (1999) *Multilevel Analysis*. Thousand Oaks, CA: Sage.
Kreft, I., & De Leeuw, J. (1998) *Introducing Multilevel Modeling*. Thousand Oaks, CA: Sage.
Heck, R., & Thomas, S. (2000) *An Introduction to Multilevel Modeling Techniques*. Mahwah, NJ: Erlbaum.
Hox, J. (2002) *Multilevel Analysis: Techniques and Applications*. Mahwah, NJ: Erlbaum.
Singer, J., & Willett, J. (2003) *Applied Longitudinal Data Analysis*. New York: Oxford University Press.
Longford, N. (1993) *Random Coefficient Models*. New York: Oxford University Press.
Goldstein, H. (1999) *Multilevel Statistical Models* (3rd ed.). London: Arnold.

The second edition of Raudenbush and Bryk's *Hierarchical Linear Models* is the best-known, most frequently cited text for multilevel analysis and growth modeling. In good part, this is due to the fact that the first edition (Bryk & Raudenbush, 1992) was the first text of its kind, and introduced specialized software, HLM, that the authors had developed for multilevel analysis.

The text is mathematically rigorous and is best suited for use by mathematically accomplished readers. Parallels between multilevel analysis and widely known statistical procedures such as multiple regression are deemphasized through presentation in a *very* condensed form. Applications are limited to use of HLM software. For most readers, this book is very difficult to use as a self-instructional tool; such difficulties are exacerbated for those lacking access to HLM software.

Snijder and Bosker's *Multilevel Analysis: An Introduction to Basic and Advanced Multilevel Modeling* is mathematically demanding but a bit more readable than Raudenbush and Bryk's text. Especially useful for beginners, however, would be a directory identifying essential material. Snijder and Bosker's text, too, fails to capitalize on parallels between multilevel analysis and better-known, more commonly used techniques. Snijder and Bosker's book covers a broad range of pertinent topics, and it is an excellent reference for readers already familiar with multilevel modeling. Again, however, for most readers it has limited value as a self-instructional text.

Kreft and De Leeuw's *Introducing Multilevel Modeling* was written to place only limited mathematical demands on readers. It includes an interesting and readable account of slopes as outcomes. However, in common with the other texts, it fails to accessibly develop parallels between multilevel modeling and more widely understood procedures. Instead, the authors' intent seems to be to highlight differences, perhaps to make the distinctiveness, virtues, and limitations of multilevel modeling clear to the reader.

Simple examples are presented for use with specialized MLn software. Models with more than two levels are not discussed. Growth models are mentioned in passing. This is a brief text that addresses some issues of importance in a Frequently Asked Questions section at the end of the book. It is not a comprehensive reference, but reads well the second time through. In addition, Kreft and De Leeuw give a good deal of attention to centering, something glossed over in most other texts.

Heck and Thomas's text, *An Introduction to Multilevel Modeling Techniques*, devotes most of its 209 pages to structural equation modeling and, earlier on, to an unusually elegant discussion of multiple regression analysis. The discussion of regression, however, is not closely tied to the comparatively brief treatment of multilevel analysis. While the joining of multilevel modeling, factor analysis, and structural equation modeling are discussed, the development of multilevel modeling itself gets less attention than one might expect from the title of the book.

Hox's *Multilevel Modeling: Techniques and Applications* covers an unusually broad range of topics, some of them fairly far removed from usual applications of multilevel analysis. Breadth of coverage, however, may have limited the amount of attention given to introducing readers to multilevel modeling as an extension of regression under specific circumstances. Hox's useful text is a bit more readable than most, but it does not develop parallels with well known techniques such as regression. It is, however, the first introductory text to acknowledge (though with just one sentence) that SPSS software now permits estimation and testing of multilevel models.

Singer and Willett's *Applied Longitudinal Data Analysis* is a recently published, oft-cited, well-written addition to the growing number of texts dealing with multilevel growth models. While this book has many virtues, including a useful website with instructive references to SAS, Stata, HLM, MLn, and SPSS, it was not written primarily as an introduction to multilevel analysis, with or without growth modeling. Instead, the emphasis throughout is on use of the multilevel framework in the study of change, and on survival analysis.

Other well-known texts include Nicholas Longford's *Random Coefficient Models* and Harvey Goldstein's *Multilevel Statistical Models*. Longford's development of concrete examples is better than that of other authors, and Goldstein's book, now in its third edition, is sometimes a useful reference. Both, however, make substantial mathematical demands on the reader, and to my knowledge neither is commonly used as an introductory text.

6

Giving OLS Regression Its Due

6.1   CHAPTER INTRODUCTION

Without question, random coefficient regression analysis and multilevel regression analysis have an important place in a broad range of disciplines. It can be disheartening, nevertheless, to have familiar statistical procedures such as OLS regression found wanting—sometimes dismissed as methodologically deficient, conceptually naïve, and simply old-fashioned. Furthermore, there is nothing new about methodological faddishness in the social and behavioral sciences (Coser, 1975). Of course, ongoing methodological advances are an integral part of the process of improving the quality of social and behavioral scientific work; even legitimate gains, however, can engender a sense of obsolescence among experienced researchers.

Put yourself in the 1960s and imagine being a veteran academician with a scholarly interest in occupational stratification and status attainment. In the middle of your career, Blau and Duncan (1967) publish *The American Occupational Structure*, a methodologically state-of-the-art, immediately influential account of social mobility in the United States. Among the monograph's strengths is application of manifest variable path analysis, a causal modeling tool borrowed from population genetics but new to the social sciences.

Blau and Duncan construct and test their relatively simple path models competently, of course. For most readers, however, the path models are obscure. It is hard to see that path analysis is firmly grounded in straightforward fashion in a statistical procedure that most researchers use and understand—OLS multiple regression analysis (Wright, 1960). Nevertheless, by the early 1970s just about every empirical piece appearing in major social science journals uses path analysis. Feelings of professional obsolescence and disaffection are made worse.

When Duncan (1975) publishes his widely adopted textbook on path modeling, most of it is devoted to fairly complex nonrecursive models of the sort not usually encountered by applied social science researchers. From the preface on, moreover, the tone of the book is admonitory—as if to say, "This is *so* basic, and you are *so* far behind your colleagues in other disciplines."

Feelings of obsolescence are reinforced by capable authors such as Hayduk (1987), who warn readers that understanding Duncan's work means understanding the "methods of the 1970s." But sadly, this knowledge does not provide a solid foundation for understanding causal modeling for the 1980s and beyond.

The quality of the work by Blau, Duncan, and Hayduk ranges from exemplary to estimable. Whatever the authors' contributions and intentions might have been, however, each added to a subtle but pervasive underestimation of the value of standard, widely used statistical tools; this is especially true with respect to OLS multiple regression analysis. In much the same way, accounts of multilevel analysis have seemed summarily dismissive of OLS regression. In spite of our "It's just regression!" disclaimer, the material presented so far may make us as culpable as anyone else.

One way to redeem ourselves is to give OLS regression a chance to show what it can do in addressing a complex, interesting, and timely issue at length. *At that point*, we can ask if multilevel analysis has anything to add. We can then correctly treat multilevel regression as a source of additional analytical opportunities, rather than a series of methodological traps waiting to be sprung on those who are naïve, unsuspecting, or over the hill.

6.2   AN EXTENDED EXERCISE WITH COUNTY-LEVEL DATA

We have made frequent use of a U.S. Bureau of the Census data set containing measures on a broad range of demographic variables for the year 2000 for 3140 U.S. counties. The county is the unit of analysis, with counties nested in states (Annie E. Casey Foundation, 2004). Conveniently, following the U.S. presidential election of November 2, 2004, *USA Today* published county-level election results for all states except Alaska (*USA Today*, 2004). Combining data from these two sources permits us to do county-level voting behavior analyses of a hotly contested presidential election.

The following example, spanning discussion of Tables 6.1 to 7.10, is unusually long. Its purpose, however, merits sustained effort. We hope to illustrate and exhaust the power and versatility of OLS multiple regression, and *only then* ask if multilevel regression analysis has anything else to offer.

6.3   TENTATIVE SPECIFICATION OF AN OLS REGRESSION MODEL

For this extended example, the dependent variable at the county level is the percentage of voters who voted for George W. Bush (Y_{BUSH}). For county-level voting behavior data, the distribution has an unexpectedly broad range, from 0.16% to 95.53%; as we see in Figure 6.1, it is approximately normal, though slightly skewed to the left.

Selection of independent variables poses familiar problems in regression model specification. Which explanatory factors should be used? What is available in our data set? Which proxies are best suited to serve as substitutes for missing variables that we really want? How can we best operationalize our choices? And what functional forms should be employed? Whether an analyst is using OLS regression, multilevel regression, or any other creditable statistical procedure, questions such as this are unavoidable.

Since the unit of analysis is the county, moreover, regression model specification is complicated by the need to avoid unwitting errors in ecological inference. With regard to selection of independent variables and interpretation of results, the ecological fallacy is an ever-present source of difficulty (Blalock, 1982). Avoiding unwitting inferences about individual behavior from county-level analyses is an important reason why we will not include gender composition among our explanatory variables.

Given the nature of our data set and a desire to keep the analysis from becoming unduly complex, we have chosen nine county-level independent variables for use in a preliminary OLS multiple regression analysis.

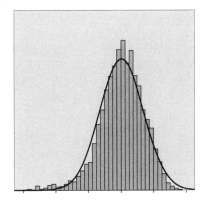

Mean = 60.41%
Standard Deviation = 13.39%

FIGURE 6.1. Percentage voting for Bush.

Independent Variables

X_{FAMILY}

We have used percentage of the population living in a traditional nuclear family as a variable in previous examples, and in the present application it is defined as the percentage of residents living in a household with husband, wife, and at least one child under age 18. We are trying to capture the journalistically pervasive but nebulous notion of **traditional family values** (Thompson, 2000), and we will use X_{FAMILY} as a proxy. We see in Figure 6.2 that the X_{FAMILY} variable very closely approximates a normal distribution.

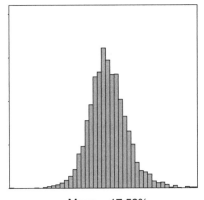

Mean = 17.52%
Standard Deviation = 3.30%

FIGURE 6.2. Percentage living in traditional nuclear family.

X_{YOUTH}

Throughout the 2004 campaign, the Democratic Party sought to tap the so-called *youth vote*, especially among those just over 18 who were voting for the first time (MoveOn.org, 2005). Supporters of John Kerry sought to kindle a temperate form of youthful idealism and bring young voters into the Democratic fold (McDonough, 2004). In our analysis, the prospective youth vote is the percentage of each county's residents ages 18–24. The X_{YOUTH} variable is skewed sharply to the right, as we see in Figure 6.3, but taking natural logarithms produces a very close approximation to a normal distribution, as displayed in Figure 6.4 (Fox, 1997).

X_{INCOME}

Students of voting behavior routinely include a standard set of demographic measures in analyses of election outcomes (Beck, Dalton, & Greene, 2001). This applies whether the unit of analysis is the individual or a geographical unit such as the county (Anatolyev, 2002). Conspicuous among these measures is family income, which we capture as a county-level median expressed in units of $1000. Income and vote for Republican candidates have historically been positively associated (Niemi & Weisberg, 2001). With the advent of the so-called Reagan revolution and the emergence of right-wing populism, however, this relationship has become uncertain (Ilbo, 2000).

Income variables are typically logged in empirical applications, but we do not log X_{INCOME} here for two reasons. First, the rightward skew of X_{INCOME} is modest, as we see in Figure 6.5. In addition, logging X_{INCOME} causes unanticipated multicollinearity problems, indicated by a condition index of just over 108.

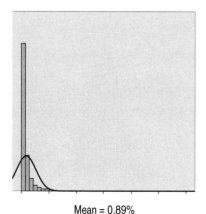

Mean = 0.89%
Standard Deviation = 1.74%

FIGURE 6.3. Percentage of county residents ages 18–24.

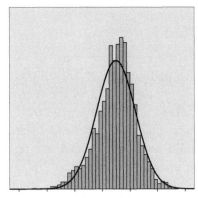

Mean = 1.02
Standard Deviation = 1.40

FIGURE 6.4. Percentage of county residents ages 18–24, logged.

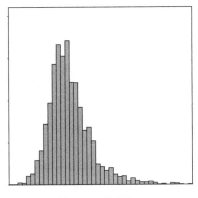

Mean = 42.140
Standard Deviation = 9.885

FIGURE 6.5. Median family income.

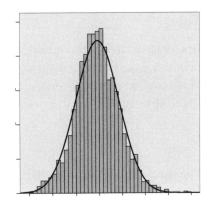

Mean = 29.22%
Standard Deviation = 9.47%

FIGURE 6.6. Percentage of county population ages 18–24 without high school diploma.

$X_{EDUCATION}$

Historically, better-educated voters have tended to vote for Democrats (Weisberg & Wilcox, 2004). However, much as with income, the past 25 years have introduced ambiguity into this traditionally reliable relationship (U.S. Politics, 2004). Our proxy for county-level educational attainment is crude: percentage of residents ages 18–24 who do not have a high school diploma. Given the limitations of our data set, we are defining educational attainment in deficit terms. This variable too has a surprisingly broad range, from 13.0% to 69.5%, and it approximates a normal distribution, as seen in Figure 6.6.

X_{BLACK}

Ethnicity can be categorized in a variety of ways, depending on time and place (Mayer, 2002). While ethnicity is often confounded with income, education, and family structure, ethnicity has independent political consequences, with members of most ethnic minority groups tending to vote for Democrats (cf. Conley, 1999).

In the United States today, an informative and manageable set of ethnic categories is White, Black, Hispanic, Asian, and Native American. In our analysis, Whites are represented by implication. The skewed-to-the-right variable X_{BLACK} is explicitly incorporated and is measured as the percentage of each county's residents who are Black.

$X_{HISPANIC}$

As X_{BLACK} does, $X_{HISPANIC}$ (the percentage of each county's residents classified as Hispanic) varies sharply from county to county, with a rightward skew.

X_{ASIAN}

Dramatic variability, though with a sharp rightward skew, also characterizes the distribution of X_{ASIAN} (the percentage of each county's residents classified as Asian). While 34% of all counties reported X_{ASIAN} values of zero, the maximum value for this variable is large, just over 54%.

X_{NATIVE}

The percentage of each county's residents who are Native American (X_{NATIVE}) is zero for 5% of all counties. Only 10% have an X_{NATIVE} value of at least 15%. Nevertheless, X_{NATIVE} has a large maximum value of 94%.

As with X_{BLACK}, $X_{HISPANIC}$, and X_{ASIAN}, the sharp rightward skew of X_{NATIVE} suggests that logging might be useful (Fox, 1997). Even with zero-valued entries, this could be done by first adding one to each county's value on each of the ethnicity variables (cf. Wooldridge, 2002). Logging, however, would still leave heavy concentrations of cases in the lowest-valued categories. We have concluded, therefore, that in their nonlogged form the ethnicity measures give us about as much information as we can get. By way of illustration, the distributions of X_{BLACK} without and with logging are reported in Figures 6.7 and 6.8, respectively. The fact that little or nothing is gained from logging seems self-evident, and applies with even greater force to the other ethnicity measures.

X_{RURAL}

Finally, the broad swath of Republican-voting states across the middle of the nation intimates that rural residents were more likely to vote for Bush than nonrural resi-

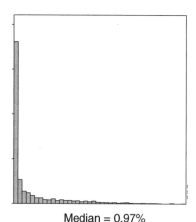

Median = 0.97%
Mean = 7.74%
Standard Deviation = 13.61%

FIGURE 6.7. Distribution of X_{BLACK}.

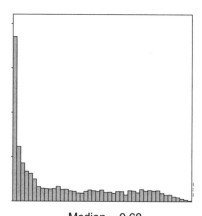

Median = 0.68
Mean = 1.24
Standard Deviation = 1.29

FIGURE 6.8. Distribution of X_{BLACK}, logged.

dents. We have already made frequent use of the urban–rural continuum used to assign county-level scores ranging from 1 to 9, with higher scores representing more rural areas (ERS, 2004b). We will use this continuum to determine if place of residence is related to Y_{BUSH}. We illustrated this irregular, very roughly horizontal distribution in Figure 3.2.

6.4   PRELIMINARY REGRESSION RESULTS

With complete data for 3090 of the 3140 counties, OLS multiple regression results are as reported in Table 6.1. Standard errors are in parentheses. Dividing each regression coefficient by its standard error yields values that exceed the critical t value ($p < .001$) for all coefficients. Because the county is the unit of analysis, interpretation of the OLS regression results is straightforward.

1. Each 1% increase in the number of county residents living in a traditionally structured family corresponds, on average, to a 1.482-point increase in percent voting for Bush.
2. Each 1% increase in the percentage of county residents between the ages of 18 and 24 corresponds, on average, to a 1.855-point increase in percent voting for Bush. Remember that this independent variable has been logged, modifying its interpretation as indicated.
3. Each $1000 increase in county median family income corresponds, on average, to a 0.242-point decrease in percent voting for Bush.
4. Each 1% increase in the number of county residents ages 18–24 who are not high school graduates corresponds, on average, to a 0.188-point increase in percent voting for Bush.
5. Each 1% increase in the number of county residents who are Black corresponds, on average, to a 0.224-point decrease in percent voting for Bush.
6. Each 1% increase in the number of county residents who are Hispanic corresponds, on average, to a 0.176-point decrease in percent voting for Bush.
7. Each 1% increase in the number of county residents who are Asian corresponds, on average, to a 0.376-point decrease in percent voting for Bush.

TABLE 6.1. Preliminary OLS Analysis of County-Level Percentage Voting for Bush

$Y_{BUSH} = 46.945 + 1.482X_{FAMILY} + 1.855X_{LNYOUTH} - 0.242X_{INCOME} + 0.188X_{EDUCATION} - 0.224X_{BLACK}$
$\quad\quad\quad (1.964) \quad (0.075) \quad\quad\quad (0.222) \quad\quad\quad\quad (0.029) \quad\quad\quad\quad (0.024) \quad\quad\quad\quad (0.017)$

$\quad\quad - 0.176X_{HISPANIC} - 0.376X_{ASIAN} - 0.409X_{NATIVE} - 0.440X_{RURAL}$
$\quad\quad\quad (0.019) \quad\quad\quad (0.093) \quad\quad (0.031) \quad\quad\quad (0.112)$

$$R^2 = 37.6\%$$
$$N = 3090$$

8. Each 1% increase in the number of county residents who are Native American corresponds, on average, to a 0.409-point decrease in percent voting for Bush.

9. Each one-level increase in the direction of increasing rurality on the urban–rural continuum corresponds, on average, to a 0.440-point decrease in percent voting for Bush.

6.5   SURPRISE RESULTS AND POSSIBLE VIOLATION OF OLS ASSUMPTIONS

We have acknowledged the emergence of right-wing populism during the last three decades (Mayer, 2000). Nevertheless, the negative X_{INCOME} coefficient in our county-level data is a surprise. A prudent response to unexpected findings is reexamination of the regression analysis with respect to the usual OLS assumptions.

Y_{BUSH} by X_{INCOME}

Upon visual examination of a scatterplot, the relationship between Y_{BUSH} and X_{INCOME} turns out to be curvilinear at the bivariate level. The relationship is positive but decelerating until X_{INCOME} reaches a value of \$41,440, and then slopes downward in accelerating fashion (Wooldridge, 2002, p. 191). R^2 for the simple linear regression is 0.6%, while the same value with a quadratic functional form is 6.6%. Figure 6.9 provides a visual comparison of efforts to capture the relationship between Y_{BUSH} and X_{INCOME}, using linear and quadratic relationships.

Even sharp departures from linearity *may* be due to failure to include needed independent variables in a regression model (Kennedy, 1998; Wooldridge, 2002; see also the discussion of the RESET test in Gujarati, 2006). With our tentatively specified complement of controls in place, as in Table 6.1, the Y_{BUSH}-by-X_{INCOME} relationship is approximately linearized, as is evident from examination of Figure 6.10.

When Y_{BUSH} and X_{INCOME} are both purged of variability due to the remaining independent variables, the R^2 value for the simple linear regression of Y_{BUSH} on X_{INCOME} is

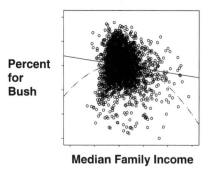

Median Family Income

FIGURE 6.9. Y_{BUSH} by X_{INCOME}, bivariate.

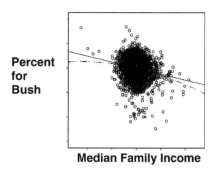

Median Family Income

FIGURE 6.10. Y_{BUSH} by X_{INCOME}, adjusted.

3.5%, and the R^2 value for the same relationship with quadratic functional form is 3.6%—a statistically nonsignificant difference (cf. Freckleton, 2002). The negative *linear* relationship between Y_{BUSH} and X_{INCOME} is retained, with departures from linearity at the bivariate level attributed to specification error in the form of excluded independent variables.

6.6   CURVILINEAR RELATIONSHIPS: Y_{BUSH} BY X_{BLACK}, $X_{HISPANIC}$, AND X_{NATIVE}

Nevertheless, examination of partial plots for all relationships makes clear that even with the full complement of independent variables, the relationships between Y_{BUSH} and three of our four measures of ethnicity (X_{BLACK}, $X_{HISPANIC}$, and X_{NATIVE}) remain curvilinear. As values of the ethnicity variables increase, relationships with percent voting for Bush curve sharply downward (see Figures 6.11, 6.12, and 6.13).

6.7   QUADRATIC FUNCTIONAL FORM

One of the virtues of OLS regression is that it is well suited to dealing with curvilinear relationships (Halcoussis, 2005). In this instance, quadratic functions have been estimated, creating a *polynomial* regression equation (Pedhazur & Schmelkin, 1991). Polynomial regression is just another useful extension of OLS regression, modifying it to deal better with our complex social world.

Use of quadratic functional forms, however, raises the issue of multicollinearity. Even though X_{BLACK}, $X_{HISPANIC}$, and X_{NATIVE} are not *linearly* related

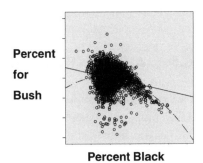

Percent Black

FIGURE 6.11. Y_{BUSH} by X_{BLACK}, adjusted.

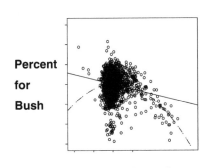

Percent Hispanic

FIGURE 6.12. Y_{BUSH} by $X_{HISPANIC}$, adjusted.

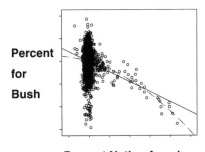

Percent Native American

FIGURE 6.13. Y_{BUSH} by X_{NATIVE}, adjusted.

TABLE 6.2. A Respecified OLS Model of Percentage Voting for Bush

Y_{BUSH} = −101.386 + 1.541X_{FAMILY} + 3.161$X_{LNYOUTH}$ − 0.173X_{INCOME} + 0.002$X_{EDUCATION}$
    (27.329)   (0.083)   (0.166)   (0.033)   (0.024)

    − 0.004X_{BLACK} − 0.009$X_{HISPANIC}$ − 0.556X_{ASIAN} − 0.001X_{NATIVE} − 0.359X_{RURAL} − 0.003X_{BLACK}^2
    (0.000)   (0.001)   (0.145)   (0.001)   (0.100)   (0.000)

    + 0.004$X_{HISPANIC}^2$ + 0.004X_{NATIVE}^2
    (0.000)   (0.055)

$$R^2 = 43.8\%$$
$$N = 3090$$

Note. Standard errors have been rounded to three decimals. Those represented by "0.000" represent extremely small values, and each corresponds to a statistically significant regression coefficient.

to their squared values, bivariate correlations among them are quite large, with r values ranging from 0.909 to 0.928.

To make approximate corrections for multicollinearity, X_{BLACK}, $X_{HISPANIC}$, and X_{NATIVE}, along with their squared values, have been centered with respect to their grand means, as have all the other independent variables. Mean centering diminishes the bivariate correlations between the ethnicity variables and their squared terms, but the associations remain strong, ranging from 0.783 to 0.863. Fortunately, our sample size is large.

6.8   A RESPECIFIED OLS REGRESSION MODEL

OLS regression results, with relationships respecified as just described, are reported in Table 6.2. All unstandardized regression coefficients except those for $X_{EDUCATION}$ and X_{NATIVE} are statistically significant. Without assigning undue importance to the R^2 summary statistic (Yuan & Loi, 1996), we can see that the increase in the value of this conventional goodness-of-fit measure from Table 6.1 to Table 6.2 is substantial, going from 37.6% to 43.9%.

For all variables except those representing percent of county residents who are Black, Hispanic, or Native American, the signs, approximate values, and substantive import of the unstandardized regression coefficients are as reported in Table 6.1. The variables X_{BLACK}, $X_{HISPANIC}$, and X_{NATIVE} and their squared values, however, require additional interpretation.

6.9   INTERPRETING QUADRATIC RELATIONSHIPS

In its simplest form, a quadratic relationship is expressed as in Table 6.3. More concretely for the relationship between Y_{BUSH} and X_{BLACK}, and with borrowing of the coefficient estimates reported in Table 6.2, the quadratic relationship is expressed as in Table 6.4.

TABLE 6.3. Specifying a Quadratic Relationship

$$Y = a + b_1X_1 + b_2X_1^2$$

TABLE 6.4. Y_{BUSH} by X_{BLACK} in Quadratic Form

$$Y_{BUSH} = a - 0.004X_{BLACK} - 0.003X_{BLACK}^2$$

TABLE 6.5. Making Sense of Quadratic Relationships: Y_{BUSH} by X_{BLACK}

Coefficient values		
X_{BLACK}	X_{BLACK}^2	Rate of change
−0.004	−0.003	$(-0.004) + (2 * [-0.003 * X_{BLACK}]) = $ Total

Variable values	
10	−0.004 − 0.060 = −0.064
20	−0.004 − 0.120 = −0.124
30	−0.004 − 0.180 = −0.184
40	−0.004 − 0.240 = −0.244
50	−0.004 − 0.300 = −0.304
60	−0.004 − 0.360 = −0.364
70	−0.004 − 0.420 = −0.424
80	−0.004 − 0.480 = −0.484
90	−0.004 − 0.540 = −0.544

Working with the information in Table 6.4, we can illustrate a simple procedure for making sense of quadratic relationships in OLS regression (Bickel & Howley, 2000). Setting up Table 6.5 is not difficult. Just insert coefficient values where indicated, and do the specified arithmetic for rate of change with illustrative values of the independent variable—in this instance, X_{BLACK}. Simply put, we multiply each illustrative value by the coefficient corresponding to X_{BLACK}, and then adjust for curvilinearity using the coefficient for X_{BLACK}^2. In this way, we start with the best-fitting linear relationship, and then make the relationship more precise by introducing departures from linearity. The values reported are sometimes referred to as *marginal increments* (Hayashi, 2000).

Via the same procedure, the quadratic relationships between Y_{BUSH} and $X_{HISPANIC}$ and Y_{BUSH} and X_{NATIVE} are clarified in Tables 6.6 to 6.9.

6.10 NONADDITIVITY AND INTERACTION TERMS

We have just seen that several quadratic relationships can be handled in the same conventional multiple regression equation in an informative and succinct manner. The

TABLE 6.6. Y_{BUSH} by $X_{HISPANIC}$ in Quadratic Form

$$Y_{BUSH} = a - 0.009X_{HISPANIC} + 0.004X_{HISPANIC}^2$$

TABLE 6.7. Making Sense of Quadratic Relationships: Y_{BUSH} by $X_{HISPANIC}$

Coefficient values		
$\underline{X_{HISPANIC}}$	$\underline{X_{HISPANIC}^2}$	$\underline{\text{Rate of change}}$
–0.009	0.004	$(-0.009) + (2 * [0.004 * X_{HISPANIC}]) = \text{Total}$

Variable values	
10	–0.009 + 0.080 = 0.071
20	–0.009 + 0.160 = 0.151
30	–0.009 + 0.240 = 0.231
40	–0.009 + 0.320 = 0.319
50	–0.009 + 0.400 = 0.391
60	–0.009 + 0.480 = 0.471
70	–0.009 + 0.560 = 0.551
80	–0.009 + 0.640 = 0.631
90	–0.009 + 0.720 = 0.711

TABLE 6.8. Y_{BUSH} by X_{NATIVE} in Quadratic Form

$$Y_{BUSH} = a + 0.004X_{NATIVE}^2$$

TABLE 6.9. Making Sense of Quadratic Relationships: Y_{BUSH} by X_{NATIVE}

Coefficient values		
$\underline{X_{NATIVE}}$	$\underline{X_{NATIVE}^2}$	$\underline{\text{Rate of change}}$
N.S.	0.004	$(2 * [0.004 * X_{NATIVE}]) = \text{Total}$

Variable values	
10	— + 0.004 = 0.004
20	— + 0.008 = 0.008
30	— + 0.012 = 0.012
40	— + 0.016 = 0.016
50	— + 0.020 = 0.020
60	— + 0.024 = 0.024
70	— + 0.028 = 0.028
80	— + 0.032 = 0.032
90	— + 0.036 = 0.036

assumption of linearity was violated, but a corrective in the form of polynomial regression was readily available.

The same is true of the assumption of additivity. This is another strength of OLS regression. By way of illustration, our analysis of county-to-county variability in percent voting for Bush offers interesting opportunities for studying same-level interaction effects or departures from additivity.

Though we are now speaking in terms of relationships that vary, in this instance we are *not* suggesting that relationships vary from state to state in a way that necessitates use of a random coefficient regression model. We are interested instead in the possibility that the relationship between Y_{BUSH} and one or more independent variables varies from level to level of another independent variable. So long as the moderator variable is a dichotomy or is measured at the interval or ratio level, this is a phenomenon that OLS regression easily accommodates (Jaccard et al., 1990).

As a concrete example, living in a traditional nuclear family commonly brings the economic advantage of two breadwinners (Lareau, 2003). This suggests that even at the county level, the relationship between Y_{BUSH} and X_{FAMILY} may vary from level to level of X_{INCOME}. Similarly, urban and rural environments may have different consequences for variability in family structure and income. It may be that the relationships between Y_{BUSH} and X_{FAMILY} and Y_{BUSH} and X_{INCOME} vary from level to level of X_{RURAL}.

As with so many of the specification decisions we have made throughout this presentation, the rationale for each of the interaction terms we plan to introduce is more speculative than we would like. Nevertheless, the posited interactions are not without commonsense justification, and they permit us to illustrate the strength of OLS multiple regression analysis in dealing with departures from additivity.

Therefore, we have added three same-level multiplicative interaction terms— $X_{INCOME} * X_{FAMILY}$, $X_{RURAL} * X_{FAMILY}$, and $X_{RURAL} * X_{INCOME}$—to our OLS multiple regression equation. To minimize multicollinearity, all variables have been centered with respect to their overall means before creation of the interaction terms.

TABLE 6.10. A Further Respecified OLS Model of Percentage Voting for Bush

$$Y_{BUSH} = -100.820 + 1.553X_{FAMILY} + 3.111X_{LNYOUTH} - 0.122X_{INCOME} + 0.010X_{EDUCATION} - 0.004X_{BLACK}$$
$$(27.351) \quad (0.084) \qquad (0.166) \qquad (0.036) \qquad (0.024) \qquad (0.000)$$

$$- 0.009X_{HISPANIC} - 0.456X_{ASIAN} + 0.001X_{NATIVE} - 0.283X_{RURAL} - 0.003X_{BLACK}^2 + 0.004X_{HISPANIC}^2$$
$$(0.001) \qquad (0.088) \qquad (0.001) \qquad (0.102) \qquad (0.000) \qquad (0.000)$$

$$- 0.331X_{NATIVE}^2 + 0.027X_{INCOME} * X_{FAMILY} + 0.030X_{RURAL} * X_{FAMILY} + 0.007X_{RURAL} * X_{INCOME}$$
$$(0.055) \qquad (0.023) \qquad\qquad (0.008) \qquad\qquad (0.008)$$

$$R^2 = 44.1\%$$
$$N = 3090$$

Note. Standard errors have been rounded to three decimals. Those represented by "0.000" represent extremely small values, and each corresponds to a statistically significant regression coefficient.

6.11 FURTHER RESPECIFICATION OF THE REGRESSION MODEL

Table 6.10 shows us the OLS regression results obtained by adding the interaction terms $X_{INCOME} * X_{FAMILY}$, $X_{RURAL} * X_{FAMILY}$, and $X_{RURAL} * X_{INCOME}$ to the equation in Table 6.2. Dividing coefficients by standard errors, we see that one of these interaction terms, $X_{RURAL} * X_{FAMILY}$, has a statistically significant coefficient. This indicates that as places of residence become more rural, the positive relationship between Y_{BUSH} and X_{FAMILY} is increased: For each one-level increase in X_{RURAL}, a 1% increase in X_{FAMILY} corresponds, on average, to an additional 0.030-point increase in Y_{BUSH}.

6.12 CLARIFYING OLS INTERACTION EFFECTS

We can clarify the meaning of interaction effects by using basically the same procedure we used with quadratic relationships. In its simplest form, a multiplicative interaction term with two variables can be represented as in Table 6.11. In the case of the interaction term involving X_{RURAL} and X_{FAMILY}, this set of relationships is made concrete in Table 6.12.

As we have just said, this means that for every one-level increase in X_{RURAL}, each 1-point increase in X_{FAMILY} corresponds, on average, to a 0.030-point increase in Y_{BUSH}. A procedure for saying the same thing more instructively is illustrated in Table 6.13. This table too is easy to construct. Just insert main-effect and interaction-effect coefficients in the table as indicated, and then introduce illustrative values of the moderator variable.

We may interpret Table 6.13 much as we did the tables representing quadratic relationships. The main-effect coefficient represents our best estimate of the relationship between Y_{BUSH} and X_{FAMILY} **without additivity**. The interaction term enables us to specify the effect of departures from additivity. Inserting coefficients from Table 6.12 into Table 6.13 enables us to better explain the interaction effect involving X_{RURAL} as the moderator variable, Y_{BUSH} as the dependent variable, and X_{FAMILY} as the independent variable. This shifting pattern of relationships is illustrated in Figures 6.14 through 6.16, with slope estimates ranging from 1.476 to 1.852 to 1.992.

TABLE 6.11. Multiplicative Interaction Term

$$Y = a + b_1X_1 + b_2X_2 + b_3X_1 * X_2$$

TABLE 6.12. X_{RURAL} Moderates Y_{BUSH} by X_{FAMILY}

$$Y_{BUSH} = a - 0.283X_{RURAL} + 1.553X_{FAMILY} + 0.030X_{RURAL} * X_{FAMILY}$$

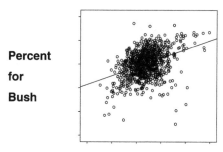

Percent Living in Traditional Nuclear Family

b = 1.476

FIGURE 6.14. Y_{BUSH} by X_{FAMILY} for urban categories of X_{RURAL}

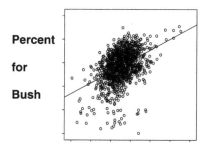

Percent Living in Traditional Nuclear Family

b = 1.853

FIGURE 6.15. Y_{BUSH} by X_{FAMILY} for middle categories of X_{RURAL}.

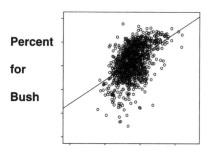

Percent Living in Traditional Nuclear Family

b = 1.992

FIGURE 6.16. Y_{BUSH} by X_{FAMILY} for rural categories of X_{RURAL}.

TABLE 6.13. Making Sense of Interaction Effects: X_{RURAL} Moderates Y_{BUSH} by X_{FAMILY}

Coefficient values		
Main effect	Interaction effect	Rate of change
+1.553	0.030	$(+1.553) + (0.030 * X_{RURAL}) = $ Total
Moderator variable values		
1		+1.553 + 0.030 = +1.583
2		+1.553 + 0.060 = +1.613
3		+1.553 + 0.090 = +1.643
4		+1.553 + 0.120 = +1.673
5		+1.553 + 0.150 = +1.703
6		+1.553 + 0.180 = +1.733
7		+1.553 + 0.210 = +1.763
8		+1.553 + 0.240 = +1.793
9		+1.553 + 0.270 = +1.823

6.13 INTERPRETING RESULTS FOR THE RESPECIFIED OLS REGRESSION EQUATION FOR COUNTY-LEVEL DATA

Given the constraints of secondary analysis with county-level data, as well as the virtues and limitations of OLS regression, the results reproduced in Table 6.14 (from Table 6.10) provide an interesting statistical account of relationships that contributed to determining the outcome of the 2004 U.S. presidential election. These results can be interpreted as follows:

1. Each 1% increase in the number of county residents living in a traditionally structured family corresponds, on average, to a 1.553-point increase in percent voting for Bush.
2. Each 1% increase in the number of county residents between the ages of 18 and 24 corresponds, on average, to a 3.111-point increase in percent voting for Bush.

TABLE 6.14. (Table 6.10, Reproduced). A Further Respecified OLS Model of Percentage Voting for Bush

$$Y_{BUSH} = -100.820 + 1.553X_{FAMILY} + 3.111X_{LNYOUTH} - 0.122X_{INCOME} + 0.010X_{EDUCATION} - 0.004X_{BLACK}$$
$$\quad\ (27.351)\ (0.084) \qquad\quad (0.166) \qquad\quad (0.036) \qquad\quad (0.024) \qquad\quad (0.000)$$

$$\quad - 0.009X_{HISPANIC} - 0.456X_{ASIAN} + 0.001X_{NATIVE} - 0.283X_{RURAL} - 0.003X_{BLACK}^2 + 0.004X_{HISPANIC}^2$$
$$\qquad (0.001) \qquad\quad (0.088) \qquad\quad (0.001) \qquad\quad (0.102) \qquad\quad (0.000) \qquad\quad (0.000)$$

$$\quad + 0.004X_{NATIVE}^2 + 0.027X_{INCOME} * X_{FAMILY} + 0.030X_{RURAL} * X_{FAMILY} + 0.007X_{RURAL} * X_{INCOME}$$
$$\qquad (0.000) \qquad\quad (0.023) \qquad\qquad\qquad (0.008) \qquad\qquad\qquad (0.008)$$

$$R^2 = 44.1\%$$
$$N = 3090$$

Note. Standard errors have been rounded to three decimals. Those represented by "0.000" represent extremely small values, and each corresponds to a statistically significant regression coefficient.

3. Each $1000 increase in county median family income corresponds, on average, to a 0.122-point decrease in percent voting for Bush. As already explained, we had not expected a negative relationship.

4. We have tentatively determined that the relationship between Y_{BUSH} and X_{BLACK} is curvilinear, usefully expressed in quadratic form. Furthermore, by dividing the coefficient for X_{BLACK} by twice the absolute value of the coefficient for X_{BLACK}^2, we can identify the value of X_{BLACK} at which the relationship curves from positive to negative (Wooldridge, 2006, p. 201). In this case, we get 0.004/0.006, or 0.67%.

5. We have also tentatively determined that the Y_{BUSH}-by-$X_{HISPANIC}$ relationship is quadratic. The relationship changes from positive to negative when $X_{HISPANIC}$ equals –0.009/0.008, or 1.13%. (The minus sign is simply deleted.)

6. The relationship between Y_{BUSH} and X_{ASIAN} has been specified as linear throughout. Based on the regression results from Table 6.10 reproduced in Table 6.14, we see that each 1% increase in the number of county residents who are Asian corresponds, on average, to a 0.456-point decrease in percent voting for Bush.

7. The Y_{BUSH}-by-X_{NATIVE} relationship has been tentatively specified as quadratic. The coefficient for X_{NATIVE} is not statistically significant, meaning that the relationship, while curvilinear, is negative for all values of the independent variable: 0.000/0.008 yields zero.

8. For every one-level increase in X_{RURAL}, each 1-point increase in X_{FAMILY} corresponds, on average, to a 0.030-point decrease in Y_{BUSH}.

6.14 SUMMING UP

Given the limitations of our county-level data set, we have pretty well exhausted the power of OLS regression in analyzing the results of the U.S. presidential election of 2004. One of the most interesting findings is that increases in the percentage of people living in traditionally structured nuclear families yielded a substantial increase in the percentage voting for Bush. If our X_{FAMILY} variable is a reasonable proxy for the ill-defined but relentlessly invoked notion of traditional family values, then popular journalistic conceptions were correct: The more pervasive this factor, the better Bush did.

We also see that insofar as percentage of county residents ages 18–24 is a useful proxy for younger prospective voters, Kerry's effort to win aggregates of voters by appealing to the youth vote seems to have failed. At the county level, as the representation of this age group increased, percent voting for Bush increased as well.

It is not surprising that increases in ethnic minority representation are negatively associated with percent voting for Bush. This is consistent with voting patterns that have prevailed since before Franklin D. Roosevelt's New Deal.

It is surprising, however, that as a county's median family income increased, percent voting for Bush decreased. It is conceivable that as a county's median family income increased the percentage of nonaffluent residents voting for Bush increased as well, and that this accounts for the negative association between percent voting for Bush and median family income. This, however, seems unlikely.

As far as we can tell, then, the Bush base was organized around traditional family values and youth. The Kerry base was organized around ethnic minorities and comparative affluence. It will be interesting to see if these findings hold up when we improve our analysis through use of multilevel regression in Chapter 7.

6.15 USEFUL RESOURCES

Johnston, R., Hagen, M., & Jamieson, K. (2004) *The 2000 Presidential Election and the Foundations of Party Politics*. New York: Cambridge University Press.

Weisberg, H., & Wilcox, C. (Eds.) (2004) *Models of Voting in Presidential Elections: The 2000 U.S. Elections*. Stanford, CA: Stanford Law and Politics.

Use of OLS regression, logistic regression, and related techniques has a long history in the study of voting behavior. The book by Johnston, Hagen, and Jamieson is an informative example. The collection of essays by Weisberg and Wilcox illustrates the broad range of issues pertinent to voting behavior research.

7

Does Multilevel Regression Have Anything to Contribute?

7.1 CHAPTER INTRODUCTION

Our OLS multiple regression analysis of county-level voting in the 2004 U.S. presidential election could be further developed in a variety of ways. After all, only three two-way interactions have been investigated, and no higher-order interactions have been considered.

There are, moreover, interesting variables in the data set that we might have used as explanatory factors but did not. Percentage of the population under age 6, for example, turns out to have a statistically significant and negative regression coefficient when added to the regression equation in Table 6.14. More interesting still is the statistically significant and positive coefficient for the interaction term created with X_{FAMILY} and X_{UNDER6}. However, since these relationships were discovered by accident and their meaning requires a good deal of speculation, they have not been incorporated into the regression model. Nevertheless, if we had a better understanding of the traditional family values concept and if we were not restricted to working with county-level data, it is likely that X_{FAMILY} could have been defined in a more informative way.

There are also high-profile variables that are not included in our data set but that belong in any analysis of this kind. These include county-level voter turnout (Flanigan & Zingale, 2002), religious affiliation (Johnston, Hagen, & Jamieson, 2004), and union membership (Weisberg & Wilcox, 2004).

Moreover, none of our independent variables is inherently cultural or social-psychological. Insofar as we are interested in the way that collectivities assign value and respond to their circumstances, we have been limited to using county-level demographic aggregates as proxies.

In addition, as we have acknowledged, using county-level data is rarely a first choice. Having measures comparable to those used in this analysis for individuals would be better suited to answering most questions concerning voting behavior. As it is, avoidance of unwarranted ecological inferences is an ever-present concern. Again, this explains why we were uncomfortable incorporating county-level gender composition into our analysis.

Nevertheless, the process that led to the results in Table 6.14 was thorough. Modifications of functional form were prompted by examination of preliminary regression results for violation of assumptions. Selection of interaction terms, while speculative, was animated by an interest in three identifiable themes: the commonplace but poorly understood notion of traditional family values; lingering uncertainty as to the negative relationship between percentage voting for Bush and median family income; and the knowledge that a large rural turnout may have been crucial in the Bush victory (see, e.g., Kaiser, 2005). When all was said and done, we sought to make good choices, avoid data dredging, be reasonably parsimonious, and make a case for the power and flexibility of OLS multiple regression analysis. A case has been made.

At this point we may ask: *Is there anything left for multilevel regression analysis to contribute?* Are there analytical opportunities we cannot use without the additional tools and correctives embodied in multilevel regression?

7.2   CONTEXTUAL EFFECTS IN OLS REGRESSION

It is immediately evident that contextual or grouping variables are missing from our analysis. We have already explained, however, that OLS is not designed to handle more than one level of analysis in the same equation. By tacitly treating all variables as if they were measures made at the same level, OLS regression denies the reality and consequences of nesting.

Nesting introduces the possibility that regression coefficients are not fixed, but should be permitted to vary from context to context. Nesting also raises the possibility that observations and residuals are dependent, accompanied by intraclass correlation and deflated standard errors. With nesting, the number of degrees of freedom needed for statistical tests varies from level to level. Nesting makes it virtually certain that contextual factors will be needed as additional independent variables. The contextual factors used to explain variability in nesting-engendered random slopes, moreover, are invariably accompanied by implied cross-level interaction terms.

None of these inherently multilevel issues can be adequately addressed by using OLS regression with fixed coefficients in a single-level framework. If contextual variables are needed in our voting behavior analysis, it would be best to use something other than OLS. We would still be doing regression, but to do it right we need a multilevel framework and the capacity to use a random coefficient regression model.

We have offered numerous examples, however, in which OLS applications have used contextual variables and cross-level interaction terms to mimic multilevel regression. For example, we could pursue our interest in relationships between Y_{BUSH} and specific explanatory factors by aggregating X_{FAMILY}, X_{INCOME}, X_{RURAL}, X_{BLACK}, $X_{HISPANIC}$, X_{NATIVE}, and X_{ASIAN} to the state level, using state means as group or contextual variables. Furthermore, we may suspect that a county-level variable such as X_{FAMILY} would behave differently in predominately rural states than in predominately urban states, or that variation in X_{INCOME} might have different consequences depending on the average income level of the state.

With these last two examples, using contextual variables and cross-level interaction terms, the notion of linked levels of analysis is very clearly introduced. As we know, however, OLS regression does not permit dealing with different levels, much less linked levels.

Nevertheless, we can continue our effort to give OLS regression its due, concretely acknowledging its strengths and limitations, by tacking on contextual variables. This may also provide a point of departure for a properly specified multilevel regression model and facilitate regression diagnostics (Leyland & McCleod, 2000; see also Kreft & De Leeuw, 1998; Snijders & Bosker, 1999). So we add the aggregated contextual variables $X_{FAMILYMEAN}$, $X_{INCOMEMEAN}$, $X_{RURALMEAN}$, $X_{BLACKMEAN}$, $X_{HISPANICMEAN}$, $X_{NATIVEMEAN}$, and $X_{ASIANMEAN}$ to the OLS regression equation from Table 6.14 and get the results in Table 7.1. (As with all the other predictors, each of the contextual variables has been centered with respect to its grand mean.)

In addition to the obvious methodological problems already discussed, the OLS multiple regression equation is now becoming quite complex. Claims to parsimony have become dubious. Moreover, even with grand-mean centering, multicollinearity has become troublesome. Nine variance inflation factors exceed the usual rule-of-thumb cutoff of 4.000, including enormous values ranging from 55.945 for X_{BLACK} to 2076.290

TABLE 7.1. OLS Analysis of Percentage Voting for Bush; Contextual Variables Included

$Y_{BUSH} = 20.705 + 1.609X_{FAMILY} + 2.273X_{LNYOUTH} - 0.189X_{INCOME} + 0.011X_{EDUCATION} - 0.005X_{BLACK}$
    (1.369) (0.083)   (0.123)   (0.035)   (0.022)   (0.003)

    $- 0.007X_{HISPANIC} - 0.622X_{ASIAN} - 0.004X_{NATIVE} - 0.143X_{RURAL} - 0.001X_{BLACK}^2 + 0.002X_{HISPANIC}^2$
    (0.004)   (0.150)   (0.019)   (0.002)   (0.000)   (0.000)

    $- 0.082X_{NATIVE}^2 + 0.018X_{INCOME} * X_{FAMILY} + 0.053X_{RURAL} * X_{FAMILY} + 0.009X_{RURAL} * X_{INCOME}$
    (0.020)   (0.007)   (0.025)   (0.008)

    $- 1.591X_{RURALMEAN} + 1.879X_{FAMILYMEAN} - 0.659X_{INCOMEMEAN} + 0.004X_{BLACKMEAN}$
    (0.221)   (0.134)   (0.041)   (0.002)

    $+ 0.001X_{HISPANICMEAN} - 0.016X_{NATIVEMEAN} - 0.272X_{ASIANMEAN}$
    (0.001)   (0.002)   (0.117)

$$R^2 = 49.9\%$$
$$N = 3090$$

Note. Standard errors have been rounded to three decimals. Those represented by "0.000" represent extremely small values, and each corresponds to a statistically significant regression coefficient.

TABLE 7.2. Squaring, Aggregation, and Collinearity

	X_{BLACK}	X_{BLACK}^2	X_{HISPANIC}	X_{HISPANIC}^2	X_{NATIVE}	X_{NATIVE}^2
X_{BLACK}^2	0.794					
$X_{\text{BLACKMEAN}}$	0.177	0.457				
X_{HISPANIC}^2			0.863			
$X_{\text{HISPANICMEAN}}$			0.000	0.505		
X_{NATIVE}^2					0.783	
$X_{\text{NATIVEMEAN}}$					0.000	0.527

for X_{NATIVE}^2! In addition, the condition index is 561.324, far larger than any published rule-of-thumb cutoff (cf. Draper & Smith, 1998; Gujarati, 2003).

No wonder. Three of the four ethnicity variables—percent Black, percent Hispanic, and percent Native American—are represented in three different terms: X_{BLACK}, X_{BLACK}^2, $X_{\text{BLACKMEAN}}$; X_{HISPANIC}, X_{HISPANIC}^2, $X_{\text{HISPANICMEAN}}$; and X_{NATIVE}, X_{NATIVE}^2, $X_{\text{NATIVEMEAN}}$. Even with grand-mean centering, correlations of squared values with county-level variables and aggregated state-level variables remain strong, as we see in Table 7.2.

With 3090 cases, we might be inclined to ignore even huge variance inflation factors. As noted in our discussion of adequate sample sizes, however, when we specify and estimate a more suitable multilevel regression alternative, multicollinearity will still be there. It will still be inflating standard errors, rendering tests of significance dubious, and making coefficient estimates unduly imprecise. Using random coefficients with REML estimators instead of OLS will not eliminate multicollinearity and its adverse consequences. In addition, multicollinearity may introduce bias into estimates of the variances of random components and their standard errors (Shier & Fouladi, 2003). What are we to do?

7.3   RESPECIFICATION AND CHANGING FUNCTIONAL FORM

Recall our discussion of the relationship between Y_{BUSH} and X_{INCOME}. We found that it was curvilinear at the bivariate level, but that addition of needed independent variables linearized the relationship—a fairly common result, though definitely not a certain one, in OLS multiple regression analysis (Kennedy, 1998; Wooldridge, 2002). If contextual variables are in fact needed for proper specification of the voting behavior regression model, inclusion of $X_{\text{RURALMEAN}}$, $X_{\text{FAMILYMEAN}}$, $X_{\text{INCOMEMEAN}}$, $X_{\text{BLACKMEAN}}$, $X_{\text{HISPANICMEAN}}$, $X_{\text{NATIVEMEAN}}$, and $X_{\text{ASIANMEAN}}$ *may* linearize the relationships between Y_{BUSH} and the independent variables X_{BLACK}, X_{HISPANIC}, and X_{NATIVE}.

As it turns out, if we purge Y_{BUSH}, X_{BLACK}, X_{HISPANIC}, and X_{NATIVE} of variability due to the remaining independent variables (excluding the squared terms but including the aggregated group variables), the relationships between Y_{BUSH} and the three ethnicity variables are in fact approximately linearized (Gujarati, 2003). Figures 7.1 through 7.3, however, illustrate the fact that linearization is far from perfect.

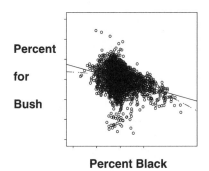

Percent for Bush

Percent Black

FIGURE 7.1. Approximate linearization of Y_{BUSH} by X_{BLACK}.

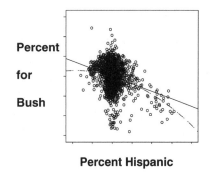

Percent for Bush

Percent Hispanic

FIGURE 7.2. Approximate linearization of Y_{BUSH} by $X_{HISPANIC}$.

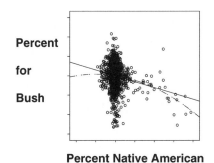

Percent for Bush

Percent Native American

FIGURE 7.3. Approximate linearization of Y_{BUSH} by X_{NATIVE}.

Nevertheless, as with our application of this procedure in examining the functional form of the Y_{BUSH}-by-X_{INCOME} relationship, values of R^2 for linear and quadratic functions vary very little, as we see in Table 7.3. This is consistent with the judgment that the relationships between Y_{BUSH} and the three ethnicity variables took nonlinear form due to specification error. Since specification error in this instance is manifest in failure to include one or more needed contextual factors, this is a compelling reason indeed to conclude that we have exhausted the utility of OLS multiple regression and should use the multilevel alternative.

TABLE 7.3. Linearizing OLS Relationships with Contextual Variables

	Linear	Quadratic
R^2 values, contextual variables controlled		
Y_{BUSH} by X_{BLACK}	6.5%	6.8%
Y_{BUSH} by $X_{HISPANIC}$	8.7%	9.6%
Y_{BUSH} by X_{NATIVE}	3.4%	3.6%
R^2 values, contextual variables not controlled		
Y_{BUSH} by X_{BLACK}	5.1%	7.3%
Y_{BUSH} by $X_{HISPANIC}$	3.5%	7.3%
Y_{BUSH} by X_{NATIVE}	5.5%	6.8%

TABLE 7.4. Final OLS Model: Percentage Voting for Bush

$$Y_{\text{BUSH}} = 60.274 + 1.612X_{\text{FAMILY}} + 2.290X_{\text{LNYOUTH}} - 0.187X_{\text{INCOME}} + 0.010X_{\text{EDUCATION}} - 0.006X_{\text{BLACK}}$$
$$\quad (0.242)\quad (0.080)\qquad\quad (0.207)\qquad\qquad (0.035)\qquad\qquad (0.022)\qquad\qquad (0.000)$$

$$\quad - 0.005X_{\text{HISPANIC}} - 0.615X_{\text{ASIAN}} - 0.005X_{\text{NATIVE}} + 0.145X_{\text{RURAL}} + 0.018X_{\text{INCOME}} * X_{\text{FAMILY}}$$
$$\quad\quad (0.000)\qquad\qquad (0.148)\qquad\quad (0.000)\qquad\quad (0.104)\qquad\quad (0.010)$$

$$\quad - 0.054X_{\text{RURAL}} * X_{\text{FAMILY}} + 0.009X_{\text{RURAL}} * X_{\text{INCOME}} + 5.040X_{\text{LNYOUTHMEAN}}$$
$$\quad\quad (0.032)\qquad\qquad\qquad (0.008)\qquad\qquad\qquad (0.409)$$

$$\quad + 0.380X_{\text{EDUCATEMEAN}} - 1.597X_{\text{RURALMEAN}} + 1.879X_{\text{FAMILYMEAN}} - 0.655X_{\text{INCOMEMEAN}}$$
$$\quad\quad (0.076)\qquad\qquad\quad (0.238)\qquad\qquad (0.134)\qquad\qquad (0.050)$$

$$\quad - 0.001X_{\text{BLACKMEAN}} + 0.002X_{\text{HISPANICMEAN}} - 0.017X_{\text{NATIVEMEAN}} - 0.184X_{\text{ASIANMEAN}}$$
$$\quad\quad (0.001)\qquad\qquad (0.000)\qquad\qquad\quad (0.002)\qquad\qquad (0.114)$$

$$R^2 = 49.9\%$$
$$N = 3090$$

Note. Standard errors have been rounded to three decimals. Those represented by "0.000" represent extremely small values, and each corresponds to a statistically significant regression coefficient.

The value of state-level contextual variables in a multilevel model is again abundantly evident. For comparative and diagnostic purposes, however, we will continue developing the inherently single-level OLS equation with contextual variables. As a result, we delete the squared terms while retaining the contextual variables. OLS regression results for the model with contextual variables but without squared terms are reported in Table 7.4. All variance inflation factors are now below 3.00, and the condition index is much smaller as well, equal to 3.97. Since the R^2 statistic in Table 7.4 is not smaller than the same measure in Table 6.14, deleting the squared terms has cost us no explanatory power. This is what we would expect if inclusion of contextual factors has linearized the formerly curvilinear relationships.

7.4   ADDRESSING THE LIMITATIONS OF OLS

Using OLS regression with contextual variables, multicollinearity has been remedied. In addition, a semblance of parsimony has been restored, including simplification of functional forms. Critical observers might judge, however, that our earlier disclaimers concerning mechanical empiricism and data dredging have been forgotten. After all, how many times can a regression model be respecified before we acknowledge that we are making too much of the peculiarities of one data set (cf. Kmenta, 1997, pp. 598–600)?

In the absence of models thoroughly grounded in well-developed theory, however, OLS regression, multilevel regression, and related techniques inevitably involve an element of uncertainty and exploration (Falk & Miller, 1992; Hamilton, 1999; Klees,

1999). To ignore this and to focus narrowly on statistical tests of inflexibly defined equations mean prematurely closing the door to discovery, turning social and behavioral research into caricatures of the so-called hard sciences (Alford, 1998; Chatterjee et al., 2000; Wooldridge, 2002). Specification and ongoing respecification of a statistical model, while subject to abuse, become matters of informed judgment (cf. Leamer, 1983).

In that spirit, we have given OLS multiple regression analysis its due. In fact, we have willfully erred and gone even further by including state-level and county-level variables in the same OLS regression equation. In the process, we have learned a lot about county-level voting behavior in the 2004 election. We are also reminded, however, that in spite of its power and flexibility, there are analytical tasks for which OLS regression is not well suited.

For nearly a century, students of regression analysis have devised effective responses to such methodological challenges, and found new opportunities for fruitful application of regression. In this instance, the remedy takes the form of multilevel modeling with random coefficients, contextual variables, and cross-level interaction terms.

7.5   COUNTIES NESTED WITHIN STATES: INTRACLASS CORRELATION

With Y_{BUSH} as the dependent variable, and random component estimates as shown in Table 7.5, the unconditional intraclass correlation for counties nested in states is large:

$$r = 71.421/(71.421 + 134.415) = 0.352$$

This tells us that 35.2% of the variability in Y_{BUSH} occurs between categories of the grouping variable, state. With an intraclass correlation coefficient this large and an average of 64 counties per state, a nominal alpha level of .05 will correspond to an actual alpha level of very roughly .70, certainly rendering inferential procedures suspect (Singer, 1987). Nesting of counties within states, in other words, poses the kinds of statistical problems that multilevel regression is designed to address.

TABLE 7.5. Random Component Estimates for Percentage Voting for Bush; Unconditional Model

Parameter	Estimate	Std. error	Wald Z	Sig. level
Residual	134.415	3.452	38.939	.000
INTERCEPT1	71.421	15.522	4.076	.000

7.6   MULTILEVEL REGRESSION MODEL SPECIFICATION: LEARNING FROM OLS

Whatever the limitations of OLS regression for the analytical task at hand, we would be foolish to ignore all that we have learned with regard to county-to-county variability in percentage voting for Bush. This is especially true of regression model specification. Our work with OLS will inform everything we do with random coefficient regression and REML estimators in a multilevel framework.

When we specified the OLS multiple regression model in Table 7.4, we provided a brief, intuitive rationale for using nine state-level contextual factors: $X_{LNYOUTHMEAN}$, $X_{EDUCATEMEAN}$, $X_{RURALMEAN}$, $X_{FAMILYMEAN}$, $X_{INCOMEMEAN}$, $X_{BLACKMEAN}$, $X_{HISPANICMEAN}$, $X_{NATIVEMEAN}$, and $X_{ASIANMEAN}$. These contextual factors were selected because we anticipated that they would contribute to explaining county-to-county variability in the dependent variable, Y_{BUSH}. This rationale still holds.

However, in multilevel regression analysis, as we now know, our expectations go further. Contextual factors and, by implication, cross-level interaction terms contribute to explaining variability in the level-one dependent variable and to explaining variability in random components corresponding to an intercept and to slopes that vary from group to group. They may also provide information used in interpreting covariances among random components.

In addition to variable selection and functional form, questions as to proper specification of a multilevel regression model include identification of coefficients that are permitted to vary across groups and coefficients that are fixed. These decisions are best made through reference to pertinent theory and thorough knowledge of substantive literature. We will *very roughly* approximate this set of circumstances by assigning random coefficients to the county-level variables that correspond to conspicuously high-profile or unexpected findings.

In this instance, X_{FAMILY} will be assigned a random slope because it is a proxy for a poorly understood but empirically consequential concept, traditional family values. It has, moreover, a strong and consistently powerful relationship with Y_{BUSH}. X_{INCOME} will be assigned a random slope because of its unexpected and consistently negative relationship with Y_{BUSH}. The intercept will also be random, reflecting the enormous diversity among states with respect to percentage voting for Bush.

Assigning random coefficients to X_{FAMILY} and X_{INCOME} has an appealing common-sense rationale—often the best sort of explanation available, though an admittedly weak one. In addition, by limiting the number of independent variables with random slopes to two, we are able to guard against undue complexity in specification of our multilevel regression model; this is something we have not consistently managed to do before.

This is certainly not the only way to go. Contextual variables measuring, say, the four categories of ethnicity, might very well be used to account for variability in slopes corresponding to income, traditional family structure, or any other level-one coefficient, including the intercept. In the absence of a compelling reason to proceed otherwise, however, the county-level variables to which we assign random slopes will be X_{FAMILY} and X_{INCOME}.

We will, moreover, treat variability in the county-level intercept as a function of each of the contextual factors: $X_{\text{LNYOUTHMEAN}}$, $X_{\text{EDUCATEMEAN}}$, $X_{\text{RURALMEAN}}$, $X_{\text{FAMILYMEAN}}$, $X_{\text{INCOMEMEAN}}$, $X_{\text{BLACKMEAN}}$, $X_{\text{HISPANICMEAN}}$, $X_{\text{NATIVEMEAN}}$, and $X_{\text{ASIANMEAN}}$. To maintain a semblance of simplicity, however, we will express variability in the two random intercepts, for FAMILY1 and INCOME1, as functions of $X_{\text{FAMILYMEAN}}$ and $X_{\text{INCOMEMEAN}}$.

Table 7.6 presents estimates of the random components of the intercept and the two random slopes, as well as covariances among the three. Each of the independent variables has been centered with respect to its grand mean, and estimates have been made without contextual factors, cross-level interaction terms, or the other independent variables in the equation.

From here on, we will adhere to the naming conventions introduced in Table 4.14 and used only sporadically since then. Variables with random coefficients are given names with all capital letters, such as ETHNIC1, and variables with fixed coefficients are given names in the form X_{ETHNIC2}. The number affixed to each variable name tells us the level—in this case, county or state—at which the variable is measured. As we have already acknowledged, this set of conventions differs from that normally used, but we have found this alternative preferable. In addition, some variable names have been simplified by deleting letters, as in EDUCATE1 rather than EDUCATION1 and ASIA1 rather than ASIAN1. This signifies nothing but a desire to fit material more easily into tables.

As we see in Table 7.6, each of the estimates of the random components is statistically significant. This is consistent with our decision to treat the INTERCEPT1 and the slopes for FAMILY1 and INCOME1 as varying from state to state rather than being fixed across states. Note, however, that even though the random components in Table 7.6 were estimated without contextual variables or cross-level interaction terms in the multilevel regression equation, none of the covariances is statistically significant. Consistent with our discussion of contextual variables and covariance structure in Chapter 3, however, we will use the unstructured option, permitting random components to vary together.

We are now in a position to specify a multilevel regression model to serve as an alternative to OLS models. Our multilevel model appears in Table 7.7, with estimated fixed component values reported in Table 7.8. The large number of independent vari-

TABLE 7.6. Random Component Estimates for Percentage Voting for Bush; Fixed Components Not Included in Equation

Parameter	Estimate	Std. error	Wald Z	Sig. level
Residual	92.427	2.410	38.348	.000
INTERCEPT1	84.777	20.764	4.083	.000
INTERCEP1 by FAMILY1	−3.229	2.007	−1.609	.108
FAMILY1	0.793	0.264	3.004	.003
INTERCEPT1 by FAMILY1	−0.943	0.843	−1.119	.263
FAMILY1 by INCOME1	−0.009	0.083	−0.110	.912
INCOME1	0.206	0.054	3.796	.000

TABLE 7.7. Multilevel Regression Model: Percentage Voting for Bush

Level-one model

$Y_{BUSH} = \beta_{0J} + \beta_{1J}FAMILY1 + \beta_{2J}INCOME1 + \gamma_{30}X_{LNYOUTH1} + \gamma_{40}X_{EDUCATE1} + \gamma_{50}X_{BLACK1} + \gamma_{60}X_{HISPANIC1}$

$\quad + \gamma_{70}X_{ASIA1} + \gamma_{80}X_{NATIVE1} + \gamma_{90}X_{RURAL1} + (u_{0J} + u_{1J} * FAMILY1 + u_{2J} * INCOME1 + e_{IJ})$

Level-two model

$\beta_{0J} = \gamma_{00} + \gamma_{01}X_{FAMILY2} + \gamma_{02}X_{INCOME2} + \gamma_{03}X_{BLACK2} + \gamma_{04}X_{HISPANIC2} + \gamma_{05}X_{ASIA2} + \gamma_{06}X_{NATIVE2}$

$\quad + \gamma_{07}X_{RURAL2} + \gamma_{08}X_{LNYOUTH2} + \gamma_{09}X_{EDUCATE2} + u_{0J}$

$\beta_{1J} = \gamma_{10} + \gamma_{11}X_{FAMILY2} + \gamma_{12}X_{INCOME2} + u_{1J}$

$\beta_{2J} = \gamma_{20} + \gamma_{21}X_{INCOME2} + \gamma_{22}X_{FAMILY2} + u_{2J}$

Full equation

$Y_{BUSH} = \gamma_{00} + \gamma_{10}FAMILY1 + \gamma_{20}INCOME1 + \gamma_{30}X_{LNYOUTH1} + \gamma_{40}X_{EDUCATE} + \gamma_{50}X_{BLACK1} + \gamma_{60}X_{HISPANIC1}$

$\quad + \gamma_{70}X_{ASIA1} + \gamma_{80}X_{NATIVE1} + \gamma_{90}X_{RURAL1} + \gamma_{01}X_{FAMILY2} + \gamma_{02}X_{INCOME2} + \gamma_{03}X_{BLACK2} + \gamma_{04}X_{HISPANIC2}$

$\quad + \gamma_{05}X_{ASIA2} + \gamma_{06}X_{NATIVE2} + \gamma_{07}X_{RURAL2} + X_{08LNYOUTH2} + X_{9EDUCATE2} + \gamma_{11}X_{FAMILY2} * FAMILY1$

$\quad + \gamma_{12}X_{INCOME2} * FAMILY1 + \gamma_{21}X_{INCOME2} * INCOME1 + \gamma_{21}X_{FAMILY2} * INCOME1 + u_{0J}$

$\quad + u_{1J} * FAMILY1 + u_{2J} * INCOME1 + e_{IJ}$

TABLE 7.8. Multilevel Regression Equation: Percentage Voting for Bush

$Y_{BUSH} = 66.500 + 1.523FAMILY1 + 2.221X_{LNYOUTH1} - 0.214INCOME + 0.034X_{EDUCATE1} - 0.008X_{BLACK1}$
$\qquad (2.592) \quad (0.111) \qquad (0.197) \qquad\quad (0.059) \qquad\qquad (0.019) \qquad\qquad (0.000)$

$\quad - 0.006X_{HISPANIC1} - 0.674X_{ASIA1} - 0.006X_{NATIVE1} + 0.098X_{RURAL1} - 0.071X_{FAMILY2} * INCOME1$
$\qquad (0.000) \qquad\quad (0.133) \qquad\quad (0.000) \qquad\quad (0.091) \qquad\quad (0.025)$

$\quad - 0.065X_{INCOME2} * FAMILY1 + 0.011X_{FAMILY2} * FAMILY1 + 0.013X_{INCOME2} * INCOME1$
$\qquad (0.020) \qquad\qquad\qquad (0.009) \qquad\qquad\qquad (0.046)$

$\quad - 0.098X_{RURAL2} + 1.368X_{FAMILY2} - 0.224X_{INCOME2} - 0.004X_{BLACK2} - 0.002X_{HISPANIC2}$
$\qquad (0.091) \qquad\quad (0.433) \qquad\quad (0.184) \qquad\quad (0.002) \qquad\quad (0.003)$

$\quad - 0.015X_{NATIVE2} - 0.101X_{ASIA2} + 6.349X_{LNYOUTH2} + 0.764X_{EDUCATE2}$
$\qquad (0.006) \qquad\quad (0.201) \qquad\quad (2.324) \qquad\qquad (0.258)$

$$R_1^2 = 56.1\%$$
$$N_1 = 3090$$
$$N_2 = 49$$

Note. Standard errors have been rounded to three decimals. Those represented by "0.000" represent extremely small values, and each corresponds to a statistically significant regression coefficient.

ables in this model, including contextual variables and cross-level interaction terms, suggests that multicollinearity may be a problem. As it turns out, 14 of the 22 variance inflation factors are less than 2.000, and another 4 are less than 3.000. Only 2 variance inflation factors—those for X_{RURAL2} (5.552) and X_{LNYOUTH2} (6.351)—are greater than 4.000, but each of these variables corresponds to a statistically significant slope. The condition index is 9.939. Multicollinearity is not the serious problem we had anticipated.

7.7   INTERPRETING THE MULTILEVEL REGRESSION EQUATION FOR COUNTY-LEVEL DATA

1. Each 1% increase in the number of county residents living in a traditionally structured family (FAMILY1) corresponds, on average, to a 1.523-point increase in percent voting for Bush. In the preliminary OLS regression analysis, the increase was almost the same, 1.482 points. In the final OLS model, the value of the FAMILY1 slope was 1.612. All told, the relationship between Y_{BUSH} and our traditional family structure variable changes little from one regression model specification to another.

2. In the preliminary OLS regression equation, each 1% increase in the natural logarithm of percentage of county residents ages 18–24 corresponded, on average, to a 1.855-point increase in Y_{BUSH}. In the final OLS model, the value of the same coefficient was 2.290; in the multilevel model, the slope for X_{LNYOUTH} is a statistically significant 2.221. In general, as the OLS specification more closely approximates adequacy, the OLS estimates become more similar to the multilevel regression results.

3. Each $1000 increase in county median family income (INCOME1) corresponds, on average, to a 0.214-point decrease in percent voting for Bush. Again, we had not expected a negative relationship. Nevertheless, this robust relationship remains statistically significant and negative, with a value similar to the preliminary and final OLS results.

4. In the preliminary OLS analysis, each 1% increase in the number of county residents ages 18–24 who are not high school graduates corresponded, on average, to a 0.188-point increase in percent voting for Bush. As regression model specification improved, however, the value of the coefficient became smaller. In the multilevel regression equation, the coefficient for X_{EDUCATE1} is no longer statistically significant, as was the case with the final OLS model.

5. Each 1% increase in the number of county residents who are Black (BLACK1) corresponds, on average, to a 0.006-point decrease in percent voting for Bush. In the preliminary OLS analysis, the value of this coefficient was a good deal larger, –0.242. We then decided that the relationship between Y_{BUSH} and X_{BLACK} was quadratic. Subsequently, after addition of contextual variables, the curvi-

linear character of the relationship was linearized, reducing the value of the coefficient for X_{BLACK} to –0.006. Clearly, specification of the multilevel regression model benefited enormously from our efforts to find the best OLS regression model.

6. For each 1% increase in the number of county residents who are Hispanic (HISPANIC1), there is, on average, a 0.006-point decrease in percent voting for Bush. This is much smaller than the coefficient value of –0.176 reported in the preliminary OLS analysis, but the same as the final OLS estimate of –0.006. We had tentatively specified the functional form of the relationship to be curvilinear, but as with X_{BLACK}, it was linearized when we introduced contextual variables. Again we see that specification of our multilevel regression model was usefully informed by our work with OLS models, and the better the OLS specification, the closer the OLS estimates to multilevel estimates.

7. For each 1% increase in the number of county residents who are Asian (ASIA1), there is, on average, a 0.674-point decrease in percent voting for Bush. This is a larger negative coefficient than the –0.537 we found with the preliminary OLS results. Nevertheless, from specification to specification, the substantive meaning of the relationship between percent voting for Bush and percent Asian is about the same. Furthermore, the consequences of gradually improved specification are evident when we compare coefficient values from equation to equation.

8. For each 1% increase in the number of county residents who are Native American (NATIVE1), percent voting for Bush decreases, on average, by 0.006 points. Though statistically significant and negative, this coefficient is much smaller than the –0.409 that we estimated in our preliminary OLS regression model, and much closer to the –0.005 in the final OLS model.

9. Three same-level interaction terms were introduced as the OLS model was respecified. In the final OLS analysis, none was statistically significant, and they were excluded from the multilevel regression model. It is true, however, that one or more of the same-level interaction terms—X_{INCOME} * X_{FAMILY}, X_{RURAL} * X_{FAMILY}, and X_{RURAL} * X_{INCOME}—might have emerged as statistically significant as a manifestation of the improved specification offered by the multilevel model. Our model, however, is quite complex even without these additional terms.

10. A primary source of multilevel regression model complexity is the presence of four implied cross-level interaction terms: $X_{FAMILY2}$ * INCOME1, $X_{INCOME2}$ * FAMILY1, $X_{FAMILY2}$ * FAMILY1, and $X_{INCOME2}$ * INCOME1. In the multilevel model, the statistically significant slopes for the first two of these terms tell us the following: For each 1% increase in $X_{FAMILY2}$, the negative relationship between Y_{BUSH} and INCOME1 moves, on average, 0.071 points closer to zero. For each 1% increase in $X_{INCOME2}$, the positive relationship between Y_{BUSH} and FAMILY1 increases, on average, by 0.133 points.

11. In the preliminary regression analysis, each one-level increase in the urban–rural continuum variable X_{RURAL1} corresponded, on average, to a 0.440-point decrease in Y_{BUSH}. In the final OLS regression analysis, however, the X_{RURAL1} coefficient had diminished to statistical nonsignificance, and it is also statistically nonsignificant in the multilevel regression analysis. Once again, as the OLS regression model specification more closely approximates adequacy, the OLS coefficient values become more similar to the multilevel coefficient values.

12. Each 1% increase in $X_{FAMILY2}$ corresponds, on average, to a 1.368-point increase in Y_{BUSH}, similar to the coefficient value of 1.612 for $X_{FAMILYMEAN}$ in the final OLS analysis. None of the other OLS analyses included contextual factors.

13. Each 1% increase in the state-level variable X_{BLACK2} corresponds, on average, to a 0.004-point decrease in Y_{BUSH}. The slope for $X_{BLACKMEAN}$ in the final OLS regression analysis was not statistically significant. This comparison is especially interesting because the multilevel coefficient for X_{BLACK2} corresponds to a sample size of 49, while $X_{BLACKMEAN}$ corresponds to a sample size of 3090. In this instance, multilevel regression detected and measured a relationship that otherwise would have been relegated to the status of statistical nonsignificance.

14. Each 1% in the aggregated contextual variable $X_{NATIVE2}$ corresponds, on average, to a 0.015-point decrease in Y_{BUSH}—nearly the same value as in the final OLS model.

15. Each 1% increase in the state-level contextual variable $X_{LNYOUTH2}$ corresponds, on average, to a 6.349-point increase in percent voting for Bush. The statistically significant slope for $X_{LNYOUTHMEAN}$ in the final OLS model was a bit smaller, 5.040, but also statistically significant.

16. Each 1% increase in $X_{EDUCATE2}$ (the percentage of state residents ages 18–24 who are not high school graduates) corresponds, on average, to a 0.764-point increase in Y_{BUSH}. This coefficient is just over twice the size of the statistically significant coefficient for $X_{EDUCATEMEAN}$ in the final OLS analysis.

7.8 KNOWING WHEN TO STOP

If we had compelling theoretical or substantive reasons, our analysis of county-level voting behavior could be developed further. In fact, thinking about this analysis forces us to recognize how many consequential specification decisions are made, even if by default, when we do multilevel regression. In the absence of a compelling rationale for changing the model specification in Table 7.8, it seems a good idea to avoid making a complex multilevel regression model even more complex. Similarly, it seems unwise to generate confusion by searching for a way to make the existing model more parsimonious; there are simply too many options available for what would be an exercise in naked empiricism.

The covariance parameter estimates for our multilevel voting behavior analysis appear in the top panel of Table 7.9. To facilitate comparison, we have also reproduced the covariance parameter estimates from Table 7.6. With or without the contextual variables and cross-level interaction terms in the analysis, none of the random component covariances is statistically significant, while all three random component variances remain statistically significant. Nevertheless, it is clear that introduction of contextual variables and cross-level interaction terms has substantially reduced the numerical value of each random component estimate.

As we have done in some of our previous analyses, we may wish to determine the range of values covered by each of our random coefficients. To do so, we can construct intervals for the random intercept and each of the two random slopes (see Table 7.10). The intervals will include intercept and slope values for 95% of the 49 states in the voting behavior data set.

The interval constructed for the slopes for $X_{FAMILY1}$ and $X_{INCOME1}$ forcibly reminds us that varying slopes may cover such a broad range as to make interpretation difficult indeed. It is all well and good to say that every \$1000 increase in median family income corresponds, on average, to a 0.214-point decrease in Y_{BUSH}. In instances such as this, however, we must bear in mind that such unambiguous statements, while true, need to be qualified. An improved multilevel regression specification might substantially reduce the width of this interval.

TABLE 7.9. Random Component Estimates for Percentage Voting for Bush; Contextual Variables and Cross-Level Interaction Terms Included in Equation

Parameter	Estimate	Std. error	Wald Z	Sig. level
Residual	64.153	1.672	38.362	.000
INTERCEPT1	28.678	7.432	3.993	.000
INTERCEPT1 by FAMILY1	−0.127	0.702	−0.181	.856
FAMILY1	0.274	0.109	2.506	.012
INTERCEPT1 by INCOME1	−0.259	0.386	−0.670	.503
FAMILY1 by INCOME1	−0.546	0.043	−1.282	.200
INCOME1	0.107	0.030	3.531	.001

TABLE 7.6, Reproduced. Random Component Estimates for Percentage Voting for Bush; Contextual Variables and Cross-Level Interaction Terms Not Included in Equation

Parameter	Estimate	Std. error	Wald Z	Sig. level
Residual	92.427	2.410	38.348	.000
INTERCEPT1	84.777	20.764	4.083	.000
INTERCEPT1 by FAMILY1	−3.229	2.007	−1.609	.108
FAMILY1	0.793	0.264	3.004	.003
INTERCEPT1 by FAMILY1	−0.943	0.843	−1.119	.263
FAMILY1 by INCOME1	−0.816	0.830	−0.983	.368
INCOME1	0.206	0.054	3.796	.000

TABLE 7.10. Multilevel Voting Behavior Analysis:
Variability with Respect to Random Components

$$a_{\text{INTERCEPT}} - t_{.05}S_{a\text{INTERCEPT}} \text{ to } a_{\text{INTERCEPT}} + t_{.05}S_{a\text{INTERCEPT}}$$

$$66.500 - 1.960(60.035)^{1/2} \text{ to } 66.500 + 1.960(60.035)^{1/2}$$

$$51.314 \text{ to } 81.686$$

$$b_{\text{FAMILY1}} - t_{.05}S_{b\text{FAMILY1}} \text{ to } b_{\text{FAMILY1}} + t_{.05}S_{b\text{FAMILY1}}$$

$$1.523 - 1.960(0.365)^{1/2} \text{ to } 1.523 + 1.960(0.365)^{1/2}$$

$$0.339 \text{ to } 2.707$$

$$b_{\text{INCOME1}} - t_{.05}S_{b\text{INCOME1}} \text{ to } b_{\text{INCOME1}} + t_{.05}S_{b\text{INCOME1}}$$

$$-0.214 - 1.960(0.136)^{1/2} \text{ to } -0.214 + 1.960(0.136)^{1/2}$$

$$-0.937 \text{ to } 0.508$$

7.9   SUMMING UP

In Table 7.11, we compare results for four regression models: the preliminary OLS specification (OLS Preliminary); the final OLS specification, with aggregated contextual variables and same-level interaction terms (OLS Final); an OLS specification, discussed here
for the first time, in which we mimic our multilevel analysis (OLS "Multilevel"); and the
multilevel regression equation itself (Multilevel Regression).

For variables that used more than one variable name, such as those with fixed coefficients in OLS equations and random coefficients in the multilevel equation, both
names are given. Results are presented only for variables that had statistically significant
regression coefficients in at least one of the four equations. Dashes (—) indicate terms
not included in a specific model. The abbreviation "n.s." means statistically nonsignificant for a specific model. The specified alpha level is .05. An R^2 value is given for
each of the OLS specifications. The value of R_1^2 is given for the multilevel regression
equation.

In Table 7.11 we see once again that there is usually little difference between coefficients estimated with OLS regression and multilevel regression. We also see that in general, the more adequate the OLS specification, the closer the estimated coefficients are to
the values of the multilevel coefficients.

Furthermore, and especially with respect to the slopes for contextual variables, even
the best OLS specification yields standard errors with a negative bias, resulting in misleading results for tests of significance. This is most obvious with respect to the unstan-
dardized slopes for $X_{\text{RURALMEAN2}}$, $X_{\text{INCOMEMEAN2}}$, and $X_{\text{HISPANICMEAN2}}$: Each slope is statistically significant in the OLS model that mimics multilevel regression, but not in the
actual multilevel model.

TABLE 7.11. Comparing Models: Percentage Voting for Bush

Variable	Preliminary OLS	Final OLS	OLS "Multilevel"	Multilevel Regression
$X_{FAMILY1}$/FAMILY1	1.482 (0.075)	1.612 (0.080)	1.644 (0.079)	1.523 (0.111)
$X_{LNYOUTH1}$	1.855 (0.222)	2.290 (0.207)	2.289 (0.218)	2.221 (0.197)
$X_{INCOME1}$/INCOME1	−0.242 (0.029)	−0.187 (0.035)	−0.231 (0.032)	−0.214 (0.059)
$X_{EDUCATION}$	0.188 (0.024)	n.s.	n.s.	n.s.
X_{BLACK1}	−0.224 (0.017)	−0.006 (0.000)	−0.006 (0.000)	−0.008 (0.000)
$X_{HISPANIC1}$	−0.176 (0.019)	−0.005 (0.000)	−0.006 (0.000)	−0.006 (0.000)
X_{ASIAN1}	−0.376 (0.093)	−0.615 (0.148)	−0.764 (0.143)	−0.674 (0.133)
$X_{NATIVE1}$	−0.409 (0.031)	−0.005 (0.000)	−0.005 (0.000)	−0.006 (0.000)
X_{RURAL1}	0.440 (0.112)	n.s.	n.s.	n.s.
$X_{LNYOUTHMEAN2}$/$X_{LNYOUTH2}$	—	5.040 (0.409)	7.209 (0.540)	6.329 (2.234)
$X_{EDUCATEMEAN2}$	—	0.380 (0.076)	0.334 (0.077)	0.764 (0.258)
$X_{RURALMEAN2}$	—	−1.597 (0.238)	−4.213 (0.301)	n.s.
$X_{FAMILYMEAN2}$/$X_{FAMILY2}$	—	1.879 (0.134)	1.659 (0.131)	1.368 (0.433)
$X_{INCOMEMEAN2}$	—	−0.655 (0.050)	−0.481 (0.049)	n.s.
$X_{HISPANICMEAN2}$	—	0.002 (0.000)	0.001 (0.000)	n.s.
$X_{NATIVEMEAN2}$	—	−0.017 (0.002)	−0.017 (0.002)	−0.015 (0.006)
X_{ASIAN2}	—	−0.184 (0.114)	n.s.	n.s.
$X_{FAMILY2}$ * INCOME1	—	—	−0.043 (0.012)	−0.071 (0.025)
$X_{INCOME2}$ * FAMILY1	—	—	0.053 (0.015)	−0.065 (0.020)
R^2/R_1^2	37.1%	49.9%	53.0%	56.1%

The best estimates of coefficients and standard errors are provided by the multilevel regression model with REML estimators. It is the only one suited to making best use of the information available in an analysis with multiple levels, where nesting has to be taken into consideration, random coefficients should be used, and contextual variables with cross-level interaction terms are intrinsic parts of the regression model. As we illustrated in Table 7.10, however, multilevel regression results merit cautionary comments peculiar to that method of analyzing data.

7.10 USEFUL RESOURCES

Steenbergen, M., & Bradford, S. (2002) Modeling Multilevel Data Structures. *American Journal of Political Science, 46,* 218–237.

Belanger, P., & Eagles, M. (2005) *The Geography of Class and Religion in Canadian Elections.* Paper Presented at the Canadian Political Science Association Conference, University of Western Ontario, London, Ontario, June 2–4.

The article by Steenbergen and Bradford is fairly dense, but it merits attention. It makes a compelling case for application of multilevel regression in comparative political analysis and in political science generally. Application of the authors' recommendation to studies of voting behavior is straightforward.

The paper by Belanger and Eagles is readable and interesting. A primary purpose of their three-level model is to demonstrate that selection of context—in this Canadian case, locality or province—is crucial. The characteristics of contexts that are remote from individuals, such as provinces, are less likely to influence individual voting behavior than more immediate contexts, such as identifiable localities. Clearly, the same applies to contextual influences on other forms of individual behavior as well.

8

Multilevel Regression Models with Three Levels

8.1 CHAPTER INTRODUCTION

Based on our county-level voting behavior example in Chapters 6 and 7, it is evident that counties within states tend to be more alike than counties between states. We have made use of this knowledge in applying a multilevel structure to our analysis and in gauging the contribution of contextual factors—specifically state-level aggregates, along with cross-level interaction terms—to explaining variability in the percentage of county residents voting for George W. Bush. In the same way, we have sought to explain state-to-state variability in random components.

Our analysis certainly would have been more informative if we had measures on individuals comparable to those on counties and states. Students of voting behavior are usually a lot more interested in how individuals behave than in how counties behave. In addition, with individual-level information we could have constructed a multilevel regression model with more than two levels. We might have treated individuals as nested in *both* counties *and* states. Our multilevel model would have become a good deal more complex, but it might have become more interesting as well.

Instructional treatments of models with three or more levels are not hard to find. The very brief account provided by Luke (2004) is especially helpful, as are the on-the-mark cautionary observations offered by Hox (2002) and Steenbergen and Bradford (2002). Snijders and Bosker (1999) develop some informative and interesting examples.

While three-level models are available for study, most of them are quite simple, and often do not include explanatory variables at level three. One reason for this is that models with more than two levels quickly become statistically cumbersome and may include implied cross-level interaction terms formed by using variables at all three levels (Hox, 2002). It is true that higher-order interaction terms are sometimes found in empirical research, but unless they have a clear rationale in theoretical or substantive literature, they may defy interpretation.

Recall the difficulties we encountered in making the numerous and difficult specification decisions we encountered with two-level models: "Which independent variables should be used? What are the proper functional forms? Which coefficients should be fixed? Which coefficients should be random? Is there reason to depart from a covariance structure that permits random components to covary?" With models that may have three or more levels, the number of decisions is even more daunting. We must answer all the questions posed by two-level models, and then continue to this one: "Do we need more than two levels?"

Once again, the power of multilevel regression is limited by our theoretical and substantive knowledge. In the case of models with more than two levels, moreover, this constraint is even more conspicuous and confining than it has been until now. Beyond that, as already noted, when we are working with more than two levels, statistical complexity itself can be an effective deterrent to unduly ambitious analytical efforts. We will illustrate this concretely as we proceed through this chapter, especially with regard to the proliferation of random terms.

In addition, when we work with more than two levels, it is common to find that plausible-sounding third- and higher-level independent variables add nothing of explanatory value, and that random components do not vary with respect to third- and higher-level grouping variables. If we look, for example, at the usual school system hierarchy—students, classrooms, schools, districts, regional agencies, states—it seems clear that the higher organizational levels are increasingly remote from the lives of individuals. Attenuation of group effects over social and geographical distance is precisely what Belanger and Eagles (2005) found in their research on voting behavior in Canada. Yes, higher levels may have substantial effects, but without the guidance of well-developed theory or rich substantive literature, unproductive guesswork, data dredging, and intractable statistical complications come to the fore.

Nevertheless, multilevel regression models with more than two levels can provide useful information. We gradually develop increasingly complex three-level models throughout the remainder of this chapter. Each example is designed to build on the one that precedes it. In this way we work toward development of three-level models that are more than just exercises in complexity.

8.2 STUDENTS NESTED WITHIN SCHOOLS AND WITHIN DISTRICTS

Just as counties are nested within states, we also know that students are nested within schools *and* within districts. As a result, multilevel regression models with more than two levels are easy to imagine. Actually estimating such models, however, can be difficult and sometimes simply not practicable. Furthermore, the amount of computer time needed to estimate models with three or more levels can be formidable.

The models developed below are based on our large Kentucky data set containing information on nearly 50,000 eighth graders nested in 347 schools that are nested in 135 districts. We have already worked with numerous examples using this data set. Now, however, we are moving toward use of three levels: students nested within schools and within districts. The individual-level dependent variable is the California Basic Educational Skills Test measure of math achievement (National Evaluation Systems, 2002).

8.3   LEVEL ONE: STUDENTS

As we have seen in previous examples, the only student-level independent variables available with this data set are gender and ethnicity. Given this, let's begin very simply, building on what we know.

Table 8.1 is just an OLS simple regression equation. We have seen specifications of this sort at various places throughout our presentation. Individual student math achievement is treated as a function of one independent variable, individual student gender (X_{GENDER}). The possibility that nesting has occurred has not been acknowledged. As always with OLS regression, the intercept and the slope are fixed. The error term is random, varying from one level-one observation to another.

In Table 8.2 we see that dividing the intercept and slope by their standard errors will give us t values that are statistically significant at any conventionally used alpha level. Interpretation of coefficients is straightforward: Since $X_{GENDER1}$ is coded 1 for females and 0 for males, females, on average, score 1.177 points lower on the math achievement test than males.

TABLE 8.1. Math Achievement: OLS (Inherently Single-Level) Regression Model

$$Y = a + bX_{GENDER} + e$$

TABLE 8.2. OLS Regression Equation: Math Achievement on Gender

$$Y = 49.258 - 1.177X_{GENDER1}$$
$$(0.084)\ (0.169)$$

$$R^2 = 0.6\%$$
$$N = 49,616$$

8.4   LEVEL TWO: SCHOOLS

An obvious question now is "Do we need more than one level?" To find out, we proceed as usual and calculate the unconditional intraclass correlation coefficient, using the information in Table 8.3. In this instance, individual students are at level one and schools are at level two.

$$r = 72.945/(72.945 + 411.823) = 0.150$$

The intraclass correlation coefficient tells us that 85% of the variability in math achievement occurs within schools, while 15% occurs between schools. Nesting of students within schools is thus cause for concern, deflating standard errors of regression coefficients, rendering tests of significance suspect, and causing uncertainty as to the correct number of degrees of freedom to use in statistical tests.

Consequently, in Table 8.4 we have taken the OLS simple regression specification from Table 8.1 and transformed it into a random coefficient regression equation. The random coefficient equation uses REML estimators and has a random intercept and a random slope. The intercept and slope used in predicting student-level reading achievement are permitted to vary from one school to another.

There are, however, no level-two predictors to explain variability in the random intercept and random slope. Instead, the random intercept is treated as a function of the average intercept over all students, γ_{00}, plus a measure of school-to-school variability in

TABLE 8.3. Do We Need More Than One Level?: Random Components

Parameter	Estimate	Std. error	Wald Z	Sig. level
Residual	411.823	2.622	156.860	.000
INTERCEPT1	72.942	6.816	10.703	.000

TABLE 8.4. Math Achievement: Random Coefficient Regression Model with Two Levels

Level-one model

$$Y_{IJ} = \beta_{0J} + \beta_{1J}\text{GENDER1} + e_{IJ}$$

Level-two model

$$\beta_{0J} = \gamma_{00} + u_{0J}$$

$$\beta_{1J} = \gamma_{10} + u_{1J}$$

Full model

$$Y_{IJ} = \gamma_{00} + \gamma_{10}\text{GENDER1} + u_{0J} + u_{1J} * \text{GENDER1} + e_{IJ}$$

TABLE 8.5. Random Coefficient Regression of Math Achievement on Gender; Two-Level Model; Fixed Components

$$Y = 45.163 - 0.999\text{GENDER1}$$
$$(0.499)\ (0.218)$$

$$R_1^2 = 0.6\%$$
$$N_1 = 46{,}770$$
$$N_2 = 347$$

TABLE 8.6. Random Coefficient Regression of Math Achievement on Gender; Two-Level Model; Random Components

Parameter	Estimate	Std. error	Wald Z	Sig. level
Residual	410.301	2.621	156.543	.000
INTERCEPT1	72.974	6.817	10.705	.000
INTERCEPT1 by GENDER1	−3.164	2.315	−1.367	.172
GENDER1	2.736	0.949	2.882	.004

the intercept, u_{0j}. Similarly, the random slope is treated as a function of the average slope over all students, γ_{10}, plus a measure of school-to-school variability in the slope, u_{1j}. In the full model, all this is joined together in a single equation, as we have come to expect.

The fixed and random component estimates for our two-level random coefficient model are reported in Tables 8.5 and 8.6. As with the OLS results in Table 8.2, the intercept and slope in Table 8.5 are statistically significant, and interpretation of fixed slope is straightforward: Females, on average, score 0.999 points lower in math achievement than males. The slope estimate differs very little from the same value in Table 8.2. The random components reported in Table 8.6 tell us that both the random intercept and the random slope have statistically significant variances, meaning that the random components vary across schools. The intercept-by-slope covariance, however, is not statistically significant.

We have yet to introduce a school-level predictor into the analysis, transforming our random coefficient regression model into a multilevel regression model. We will, of course, do so when we try to explain variability in the random terms. So far, however, we have used the school level only to permit the random intercept and random slope to manifest measurable variability.

8.5   LEVEL THREE: DISTRICTS

Before introducing one or more contextual variables from the school level, we may ask if there is reason to introduce yet another level, districts. Suppose, for example, we suspect that the level-one intercept and slope are best construed as random with respect to ***both***

TABLE 8.7. Do We Need More Than Two Levels?: Random Components

Parameter	Estimate	Std. error	Wald Z	Sig. level
Residual: Variability within schools	415.728	2.695	154.245	.000
INTERCEPT at level two: Variability between schools within districts	31.605	3.900	8.104	.000
INTERCEPT at level three: Variability between districts	7.420	3.109	2.326	.020

schools *and* districts. We can make a judgment as to whether or not there is nakedly empirical merit to this view by using the information in Table 8.7. Again we compute an unconditional intraclass correlation coefficient. Now, however, we want to know if math achievement, in addition to varying within schools and between schools, also varies *between districts*.

Given this decomposition of math achievement variability across three levels, we may ask if students in the same district are more alike than students in other districts. To find out, we take the random component variances for all three levels and sum them. Then we divide this sum into the estimated variance between districts. This is a straightforward extension of the simple procedure used to estimate the unconditional intraclass correlation for a two-level model.

$$r = \text{Between-districts variance/(Within-schools variance}$$
$$+ \text{Between-schools-within-districts variance}$$
$$+ \text{Between-districts variance)}$$
$$r = \text{Between-districts variance/Total variance}$$
$$r = 7.420/(415.728 + 31.605 + 7.420) = 0.016$$

Since the between-districts variance is statistically significant, we know that the intraclass correlation is statistically significant as well (Snijders & Bosker, 1999). As a practical matter, however, we should acknowledge that only 1.6% of the total variability in math achievement occurs between districts. Individual students in the same district tend to be more like each other than like students in other districts, but the association is quite weak.

Snijders and Bosker (1999) introduce a variety of useful intraclass correlation coefficients that we can apply, using different combinations of levels from Table 8.7. If we wish, for example, we may calculate the intraclass correlation coefficient that measures the degree to which schools within the same district tend to be more like each other than like schools in other districts. We simply divide the between-schools-within-districts variance by the sum of the between-schools-within-districts variance and the between-districts variance.

$$r = \text{Between-schools-within-districts variance/}$$
$$\text{(Between-schools-within-districts variance + Between-districts variance)}$$

$$r = 7.420/(31.605 + 7.420) = 0.190$$

In this instance, the intraclass correlation means that 19% of the between-schools variance in math achievement occurs across districts.

Similarly, if we want to know the total amount of variability in individual student math achievement that is due to grouping within schools *and* within districts, it is not difficult to modify the formula for the intraclass correlation to compute this value.

$$r = \text{(Between-schools-within-districts variance}$$
$$+ \text{Between-districts variance)/Total variance}$$

$$r = (31.605 + 7.420)/454.753 = 0.086$$

In other words, 8.6% of the total variability in math achievement is due to students' being grouped in schools and in districts.

These variations on the same simple measure begin to suggest the complexity we analysts encounter when working with three-level models. Are we interested in students nested within schools? Students nested within districts? Students nested in both schools and districts? Students nested in schools and schools nested in districts? Schools nested in districts? Complex indeed!

In our illustrations of three-level models, we will give most of our attention to the simultaneous grouping of students within schools and districts. Specifically, we will begin with and develop a model in which the intercept and the GENDER1 slope are random with respect to both schools and districts. This is really just a three-level random coefficient regression model.

8.6   NOTATION AND SUBSCRIPT CONVENTIONS FOR SPECIFYING A THREE-LEVEL MODEL

With three levels, notation becomes a bit more complex than with two levels. Furthermore, notational conventions for three-level models vary markedly from one source to another (compare, e.g., Snijders & Bosker, 1999; Raudenbush & Bryk, 2002; Steenbergen & Bradford, 2002; Singer & Willett, 2003; Luke 2004; Belanger & Eagles, 2005).

Most accounts of three-level models augment the use of beta and gamma notation by using different symbols for variables and parameter estimates at each level. Rather than using different symbols, however, we will rely on subscripts to indicate the level-specific nature of each variable and each parameter estimate.

For the level-one model in Table 8.8, the math achievement dependent variable is represented by Y_{IJK}. This means that each math achievement score refers to a specific stu-

TABLE 8.8. Math Achievement: Random Coefficient Regression with Three Levels; One Student-Level Predictor; Random Intercept and Random Slope at Level Two and Level Three

<u>Level-one model</u>

$$Y_{IJK} = \beta_{0JK} + \beta_{1JK}GENDER1 + e_{IJK}$$

<u>Level-two model</u>

$$\beta_{0JK} = \beta_{00K} + u_{0JK}$$

$$\beta_{1JK} = \beta_{10K} + u_{1JK}$$

<u>Level-three model</u>

$$\beta_{00K} = \gamma_{000} + u_{00K}$$

$$\beta_{10K} = \gamma_{100} + u_{10K}$$

<u>Full model</u>

$$Y_{IJK} = \gamma_{000} + \gamma_{100}GENDER1 + u_{00K} + u_{0JK} + u_{10K} * GENDER1 + u_{1JK} * GENDER1 + e_{IJK}$$

dent (I) in a specific school (J) in a specific district (K). The same subscripts are attached to the level-one residual, e_{IJK}. Each level-one residual refers to the difference between observed and predicted math achievement scores for a specific student (I) located in a specific school (J) located in a specific district (K).

The random intercept is represented by a beta coefficient, β_{0JK}. The subscripts tell us that the intercept has the same value for individual students (0) in school J in district K. Since the intercept varies across schools and districts, β_{0JK} is the mean score for students in school J and district K. Similarly, the random slope for GENDER1, β_{1JK}, measures the average difference between males and females on Y_{IJK}. The subscripts tells us that this is the slope for a student-level predictor (1) for school J in district K. If there were two or more student-level predictors, their slopes would be numbered sequentially (1, 2, . . . , I). β_{1JK} is random across schools (J) and districts (K). In other words, it is the effect of GENDER1 on math achievement for a student located in school J and district K.

For the level-two model, β_{00K} tells us the common value of the school-level random intercept, β_{0JK}, for each student (0) in each school (J) in each district (K). In other words, β_{00K} is the school-level group effect for the intercept. School-specific variation around this value is represented by u_{0JK}. β_{10K} tells us the common value of the school-level random slope, β_{1JK}, for each student (1) in each school (J) in district (K). In other words, β_{10K} is the school-level group effect for the slope. School-specific variation around this value is represented by u_{1JK}.

For the level-three model, γ_{000} tells us the common value of the random intercept for each student (0) in each school (0) in each district (0). The string of three zeroes constituting the subscripts indicates that γ_{000} is the grand mean for math achievement. District-specific variation around this value is represented by u_{00K}. Similarly, γ_{100} tells us the common value of the random slope for each student (1) in each school (0) in each district (0). District-specific variation around this common value is represented by u_{10K}.

As we develop our discussion of three-level models, we will provide additional information concerning notation and subscripts. The modifications we will make, however, are just extensions of the basic scheme we have just presented. Proper use of subscripts in three-level models takes some getting used to, or at least that has been my experience.

8.7   ESTIMATING A THREE-LEVEL RANDOM COEFFICIENT MODEL

Fixed components for this three-level model are reported in Table 8.9, and random components are reported in Table 8.10. As with the two-level equation in Table 8.5, the fixed component estimates of the intercept and slope are statistically significant. Females, on average, score 0.840 points lower than males—an estimate with an absolute value a bit lower than the OLS and two-level REML estimates.

Though we still have only one predictor, the complexity of three-level models has begun to show itself in the random component estimates, with four variances and two intercept-by-slope covariances. As with the two-level model reported in Tables 8.4 through 8.6, the variances for the intercept and the GENDER1 slope are statistically sig-

TABLE 8.9. Math Achievement: Random Coefficient Regression with Three Levels; One Student-Level Predictor; Random Intercept and Random Slope at Level Two and Level Three; Fixed Components

$$Y = 49.281 - 0.840\text{GENDER1}$$
$$(0.481)\ (0.247)$$

$$R_1^2 = 0.6\%$$
$$N_1 = 46,770$$
$$N_2 = 347$$

TABLE 8.10. Math Achievement: Random Coefficient Regression with Three Levels; One Student-Level Predictor; Random Intercept and Random Slope at Level Two and Level Three; Estimates of Covariance Parameters

Parameter	Estimate	Std. error	Wald Z	Sig. level
Residual	414.645	2.693	156.952	.000
INTERCEPT1 variance at level two	31.217	3.808	8.198	.000
INTERCEPT1-by-GENDER1 covariance at level two	−1.530	1.278	−1.197	.231
GENDER1 variance at level two	2.736	0.949	2.882	.004
INTERCEPT1 variance at level three	7.900	3.155	2.504	.012
INTERCEPT1-by-GENDER1 covariance at level three	−1.496	1.017	−1.471	.141
GENDER1 variance at level three	1.210	0.594	2.308	.042

nificant at level two. In addition, we see that the variances for the intercept and the GENDER1 slope are also statistically significant at level three. The random intercept and the random slope vary across schools *and* across districts. Neither covariance, however, is statistically significant.

Clearly, there is a lot more information in the random component results reported in Table 8.10 than in Table 8.6. Furthermore, we can be confident that the random component estimates at level two better reflect the way the world works, since we have permitted their variability to be apportioned across both schools and districts. Nevertheless, given the modest differences between the fixed component estimates in Tables 8.9 and 8.5, it may still be unclear that we have gained much from the work and computer time needed to specify and estimate a three-level model.

SPSS remains easy to use with three levels. The instructions in SPSS Routine 8.1 are only a little more complicated than those in SPSS Routines 1.1, 2.1, 2.2, and 2.3.

If we reestimate the level-two and level-three models with ML rather than REML, we can use the deviance difference statistic and the information criteria routinely pro-

---

SPSS Routine 8.1. Three-Level Regression Model for Math Achievement

1. Open the SPSS data file; click on ANALYZE.
2. Go to MIXED MODELS and click on LINEAR.
3. Insert the school identifier and the district identifier into the SUBJECTS box.
4. Click on CONTINUE, insert math achievement into the DEPENDENT variable box, and insert GENDER1 into the COVARIATES box.
5. Click on FIXED. In the small box in the middle of the screen change FACTORIAL to MAIN EFFECTS.
6. Move the independent variable from the FACTORS and COVARIATE(S) box to the MODEL box.
7. Click on CONTINUE.
8. Click on the RANDOM button in the middle of the screen. Move the school identifier from the SUBJECTS box to the COMBINATIONS box. In the small box in the middle of the screen, change FACTORIAL to MAIN EFFECTS. Click on INCLUDE INTERCEPT and move the independent variable GENDER1 into the MODEL box.
9. Just above INCLUDE INTERCEPT select UNSTRUCTURED.
10. Click on NEXT. Move the district identifier from the SUBJECTS box to the COMBINATIONS box.
11. Change FACTORIAL to MAIN EFFECTS. Click on INCLUDE INTERCEPT, and move GENDER1 into the MODEL box.
12. Just above INCLUDE INTERCEPT select UNSTRUCTURED.
13. Click on CONTINUE, and then click on the STATISTICS button.
14. On the left, under MODEL STATISTICS, select PARAMETER ESTIMATES and TESTS FOR COVARIANCE PARAMETERS.
15. Click on CONTINUE and click on OK.

TABLE 8.11. Information Criteria for Tables 8.5 and 8.9

Criterion	Three-Level Model	Two-Level Model
–2 log likelihood	*424579.1*	424599.4
Akaike's Information Criterion	*424597.1*	424611.4
Hurvich and Tsai's Criterion	*424597.1*	424611.4
Bozdogan's Criterion	424685.0	*424670.0*
Schwarz's Bayesian Criterion	424676.0	*424664.0*

Note. The smaller value for each measure is boldfaced and italicized.

vided by SPSS (see Table 8.11) to make a better-informed judgment as to whether or not the three-level model is really a better-fitting one.

$$\text{Deviance difference} = 424599.4 - 424579.1 = 20.3$$
$$df = 9 - 6 = 3$$

In this case, the deviance difference is statistically significant ($p < .05$), indicating that the three-level model provides a better fit. The four information criteria, however, give inconsistent results—an outcome with which we have become familiar. When we refer to the most commonly used criteria, Akaike's Information Criterion indicates that the three-level model is the better-fitting one, while Schwarz's Bayesian Criterion indicates that the two-level model provides a better fit to the Kentucky data. If we refer to the less commonly used information criteria, we are faced with the same sort of ambiguity.

Rather than anguish over which model *really* provides the better fit, we will simply acknowledge that each is an obvious oversimplification. No one imagines that gender is the only factor contributing to student-level difference in math achievement. Furthermore, it seems extremely unlikely that coefficients estimated with student-level gender as the only predictor will not be compromised by misspecification. We would do well to move toward a closer approximation of real-world complexity in explaining math achievement differences.

Nevertheless, it is important to recognize what we have accomplished: We have estimated a three-level random coefficient model in which the intercept and slope are random for both schools and districts. We have found, moreover, that the intercept and slope do in fact vary with respect to both level two and level three. We will use this three-level model as a point of departure as we add predictors at all levels.

8.8   ADDING A SECOND LEVEL-ONE PREDICTOR

The three-level model specified in Table 8.12 contains an additional level-one predictor with a random slope, ETHNIC1 (coded 1 for Blacks and 0 otherwise). The notation and subscript conventions for this model are straightforward extensions of the model specified in Table 8.8.

TABLE 8.12. Math Achievement: Random Coefficient Regression with Three Levels; Adding a Second Level-One Predictor; Random Intercept and Random Slope at Level Two and Level Three

Level-one model

$$Y_{IJK} = \beta_{0JK} + \beta_{1JK}GENDER1 + \beta_{2JK}ETHNIC1 + e_{IJK}$$

Level-two model

$$\beta_{0JK} = \beta_{00K} + u_{0JK}$$

$$\beta_{1JK} = \beta_{10K} + u_{1JK}$$

$$\beta_{2JK} = \beta_{20K} + u_{2JK}$$

Level-three model

$$\beta_{00K} = \gamma_{000} + u_{00K}$$

$$\beta_{10K} = \gamma_{100} + u_{10K}$$

$$\beta_{20K} = \gamma_{200} + u_{20K}$$

Full model

$$Y_{IJK} = \gamma_{000} + \gamma_{100}GENDER1 + \gamma_{200}ETHNIC1 + u_{00K} + u_{0JK} + u_{10K} * GENDER1 + u_{1JK} * GENDER1$$
$$+ u_{20K} * ETHNIC1 + u_{2JK} * ETHNIC1 + e_{IJK}$$

In the level-one model, the subscripts for the ETHNIC1 random slope, β_{2JK}, tell us that this is the slope for our second student-level predictor (2) and that it is random across schools (*J*) and districts (*K*). The level-two model tells us that β_{2JK} is a function of two factors: β_{20K}, the common value of the school-level random slope, β_{2JK}, for each student (2) in school *J* in district *K*; and u_{2JK}, school-specific variation around this common value. In the level-three model, we see that β_{20K} is a function of two factors: γ_{200}, the common value of the random intercept for each student (2) in each school (0) in district *K*; and u_{20K}, district-specific variation around this common value.

Fixed components for this three-level model are reported in Table 8.13, and random components are reported in Table 8.14. All coefficients in Table 8.13 are statistically sig-

TABLE 8.13. Math Achievement: Random Coefficient Regression with Three Levels; Adding a Second Level-One Predictor; Random Intercept and Random Slope at Level Two and Level Three; Fixed Components

$$Y = 49.285 - 0.811GENDER1 - 8.046ETHNIC1$$
$$(0.483)\ (0.238) \qquad\qquad (0.697)$$

$$R_1^2 = 2.7\%$$
$$N_1 = 46{,}770$$
$$N_2 = 347$$

TABLE 8.14. Math Achievement: Random Coefficient Regression with Three Levels; Adding a Second Level-One Predictor; Random Intercept and Random Slope at Level Two and Level Three; Same-Level Interaction Term Included; Fixed Components

$$Y = 49.265 - 0.808\text{GENDER1} - 8.046\text{ETHNIC1} + 0.550\text{GENDER1} * \text{ETHNIC1}$$
$$(0.483)\ (0.238)\qquad\quad (0.697)\qquad\quad (0.874)$$

$$R_1^2 = 2.7\%$$
$$N_1 = 46{,}770$$
$$N_2 = 347$$

nificant, and interpretation is straightforward: Female students, on average, score 0.811 points below male students in math achievement. Black students, on average, score 8.046 points below White students.

In Table 8.14 we see that, just as two-level models do, three-level regression models give us a good deal of discretion with regard to including interaction terms not implied by model specification. In this instance, we have created a same-level multiplicative interaction term with GENDER1 and ETHNIC1. The fixed slope for GENDER1 * ETHNIC1 turns out not to be statistically significant. Nevertheless, the notion that the relationship between gender and math achievement varies from category to category of ethnicity seems worthy of investigation.

If there had been any doubt as to whether or not the same-level interaction term should be retained, we could have reestimated the equations in Tables 8.13 and 8.14 with ML, and then used the deviance difference and information criteria, as given in Table 8.15.

$$\text{Deviance difference} = 413565.9 - 431565.1 = 0.08$$
$$df = 15 - 14 = 1$$

With the significance level set at .05, the deviance difference is not statistically significant. This indicates that both models fit the Kentucky data equally well, which we interpret to mean that nothing was gained by adding the GENDER1 * ETHNIC1 interaction term. Nevertheless, each of the smaller-is-better information criteria tells us that the

TABLE 8.15. Information Criteria for Tables 8.13 and 8.14

Criterion	Without interaction term	With interaction term
−2 log likelihood	*413565.1*	413565.9
Akaike's Information Criterion	*413597.9*	424611.4
Hurvich and Tsai's Criterion	*413597.9*	424611.4
Bozdogan's Criterion	*413753.9*	424670.0
Schwarz's Bayesian Criterion	*413737.9*	424664.0

Note. The smaller value for each measure is boldfaced and italicized.

model without the same-level interaction term is the better-fitting one, although differences between criteria estimated for the models with and without the interaction term are small.

We conclude that there is no gender-by-ethnicity interaction. However, investigating this possibility has shown us that discretionary use of same-level interactions is another way in which we may develop three-level models to make them more instructive.

Still more interesting—some might say alarming!—with regard to the model specified in Table 8.12 are the random components reported in Table 8.16. This table is *far* more complex than anything we have seen before, giving values for six random component variances and six random component covariances. And we still have only two predictors, both at level one!

The variances for INTERCEPT1 at levels two and three are statistically significant, indicating that the intercept does in fact vary across both schools and districts. In addition, the variance of the random component of the slope for ETHNIC1 is statistically significant at level two, and the variance of the random slope for GENDER1 is statistically significant at level three. This means that the ETHNIC1 slope does in fact vary across schools, and the GENDER1 slope does in fact vary across districts.

In addition, the negative INTERCEPT1-by-ETHNIC1 covariance is statistically significant at the school level: At level two, the random components for the intercept and the ETHNIC1 slope vary in opposite directions. This suggests that as school mean math achievement increases, the comparative math achievement disadvantage associated with

TABLE 8.16. Math Achievement: Random Coefficient Regression with Three Levels; Adding a Second Level-One Predictor; Random Intercept and Random Slope at Level Two and Level Three; Estimates of Covariance Parameters

Parameter	Estimate	Std. error	Wald Z	Sig. level
Residual	399.771	2.632	151.913	.000
INTERCEPT1 variance at level two	31.481	3.860	8.156	.000
INTERCEPT1-by-GENDER1 covariance at level two	−1.771	1.232	−1.438	.150
GENDER1 variance at level two	0.996	0.827	1.205	.228
INTERCEPT1-by-ETHNIC1 covariance at level two	−9.359	3.461	−2.704	.007
GENDER1-by-ETHNIC1 covariance at level two	−2.183	1.877	−1.163	.245
ETHNIC1 variance at level two	26.577	7.850	3.386	.001
INTERCEPT1 variance at level three	7.907	3.217	2.458	.014
INTERCEPT1-by-GENDER1 covariance at level three	−1.234	1.006	−1.236	.216
GENDER1 variance at level three	1.168	0.666	1.754	.083
INTERCEPT-by-ETHNIC1 covariance at level three	−1.035	3.634	−0.285	.776
GENDER1-by-ETHNIC1 covariance at level three	2.553	1.526	1.672	.094
ETHNIC1 variance at level three	9.577	8.488	1.128	.259

being Black decreases. Higher-achieving schools, in other words, may do a better job of closing the Black–White achievement gap.

The fact remains, however, that there is a good deal of random component variability to be explained in Table 8.16. As is often the case, we have little theoretical or substantive information to guide our efforts. An obvious way to simplify Table 8.16 is to use the variance components covariance structure, constraining random components not to covary (cf. Hox, 2002). Another obvious tack is to use fewer random terms. As we move through this chapter, we will adopt the second strategy, exercising a good deal more caution in assigning random slopes to predictors.

8.9   ADDING A LEVEL-TWO PREDICTOR

In the multilevel regression model specified in Table 8.17, we have introduced a level-two variable, school size (X_{SIZE2}), into the three-level equation. Based on literature concerning the politically charged school size issue, we suspect that school size may help to account for variability in the random intercept at the school level and in the random slopes for GENDER1 and ETHNIC1 at the school level (Bickel et al., 2002; Johnson, Howley, & Howley, 2002).

TABLE 8.17. Math Achievement: Multilevel Regression with Three Levels; Two Student-Level Predictors; One School-Level Predictor; Random Intercept and Random Slope at Level Two and Level Three

Level-one model

$$Y_{IJK} = \beta_{0JK} + \beta_{1JK}GENDER1 + \beta_{2JK}ETHNIC1 + e_{IJK}$$

Level-two model

$$\beta_{0JK} = \beta_{00K} + \gamma_{010}X_{SIZE2} + u_{0JK}$$

$$\beta_{1JK} = \beta_{10K} + \gamma_{110}X_{SIZE2} + u_{1JK}$$

$$\beta_{2JK} = \beta_{20K} + \gamma_{210}X_{SIZE2} + u_{2JK}$$

Level-three model

$$\beta_{00K} = \gamma_{000} + u_{00K}$$

$$\beta_{10K} = \gamma_{100} + u_{10K}$$

$$\beta_{20K} = \gamma_{200} + u_{20K}$$

Full model

$$Y_{IJK} = \gamma_{000} + \gamma_{100}GENDER1 + \gamma_{200}ETHNIC1 + \gamma_{010}X_{SIZE2} + \gamma_{120}X_{SIZE2} * GENDER1$$

$$+ \gamma_{220}X_{SIZE2} * ETHNIC2 + u_{00K} + u_{0JK} + u_{10K} * GENDER1 + u_{1JK} * GENDER1$$

$$+ u_{0JK} * ETHNIC1 + e_{IJK} + u_{2JK} * ETHNIC1 + e_{IJK}$$

Admittedly, this is a very cautious first step toward accounting for random components and introducing a measure of real-world complexity into the three-level model. This move does, however, have a point of departure in substantive literature, and we are proceeding as promised: developing the three-level model slowly, while acknowledging that its complexity is an invitation to error and misunderstanding.

We now have three predictors: GENDER1 and ETHNIC1 at level one, and X_{SIZE2} at level two. Both level-one predictors have been assigned random slopes, with the GENDER1 and ETHNIC1 random slopes varying across both schools and districts. In addition, the level-one intercept is random, also varying across schools and across districts. The slope for X_{SIZE2} is fixed.

The subscript conventions for the three-level model in Table 8.17 are the same as for Tables 8.8 and 8.12. For the first time, however, we have a predictor at level two: X_{SIZE2}, school size with a fixed slope. The coefficient γ_{010} represents the contribution of X_{SIZE2} to the common value of the random intercept, β_{0JK}. The coefficients γ_{120} and γ_{220} represent the contribution of X_{SIZE2} to the common values of the random slopes for GENDER1, β_{1JK}, and ETHNIC1, β_{2JK}.

The fixed component estimates in Table 8.18 can be interpreted as follows:

1. Black students, on average, score 6.515 points lower in math achievement than White students.
2. For each 100-student increase in school size, student math achievement increases, on average, by 1.171 points.
3. For each 100-student increase in school size, Black students' disadvantage relative to White students increases by 2.179 points.

By introducing school size at level two, along with two implied cross-level interaction terms, we have begun to clarify the relationships between the math achievement dependent variable and the gender and ethnicity independent variables. As is often the case, the most interesting finding pertains to a cross-level interaction term: As school

TABLE 8.18. Math Achievement: Multilevel Regression with Three Levels; Two Student-Level Predictors; One School-Level Predictor; Random Intercept and Random Slope at Level Two and Level Three; Fixed Components

$Y = 48.677 - 0.737 \text{GENDER1} - 6.515 \text{ETHNIC1} + 1.171 X_{SIZE2} - 0.136 X_{SIZE2} * \text{GENDER1}$
$\quad (0.535)\ (0.396) \qquad\quad (0.928) \qquad\qquad (0.460) \qquad\quad (0.382)$

$\quad - 2.179 X_{SIZE2} * \text{ETHNIC1}$
$\quad (0.830)$

$$R_1^2 = 3.2\%$$
$$N_1 = 46{,}770$$
$$N_2 = 347$$

size increases, the math achievement disadvantage for Black students is exacerbated. Increases in school size, on average, are associated with increased achievement. This gain, however, comes at a relative cost to Blacks.

At first look, this finding seems to be at odds with our tentative interpretation of the INTERCEPT1-by-ETHNIC1 negative covariance in Table 8.16. We interpreted that association between random components to mean that as average achievement increases, the Black–White achievement gap decreases. Let's think about it. Suppose that school size is confounded with math achievement and ethnicity, such that overall math achievement increases with school size, *and* the math achievement gap between Blacks and Whites also increases with school size. If this were happening, we would expect the statistically significant X_{SIZE2} * ETHNIC1 interaction effect in Table 8.18, *and* we would expect that introducing school size as an independent variable would diminish the absolute value of the INTERCEPT1-by-ETHNIC1 covariance, because school size is now controlled.

As it turns out, the only random term that is substantially reduced by introduction of X_{SIZE2} is indeed the INTERCEPT1-by-ETHNIC1 covariance. Otherwise, we see in Table 8.19 that we have gained very little with regard to explaining random component variances and covariances. There have been very small reductions in the statistically significant variances and covariances from Table 8.16. The district-level random component variance for GENDER1 is no longer statistically significant, but this has been accomplished in spite of the fact that the GENDER1 variance has been reduced very lit-

TABLE 8.19. Math Achievement: Multilevel Regression with Three Levels; Two Student-Level Predictors; One School-Level Predictor; Random Intercept and Random Slope at Level Two and Level Three; Estimates of Covariance Parameters

Parameter	Estimate	Std. error	Wald Z	Sig. level
Residual	399.795	2.632	151.901	.000
INTERCEPT1 variance at level two	31.481	3.860	8.156	.000
INTERCEPT1-by-GENDER1 covariance at level two	−1.683	1.234	−1.221	.222
GENDER1 variance at level two	1.104	0.831	1.221	.222
INTERCEPT1-by-ETHNIC1 covariance at level two	−7.641	3.402	−2.246	.025
GENDER1-by-ETHNIC1 covariance at level two	−2.306	1.867	−1.235	.217
ETHNIC1 variance at level two	25.277	8.007	3.157	.002
INTERCEPT1 variance at level three	7.734	3.105	2.490	.013
INTERCEPT1-by-GENDER1 covariance at level three	−1.110	0.997	−1.113	.266
GENDER1 variance at level three	1.057	0.671	1.575	.124
INTERCEPT-by-ETHNIC1 covariance at level three	−1.153	3.695	−0.312	.755
GENDER1-by-ETHNIC1 covariance at level three	2.377	1.609	1.478	.140
ETHNIC1 variance at level three	11.127	9.723	1.144	.252

tle. Beyond that, with the exception of the INTERCEPT1-by-ETHNIC1 covariance, any real gains in accounting for these values will have to come from further respecifications of the three-level regression model.

8.10 ADDING A SECOND PREDICTOR AT LEVEL TWO AND A PREDICTOR AT LEVEL THREE

The subscript conventions for the three-level model in Table 8.20 are the same as for those used previously. For the first time, however, we have a predictor at level three: X_{SIZE3}, school size with a fixed slope. The coefficient γ_{001} represents the contribution of X_{SIZE3} to β_{00K}, which is the common value of the random intercept, β_{0JK}, as it varies across districts. The coefficient γ_{201} represents the contribution of X_{SIZE3} to β_{20K}, which is the common value of the random slope, β_{2JK}, as it varies across districts.

We have also assigned GENDER1 (now $X_{GENDER1}$) a fixed slope rather than a random slope. This is consistent with Table 8.19, in which we found that the district-level variance component for GENDER1 is no longer statistically significant. It is also a big step in the direction of simplification, resulting in fewer random terms.

Moreover, we have added another school-level predictor: percentage of students who are eligible for free/reduced cost lunch (X_{POOR2}), with a fixed slope. As with the other level-two predictors, X_{POOR2} and its implied cross-level interaction term (X_{POOR2} *

TABLE 8.20. Math Achievement: Multilevel Regression with Three Levels; Two Student-Level Predictors; Two School-Level Predictors; One District-Level Predictor; Random Intercept and Random Slope at Level Two and Level Three

Level-one model

$$Y_{IJK} = \beta_{0JK} + \gamma_{100}X_{GENDER1} + \beta_{2JK}ETHNIC1 + e_{IJK}$$

Level-two model

$$\beta_{0JK} = \beta_{00K} + \gamma_{010}X_{SIZE2} + \gamma_{020}X_{POOR2} + u_{0JK}$$

$$\beta_{2JK} = \beta_{20K} + \gamma_{210}X_{SIZE2} + \gamma_{220}X_{POOR2} + u_{2JK}$$

Level-three model

$$\beta_{00K} = \gamma_{000} + \gamma_{001}X_{SIZE3} + u_{00K}$$

$$\beta_{20K} = \gamma_{200} + \gamma_{201}X_{SIZE3} + u_{20K}$$

Full model

$$Y_{IJK} = \gamma_{000} + \gamma_{100}X_{GENDER1} + \gamma_{002}ETHNIC1 + \gamma_{010}X_{SIZE2} + \gamma_{020}X_{POOR2} + \gamma_{001}X_{SIZE3}$$

$$+ \gamma_{210}X_{SIZE2} * ETHNIC1 + \gamma_{220}X_{POOR2} * ETHNIC1 + \gamma_{201}X_{SIZE3} * ETHNIC1$$

$$+ u_{00K} + u_{0JK} + u_{20K} * ETHNIC1 + u_{2JK} * ETHNIC1 + e_{IJK}$$

TABLE 8.21. Math Achievement: Multilevel Regression with Three Levels; Two Student-Level Predictors; Two School-Level Predictors; One District-Level Predictor; Random Intercept and Random Slope at Level Two and Level Three; Fixed Components

$$Y = 46.061 - 1.155X_{GENDER1} - 7.105ETHNIC1 + 0.391X_{SIZE2} - 0.278X_{POOR2} - 0.890X_{SIZE3}$$
$$\quad (0.386)\ (0.186) \qquad\qquad (1.110) \qquad\qquad (0.493) \qquad\quad (0.016) \qquad\quad (0.382)$$

$$- 0.136X_{SIZE2} * ETHNIC1 + 0.075X_{POOR2} * ETHNIC1 + 0.773X_{SIZE3} * ETHNIC1$$
$$\quad (0.874) \qquad\qquad\qquad (0.039) \qquad\qquad\qquad (0.971)$$

$$R_1^2 = 8.4\%$$
$$N_1 = 46{,}770$$
$$N_2 = 347$$
$$N_3 = 135$$

ETHNIC1) are being used to account for variability in the random intercept, β_{0JK}, and the random slope, β_{0JK}.

As with the fixed components for the other random coefficient and multilevel regression analyses, interpretation of the fixed component results shown in Table 8.21 is easy:

1. Female students, on average, score 1.155 points lower in math achievement than male students. This coefficient was not statistically significant in Table 8.18, when gender had a random slope corresponding to a sample size of 347 schools. Now that the slope is fixed, it corresponds to a sample size of 46,770 schools, and it is statistically significant.

2. Black students, on average, score 7.105 points lower on math achievement than White students.

3. For each 1-point increase in the percentage of a school's students who are eligible for free/reduced cost lunch (X_{POOR2}), individual student math achievement scores are decreased, on average, by 0.278 points.

4. District school size is expressed in natural logarithms, meaning that for each 1% increase in district enrollment, individual student math achievement decreases, on average, by 0.890 points.

Though we have added a level-two predictor, X_{POOR2}, and a level-three predictor, X_{SIZE3}, there are only half as many random terms in Table 8.22. This is a welcome consequence of replacing the random slope for GENDER1 with a fixed slope for $X_{GENDER1}$.

We see, furthermore, that three of the four random component variances and both covariances have been substantially diminished. With the addition of X_{POOR2}, X_{SIZE3}, and the implied interaction terms $X_{POOR2} * ETHNIC1$ and $X_{SIZE3} * ETHNIC1$, we are accounting for much more of the variability in the random component variances and covariances. Nevertheless, the random component for ETHNIC1 at the district level has actually gotten larger and is now statistically significant. This suggests that variability in

TABLE 8.22. Math Achievement: Multilevel Regression with Three Levels; Two Student-Level Predictors; Two School-Level Predictors; One District-Level Predictor; Random Intercept and Random Slope at Level Two and Level Three; Estimates of Covariance Parameters

Parameter	Estimate	Std. error	Wald Z	Sig. level
Residual	400.411	2.630	152.223	.000
INTERCEPT1 variance at level two	12.824	1.686	7.607	.000
INTERCEPT1-by-ETHNIC1 covariance at level two	–3.171	2.312	–1.372	.170
ETHNIC1 variance at level two	20.756	6.698	3.099	.002
INTERCEPT1 variance at level three	1.119	1.106	1.012	.312
INTERCEPT1-by-ETHNIC1 covariance at level three	–1.208	2.296	–0.526	.599
ETHNIC1 variance at level three	18.239	8.647	2.109	.035

district size masks district-to-district variability in the relationship between math achievement and ethnicity.

8.11 DISCRETIONARY USE OF SAME-LEVEL INTERACTION TERMS

School size and district size seem to be implicated in educational achievement processes in consequential ways that are only imperfectly understood (see, e.g., Bickel & Howley, 2000; Bickel et al., 2001; Strange, Howley, & Bickel, 2001). This is most conspicuously manifest in the form of same-level interaction terms involving school size and percentage of a school's students eligible for free/reduced cost lunch (Johnson et al., 2002; Howley & Howley, 2004; A. Howley & Howley, 2006). Specifically, as school size increases, the achievement test score costs associated with being in a school with economically disadvantaged students increase. Less often, a same-level interaction term created with district size and percentage of a district's students eligible for free/reduced lunch has yielded similar results.

By way of more effectively demonstrating some of the discretion and flexibility that an analyst enjoys when working with three-level models, we will use the model specified in Table 8.20 and estimated in Tables 8.21 and 8.22 as a point of departure. Guided by substantive literature, we will add the two cross-level interaction terms just discussed and make an assessment of their value in this context.

Interpretation of the fixed components in the multilevel model augmented by the discretionary addition of two same-level interaction terms (see Table 8.23) is as follows:

1. Female students, on average, score 1.155 points lower in math achievement than male students.
2. Black students, on average, score 6.924 points lower in math achievement than White students.

TABLE 8.23. Math Achievement: Multilevel Regression with Three Levels; Two Student-Level Predictors; Two School-Level Predictors; One District-Level Predictor; Random Intercept and Random Slope at Level Two and Level Three; Same-Level Interaction Terms Included; Fixed Components

$$Y = 46.197 - 1.155X_{GENDER1} - 6.924ETHNIC1 + 0.394X_{SIZE2} - 0.226X_{POOR2} - 1.056X_{SIZE3}$$
$$(0.380)\ (0.186) \qquad (1.020) \qquad\quad (0.522) \qquad\quad (0.019) \qquad\quad (0.319)$$

$$- 0.942X_{SIZE2} * ETHNIC1 + 0.080X_{POOR2} * ETHNIC1 + 0.892X_{SIZE3} * ETHNIC1$$
$$(0.863) \qquad\qquad\qquad (0.038) \qquad\qquad\qquad (0.801)$$

$$- 0.097\ X_{SIZE2} * X_{POOR2} + 0.019X_{SIZE3} * X_{POOR3}$$
$$(0.024) \qquad\qquad\quad (0.021)$$

$$R_1^2 = 8.7\%$$
$$N_1 = 46,770$$
$$N_2 = 347$$
$$N_3 = 135$$

3. For each 1% increase in a school's students eligible for free/reduced cost lunch, individual student math achievement is decreased, on average, by 0.226 points.

4. For each 1% increase in district size, individual student math achievement is decreased, on average, by 1.056 points.

5. For each 1% increase in a school's students eligible for free/reduced cost lunch, Black students' disadvantage in math achievement is decreased by 0.080 points.

6. For each 100-student increase in school size, the math achievement disadvantage corresponding to a 1% increase in students who are economically disadvantaged increases by 0.097 points.

As we see, the same-level interaction term has worked as expected for schools but not for districts. If there are doubts as to whether or not inclusion of the same-level interaction has improved model fit, these may be addressed by using the deviance difference and the usual information criteria, as given in Table 8.24.

$$\text{Deviance difference} = 413386.8 - 413370.0 = 16.8$$
$$df = 18 - 16 = 2$$

TABLE 8.24. Information Criteria for Tables 8.21 and 8.23

Criterion	With interaction term	Without interaction term
−2 log likelihood	413386.8	*413370.0*
Akaike's Information Criterion	413418.8	*413406.0*
Hurvich and Tsai's Criterion	413418.8	*413406.0*
Bozdogan's Criterion	*413574.8*	413581.5
Schwarz's Bayesian Criterion	*413558.8*	413563.5

Note. The smaller value for each measure is boldfaced and italicized.

After rerunning the analyses with ML, we get mixed results with regard to which model provides the better fit. The deviance difference and two of the information criteria indicate that the model without the same-level interaction terms provides the better fit. The other two information criteria, however, find that the model with the same-level interaction terms is the better-fitting one.

We have seen this sort of split decision several times, and it remains a source of confusion and uncertainty. For now, however, let's focus on the same-level interaction term for schools; acknowledge that our results are consistent with those presented in numerous research reports; and judge this to be consistent with the observation that as school size increases, the achievement test score costs of economic disadvantage increase as well.

8.12 ONGOING RESPECIFICATION OF A THREE-LEVEL MODEL

There are many ways in which we might seek to improve the three-level model specification in Table 8.20. Given the limitations of our Kentucky data set, we have exhausted the list of level-one predictors. At levels two and three, however, additional, potentially informative independent variables are available. In Table 8.25 we have added $X_{ETHNIC2}$ (ethnicity aggregated to the school level) and X_{POOR3} (the percentage of students eligible for free/reduced cost lunch, computed at the district level). Both $X_{ETHNIC2}$ and X_{POOR3}

TABLE 8.25. Math Achievement: Multilevel Regression with Three Levels; Two Student-Level Predictors; Three School-Level Predictors; Two District-Level Predictors; Random Intercept and Random Slope at Level Two and Level Three

<u>Level-one model</u>

$$Y_{IJK} = \beta_{0JK} + \gamma_{100}X_{GENDER1} + \beta_{2JK}ETHNIC1 + e_{IJK}$$

<u>Level-two model</u>

$$\beta_{0JK} = \beta_{00K} + \gamma_{010}X_{SIZE2} + \gamma_{020}X_{POOR2} + \gamma_{030}X_{ETHNIC2} + u_{0JK}$$

$$\beta_{2JK} = \beta_{20K} + \gamma_{210}X_{SIZE2} + \gamma_{220}X_{POOR2} + \gamma_{230}X_{ETHNIC2} + u_{1JK}$$

<u>Level-three model</u>

$$\beta_{00K} = \gamma_{000} + \gamma_{001}X_{SIZE3} + \gamma_{002}X_{POOR3} + u_{00K}$$

$$\beta_{20K} = \gamma_{002} + \gamma_{201}X_{SIZE3} + \gamma_{202}X_{POOR3} + u_{10K}$$

<u>Full model</u>

$$Y_{IJK} = \gamma_{000} + \gamma_{100}X_{GENDER1} + \gamma_{200}ETHNIC1 + \gamma_{010}X_{SIZE2} + \gamma_{020}X_{POOR2} + \gamma_{020}X_{ETHNIC2}$$

$$+ \gamma_{001}X_{SIZE3} + \gamma_{002}X_{POOR3} + \gamma_{210}X_{SIZE2} * ETHNIC1 + \gamma_{220}X_{POOR2} * ETHNIC1$$

$$+ \gamma_{230}X_{ETHNIC2} * ETHNIC1 + \gamma_{201}X_{SIZE3} * ETHNIC1 + \gamma_{202}X_{POOOR3} * ETHNIC1$$

$$+ u_{00K} + u_{0JK} + u_{20K} * ETHNIC1 + u_{2JK} * ETHNIC1 + e_{IJK}$$

have fixed slopes. The intercept remains random at the school and district levels, as does the slope for ETHNIC1. The respecified three-level model is reported in Table 8.25. Interpretation of fixed components (see Table 8.26) is much as for Table 8.21:

1. Female students, on average, score 1.155 points lower in math achievement than male students.
2. Black students, on average, score 6.506 points lower in math achievement than White students.
3. For each 1% increase in a school's students eligible for free/reduced cost lunch, individual student math achievement is decreased, on average, by 0.263 points.
4. For each 1% increase in district size, individual student math achievement is decreased, on average, by 0.713 points.
5. For each 1% increase in a school's students eligible for free/reduced cost lunch, Black students' disadvantage in math achievement is decreased by 0.094 points.
6. For each 1% increase in the number of a school's students who are Black, the math achievement disadvantage for Black students is increased by 21.188 points. Until now, this consequential finding has gone undetected. An important reason why the coefficient is so large is naturally limited variability in X_{ETHNIC2}, with a coefficient of variation of only 3.3%.

When we examine random components (see Table 8.27), we find that model respecification has not diminished the magnitude of the random terms at the school level. The variance of INTERCEPT1 at the school level is still statistically significant, and has actually increased in value. The same is true for the random component variance of the slope for ETHNIC1: still statistically significant at the school level, and larger than in Table 8.22.

TABLE 8.26. Math Achievement: Multilevel Regression with Three Levels; Two Student-Level Predictors; Three School-Level Predictors; Two District-Level Predictors; Random Intercept and Random Slope at Level Two and Level Three; Fixed Components

$$Y = 46.167 - 1.155X_{\text{GENDER1}} - 6.506\text{ETHNIC1} + 0.148X_{\text{SIZE2}} - 0.263X_{\text{POOR2}} - 2.385X_{\text{ETHNIC2}}$$
$$(0.470)\ (0.186)\qquad\quad (1.066)\qquad\quad (0.581)\qquad (0.028)\qquad\quad (2.335)$$

$$\quad - 0.713X_{\text{SIZE3}} - 0.021X_{\text{POOR3}} + 0.094X_{\text{POOR2}} * \text{ETHNIC1} - 1.361X_{\text{SIZE2}} * \text{ETHNIC1}$$
$$\quad (0.345)\qquad (0.031)\qquad (0.040)\qquad\qquad\qquad (1.360)$$

$$\quad - 21.188X_{\text{ETHNIC2}} * \text{ETHNIC1} + 0.932X_{\text{SIZE3}} * \text{ETHNIC1}$$
$$\quad (0.451)\qquad\qquad\qquad (0.684)$$

$$R_1^2 = 9.1\%$$
$$N_1 = 46{,}770$$
$$N_2 = 347$$
$$N_3 = 135$$

TABLE 8.27. Math Achievement: Multilevel Regression with Three Levels; Two Student-Level Predictors; Three School-Level Predictors; Two District-Level Predictors; Random Intercept and Random Slope at Level Two and Level Three; Estimates of Covariance Parameters

Parameter	Estimate	Std. error	Wald Z	Sig. level
Residual	400.402	2.630	152.234	.000
INTERCEPT1 variance at level two	13.032	1.748	7.455	.000
INTERCEPT1-by-ETHNIC1 covariance at level two	−4.459	2.517	−1.772	.076
ETHNIC1 variance at level two	26.251	7.885	3.329	.001
INTERCEPT1 variance at level three	0.861	1.145	0.752	.452
INTERCEPT1-by-ETHNIC1 covariance at level three	−0.607	1.988	−0.305	.760
ETHNIC1 variance at level three	3.301	7.259	0.455	.649

None of the district-level random components, however, is statistically significant. Respecification of the three-level model has accounted for the district-level variance of the random component for ETHNIC1, which had been statistically significant and more than five times as large in Table 8.22.

Including the $X_{SIZE2} * X_{POOR2}$ and $X_{SIZE3} * X_{POOR3}$ same-level interaction terms in this three-level equation makes little difference in the other fixed component values (see Table 8.28). Once again, however, we see that the slope for $X_{SIZE2} * X_{POOR2}$ is statistically significant: For each 100-student increase in school size, the math achievement disadvantage corresponding to a 1% increase in students who are economically disadvantaged increases by 0.095 points. This is almost exactly the same value reported in Table 8.26.

As in our use of Table 8.24, we again get inconsistent results from application of the deviance difference and the information criteria (see Table 8.29). In this instance, the deviance difference indicates that the model with same-level interaction terms is the better-fitting one. The information criteria, however, again give us a split decision.

TABLE 8.28. Math Achievement: Multilevel Regression with Three Levels; Two Student-Level Predictors; Three School-Level Predictors; Two District-Level Predictors; Random Intercept and Random Slope at Level Two and Level Three; Same-Level Interaction Terms Included; Fixed Components

$$Y = 46.369 - 1.155X_{GENDER1} - 6.336ETHNIC1 + 0.115X_{SIZE2} - 0.208X_{POOR2} - 1.374X_{ETHNIC2} - 0.953X_{SIZE3}$$
$$\quad (0.470) \ (0.186) \qquad (1.071) \qquad (0.186) \qquad (0.032) \qquad (2.329) \qquad (0.353)$$

$$\quad - 0.027X_{POOR3} + 0.099X_{POOR2} * ETHNIC1 - 1.572X_{SIZE2} * ETHNIC1 - 21.044X_{ETHNIC2} * ETHNIC1$$
$$\quad (0.032) \qquad (0.040) \qquad\qquad (1.369) \qquad\qquad (0.454)$$

$$\quad + 1.054X_{SIZE3} * ETHNIC1 - 0.095X_{SIZE2} * X_{POOR2} + 0.019X_{SIZE3} * X_{POOR3}$$
$$\quad (0.703) \qquad\qquad (0.025) \qquad\qquad (0.022)$$

$$R_1^2 = 9.1\%$$
$$N_1 = 46,770$$
$$N_2 = 347$$
$$N_3 = 135$$

TABLE 8.29. Information Criteria for Tables 8.26 and 8.28

Criterion	With interaction term	Without interaction term
–2 log likelihood	*413341.6*	413360.6
Akaike's Information Criterion	*413383.6*	413398.6
Hurvich and Tsai's Criterion	*413383.6*	413398.6
Bozdogan's Criterion	413588.4	*413583.9*
Schwarz's Bayesian Criterion	413567.4	*413564.9*

Note. The smaller value for each measure is boldfaced and italicized.

$$\text{Deviance difference} = 413360.6 - 413341.6 = 19.0$$
$$df = 21 - 19 = 2$$

As before, we acknowledge that it is not clear that either model, with or without same-level interaction terms, fits the data better than the other. At the same time, the consistency with which the same-level interaction term $X_{SIZE2} * X_{POOR2}$ has yielded statistically significant and negative results in this research and in numerous analyses reported by others gives it a good deal of credibility.

8.13 A LEVEL-TWO RANDOM SLOPE AT LEVEL THREE

Any terms included in the level-two model may be considered random at level three (Luke, 2004). This is easy enough to say, but how do we actually make this happen? Suppose that in developing our three-level model we decide to permit γ_{020}—the slope for X_{POOR2} in the equation for the random intercept, β_{0JK}—to be random with respect to districts. In addition, we decide that the random component estimates in Table 8.27 indicate that the random slope for ETHNIC1 should vary across schools, but not across districts. Lastly, we permit the intercept to continue to be random with respect to both schools and districts. What will our model look like?

Using Table 8.25 as a point of departure and making the changes in random terms just indicated, we get the model specified in Table 8.30. At level two we see that the equation for the random intercept, β_{0JK}, contains a random slope, β_{02K}, for the predictor POOR2. The subscripts for β_{02K} indicate that it is the contribution of POOR2 to the random intercept, β_{0JK}, as it varies across districts. β_{02K} is a function of its common value, γ_{020}, and the district-level effects of X_{SIZE3} (γ_{021}) and X_{POOR3} (γ_{022}). The district-specific variability is represented by u_{02K}.

The same-level interaction terms $X_{SIZE2} * X_{POOR2}$ and $X_{SIZE3} * X_{POOR3}$, which have received a good deal of attention in previous analyses, have been excluded to avoid multicollinearity. When the same-level interaction terms were added to an OLS regression equation specified to simulate the multilevel equation in Table 8.31, seven condition indices exceeded the usual cutoff of 4, with one condition index exceeding 10.0 (Fox, 1997).

TABLE 8.30. Math Achievement: Random Coefficient Regression with Three Levels; Two Student-Level Predictors; Two School-Level Predictors; Two District-Level Predictors; Random Intercept and Random Slope at Level Two and Level Three

<u>Level-one model</u>

$$Y_{IJK} = \beta_{0JK} + \gamma_{100}X_{GENDER1} + \beta_{2J0}ETHNIC1 + e_{IJK}$$

<u>Level-two model</u>

$$\beta_{0JK} = \beta_{00K} + \gamma_{010}X_{SIZE2} + \beta_{02K}POOR2 + \gamma_{030}X_{ETHNIC2} + u_{0JK}$$

$$\beta_{2J0} = \gamma_{200} + \gamma_{210}X_{SIZE2} + \gamma_{220}X_{POOR2} + \gamma_{230}X_{ETHNIC2} + u_{2J0}$$

<u>Level-three model</u>

$$\beta_{00K} = \gamma_{000} + \gamma_{001}X_{SIZE3} + \gamma_{002}X_{POOR3} + u_{00K}$$

$$\beta_{02K} = \gamma_{020} + \gamma_{021}X_{SIZE3} + \gamma_{022}X_{POOR3} + u_{02K}$$

<u>Full model</u>

$$Y_{IJK} = \gamma_{000} + \gamma_{100}X_{GENDER1} + \gamma_{200}ETHNIC1 + \gamma_{010}X_{SIZE2} + \gamma_{002}X_{POOR2} + \gamma_{030}X_{ETHNIC2} + \gamma_{001}X_{SIZE3}$$

$$+ \gamma_{002}X_{POOR3} + \gamma_{210}X_{SIZE2} * ETHNIC1 + \gamma_{220}X_{POOR2} * ETHNIC1 + \gamma_{230}X_{ETHNIC2} * ETHNIC1$$

$$+ \gamma_{021}X_{SIZE3} * POOR2 + \gamma_{022}X_{POOR3} * POOR2 + u_{00K} + u_{0JK} + u_{02K} * POOR2 + u_{2J0} * ETHNIC1 + e_{IJK}$$

TABLE 8.31. Math Achievement: Random Coefficient Regression with Three Levels; Two Student-Level Predictors; Two School-Level Predictors; Two District-Level Predictors; Random Intercept and Random Slope at Level Two and Level Three; Fixed Components

$$Y = 46.769 - 1.154X_{GENDER1} - 6.528ETHNIC1 + 0.311X_{SIZE2} - 0.177POOR2 - 1.091X_{ETHNIC2}$$
$$(0.578)\ (0.186) \qquad (1.045) \qquad\qquad (0.541) \qquad\quad (0.034) \qquad\quad (2.204)$$

$$- 1.707X_{SIZE3} - 0.067X_{POOR3} + 0.103POOR2 * ETHNIC1 - 0.289X_{SIZE2} * ETHNIC1$$
$$(0.382) \qquad\quad (0.038) \qquad\quad (0.040) \qquad\qquad\qquad (1.064)$$

$$- 19.774X_{ETHNIC2} * ETHNIC1 - 0.063\ X_{SIZE3} * POOR2 + 0.001X_{POOR3} * POOR2$$
$$(3.635) \qquad\qquad\qquad (0.014) \qquad\qquad\quad (0.001)$$

$$R_1^2 = 9.2\%$$
$$N_1 = 46,770$$
$$N_2 = 347$$
$$N_3 = 135$$

Interpretation of this three-level model follows a by-now-familiar pattern:

1. Female students, on average, score 1.154 points lower in math achievement than male students.
2. Black students, on average, score 6.258 points lower in math achievement than White students.
3. For each 1% increase in the number of a school's students eligible for free/reduced cost lunch, individual student math achievement decreases, on average, by 0.177 points.
4. For each 1% increase in district size, individual student math achievement decreases, on average, by 1.707 points.
5. For each 1% increase in the number of a school's students eligible for free/reduced cost lunch, the math achievement disadvantage for Black students relative to Whites decreases, on average, by 0.103 points.
6. For each 1% increase in the number of a school's students who are Black, individual Black students' math achievement disadvantage relative to Whites increases, on average, by 19.744 points.
7. Each 1% increase in district size corresponds, on average, to a 0.063-point increase in the negative relationship between math achievement and the percentage of a school's students eligible for free/reduced lunch.

In Table 8.32 we see that the intercept at level one and the ETHNIC1 random slope remain statistically significant. The ETHNIC1 random slope, in fact, has been immune to substantial diminution over the various specifications in which it has been included. Even though this is a very complex model, it is not difficult to run with SPSS. Look at the screen and follow the steps in SPSS Routine 8.2.

It is instructive to compare Table 8.32 with Table 8.33. The random component variances and covariances in the latter table have been estimated after exclusion of all

TABLE 8.32. Math Achievement: Random Coefficient Regression with Three Levels; Two Student-Level Predictors; Two School-Level Predictors; Two District-Level Predictors; Random Intercept and Random Slope at Level Two and Level Three; Estimates of Covariance Parameters

Parameter	Estimate	Std. error	Wald Z	Sig. level
Residual	400.437	2.630	152.229	.000
INTERCEPT1 variance at level two	8.936	1.361	6.564	.000
INTERCEPT1-by-ETHNIC1 covariance at level two	−1.863	2.028	−0.919	.358
ETHNIC1 variance at level two	27.767	6.504	4.269	.000
INTERCEPT1 variance at level three	1.449	1.165	1.244	.214
INTERCEPT1-by-POOR2 covariance at level three	0.048	0.044	1.089	.276
POOR2 variance at level three	0.004	0.003	1.301	.193

SPSS Routine 8.2. Random Slope at Level Two and Level Three

1. Open the SPSS data file and click on ANALYZE.
2. Go to MIXED MODELS and click on LINEAR.
3. Insert the school identifier and the district identifier into the SUBJECTS box.
4. Click on CONTINUE; insert math achievement into the DEPENDENT VARIABLE box; insert the independent variables and cross-level interaction terms into the COVARIATE(S) box.
5. Click on FIXED; change FACTORIAL to MAIN EFFECTS. Move the independent variables and cross-level interaction terms from the FACTORS AND COVARIATES box to the MODEL box.
6. Click on CONTINUE.
7. Click on RANDOM. Move the school identifier from the from the SUBJECTS box to the COMBINATIONS box.
8. Change FACTORIAL to MAIN EFFECTS.
9. Click on INCLUDE INTERCEPT, and move ETHNIC1 into the MODEL box.
10. Just above INCLUDE INTERCEPT and to the right of COVARIANCE TYPE, select UNSTRUCTURED. Click on NEXT.
11. Move the district identifier from the SUBJECTS box to the COMBINATIONS box. Change FACTORIAL to MAIN EFFECTS.
12. Click on INCLUDE INTERCEPT and move the POOR2 into the MODEL box.
13. Just above INCLUDE INTERCEPT and to the right of COVARIANCE TYPE, select UNSTRUCTURED.
14. Click on CONTINUE, and the click on the STATISTICS button.
15. Under MODEL STATISTICS select PARAMETER ESTIMATES and TESTS FOR COVARIANCE PARAMETERS.
16. Click on CONTINUE and click on OK.

TABLE 8.33. Math Achievement: Random Coefficient Regression with Three Levels; Two Student-Level Predictors; Contextual Variables and Cross-Level Interaction Terms Not Included; Random Intercept and Random Slope at Level Two and Level Three; Estimates of Covariance Parameters

Parameter	Estimate	Std. error	Wald Z	Sig. level
Residual	400.416	2.631	152.214	.000
INTERCEPT1 variance at level two	9.029	1.419	6.363	.000
INTERCEPT1-by-ETHNIC1 covariance at level two	−3.336	2.389	−1.396	.183
ETHNIC1 variance at level two	39.424	7.664	5.144	.000
INTERCEPT1 variance at level three	4.585	1.614	2.842	.008
INTERCEPT1-by-POOR2 covariance at level three	0.152	0.064	2.359	.018
POOR2 variance at level three	0.007	0.003	2.110	.035

fixed effects that do not correspond to a random coefficient. When contextual variables (other than X_{POOR2}) and all cross-level interaction terms are excluded, the random component variances and covariances are substantially larger. As we can now see, the variance of the random slope for ETHNIC1 is substantially diminished when contextual variables and cross-level interaction terms are included.

8.14   SUMMING UP

It is true that anyone who can specify and estimate a two-level model can learn to specify and estimate a three-level model. In my experience, however, the amount of work required to make the transition from two-level to three-level models is underestimated in most instructional accounts. Part of the problem inheres in making more and more difficult model specification decisions in the absence of readily interpretable guidance from pertinent theoretical and substantive literature.

Beyond that, however, models with three or more levels quickly become very complex statistically. The number of random component variances and covariances increases dramatically with the addition of predictors with random slopes. Parallels between two-level and three-level models are a good deal less obvious when it comes to actually specifying a three-level model. Model-building facility takes practice.

Three-level models can be informative, providing insights that otherwise would not be available. However, off-handed assertions that three-level regression models are just straightforward extensions of two-level models may lead us to expect too much. Three-level models are uniquely complex, and their effective application demands more theoretical and substantive knowledge than typically is available.

8.15   USEFUL RESOURCES

Hox, J. (2002) *Multilevel Analysis.* Mahwah, NJ: Erlbaum.
Luke, D. (2004) *Multilevel Modeling.* Thousand Oaks, CA: Sage.
Raudenbush, S., & Bryk, A. (2002) *Hierarchical Linear Models* (2nd ed.). Thousand Oaks, CA: Sage.
Snijders, T., & Bosker, R. (1999) *Multilevel Analysis.* Thousand Oaks, CA: Sage.

Hox (2002) gives only one page to three-level models, but his cautionary comments are invaluable. He persuasively alerts the reader to the intractable statistical complexity that is occasioned by unduly ambitious three-level models.

Luke (2004) devotes only four pages to three-level models, but his examples are the most instructive to be found. Understanding Luke's examples lends a modicum of credibility to the off-handed judgment that three-level models are almost as easy to specify, estimate, and understand as two-level models.

Raudenbush and Bryk (2002) devote a chapter of their widely used textbook to three-level models. A brief discussion is also provided by Snijders and Bosker (1999). The examples used by

Snijders and Bosker are especially interesting. As we have noted before, however, these texts make for difficult reading.

Belanger, P., & Eagles, M. (2005) *The Geography of Class and Religion in Canadian Elections*. Paper Presented at the Canadian Political Science Association Conference, University of Western Ontario, London, Ontario, June 2–4.

Romano, E., Tremblay, R., Boulerice, B., & Swisher, R. (2005) Multilevel Correlates of Childhood Physical Aggression and Prosocial Behavior. *Journal of Abnormal Child Psychology, 33,* 565–578.

Wiggins, R., Joshi, H., Bartley, M., Gleave, S., Lynch, K., & Cullis, A. (2002) Place and Personal Circumstances in a Multilevel Account of Women's Long-Term Illness. *Social Science and Medicine, 54,* 827–838.

Clearly written article-length accounts provide some of the best material for learning about three-level models. A primary virtue of the paper by Belanger and Eagles is their demonstration that the choice of variables to constitute levels in a three-level analysis can have a dramatic effect on results. The three levels in their Canadian voting behavior research are individual, locality, and province. When they compare their results with analyses that used the province rather than the locality at level two, they find that the social and geographical distance between individual and province failed to reveal important group effects peculiar to localities.

Romano and colleagues (2005) address the role of individual, family, and neighborhood factors affecting unduly aggressive and socially acceptable behavior among adolescent males. Their work is methodologically instructive because of the clarity with which the authors present their analysis. Their identification of level-three neighborhood characteristics as correlates of aggressive behavior is especially interesting because we have used similar measures, including gauges of neighborhood quality, to account for student achievement differences in some of our two-level models.

Wiggins et al.'s interesting application of multilevel regression analysis with three levels is characterized by an unusually large sample of 76,374 women nested in 9539 local wards and 401 larger districts. Table 3 on page 838 of their article provides a remarkably clear and straightforward summary example of instructive reporting of fixed effects in a complex model. Level-three factors related to the frequency of long-term illnesses among women in England and Wales are numerous and easy to understand. Though their models are complex, the authors use no random slopes, just random intercepts. This too is easy to see and interpret in their presentation. It is instructive to learn that the authors used principal components analysis in constructing five of their level-two independent variables. This is exactly the sort of variable construction approach often used with OLS regression, and it lends itself just as readily to multilevel regression.

Familiar Measures
Applied to Three-Level Models

9.1   CHAPTER INTRODUCTION

As we have repeatedly emphasized, the intraclass correlation coefficient is an indispensable tool. Without it, judgments as to whether or not multilevel regression is applicable to the analytical task at hand would be a good deal less certain. Fortunately, as with the other measures discussed in this brief chapter, calculation and interpretation of the intraclass correlation coefficient are just as easy for three-level models as for two-level models. This assertion holds for both the unconditional and conditional versions of this informative statistic.

Reading empirical research in journals representing a variety of disciplines affirms Kreft and De Leeuw's (1998) judgment that the deviance is treated as if it were the most important summary statistic. It is quite uncommon to find a research report using multilevel analysis that does not use the deviance statistic, if only to demonstrate that a specific conditional model provides a better fit than the unconditional model. This is accomplished by using the deviance difference to compare nested models.

The R_1^2 summary measure, by contrast, is reported sporadically. As with contemporary applications of OLS regression, there is a good deal more interest in the value of fixed coefficients than in reduction in errors of prediction. The fact that R_1^2 is of dubious value as a decision-making tool when we are comparing differently specified models may help to explain its irregular use. Some authors, moreover, prefer reporting reductions in within-group variance and between-group variance without also using an overall summary statistic.

While the utility of the deviance for choosing among competing models helps to account for its popularity, we have already noted some of its limitations. Comparing models by using the deviance difference should be done only with nested models (cf.

248

SAS Institute, 1999). In addition, the deviance is sensitive to the number of parameters estimated: The more parameters used, the easier it is to find a statistically significant difference between two deviance values. As still another caution, the deviance is sensitive to sample size: The larger the sample, the easier it is to find a statistically significant difference between two deviance values.

However, application of the information criteria routinely reported by SPSS—Akaike's Information Criterion, Hurvich and Tsai's Criterion, Bozdogan's Criterion, and Schwarz's Bayesian Criterion—need share none of these limitations. They can be used to compare either nested or non-nested models; they impose penalties for estimating additional parameters; and Schwarz's Bayesian Criterion adjusts for sample size.

The smaller-is-better interpretations of the information criteria, however, lack the intuitive appeal of the R_1^2 summary measure. In addition, the information criteria do not provide the decisive appearance of a formal statistical test, while the deviance difference does grant this kind of statistical authority. Nevertheless, the information criteria, especially Akaike's Information Criterion and Schwarz's Bayesian Criterion, are versatile and commonly used measures. They do not share the ubiquity of the deviance in the empirical literature on multilevel regression, but, as we have seen, they can be used to address questions for which the deviance is not well suited.

Whatever their purpose and pervasiveness, all the measures discussed in this chapter—the intraclass correlation, R_1^2, the deviance and the deviance difference, and the information criteria—play exactly the same role with three-level models as with two-level models. Increasing the number of levels in our model, moreover, does not make these statistics more difficult to compute.

9.2   THE INTRACLASS CORRELATION COEFFICIENT REVISITED

We have already seen that computation of the unconditional intraclass correlation for a two-level model is not difficult. For example, if we use vocabulary achievement at the end of kindergarten with the 18 classrooms in our 12-school West Virginia data set, we get the information in Table 9.1.

As always, the unconditional intraclass correlation is computed as follows:

$$r = \text{Variability between groups/total variability}$$
$$r = 3.815/(3.815 + 17.772) = 0.175$$

TABLE 9.1. Computing the Unconditional Intraclass Correlation Coefficient: Students Nested in Classrooms; Random Component Estimates for Null Model

Parameter	Estimate	Std. error	Wald Z	Sig. level
Residual	17.772	1.432	12.409	.000
INTERCEPT1	3.815	1.699	2.246	.025

As we know, this means that 17.5% of the variability in vocabulary achievement occurs between classrooms, while the rest occurs within classrooms. A useful way to say the same thing is to note that between-group variability is explained simply by virtue of the fact that individuals are placed into a set of categories, while within-group variability is not explained by the process of categorization.

We know, of course, that the unconditional intraclass correlation coefficient is computed with no predictors other than the random intercept. In other words, there are no independent variables. However, after one or more independent variables have been introduced, the unconditional intraclass correlation coefficient gives way to the *conditional* intraclass correlation coefficient.

The information in Table 9.2, for example, has been obtained by including independent variables representing family income at the classroom level and a cross-level interaction term created by using this contextual variable and its level-one counterpart.

$$r = 3.467/(3.467 + 17.059) = 0.169$$

As we expect, the conditional intraclass correlation is smaller than its unconditional counterpart. The contextual variable and the cross-level interaction term have accounted for some, though not very much, of the between-group variability in end-of-kindergarten reading achievement.

The information in Table 9.3 has been obtained by adding another contextual variable. This second group-level variable has been created by aggregating beginning-of-kindergarten reading achievement to the classroom level. In addition, a cross-level interaction term created by multiplying this contextual variable by its level-one counterpart has been introduced. Again, between-group variability in the dependent variable has been diminished, and the overall consequence is further reduction in the magnitude of the conditional intraclass correlation coefficient:

TABLE 9.2. Computing the Conditional Intraclass Correlation Coefficient: Students Nested in Classrooms; Random Component Estimates for Conditional Model

Parameter	Estimate	Std. error	Wald Z	Sig. level
Residual	17.059	1.411	12.089	.000
INTERCEPT1	3.467	1.656	2.093	.036

TABLE 9.3. Computing the Conditional Intraclass Correlation Coefficient; Students Nested in Classrooms; Random Component Estimates for a More Complex Model

Parameter	Estimate	Std. error	Wald Z	Sig. level
Residual	8.296	0.669	12.393	.000
INTERCEPT1	0.411	0.562	0.721	.465

$$r = 0.411/(0.411 + 8.296) = 0.047$$

Notice that INTERCEPT1, our measure of between-classroom variability, is no longer statistically significant. This means that we have succeeded in accounting for all but an incidental, sample-specific amount of the between-classroom variability in end-of-kindergarten reading achievement. If we had gotten a nonsignificant value for INTERCEPT1 when computing the *unconditional* intraclass correlation, we would have concluded that multilevel regression was not needed, and we would have continued with OLS.

As we illustrated in Chapter 8, with more than two levels, there will be more than one unconditional intraclass correlation. To clarify this with another example, we have structured Table 9.4 in the same way as Table 8.7, though we have added a fourth level. In this instance we are using a second West Virginia data set, this one assembled by the National Institute for Early Education Research (NIEER) for evaluating early childhood education programs (Lamy, Barnett, & Jung, 2005). The data set includes 750 students nested in 164 classrooms nested in 92 schools nested in 34 districts (Lamy et al., 2005). The dependent variable is a measure of skill in sound blending or phonics from the Preschool Comprehensive Test of Phonological and Print Processing, used to measure reading readiness at the beginning of kindergarten (Lonigan, Wagner, Torgesen, & Rashotte, 2002).

Following our cautionary comments regarding the sometimes troublesome complexity of three-level models in Chapter 8, invoking four levels may seem excessive. However, we will use the information in Table 9.4 only to illustrate the ease with which a variety of different unconditional intraclass correlation coefficients may be computed (Snijders & Bosker, 1999).

If we are interested in the intraclass correlation for individual students nested in classrooms, the procedure is by now quite familiar:

$$r = 2.756/(2.756 + 13.316) = 0.171$$

TABLE 9.4. Phonics (Sound-Blending): Students in Classrooms in Schools in Districts; the Unconditional Intraclass Correlation with More Than Two Levels; Random Component Estimates

Parameter	Estimate	Std. error	Wald Z	Sig. level
Residual variability within schools	13.316	0.807	16.496	.000
INTERCEPT at level two: Variability between classrooms within schools	2.756	0.971	2.839	.005
INTERCEPT at level three: Variability between schools within districts	0.793	0.912	0.870	.384
INTERCEPT at level four: Variability between districts	8.321	2.528	3.291	.001

As we know, this means that 17.1% of the variability in reading readiness occurs between classrooms.

If we are interested in the intraclass correlation for individuals nested in classrooms, schools, and districts, a straightforward variation on the same procedure is easy to apply:

$$r = (2.796 + 0.794 + 8.321)/(2.796 + 0.794 + 8.321 + 13.316) = 0.472$$

This means that 47.2% of the variability in reading readiness is due to grouping in classrooms, schools, and districts, while 52.8% of the variability occurs between individual students.

It is interesting to see, by the way, that most of the variability due to grouping occurs at the district level, farther removed from individual students than classrooms or schools. This unexpected finding indicates that 69.9% of the reading readiness variability attributable to grouping occurs at the district level. We calculate this percentage by using another straightforward variation on the usual formula for the intraclass correlation coefficient:

$$r = 8.321/(2.796 + 0.794 + 8.321) = 0.699$$

Clearly, working with more than two levels gives rise to patterns of nesting that we otherwise would not anticipate. Furthermore, we now see that increasing the organizational distance between students and a grouping variable does not always mean that groups become internally less homogeneous.

It is also interesting that variability between schools within districts is not statistically significant. If we were contemplating a multilevel regression analysis using school-level data, we would not have to worry about the nesting of schools in districts; as a practical matter, there is none! The statistically nonsignificant variance component at the school level tells us that the intraclass correlation coefficient for an analysis of this sort would also be statistically nonsignificant. In this case, we could use traditional OLS regression.

9.3   PERCENTAGE OF VARIANCE EXPLAINED IN A LEVEL-ONE DEPENDENT VARIABLE

We have also seen that R_1^2 is easy to compute. Say, for example, that we want to examine the relationship between individual reading readiness and age in months among beginning kindergarten students. We use the West Virginia data set introduced in the preceding section, and specify a three-level model. With 750 students nested in 164 classrooms and 34 districts, we make the intercept and the age-in-months slope random at both the classroom and district levels. This gives us the three-level model specified in Table 9.5.

When we run the analysis, we get the results reported in Tables 9.6 and 9.7. In Table 9.6 we see that for each 1-month increase in age, the value of the measure of phonics or

TABLE 9.5. Phonics: Random Coefficient Regression with Three Levels; One Student-Level Predictor; Random Intercept and Random Slope at Level Two and Level Three

Level-one model

$$Y_{IJK} = \beta_{0JK} + \beta_{1JK}AGE1 + e_{IJK}$$

Level-two model

$$\beta_{0JK} = \beta_{00K} + u_{0JK}$$

$$\beta_{1JK} = \beta_{10K} + u_{1JK}$$

Level-three model

$$\beta_{00K} = \gamma_{000} + u_{00K}$$

$$\beta_{10K} = \gamma_{100} + u_{10K}$$

Full model

$$Y_{IJK} = \gamma_{000} + \gamma_{100}AGE1 + u_{00K} + u_{0JK} + u_{10K} * AGE1 + u_{1JK} * AGE1 + e_{IJK}$$

TABLE 9.6. Phonics: Random Coefficient Regression with Three Levels; One Student-Level Predictor; Random Intercept and Random Slope at Level Two and Level Three; Fixed Components

$$Y = 14.968 + 0.156AGE1$$
$$(0.350)\ (0.225)$$

$$R_1^2 = 5.3\%$$
$$N = 46,770$$

TABLE 9.7. Phonics: Random Coefficient Regression with Three Levels; One Student-Level Predictor; Random Intercept and Random Slope at Level Two and Level Three; Estimates of Covariance Parameters

Parameter	Estimate	Std. error	Wald Z	Sig. level
Residual	12.158	0.791	15.832	.000
INTERCEPT variance at level two	0.303	0.867	0.350	.726
INTERCEPT-by-AGE1 covariance at level two	0.005	0.051	0.095	.925
AGE1 variance at level two	0.014	0.014	0.994	.320
INTERCEPT variance at level three	9.488	1.826	5.197	.000
INTERCEPT-by-AGE1 covariance at level three	0.206	0.095	2.165	.030
AGE1 variance at level three	0.005	0.008	0.594	.552

sound-blending skills increases, on average, by 0.156 points. In Table 9.7 we see that the level-two intercept variance that contributed substantially to the values we calculated for unconditional intraclass correlation coefficients following Table 9.4 has been reduced to statistical nonsignificance. In fact, the only statistically significant random terms are the intercept and the intercept-by-slope covariance at the district level.

For present purposes, however, the important question concerns R_1^2 in Table 9.6. Specifically, how did we determine the value of this summary measure? My notation is clumsy, but the formula is as follows (Snijders & Bosker, 1999):

$$R_1^2 = (1 - [\text{RESIDUAL}_{\text{FIXED}} + \text{INTERCEPT2}_{\text{FIXED}} + \text{INTERCEPT3}_{\text{FIXED}})/$$

$$(\text{RESIDUAL}_{\text{NULL}} + \text{INTERCEPT3}_{\text{NULL}} + \text{INTERCEPT3}_{\text{NULL}})]) * 100$$

In other words, we first estimate the null model, permitting the intercept to be random at both level two and level three. Then we sum the random components, and we have the denominator for the formula above. Next, we estimate the conditional model permitting the intercept to be random at levels two and three, but make all slopes fixed. We then sum the random components, and we have the numerator in the formula above. After dividing, we subtract the result from 1.00 and multiply by 100. This gives us R_1^2 for a three-level model, percentage of reduction of errors in prediction for the dependent variable. This is just a straightforward extension of the formula we used in calculating R_1^2 for two-level models. Now, however, we have more levels.

The information needed to compute R_1^2 for Table 9.6 is reported in Tables 9.8 and 9.9. With this information, we can do so as follows:

$$R_1^2 = 1 - [(13.068 + 1.050 + 8.943)/(13.092 + 2.845 + 8.983)] * 100 = 5.3\%$$

TABLE 9.8. Phonics: Random Coefficient Regression with Three Levels; One Student-Level Predictor; Estimates of Covariance Parameters; Unconditional (Null) Model

Parameter	Estimate	Std. error	Wald Z	Sig. level
Residual	13.092	0.802	16.328	.000
INTERCEPT variance at level two	2.845	1.022	2.783	.005
INTERCEPT variance at level three	8.983	1.852	4.849	.000

TABLE 9.9. Phonics: Random Coefficient Regression with Three Levels; One Student-Level Predictor; Estimates of Covariance Parameters; Conditional Model with Fixed Slope

Parameter	Estimate	Std. error	Wald Z	Sig. level
Residual	13.068	0.798	16.383	.000
INTERCEPT variance at level two	1.050	0.751	1.398	.162
INTERCEPT variance at level three	8.943	1.687	5.302	.000

Relative to the null model, the conditional model has reduced errors in predicting the value of individual students' sound-blending scores by 5.3%.

Suppose we add another level-one predictor, a measure of student social skills at the beginning of kindergarten ($X_{SOCIAL1}$) (Gresham & Elliott, 1990). As a rationale for this additional student-level predictor, we surmise that social skills are an essential prerequisite for learning, both in school and out of school. Social skills deficits, in fact, have been construed as a primary learning disability (Gresham & Elliott, 1989). We assign $X_{SOCIAL1}$ a fixed slope. The only difference between the respecified three-level model in Table 9.10 and the original three-level specification in Table 9.5 occurs in the level-one model with the addition of the predictor $X_{SOCIAL1}$ and its fixed slope, γ_{200}.

When we examine Table 9.11, we see that both slopes are statistically significant with large t values. For each 1-month increase in student age (AGE1), beginning-of-kindergarten phonics achievement increases, on average, by 0.156 points. In addition, for each 1-unit increase in social skills ($X_{SOCIAL1}$), beginning-of-kindergarten phonics achievement increases, on average, by 0.795 points.

TABLE 9.10. Phonics: Random Coefficient Regression with Three Levels; Two Student-Level Predictors; Random Intercept and Random Slope at Level Two and Level Three

Level-one model

$$Y_{IJK} = \beta_{0JK} + \beta_{1JK}AGE1 + \gamma_{200}X_{SOCIAL1} + e_{IJK}$$

Level-two model

$$\beta_{0JK} = \beta_{00K} + u_{0JK}$$
$$\beta_{1JK} = \beta_{10K} + u_{1JK}$$

Level-three model

$$\beta_{00K} = \gamma_{000} + u_{00K}$$
$$\beta_{10K} = \gamma_{100} + u_{10K}$$

Full model

$$Y_{IJK} = \gamma_{000} + \gamma_{100}AGE1 + u_{00K} + u_{0JK} + u_{10K} * AGE1 + u_{1JK} * AGE1 + e_{IJK}$$

TABLE 9.11. Phonics: Random Coefficient Regression with Three Levels; Two Student-Level Predictors; Random Intercept and Random Slope at Level Two and Level Three; Fixed Components

$$Y = 14.890 + 0.156AGE1 + 0.795X_{SOCIAL1}$$
$$(0.372) \quad (0.023) \qquad (0.016)$$

$$R_1^2 = 8.8\%$$
$$N = 46,770$$

Random component variances and covariances are reported in Table 9.12. Introduction of $X_{SOCIAL1}$ as an additional predictor has reduced the INTERCEPT-by-AGE1 covariance to statistical nonsignificance. The variance of the random component of the intercept at the district level, however, remains statistically significant and has actually gotten a bit larger. None of the other random terms were statistically significant in Table 9.7 with only AGE1 as a predictor, and they remain statistically nonsignificant in Table 9.12.

More important for present purposes, however, are the random component estimates in Table 9.13. This information was computed for the conditional model in Table 9.11, with all slopes fixed. We divide this by the random components already computed for the null model in Table 9.8, and we can calculate R_1^2 in the usual way. Addition of $X_{SOCIAL1}$ as a second predictor has increased the value of R_1^2 from 5.3% to 8.8%. In other words, by using AGE1 and $X_{SOCIAL1}$ as explanatory factors, we reduce errors in prediction of the dependent variable by 8.8%.

$$R_1^2 = 1 - [(12.125 + 1.000 + 8.696)/(13.092 + 2.845 + 8.983)] * 100 = 8.8\%$$

Summary measures such as the conventional R^2 statistic have a long history among users of multiple regression analysis. While reporting such goodness-of-fit measures is customary, the information they provide is sometimes of dubious value (Wittink, 1988).

TABLE 9.12. Phonics: Random Coefficient Regression with Three Levels; Two Student-Level Predictors; Random Intercept and Random Slope at Level Two and Level Three; Estimates of Covariance Parameters

Parameter	Estimate	Std. error	Wald Z	Sig. level
Residual	11.288	0.736	15.342	.000
INTERCEPT variance at level two	0.849	0.000	—	—
INTERCEPT-by-AGE1 covariance at level two	0.072	0.120	0.605	.545
AGE1 variance at level two	0.048	0.000	—	—
INTERCEPT variance at level three	9.741	1.994	4.885	.000
INTERCEPT-by-AGE1 covariance at level three	0.186	0.137	1.353	.176
AGE1 variance at level three	0.004	0.000	—	—

Note. A dash (—) indicates a value too small to measure.

TABLE 9.13. Phonics: Random Coefficient Regression with Three Levels; Two Student-Level Predictors; Estimates of Covariance Parameters; Conditional Model with Fixed Slopes

Parameter	Estimate	Std. error	Wald Z	Sig. level
Residual	12.125	0.783	15.479	.000
INTERCEPT variance at level two	1.000	0.766	1.306	.192
INTERCEPT variance at level three	8.696	1.807	5.367	.000

Historically, OLS regression analysis has too often devolved into an effort to maximize values of summary statistics (notably R^2 as used in OLS regression analysis), with little attention to substantive importance or theoretical development (Blalock, 1964).

During the past four decades, however, the search for unstandardized partial regression coefficients that reflect approximately uniform relationships from time to time and place to place has taken precedence over efforts to maximize R^2 values (Blalock, 1964; Duncan, 1975; Wittink, 1988; Tacq, 1997; Wooldridge, 2002). Nevertheless, measures comparable to the conventional R^2, when interpreted judiciously, can be informative.

Our application of R_1^2 is premised on the assumption that we are interested in determining the percentage of reduction in errors of prediction for the first-level dependent variable, and we have less interest in using a comparable measure at other levels, though such measures exist. In addition, while R_1^2 provides a close approximation of this percentage, a more accurate measure would take into consideration the fact that some slopes are random. Such measures are available, but their computation is complex, and they are not included with general purpose statistical software such as SPSS.

9.4 OTHER SUMMARY MEASURES USED WITH MULTILEVEL REGRESSION

Throughout this presentation we have had to make some difficult choices among alternative multilevel regression model specifications. Often, as we have seen, we had no firm statistical basis for doing so, and very thin substantive criteria were brought to bear in making difficult decisions. Nevertheless, it was always reassuring to know that, whatever our choice, it was not wildly at odds with application of the deviance difference or the four information criteria routinely reported by SPSS. This holds true for three-level models as well as for two-level models.

We will once again use the Kentucky data set to formulate three-level regression models. The dependent variable will be reading achievement as measured by the California Basic Educational Skills Test. Our objective is to illustrate application of the deviance difference and the four information criteria routinely provided by SPSS in comparing differently specified models.

All comparisons will be made with nested models. In this context, *nesting* means than one of the models being compared has more specified parameters than the other. The deviance difference, as we noted above, is intended for use only with nested models (SAS Institute, 1999).

In addition, the deviance difference assumes use of ML rather than REML. Since we will be estimating parameter values for our three-level models with REML, obtaining deviance values for use in computing the deviance difference will mean running each model a second time with ML. In contrast to the deviance difference, the information criteria may be used with either nested or non-nested models (Singer & Willett, 2003). As with the deviance difference, however, the information criteria presuppose use of ML rather than REML.

In the three-level reading achievement model specified in Table 9.14, ethnicity (ETHNIC1, coded 1 for Black and 0 for White) is the only level-one predictor. It has been assigned a random slope that varies across both schools and districts. The intercept too is random, varying across schools and districts. $X_{ETHNIC2}$, ethnicity aggregated to the school level, is the only level-two predictor. It has been assigned a fixed slope. There are no predictors at the district level.

When we estimate fixed and random components for the model in Table 9.14, we get the results reported in Tables 9.15 and 9.16. The fixed components in Table 9.15 tell us that Black students, on average, score 5.932 points lower than White students in reading achievement. The cross-level interaction term tells us that for each 1% increase in the number of Black students in a school, the reading achievement disadvantage for individual Black students is increased by 17.024 points. As we have already explained,

TABLE 9.14. Reading Achievement: Multilevel Regression with Three Levels; One Student-Level Predictor; One School-Level Predictor; Random Intercept and Random Slope at Level Two and Level Three

Level-one model

$$Y_{IJK} = \beta_{0JK} + \beta_{1JK}ETHNIC1 + e_{IJK}$$

Level-two model

$$\beta_{0JK} = \beta_{00K} + \gamma_{010}X_{ETHNIC2} + u_{0JK}$$

$$\beta_{1JK} = \beta_{10K} + \gamma_{110}X_{ETHNIC2} + u_{1JK}$$

Level-three model

$$\beta_{00K} = \gamma_{000} + u_{00K}$$

$$\beta_{10K} = \gamma_{100} + u_{10K}$$

Full model

$$Y_{IJK} = \gamma_{000} + \gamma_{100}ETHNIC1 + \gamma_{020}X_{ETHNIC2} + \gamma_{120}X_{ETHNIC} * ETHNIC1$$

$$+ u_{00K} + u_{0JK} + u_{10K} * ETHNIC1 + u_{1JK} * ETHNIC1 + e_{IJK}$$

TABLE 9.15. Reading Achievement: Multilevel Regression with Three Levels; One Student-Level Predictor; One School-Level Predictor; No District-Level Predictors; Random Intercept and Random Slope at Level Two and Level Three; Fixed Components

$$Y = 51.187 - 5.932ETHNIC1 - 5.024X_{ETHNIC2} - 17.024X_{ETHNIC2} * ETHNIC1$$
$$(0.411)\ (0.572) \qquad\qquad (2.945) \qquad\qquad (3.422)$$

$$R_1^2 = 2.1\%$$
$$N_1 = 46,770$$
$$N_2 = 347$$
$$N_3 = 135$$

TABLE 9.16. Reading Achievement: Multilevel Regression with Three Levels; One Student-Level Predictor; One School-Level Predictor; No District-Level Predictors; Random Intercept and Random Slope at Level Two and Level Three; Estimates of Covariance Parameters

Parameter	Estimate	Std. error	Wald Z	Sig. level
Residual	331.757	2.177	152.401	.000
INTERCEPT variance at level two	22.843	3.587	6.368	.000
INTERCEPT-by-ETHNIC1 covariance at level two	−5.788	3.256	−1.778	.075
ETHNIC1 variance at level two	24.193	6.722	3.599	.000
INTERCEPT variance at level three	3.993	3.077	1.298	.194
INTERCEPT-by-ETHNIC1 covariance at level three	−2.644	3.156	−0.837	.403
ETHNIC1 variance at level three	1.774	0.000	—	—

Note. A dash (—) indicates a value too small to measure.

one reason why the unstandardized slope for the $X_{ETHNIC2}$ * ETHNIC1 is so large is naturally limited school-to-school variation in $X_{ETHNIC2}$.

The random components in Table 9.16 include statistically significant variances for the random intercept at level one and the ETHNIC1 random slope at level one. One objective of subsequent respecifications of this model will be explanation of random component values. As we know, this is accomplished through introduction of contextual variables and cross-level interaction terms.

For now, however, we will begin by introducing gender ($X_{GENDER1}$) with a fixed slope in the three-level model specified in Table 9.17. Perhaps introduction of a second level-

TABLE 9.17. Reading Achievement: Multilevel Regression with Three Levels; Two Student-Level Predictors; One School-Level Predictor; No District-Level Predictors; Random Intercept and Random Slope at Level Two and Level Three

Level-one model

$$Y_{IJK} = \beta_{0JK} + \beta_{1JK}ETHNIC1 + \gamma_{200}X_{GENDER1} + e_{IJK}$$

Level-two model

$$\beta_{0JK} = \beta_{00K} + \gamma_{010}X_{ETHNIC2} + u_{0JK}$$

$$\beta_{1JK} = \beta_{10K} + \gamma_{121}X_{ETHNIC2} + u_{1JK}$$

Level-three model

$$\beta_{00K} = \gamma_{000} + u_{00K}$$

$$\beta_{10K} = \gamma_{100} + u_{10K}$$

Full model

$$Y_{IJK} = \gamma_{000} + \gamma_{100}ETHNIC1 + \gamma_{200}X_{GENDER1} + \gamma_{020}X_{ETHNIC2} + \gamma_{120}X_{ETHNIC2} * ETHNIC1$$

$$+ u_{00K} + u_{0JK} + u_{10K} * ETHNIC1 + u_{1JK} * ETHNIC1 + e_{IJK}$$

one predictor will increase the predictive efficacy of our equation, thereby increasing the value of R_1^2. In Table 9.18, we see that introduction of gender as a second level-one predictor has indeed increased the value of R_1^2, from 2.2% to 5.8%. The slope for $X_{GENDER1}$ tells us that females, on average, score 7.405 points higher than males in reading achievement. The coefficients for ETHNIC1, $X_{ETHNIC2}$, and $X_{ETHNIC2} *$ ETHNIC1 are similar to those reported in Table 9.15, before $X_{GENDER1}$ was introduced.

The random component variances and covariances in Table 9.19 are little different from those reported in Table 9.16. This finding is not surprising, because the only change in model specification has been addition of a predictor at level one. Had we added contextual variables at level two—say, $X_{GENDER2}$ and X_{POOR2}—we might have substantially reduced the random component variances and covariances, as we illustrate in Table 9.20. Inclusion of these contextual variables as level-two predictors substantially reduces each of the random terms.

The more important point for present purposes, however, is that the fixed component results make a compelling case for the model that includes $X_{GENDER1}$ as the better-fitting one. This is certainly consistent with the increase in R_1^2 in Table 9.18. If we want additional evidence to use in deciding which model provides the better fit, we have

TABLE 9.18. Reading Achievement: Multilevel Regression with Three Levels; Two Student-Level Predictors; One School-Level Predictor; No District-Level Predictors; Random Intercept and Random Slope at Level Two and Level Three; Fixed Components

$$Y = 51.222 - 5.977ETHNIC1 + 7.405X_{GENDER1} - 4.870X_{ETHNIC2} - 17.015X_{ETHNIC2} * ETHNIC1$$
$$\quad (0.418) \quad (0.566) \qquad (0.166) \qquad\qquad (2.998) \qquad\quad (3.382)$$

$$R_1^2 = 5.8\%$$
$$N_1 = 46{,}770$$
$$N_2 = 347$$
$$N_3 = 135$$

TABLE 9.19. Reading Achievement: Multilevel Regression with Three Levels; Two Student-Level Predictors; One School-Level Predictor; No District-Level Predictors; Random Intercept and Random Slope at Level Two and Level Three; Estimates of Covariance Parameters

Parameter	Estimate	Std. error	Wald Z	Sig. level
Residual	317.591	2.088	152.053	.000
INTERCEPT variance at level two	23.275	3.733	6.236	.000
INTERCEPT-by-ETHNIC1 covariance at level two	−5.493	3.400	−1.616	.106
ETHNIC1 variance at level two	25.099	7.012	3.579	.000
INTERCEPT variance at level three	4.294	3.319	1.294	.196
INTERCEPT-by-ETHNIC1 covariance at level three	−2.377	3.708	−0.641	.521
ETHNIC1 variance at level three	1.346	0.000	—	—

Note. A dash (—) indicates a value too small to measure.

TABLE 9.20. Reading Achievement: Multilevel Regression with Three Levels; Two Student-Level Predictors; One School-Level Predictor; No District-Level Predictors; Random Intercept and Random Slope at Level Two and Level Three; Estimates of Covariance Parameters

Parameter	Estimate	Std. error	Wald Z	Sig. level
Residual	317.249	2.084	152.266	.000
INTERCEPT variance at level two	8.233	1.149	7.156	.000
INTERCEPT-by-ETHNIC1 covariance at level two	−1.861	1.563	−1.191	.234
ETHNIC1 variance at level two	18.393	4.389	4.191	.000
INTERCEPT variance at level three	0.515	0.650	0.792	.428
INTERCEPT-by-ETHNIC1 covariance at level three	−0.356	0.892	−0.399	.690
ETHNIC1 variance at level three	0.248	0.000	—	—

Note. A dash (—) indicates a value too small to measure.

ready access to the deviance difference and the four information criteria, as given in Table 9.21.

$$\text{Deviance difference} = 406503.6 - 402773.9 = 3729.7$$
$$df = 12 - 11 = 1$$

When we compare the three-level models from Tables 9.15 and 9.18, the deviance difference is statistically significant at any commonly used alpha level. This is consistent with the claim that the three-level model including $X_{GENDER1}$ as a second individual-level predictor is the better-fitting one. In addition, and in contrast with some of the split decisions we have found in other examples, the value for each of the smaller-is-better information criteria is consistent with the judgment that the model with $X_{GENDER1}$ provides the better fit.

We have used the information criteria fairly often, explaining that one of their virtues, when compared with the deviance, is that they punish analysts for using additional degrees of freedom in specifying statistical models. We have not, however, described how this is accomplished. Formulas for the most commonly cited information criteria, Akaike's Information Criterion and Schwarz's Bayesian Criterion, make it easy to see

TABLE 9.21. Information Criteria for Tables 9.15 and 9.18

Criterion	With $X_{GENDER1}$	Without $X_{GENDER1}$
−2 log likelihood	*402773.9*	406503.6
Akaike's Information Criterion	*402797.9*	406525.6
Hurvich and Tsai's Criterion	*402797.9*	406525.6
Bozdogan's Criterion	*402914.9*	406632.9
Schwarz's Bayesian Criterion	*402902.9*	406621.9

Note. The smaller value for each measure is boldfaced and italicized.

why using additional degrees of freedom is costly. In the formula for Schwarz's Bayesian Criterion, $ln(N)$ is the natural logarithm of the level-one sample size (Luke, 2004).

Akaike's Information Criterion = –2 log likelihood + (2 * number of parameters)
402797.9 = 402773.9 + (2 * 12)

Schwarz's Bayesian Criterion = –2 log likelihood + number of parameters * $ln(N)$
402902.9 = 402773.9 + 12 * 10.753

Both criteria use the –2 log likelihood or deviance as a point of departure. As more parameters are added, the criteria become larger. This is a safeguard against using additional parameters to provide the *appearance* of a better fit to the data, when in fact little or nothing has been accomplished. In the sense, the information criteria are analogous to adjusted R^2 as it is used in OLS regression.

Schwarz's Bayesian Criterion increases not only in response to an increase in the number of parameters estimated, but as a function of level-one sample size as well. As sample size increases, deviance values become larger, and the deviance difference is more likely to be statistically significant. Schwarz's Bayesian Criterion provides a hedge against deviance values that are inflated due to large sample sizes.

We can illustrate use of the deviance difference and information criteria again by adding two level-three predictors, $X_{ETHNIC3}$ and X_{POOR3}, to the model specified in Table 9.17. This change in model specification is manifest in the level-three model and the full model in Table 9.22.

TABLE 9.22. Reading Achievement: Multilevel Regression with Three Levels; Two Student-Level Predictors; One School-Level Predictor; Two District-Level Predictors; Random Intercept and Random Slope at Level Two and Level Three

Level-one model

$$Y_{IJK} = \beta_{0JK} + \beta_{1JK}ETHNIC1 + \gamma_{200}X_{GENDER1} + e_{IJK}$$

Level-two model

$$\beta_{0JK} = \beta_{00K} + \gamma_{010}X_{ETHNIC2} + u_{0JK}$$

$$\beta_{1JK} = \beta_{10K} + \gamma_{110}X_{ETHNIC2} + u_{1JK}$$

Level-three model

$$\beta_{00K} = \gamma_{000} + \gamma_{001}X_{ETHNIC3} + \gamma_{002}X_{POOR3} + u_{00K}$$

$$\beta_{10K} = \gamma_{100} + \gamma_{101}X_{ETHNIC3} + \gamma_{102}X_{POOR3} + u_{10K}$$

Full model

$$Y_{IJK} = \gamma_{000} + \gamma_{100}ETHNIC1 + \gamma_{200}X_{GENDER1} + \gamma_{010}X_{ETHNIC2} + {}_{001}X_{ETHNIC3} + \gamma_{002}X_{POOR3}$$

$$+ \gamma_{110}X_{ETHNIC2} * ETHNIC1 + \gamma_{101}X_{ETHNIC3} * ETHNIC1 + \gamma_{102}X_{POOR3} * ETHNIC1$$

$$+ u_{00K} + u_{0JK} + u_{10K} * ETHNIC1 + u_{1JK} * ETHNIC1 + e_{IJK}$$

When we estimate fixed and random components for the full model, we get the values reported in Tables 9.23 and 9.24. From Table 9.23, we can conclude the following:

1. Female students, on average, score 7.406 points higher in verbal achievement than males.
2. Each 1% increase in the number of a school's students who are Black corresponds, on average, to an 8.819-point decrease in individual student reading achievement.
3. Each 1% increase in the number of a school's students eligible for free/reduced cost lunch corresponds, on average, to a 0.174-point decrease in individual student reading achievement.
4. Each 1% increase in the number of a district's students who are Black corresponds, on average, to an 11.952-point exacerbation of the reading achievement disadvantage for individual Black students.

TABLE 9.23. Reading Achievement: Multilevel Regression with Three Levels; Two Student-Level Predictors; One School-Level Predictor; Two District-Level Predictors; Random Intercept and Random Slope at Level Two and Level Three; Fixed Components

$$Y = 46.372 - 6.599\text{ETHNIC1} + 7.406X_{\text{GENDER1}} - 8.819X_{\text{ETHNIC2}} + 4.489X_{\text{ETHNIC3}} - 0.174X_{\text{POOR3}}$$
$$\quad (4.259) \ (5.994) \qquad\qquad (0.166) \qquad\quad (4.346) \qquad\quad (4.026) \qquad\quad (0.020)$$

$$\quad - 6.220X_{\text{ETHNIC2}} * \text{ETHNIC1} - 11.952X_{\text{ETHNIC3}} * \text{ETHNIC1} + 0.046X_{\text{POOR3}} * \text{ETHNIC1}$$
$$\quad (5.872) \qquad\qquad\qquad\quad (5.267) \qquad\qquad\qquad\quad (0.461)$$

$$R_1^2 = 8.2\%$$
$$N_1 = 46{,}770$$
$$N_2 = 347$$
$$N_3 = 135$$

TABLE 9.24. Reading Achievement: Multilevel Regression with Three Levels; Two Student-Level Predictors; One School-Level Predictor; Two District-Level Predictors; Random Intercept and Random Slope at Level Two and Level Three; Estimates of Covariance Parameters

Parameter	Estimate	Std. error	Wald Z	Sig. level
Residual	331.511	2.088	152.074	.000
INTERCEPT variance at level two	22.497	5.155	4.170	.000
INTERCEPT-by-ETHNIC1 covariance at level two	−3.018	3.458	−0.873	.383
ETHNIC1 variance at level two	25.919	8.677	2.987	.000
INTERCEPT variance at level three	0.286	0.000	—	—
INTERCEPT-by-ETHNIC1 covariance at level three	−0.102	4.526	−0.023	.982
ETHNIC1 variance at level three	1.440	0.000	—	—

Note. A dash (—) indicates a value too small to measure.

TABLE 9.25. Information Criteria for Tables 9.18 and 9.24

Criterion	Level-three predictors	No level-three predictors
−2 log likelihood	*402662.2*	402773.9
Akaike's Information Criterion	*402694.2*	402797.9
Hurvich and Tsai's Criterion	*402694.2*	402797.9
Bozdogan's Criterion	*402850.2*	402914.9
Schwarz's Bayesian Criterion	*402834.2*	402902.9

Note. The smaller value for each measure is boldfaced and italicized.

We also see that inclusion of the two district-level predictors has increased the R_1^2 value from 5.8% to 8.2%.

From Table 9.25, we see that the deviance difference for models with and without the district-level predictors is statistically significant at any commonly used alpha level, indicating that the district-level predictors improve model fit. In addition, each of the information criteria gives a smaller value for the model with the district-level predictors.

$$\text{Deviance difference} = 402773.9 - 402662.2 = 111.7$$

$$df = 16 - 12 = 4$$

9.5   SUMMING UP

The measures discussed in this chapter—the intraclass correlation coefficient, R_1^2, the deviance statistic, and the information criteria—are staples of multilevel regression analysis. Conveniently, their use with models that have three or more levels varies very little in application and interpretation from their use with two-level models.

The intraclass correlation coefficient tells us whether or not multilevel regression is needed. R_1^2 is a summary statistic analogous to R^2 in OLS regression. The deviance difference enables us to make formal comparisons of nested models. The information criteria, especially Akaike's Information Criterion and Schwarz's Bayesian Criterion, enable us to compare both nested and non-nested models. Since they include penalties for the number of parameters estimated, they give the nod to simple models.

9.6   USEFUL RESOURCES

UCLA Academic Technology Services (2006) *Statistical Computing Seminar: Introduction to Multilevel Modeling Using SAS.* Retrieved from www.ats.ucla.edu/STAT/seminars/sas_mlm/mlm_sas_seminar.htm

Snijders, T., & Boesker, R. (1999) *Multilevel Analysis.* Thousand Oaks, CA: Sage.

Kreft, I., & De Leeuw, J. (1998) *Introducing Multilevel Modeling.* Thousand Oaks, CA: Sage.

Luke, D. (2004) *Multilevel Modeling*. Thousand Oaks, CA: Sage.

SAS Institute (1999) *SAS/STAT User's Guide: The Mixed Procedure*. Cary, NC: Author.

Leyland, A. (2004) *A Review of Multilevel Modeling in SPSS*. Glasgow, UK: University of Glasgow.

Abdulnabi, R. (1999) *Using Model Fitting Information and PROC PLOT to Select the Type of Variance–Covariance Structure for Repeated Measures*. Ann Arbor, MI: Clinical Biostatistics, Pfizer.

The unconditional and conditional intraclass correlation coefficients are ubiquitous. However, formulas (especially for the latter measure) are sometimes difficult to find, and not even noted in textbook indices. The valuable UCLA statistical consulting website contains a wealth of information on multilevel regression and related topics. It includes simply presented and easy-to-find formulas for both the unconditional and conditional intraclass correlation coefficients, along with examples of each.

Extension of these measures to more than two levels is explained and illustrated in Snijders and Bosker's valuable text. Snijders and Bosker also provide an easy-to-follow account of the R_1^2 summary statistic as applied to measures with two or more levels. The authors explain limitations of their version of this statistic when applied to models with one or more random slopes. Their account of the interpretation of R_1^2 is straightforward and clear.

Kreft and De Leeuw (1998) make the strong assertion that the deviance is the most important statistic in multilevel modeling. Whether or not this is an overstatement, they clearly discuss the meaning and calculation of the deviance statistic, and they apply it to numerous models. We have found the deviance difference to be a useful, even if imperfect, decision-making tool.

We have explained that Akaike's Information Criterion and Schwarz's Bayesian Criterion are the most commonly used information criteria. Formulas for both measures have been presented and can be found in Luke's book. Formulas for all four information criteria are included in the PROC MIXED section of the SAS Institute's guide (1999) and in Leyland's review.

Abdulanabi's procedure for using Akaike's Information Criterion and Schwarz's Bayesian Criterion in selecting the most suitable covariance structure is useful in illustrating interesting ways in which these information criteria can be applied.

10

Determining Sample Sizes for Multilevel Regression

10.1 CHAPTER INTRODUCTION

In Section 2.6, "Nesting and Effective Sample Size," we have already begun to explain that *effective* sample size determination is a much more complex issue when we are working with a multilevel regression model than when we are working with an inherently single-level OLS regression model. We can illustrate this a bit more emphatically with an extravagant example, one with four levels.

As we have reported earlier, the NIEER West Virginia data set includes 750 kindergarten students nested in 164 classrooms (Lamy et al., 2005). The classrooms are nested in 92 schools, and the schools are nested in 34 districts. We used this data set in Chapter 9 to illustrate computing the intraclass correlation and summary measures for three-level models.

If we use phonics scores on a reading readiness test as the dependent variable and construe students as nested in classrooms, classrooms as nested in schools, and schools as nested in districts, we may have reason to do a variety of different analyses with two levels at a time. Each pair of levels, moreover, will give us a different value for the intraclass correlation coefficient.

If we work with students nested in classrooms, disregarding the other levels, the variance components in Table 10.1 will give us the unconditional intraclass correlation coefficient:

$$r = 14.012/(14.012 + 11.191) = 0.44$$

TABLE 10.1. Phonics: Students Nested in Classrooms; Estimates of Covariance Parameters

Parameter	Estimate	Std. error	Wald Z	Sig. level
Residual	11.191	1.624	6.889	.000
INTERCEPT at classroom level	14.012	0.838	16.719	.000

If we work with classrooms nested in schools, disregarding the other levels, the unconditional intraclass correlation coefficient can be computed by using the variance components in Table 10.2:

$$r = 11.084/(3.859 + 11.084) = 0.74$$

If we work with schools nested in districts, disregarding the other levels, the unconditional intraclass correlation coefficient can be computed by using the variance components in Table 10.3:

$$r = 11.036/(2.597 + 11.036) = 0.81$$

Given these unconditional intraclass correlations and the number of observations at each level, we can easily calculate sample design effects by using the formula from Table 2.27: students nested in classrooms = 2.59; classrooms nested in schools = 1.56; and schools nested in districts = 2.26. Now that we know the design effects, we can use the formula from Table 2.29 and easily calculate effective sample size for each level: students = 290; classrooms = 104; schools = 41. Since districts are not nested within a larger unit, the nominal and effective sample sizes at the district level are the same: 34.

Based on previous work, however, we also know that effective sample size calculated with the unconditional intraclass correlation coefficient may be very misleading. If we introduce one or more higher-level contextual variables, we may explain some or all of the between-group variability in the dependent variable. This will enable us to com-

TABLE 10.2. Phonics: Classrooms Nested in Schools; Estimates of Covariance Parameters

Parameter	Estimate	Std. error	Wald Z	Sig. level
Residual	3.859	0.214	18.051	.000
INTERCEPT at school level	11.084	1.679	6.602	.000

TABLE 10.3. Phonics: Schools Nested in Districts; Estimates of Covariance Parameters

Parameter	Estimate	Std. error	Wald Z	Sig. level
Residual	2.597	0.138	18.864	.000
INTERCEPT at district level	11.036	2.622	4.208	.000

pute the conditional intraclass correlation coefficient, which is usually smaller than the unconditional intraclass correlation. As a result, design effects will be smaller, and the effective sample sizes will be larger.

All of this is useful to know, but it leaves a really essential question unanswered: How big does the sample size have to be at each level to provide efficient and unbiased estimates of both fixed and random components? Rules of thumb are not hard to find, but they are rarely convincing and usually based on guesswork. We will try to clarify the sample size issue in this chapter.

10.2   INTEREST IN SAMPLE SIZE IN OLS AND MULTILEVEL REGRESSION

Many evaluators, policy analysts, and applied researchers from a broad range of disciplines have learned regression analysis by using literature taken from econometrics. Econometrics textbooks exhibit a good deal of variability with respect to coverage, mathematical sophistication, and demands placed on the reader (compare, e.g., Kmenta, 1997; Kennedy, 1998; Gujarati, 2003, 2006; Halcoussis, 2005; Hayashi, 2000; Wooldridge, 2006).

One characteristic shared by these different sources, however, is lack of interest in statistical power. As a result, discussions of suitable sample size are hard to find and underdeveloped. With a few exceptions, such as Cohen, Cohen, West, and Aiken (2002), much the same is true of most treatments of regression analysis produced by authors not writing in the econometrics tradition.

In multilevel regression, by contrast, there is a good deal of interest in determining suitable sample size and gauging statistical power (Maas & Hox, 2005). In large measure, this may be due to the fact that multilevel regression is inevitably complicated by the need to acknowledge at least two different sample sizes: the number of observations at level one and the number of observations at level two. As we have seen in Chapter 8, moreover, we may have to concern ourselves with sample sizes at level three and even higher levels. In any application of multilevel analysis, therefore, the inferential properties of our data will differ from level to level.

The number of cases and the effective sample size at level one may seem obviously large enough to meet the statistical power needs of any application. At level two, however, things may be a lot less clear (Mok, 1995). And what about cross-level interaction terms?

For example, if we do a two-level reading achievement analysis with the Kentucky data set, the student-level *effective* sample size at level one is just under 2800 cases without explanatory factors in the model. This stands in sharp contrast to the nearly 50,000 cases that we have reported again and again. The computations involved in arriving at Table 10.4 were introduced in Tables 2.28 and 2.29.

As we add independent variables and use the conditional intraclass correlation rather than the unconditional intraclass correlation, design effects will decrease, and

TABLE 10.4. Individual-Level Effective Sample Size

Design effect = 1 + (n − 1) * intraclass correlation

17.730 = 1 + (143.99 − 1) * 0.117

Effective sample size = N/design effect

2798.42 = 49,616/17.730

effective sample sizes will increase. Insofar as we are able to account for intraclass correlation, design effects get smaller, and effective sample sizes get larger (Mok, 1995). We see this again by referring to Tables 10.5 through 10.8. For the two-level model specified in Table 10.5 and estimated in Tables 10.6 and 10.7, the *conditional* intraclass correlation at level one is now only 0.025. The effective sample size at the individual level is 10,847.

Can we find comparable numbers for the school level in a three-level model? Using exactly the same procedures described in Tables 2.28 and 2.29, we get Table 10.9. In this table, n is the mean group size (where groups are now districts), and N is the total num-

TABLE 10.5. Reading Achievement: Model for Computing Effective Sample Size at Level One

Level-one model

$$Y = \beta_{0J} + \beta_{1J}\text{ETHNIC1} + e_{IJ}$$

Level-two model

$$\beta_{0J} = \gamma_{00} + \gamma_{01}X_{\text{ETHNIC2}} + \gamma_{02}X_{\text{SIZE2}} + \gamma_{03}X_{\text{POOR2}} + u_{0J}$$

$$\beta_{1J} = \gamma_{10} + \gamma_{11}X_{\text{ETHNIC2}} + \gamma_{12}X_{\text{SIZE2}} + \gamma_{13}X_{\text{POOR2}} + u_{1J}$$

Full equation

$$Y = \gamma_{00} + \gamma_{01}X_{\text{ETHNIC2}} + \gamma_{02}X_{\text{SIZE2}} + \gamma_{03}X_{\text{POOR2}} + \gamma_{020}X_{\text{SIZE2}} + \gamma_{10}\text{ETHNIC1} + \gamma_{11}X_{\text{ETHNIC2}} * \text{ETHNIC1}$$
$$+ \gamma_{12}X_{\text{SIZE2}} * \text{ETHNIC1} + \gamma_{13}X_{\text{POOR2}} * \text{ETHNIC1} + (u_{0J} + u_{1J} * \text{ETHNIC1} + e_{IJ})$$

TABLE 10.6. Reading Achievement Equation for Computing Effective Sample Size at Level One; Fixed Components

$$Y = 49.148 - 4.4302X_{\text{ETHNIC2}} - 0.684X_{\text{SIZE2}} - 0.200X_{\text{POOR2}} - 4.637\text{ETHNIC1}$$
$$(0.321)\ (0.873) \qquad (0.362) \qquad (0.013) \qquad (0.874)$$

$$- 17.865\ X_{\text{ETHNIC2}} * \text{ETHNIC1} - 0.086X_{\text{SIZE2}} * \text{ETHNIC1} - 0.101*X_{\text{POOR2}}\text{ETHNIC1}$$
$$(2.898) \qquad\qquad (0.872) \qquad\qquad (0.032)$$

$$R_1^2 = 5.6\%$$
$$N_1 = 46,770$$
$$N_2 = 347$$

TABLE 10.7. Reading Achievement: Computing Effective Sample Size at Level One; Estimates of Covariance Parameters

Parameter	Estimate	Std. error	Wald Z	Sig. level
Residual	331.400	2.173	152.628	.000
INTERCEPT1	8.347	0.967	8.633	.000
INTERCEPT1 by ETHNIC1	−1.037	1.291	−0.803	.422
ETHNIC1	14.574	3.721	3.917	.000

TABLE 10.8. Individual-Level Effective Sample Size

Design effect = 1 + (n − 1) * intraclass correlation

4.574 = 1 + (143.99 − 1) * 0.025

Effective sample size = N/design effect

10,847 = 49,616/4.574

TABLE 10.9. School-Level Effective Sample Size

Design effect = 1 + (n − 1) * unconditional intraclass correlation

1.810 = 1 + (2.630 − 1) * 0.494

Effective sample size = N/design effect

192 = 347/1.810

ber of groups. The unconditional intraclass correlation in this instance is computed for schools nested within districts and still pertains to reading achievement. Though the unconditional intraclass correlation coefficient is more than four times larger than it was for students nested within schools, the design effect is much smaller. This is because there are, on average, comparatively few schools nested within districts. This leaves us with an effective sample size of 192 cases at level two.

Again, if we introduce explanatory factors, as with the model specified in Table 10.10 and estimated in Tables 10.11 and 10.12, the conditional intraclass correlation will be diminished, the design effect will be diminished, and effective sample size will increase.

$$r = 8.210/(8.210 + 11.144) = 0.423$$

When the unconditional intraclass correlation in Table 10.9 is replaced by the conditional intraclass correlation in Table 10.13, the effective level-two sample size increases from 192 to 205. This is exactly the sort of thing we found at level one. However we construe it, we have two very different effective sample sizes at the individual level

TABLE 10.10. Reading Achievement: Model for Computing Effective Sample Size at Level Two

<u>Level-one model</u>

$$Y = \beta_{0J} + \beta_{1J}\text{ETHNIC2} + e_{IJ}$$

<u>Level-two model</u>

$$\beta_{0J} = \gamma_{00} + \gamma_{01}X_{\text{ETHNIC3}} + \gamma_{02}X_{\text{SIZE3}} + \gamma_{03}X_{\text{POOR3}} + u_{0J}$$

$$\beta_{1J} = \gamma_{10} + \gamma_{11}X_{\text{ETHNIC3}} + \gamma_{12}X_{\text{SIZE3}} + \gamma_{13}X_{\text{POOR3}} + u_{1J}$$

<u>Full equation</u>

$$Y = \gamma_{00} + \gamma_{01}X_{\text{ETHNIC3}} + \gamma_{02}X_{\text{SIZE3}} + \gamma_{03}X_{\text{POOR3}} + \gamma_{10}\text{ETHNIC2} + \gamma_{11}X_{\text{ETHNIC3}} * \text{ETHNIC2}$$

$$+ \gamma_{12}X_{\text{SIZE3}} * \text{ETHNIC2} + \gamma_{13}X_{\text{POOR3}} * \text{ETHNIC2} + (u_{0J} + u_{1J} * \text{ETHNIC2} + e_{IJ})$$

TABLE 10.11. Reading Achievement: Equation for Computing Effective Sample Size at Level Two; Fixed Components

$$Y = 51.400 - 4.355X_{\text{ETHNIC3}} - 0.160X_{\text{SIZE3}} - 0.124X_{\text{POOR3}} + 2.238\text{ETHNIC2} + 0.004X_{\text{ETHNIC3}} * \text{ETHNIC2}$$
$$\;\;\;(0.264)\;(1.768)\qquad\;\;(0.266)\qquad\;\;(0.004)\qquad\;\;(0.524)\qquad\;\;\;(0.188)$$

$$- 8.076X_{\text{SIZE3}} * \text{ETHNIC2} + 0.453X_{\text{POOR3}} * \text{ETHNIC2}$$
$$\;\;(0.173)\qquad\qquad\quad(0.032)$$

$$R_1^2 = 31.3\%$$
$$N_1 = 347$$
$$N_2 = 135$$

TABLE 10.12. Reading Achievement: Computing Effective Sample Size at Level Two; Estimates of Covariance Parameters

Parameter	Estimate	Std. error	Wald Z	Sig. level
Residual	11.144	0.072	154.556	.000
INTERCEPT1	8.210	1.036	7.924	.000

TABLE 10.13. School-Level Effective Sample Size

Design effect = $1 + (n - 1)$ * conditional intraclass correlation

$$1.689 = 1 + (2.630 - 1) * 0.423$$

Effective sample size = N/design effect

$$205 = 347/1.689$$

and the school level. At both levels, moreover, effective sample size varies with changing multilevel regression model specification.

Things get more complex still when we acknowledge that a three-level model will have three effective sample sizes. With the Kentucky data set, the 135 districts will constitute the sample size at level three. Since there is no grouping variable higher than the district, the effects of intraclass correlation are not measurable at the district level. The effective sample size will remain 135.

When we are working with fixed components in multilevel regression analysis, the likelihood that we will detect a relationship if one exists is a function of four factors: the strength of the relationship, the designated alpha level, the magnitude of correlations among independent variables, and effective sample size. We see therefore that with the first three factors held constant, effective sample size is a powerful determinant of statistical power. We also see that in the same multilevel analysis, statistical power may vary enormously from level to level. How do we address this issue?

10.3 SAMPLE SIZE: RULES OF THUMB AND DATA CONSTRAINTS

The most commonly offered rule of thumb with regard to sample size for multilevel models is at least 20 groups and at least 30 observations per group (Heck & Thomas, 2000). An alternative recommendation, cited almost as frequently, is 30 groups and 30 observations per group (Hox, 2002). Almost invariably, however, such recommendations are heavily qualified. It soon becomes clear that sample size and sample structure are complex and underresearched issues in multilevel analysis (Mok, 1995; Hox, 1998; Maas & Hox, 2004).

Even without immersing ourselves in the growing and difficult technical literature on sample size and statistical power in multilevel analysis, the "20/30" and "30/30" rules of thumb merit a closer look. With 20—or even 30—observations at the second level of a multilevel analysis, tests of significance and construction of confidence intervals for level-two regression coefficients will be based on a dangerously small number of cases.

As a rather extreme but quite real case, recall the data set we have used that contains measures on 331 beginning kindergarten students in 18 classrooms in 12 randomly selected West Virginia elementary schools. Clearly, there are three levels that might be used in an analysis of this information: the individual student, the classroom, and the school. With 331 students, at first glance, the sample size seems not to be unduly small.

Again, however, if we use multilevel regression, the nominal sample size at the classroom level is only 18, and the effective sample size at the school level is only 12! These are constraints that came with the data set and over which we have no control. At levels two and three, therefore, actual sample size constraints are even more severe than those embedded in the dubious 20/30 and 30/30 rules of thumb.

To make matters worse, classrooms and schools are badly confounded in the West Virginia data set. Seven of the schools have only one kindergarten classroom, making school and classroom coterminous. No, this is not the best way to do a compelling multilevel analysis—but especially in applied settings, we often have little control over the data we analyze and even the way we analyze it.

With 18 classrooms at level two, how many school-level explanatory factors could we use? In addition, are 18 classrooms enough second-level units to permit interpretable use of random coefficients in analyzing varying relationships between a level-one dependent variable and even one or two level-one independent variables? And what about 12 schools at level three?

These kinds of questions, in simplified form and pertaining to only one level and to fixed coefficients, are well known in OLS regression analysis (Maxwell, 2000). It is not difficult to see that the usual OLS issues have easy-to-identify, though more complex analogues in multilevel regression.

Continuing with the West Virginia data, because of the confounding of levels, we decide to work with students at level one and schools at level two, ignoring classrooms. We run a multilevel analysis using a standardized measure of vocabulary achievement as the dependent variable (Woodcock & Johnson, 1990). The test was administered at the end of the kindergarten year.

We treat the intercept as random—a function of the contextual variable X_{BEGIN2}, the beginning-of-kindergarten test score aggregated to the school level, and the cross-level interaction term $X_{BEGIN2} * X_{BEGIN1}$. The cross-level interaction term is created in the usual way, by multiplying the variable representing beginning-of-kindergarten test score at the student level by the same variable aggregated to the school level. X_{BEGIN1} is the only student-level independent variable. Since all slopes are fixed, the cross-level interaction term is not implied by our multilevel regression model. Instead, we use it at our discretion.

The case for using multilevel analysis in this example is based on the information in Table 10.14. The intercept variance is statistically significant, and the unconditional intraclass correlation is as follows:

$$r = 0.025/(0.025 + 0.089) = 0.219$$

Unstandardized regression coefficients and standard errors for this illustrative analysis are reported in Table 10.15, with random components reported in Table 10.16. With only 12 schools—12 observations—at level two, it comes as no surprise that the slope for the contextual variable X_{BEGIN2} is not statistically significant. This is exactly the sort of thing we have just been discussing. Similarly, since our level-one independent variable

TABLE 10.14. Reading Achievement for 12 West Virginia Schools: Unconditional (Null) Model; Estimates of Covariance Parameters

Parameter	Estimate	Std. error	Wald Z	Sig. level
Residual	0.089	0.005	18.106	.000
INTERCEPT1	0.025	0.011	2.230	.026

TABLE 10.15. Reading Achievement for 12 West Virginia Schools: Random Intercept with All Slopes Fixed; Fixed Components

$$Y = 2.446 + 0.471X_{BEGIN1} - 0.197X_{BEGIN2} + 0.439X_{XBEGIN2} * X_{BEGIN1}$$
$$\quad (0.019) \ (0.023) \qquad (0.099) \qquad (0.176)$$

$$R_1^2 = 50.1\%$$
$$N_1 = 331$$
$$N_2 = 12$$

TABLE 10.16. Reading Achievement for 12 West Virginia Schools: Random Intercept with All Slopes Fixed; Estimates of Covariance Parameters

Parameter	Estimate	Std. error	Wald Z	Sig. level
Residual	0.054	0.003	17.988	.000
INTERCEPT1	0.003	0.002	1.520	.129

has a fixed coefficient, there is nothing exceptional about our level-one results: With 331 level-one observations, and given the nature of the relationship—posttest scores regressed on pretest scores—the coefficient is almost certain to be statistically significant.

In addition, the number of degrees of freedom for a cross-level interaction term created from independent variables with fixed slopes is the same as the number of degrees of freedom for a level-one independent variable with a fixed slope. So, with 331 cases at level one, a statistically significant coefficient for the cross-level interaction term is not unexpected.

In Tables 10.17 and 10.18, however, we estimate the same multilevel regression model—but this time, in addition to the intercept, the slope for X_{BEGIN1} (now BEGIN1) is random. This, as we know, yields a larger standard error for the fixed component of the slope for BEGIN1. In addition, it means that we have many fewer degrees of freedom when we test the slopes for BEGIN1 and X_{BEGIN2} * BEGIN1 for statistical significance. Instead of $N_1 - k - 1 = 327$ degrees of freedom, we have $N_2 - k - 1 = 8$ degrees of freedom

TABLE 10.17. Reading Achievement for 12 West Virginia Elementary Schools: Random Intercept and One Random Slope; Fixed Components

$$Y = 2.441 + 0.495BEGIN1 - 0.188X_{BEGIN2} + 0.440X_{BEGIN2} * BEGIN1$$
$$\quad (0.021) \ (0.035) \qquad (0.109) \qquad (2.000)$$

$$R_1^2 = 50.1\%$$
$$N_1 = 331$$
$$N_2 = 12$$

TABLE 10.18. Reading Achievement for 12 West Virginia Elementary Schools: Random Intercept and One Random Slope; Estimates of Covariance Parameters

Parameter	Estimate	Std. error	Wald Z	Sig. level
Residual	0.053	0.003	17.812	.000
INTERCEPT1	0.004	0.003	1.322	.186
INTERCEPT1 by BEGIN1	−0.003	0.003	−0.870	.384
BEGIN1	0.006	0.008	0.779	.436

for each test. Inferential tests for BEGIN1 and X_{BEGIN2} * BEGIN1 now correspond to a sample size of 12, the number of schools, rather than 331, the number of students.

The slope for BEGIN1 remains statistically significant. With the alpha level set at .05, however, the slope for X_{BEGIN2} * BEGIN1 is not significant. This holds in spite of the fact that the t value for the X_{BEGIN2} * BEGIN1 is 2.204. With 8 degrees of freedom, the critical value for t for a two-tailed test is 2.306 (Levin & Fox, 2002). With only 12 schools at level two, statistical significance is hard to get.

Even if we got statistically significant results for the slopes for X_{BEGIN2} and X_{BEGIN2} * BEGIN1, what would we make of them? With such a small sample at the school level, how much confidence can we have in our slope estimates? If we were using OLS regression to work with a sample size of only 12, we would be quite dubious as to the value of coefficient estimates, even if they were statistically significant. Our doubts with regard to the value of level-two fixed slopes estimated with so few cases are consistent with recent work by Maas and Hox (2005). They have reported that approximately 50 level-two cases are needed to justify claims as to the absence of bias in standard error estimates for level-two slopes.

10.4 ESTIMATION AND INFERENCE FOR UNSTANDARDIZED REGRESSION COEFFICIENTS

As with OLS multiple regression, most applications of multilevel regression are aimed at estimation and inference for unstandardized regression coefficients, and sample size is an important consideration. We want unbiased, efficient estimates of the coefficients themselves and of their standard errors. This is perfectly obvious with OLS regression. With multilevel regression, however, we have seen that more parameters of varying kinds are estimated, and that they are estimated at more than one level.

Using knowledge acquired from working with OLS regression as a point of departure, we will try to make the inevitably complex issue of multilevel sample size more tractable. In the process, much as with the examples just presented, we tentatively conclude that OLS-engendered commonsense can be a useful (even if preliminary and incomplete) guide to approximating answers to some practical questions concerning sample size in applied multilevel analysis.

10.5   MORE THAN ONE LEVEL OF ANALYSIS MEANS MORE THAN ONE SAMPLE SIZE

When using OLS regression, we are accustomed to dealing with the total number of observations—in other words, the number of observations at level one. With multilevel analysis, however, we must consider at least two sample sizes: the number of observations at level one, or the total sample size; and the number of observations at level two, or the number of groups.

In truth, even with just two levels, there is a third sample size that has been conspicuously evident in our account of effective sample size: the mean number of level-one observations nested in each level-two group. With more than two levels, this framework becomes even more complex.

We have already discussed computation of the standard error of an unstandardized regression coefficient estimated with OLS. We have seen in Tables 2.22 through 2.33 that in the presence of nesting or clustering, effective total sample size must be adjusted for the absence of independence among observations.

Using the subset of the High School and Beyond data set, we will again illustrate the effect of nesting on effective sample size, much as we did in with occupational group data in Tables 2.22 through 2.33. When working with multilevel regression, we now know that there are two kinds of regression coefficients: fixed and random. In addition, we know that a random regression coefficient has two components: a fixed component and a random component. As a result, multilevel analysis requires three different kinds of estimates specific to regression coefficients: fixed coefficients; fixed components of random coefficients; and random components of random coefficients. Furthermore, fixed coefficients, fixed components, and random components may occur at more than one level of our model.

In addition, peculiar to multilevel analysis are cross-level interaction terms, created by using variables at two levels. Cross-level interaction terms, too, have fixed regression coefficients to be estimated and tested.

At the risk of redundancy, we will further develop these issues with analyses similar to the one spelled out in Tables 2.22 through 2.33. In this instance, however, the sample has a much larger number of second-level observations—160 high schools, with 7185 students at level one.

In Table 10.19, we reproduce from Table 2.22 the formula for the standard error of an unstandardized regression coefficient. We then restate the S_R^2 term, the variance of

TABLE 10.19. Standard Error of an OLS Slope: Expanded Formula

$$S_b = (((S_R^2)/SS_X) * VIF)^{1/2}$$

$$S_R^2 = \Sigma \text{ residuals}^2/(N - k - 1)$$

$$S_b = (((\Sigma \text{ residuals}^2/(N - k - 1))/SS_X) * VIF)^{1/2}$$

TABLE 10.20. Standard Error and Effective Sample Size

Design effect = $1 + (n - 1)$ * intraclass correlation

Effective sample size = N/design effect

$S_b = (((\Sigma \text{ residuals}^2/(N/[\text{design effect}] - k - 1))/SS_X) * VIF)^{1/2}$

TABLE 10.21. Unconditional Intraclass Correlation for High School and Beyond Subset

Intraclass correlation = Explained/(error + explained)

Intraclass correlation = $8.61/(39.1 + 8.61) = 0.18$

TABLE 10.22. Effective Sample Size for High School and Beyond Subset

Design effect = $1 + (n - 1)$ * intraclass correlation

$8.90 = 1 + (44.9 - 1) * 0.18$

Effective sample size = N/design effect

$807.30 = 7185/8.90$

the residuals, to clarify the role of sample size in estimating the standard error. With the formula for S_b expanded in this way, it is clear that as sample size increases, S_b gets smaller and statistical power is legitimately increased. Table 10.20, however, reminds us again that *effective* sample size with nested data is determined only after we incorporate the cluster-engendered intraclass correlation, in the form of a design effect, into our calculations for S_b.

This is getting to be an uncomfortably complex formula. Nevertheless, applying it is not difficult. For example, with our High School and Beyond subset, the intraclass correlation coefficient for math achievement is calculated in Table 10.21. With an average of 44.91 students per school, the design effect and effective sample size can be computed as in Table 10.22.

10.6   AN INDIVIDUAL-LEVEL OLS ANALYSIS WITH A LARGE SAMPLE

We can illustrate application of the information in Tables 10.19 through 10.22 with the OLS multiple regression analysis reported in Table 10.23. The dependent variable is math achievement (Y_{MATH}). The independent variables are SES (X_{SES}); gender (X_{FEMALE}), with females coded 1 and males coded 0; and ethnic minority status ($X_{MINORITY}$), with

TABLE 10.23. Illustrative OLS Analysis with High School and Beyond Subset

$$Y_{MATH} = 14.254 + 0.2.683X_{SES} - 1.377X_{FEMALE} - 2.837X_{MINORITY}$$
$$(0.119)\ (0.199) \qquad (0.148) \qquad\quad (0.172)$$

$$R^2 = 17.1\%$$
$$N = 7185$$

TABLE 10.24. OLS Standard Errors Corrected for Design Effects

$$S_b = (((\Sigma\ \text{residuals}^2/(N/[\text{design effect}] - k - 1))/SS_X) * VIF)^{1/2}$$

$$S_{SES} = 0.300 = (((286651.59/(7185/[8.90] - 3 - 1))/4363.52) * 1.084)^{1/2}$$

$$S_{FEMALE} = 0.671 = (((286651.59/(7185/[8.90] - 3 - 1))/1790.54) * 1.005)^{1/2}$$

$$S_{MINORITY} = 0.778 = (((286651.59/(/[8.90] - 3 - 1))/1431.67) * 1.080)^{1/2}$$

members of ethnic minority groups coded 1 and Whites coded 0. Dividing each unstandardized slope by its standard error yields t values that are all greater than 9.000, well above the usual critical value of 1.960 for a large sample.

In Table 10.24, however, we have corrected the OLS standard errors for design effects. Table 10.25 reports the regression results from Table 10.23, but with corrected standard errors of OLS slopes inserted in brackets and boldfaced beneath the uncorrected standard errors. Since we still have an effective sample size of 807 observations, it is not surprising that all coefficients are still statistically significant (alpha = .05). Nevertheless, we can easily see that the corrected standard errors are larger, and that each of the t values will be smaller.

10.7 A GROUP-LEVEL OLS ANALYSIS WITH A SMALL SAMPLE

As is often the case, if we estimate an OLS multiple regression equation using the same variables as in Table 10.25 but **aggregated** to the **group** level, we get results that are very different from those obtained with the individual as the unit of analysis. While in this

TABLE 10.25. OLS Illustrative Analysis with Uncorrected and Corrected Standard Errors

$$Y_{MATH} = 14.254 + 0.2.683\ X_{SES} - 1.377X_{FEMALE} - 2.837X_{MINORITY}$$
$$(0.119)\ (0.199) \qquad (0.148) \qquad\quad (0.172)$$
$$\mathbf{[0.300]} \qquad\quad \mathbf{[0.671]} \qquad\quad \mathbf{[0.778]}$$

$$R^2 = 17.1\%$$
$$\text{Corrected } N = 807$$

TABLE 10.26. OLS Aggregated Group-Level Analysis

$$Y_{MATHu} = 14.060 + 5.201X_{SESu} - 1.901\ X_{FEMALEu} - 1.515X_{MINORITYu}$$
$$(6.572)\ (0.296)\qquad (0.513)\qquad\qquad (6.572)$$

$$R^2 = 65.6\%$$
$$N = 160$$

instance signs of the regression coefficients are the same and tests of significance yield the same results, coefficient sizes from Tables 10.25 and 10.26 are very different, as is the value of R^2.

Should the group-level standard errors be adjusted for design effects due to nesting, much as the individual-level standard errors were adjusted? We made this sort of adjustment when working with the Kentucky data set. However, since the High School and Beyond subset does not include a grouping variable above the school level, no adjustment can be made. Perhaps an adjustment *should* be made, since it is safe to assume that schools are grouped within districts; however, we do not know which schools belong in the same and different districts, so an adjustment for intraclass correlation is not possible. The effective sample size at the school level, therefore, will be the same as the nominal sample size: 160.

10.8 STANDARD ERRORS: CORRECTED AND UNCORRECTED, INDIVIDUAL AND GROUP LEVELS

Of special pertinence for present purposes, the standard errors for the unstandardized OLS group-level slopes are reported correctly in Table 10.26. However, we can compare the uncorrected and corrected individual-level standard errors, along with the group-level standard errors, using the information in Table 10.27. The group-level standard errors are much larger than the individual-level standard errors that have not been corrected for clustering or nesting. Differences between the group-level standard errors and the corrected individual-level standard errors, however, are much smaller, and for X_{SESu} (X_{SES}) and $X_{FEMALEu}$ (X_{FEMALE}) the group-level standard errors are actually smaller than the individual-level standard errors.

The important point is that the effective sample size at the group level is only 160 cases. If we do multilevel regression without bearing in mind that the number of second-level observations is the number of second-level groups (in this instance, schools), we may badly overestimate the statistical power of our analysis, winding up with standard errors much larger than we had off-handedly anticipated.

Perhaps we have made this point too often and illustrated it in a needlessly wordy and otherwise cumbersome way. When we are making the transition from OLS regression and its more conventional correctives to multilevel regression, however, it is a point that is easy to forget, and its importance and ubiquitous character make it worth repeating.

TABLE 10.27. Standard Errors of OLS Slopes for Three Different Circumstances

Uncorrected individual-level		
X_{SES}	X_{FEMALE}	$X_{MINORITY}$
0.199	0.148	0.172
Corrected individual-level		
X_{SES}	X_{FEMALE}	$X_{MINORITY}$
0.300	0.671	0.778
Group-level		
X_{SESu}	$X_{FEMALEu}$	$X_{MINORITYu}$
0.555	0.578	0.407

10.9 WHEN OUTPUT IS NOT FORTHCOMING!

Let's take another extreme case. Suppose we do the occupation and income analysis from Table 2.26, but with data aggregated to the group level. The level-two grouping variable is occupational category. That means that there will be only nine second-level groups.

With the group as the unit of analysis, we see in Table 10.28 that we get values for OLS regression coefficients that are very different from those reported in Table 2.26 with the individual as the unit of analysis. We also get a wildly implausible R^2 value: 100%!

But where are the standard errors for the group-level analysis? Since our eight independent variables have used up all nine available degrees of freedom ($df = N - k - 1 = 0$), SPSS is unable to compute inferential statistics. Even after we adjust for design effects, and with a comparatively large number of independent variables, we have enough cases to do an interpretable (even if not statistically powerful) individual-level hourly-wage analysis. But we do not have enough occupational categories to get interpretable output at the group level.

TABLE 10.28. OLS Group-Level Results: Too Few Degrees of Freedom

$$Y_{WAGEu} = 9.852 - 8.279X_{EDUCATIONu} - 3.599X_{YEARSu} - 51.766X_{BLACKu} - 55.987X_{UNIONu}$$
$$(\quad) \; (\quad) \qquad (\quad) \qquad (\quad) \qquad (\quad)$$

$$- 3.276X_{MARRYu} - 163.953X_{BLACKEDu} - 9.022X_{BLACKYRSu} - 1157.306X_{BLACKUNu}$$
$$(\quad) \qquad (\quad) \qquad (\quad) \qquad (\quad)$$

$$R^2 = 100\%$$
$$N = 9$$
$$df = 0$$

10.10 SAMPLE SIZES AND OLS-BASED COMMONSENSE IN MULTILEVEL REGRESSION

Given the foregoing, imagine that we use the occupation-and-income data set to estimate a *multilevel* regression equation. The dependent variable is hourly wage, and the independent variables at the individual level are $X_{EDUCATION}$, X_{YEARS}, X_{BLACK}, X_{UNION}, and X_{MARRY}, as well as the interaction terms $X_{BLACKED}$, $X_{BLACKYRS}$, and $X_{BLACKUN}$. At the group level, we include aggregates of each of the five main-effect variables.

After we correct the total sample size for clustering or nesting by invoking design effects, we have many fewer effective cases at the individual level than we had thought. At the group level, however, things are much worse. We have only nine cases, and only four degrees of freedom that we have not used up. With so few group-level observations, even though estimates of unstandardized regression coefficients will be forthcoming, they will be extremely imprecise, and the analysis will be very short on statistical power.

As a less extreme example, recall the extended county-level voting behavior analysis that culminated in the multilevel regression equation specified in Table 7.8. At this point, a pertinent question is the following: Just what are the effective sample sizes at the county and state levels? We have 3140 counties nested within 49 states, meaning that the average number of county-level observations per state is 64.1. With a conditional intraclass correlation of 0.153, we see in Table 10.29 that our effective sample size at the county level is not 3140, as we had understandably assumed, but only 291! Another nasty surprise! The effective sample size at the state level remains 49.

Imagine that we are using OLS estimators. Would we be equally comfortable with effective sample sizes of 3140, 291, and 49? There is more to the sample size issue in multilevel regression than OLS-based questions such as this, but this is a good point of departure. If we have serious statistical power reservations prompted by sample sizes used with OLS regression, these concerns will be **at least** as serious with multilevel regression, and this assertion will apply to all levels of the analysis. After all, since multilevel estimates are adjusted for negative bias due to nesting-engendered intraclass correlation, their standard errors are typically larger than OLS standard errors (Angeles & Mroz, 2001).

TABLE 10.29. *Effective* Sample Size for Extended Voting Behavior Example

Design effect = 1 + (n − 1) * conditional intraclass correlation

$$10.79 = 1 + (n - 1) * 0.153$$

Effective sample size = N/design effect

$$291 = 3140/10.79$$

10.11 SAMPLE SIZE GENERALIZATIONS PECULIAR TO MULTILEVEL REGRESSION

Most of the sample size illustrations produced so far have been based on OLS estimators. As we know, however, when estimating coefficients for multilevel models, we have been using REML estimators. While there is a good deal of overlap with regard to sample size considerations, with REML estimators there is no straightforward, generally applicable formula for the standard error, such as that introduced for OLS coefficients (cf. Cohen, 1998).

Nevertheless, as with OLS, the statistical power of REML estimators in a multilevel analysis is improved as level-specific sample sizes increase. Statistical power also improves as relationships become stronger, as the alpha level is made larger, as the associations among independent variables diminish, and as the intraclass correlation is diminished. Beyond that, the following observations are worth remembering.

10.12 LEVEL-ONE SAMPLE SIZE AND LEVEL-TWO STATISTICAL POWER

Increasing the sample size at level one does nothing to enhance statistical power at level two. Instead, as far as sample size is concerned, improving power at level two is accomplished only by increasing the number of observations at that level. As a result, it is entirely possible to have an enormous total sample, but still have too few group-level observations to obtain creditable coefficient estimates—or any estimates at all!—for the group level.

10.13 THE IMPORTANCE OF SAMPLE SIZE AT HIGHER LEVELS

In general, *for any fixed sample size*, results of multilevel analyses are improved by making the number of groups as large as possible, thereby diminishing the number of cases for each group (Snijders & Bosker, 1999). Say we take the oft-cited rule of thumb that doing a multilevel analysis requires at least 20 groups and 30 observations per group, meaning a total of 600 level-one observations. The 600 cases would actually give better estimates of unstandardized regression coefficients and standard errors at the group level if we had 30 groups and an average of 20 observations per group. Better still for group-level estimates would be 60 groups and an average of 10 observations per group. Even then, how comfortable would we be with a conventional OLS analysis based on 60 observations? At the very least, we would feel obliged to use a small number of independent variables.

What about level-one estimates with fixed regression coefficients? As we have seen, the more level-one cases we have for each level-two group or cluster, the more our effective sample size is diminished. It is easy to forget, moreover, that the effective sample size for level-one *random* regression coefficients is equal to the **number of groups** at the second level. This makes sense if we recall that the random component of a random regression coefficient is an estimate of the variability of the coefficient across the number of groups with which we are working. The fixed component, moreover, is a weighted average taken across the same number of groups. Clearly, when we are estimating random coefficients, the number of groups is a crucial consideration.

Where does this leave us with regard to workable prescriptions for sample sizes in a multilevel regression analysis? Think of the sample sizes at each of the different levels of a multilevel model as providing or not providing the basis for reasonably precise estimates and adequate statistical power. OLS-based commonsense can be a useful tool for thinking this through.

10.14 SUMMING UP

An obvious problem with the material presented in this chapter is the absence of strict rules for determining adequate sample size at any level. This again reflects the under-researched and poorly understood character of sample size determination in multilevel analysis. It is useful to point out, nevertheless, that similar concerns are often expressed with regard to conventional applications of OLS multiple regression. With OLS regression, however, decades of applications, along with acknowledgment of the importance of design effects and increased concern for the consequences of multicollinearity, have imbued experienced analysts with a useful feel or intuition as to the number of cases needed to do creditable work (Gujarati, 2003).

My approach to judgments as to suitable sample size in multilevel analysis is to lean heavily on this OLS-engendered conventional wisdom. For example, in the exemplary work by Maas and Hox (2005) they have found that in a two-level model, at least 50 level-two observations are needed to assure that standard error estimates for fixed components are unbiased. We should ask ourselves, however, if 50 cases would be enough to give us confidence in OLS estimates of fixed components. Or would we be inclined to suspect that with only 50 cases, standard errors would be unduly large, confidence intervals unduly wide, and tests of significance unduly likely to prompt us to reject the null hypothesis? After all, even if estimates are unbiased, they may be misleading (Kennedy, 2003).

10.15 USEFUL RESOURCES

Kish, L. (1995) *Survey Sampling*. New York: Wiley. (Original work published 1965)

Kish's text is a widely read classic on survey sampling and sample design; it remains accessible and informative. Many readers first encountered concepts such as clustering, within-group homogeneity, design effects, and effective as opposed to nominal sample size by reading Kish.

Insofar as what I have termed OLS-engendered commonsense is useful in determining suitable sample size in multilevel models, it is due to the value of concepts ably discussed in this survey research classic.

Mok, M. (1995) Sample Size Requirements for 2-Level Designs in Educational Research. *Multilevel Modelling Newsletter, 7*, 11–15.

Maas, C., & Hox, J. (2004) Robustness Issues in Multilevel Regression Analysis. *Statistica Neerlandica, 58*, 127–137.

Maas, C., & Hox, J. (2005) Sufficient Sample Sizes for Multilevel Modeling. *Methodology, 1*, 86–92.

Hox, J. (2002) *Multilevel Analysis: Techniques and Applications*. Mahwah, NJ: Erlbaum.

Mok's brief article is one of the most frequently cited discussions of sample size in the literature on multilevel regression. Though no less difficult to read than the other research reports appearing in the *Multilevel Modelling Newsletter*, Mok's paper merits the effort required to work through her sometimes idiosyncratic mode of presentation.

For our purposes, Mok's most important finding is that what I have termed OLS-engendered commonsense works quite well for both fixed and random components of random regression coefficients. She also affirms that the efficiency of coefficient estimates is maximized and bias is minimized as the number of higher-level units is increased.

Mok emphasizes the distinction between nominal and effective sample size. She also makes clear that introduction of one or more predictors necessarily shifts attention from the unconditional intraclass correlation coefficient to the conditional version of this measure.

Maas and Hox have made a sustained effort to develop the literature on sample size and statistical power in multilevel modeling. In various papers, including those cited here, they have begun to accumulate a useful set of findings with regard to sample size and statistical power.

Maas and Hox have effectively questioned the 30/30 rule, finding that 30 cases at the group level are too few to avoid misleading results from tests of significance for random components. In the same vein, they have found that estimates of group-level standard errors are likely to be biased if there are fewer than 50 group-level observations. In addition, Maas and Hox's research has demonstrated that estimation of standard errors of random components is extremely sensitive to violation of the normality assumption for group-level residuals, while estimation of standard errors of fixed components is robust with regard to violation of the same assumption.

11

Multilevel Regression Growth Models

11.1 CHAPTER INTRODUCTION

The literature on multilevel regression is conceptually diverse and difficult. Even beginners, however, can occasionally find a crucial idea that seems *not* to be still another source of never-ending confusion. One of these concepts is nesting. Students within schools, schools within districts, employees within occupational groups, riflemen within squads, squads within platoons, platoons within companies … a wonderfully obvious and useful idea. But what about this: *measures nested within individual-level units?* The first few examples are obvious indeed. But *measures nested within individual-level units?* What does that mean? For readers not accustomed to working with repeated measures, this view of nesting may be confusing.

By way of illustration, suppose we are interested in evaluating a program designed to maintain achievement gains due to participation in Head Start. We hope to maintain gains through the first 4 years of elementary school (Penn, 2004). Using the Woodcock–Johnson 22 standardized test of vocabulary achievement (Woodcock & Johnson, 1990), we measure 331 students from 12 randomly selected elementary schools in two contiguous districts at the beginning of kindergarten, the end of kindergarten, the end of first grade, the end of second grade, and the end of third grade. When data collection is finished, we have longitudinal data consisting of five measures on each student. In a very real sense, *individual students are the grouping variable, and test scores are nested within students. The individual student is at level two, with the repeated measures at level one!*

From the beginning of kindergarten until the end of third grade, we certainly expect attrition (Fitzgerald, Gottschalk, & Moffitt, 2002). Families move, students are placed in private schools, parents decide to home-school their youngsters, and especially unfortunate children become chronically ill or die in accidents. In many areas of the United States, moreover, students drop out long before they get to middle school, and truant officers are but a quaint recollection from decades past (Bickel & Papagiannis, 1988; Bickel, 1989; Bickel & Lange, 1995).

Nevertheless, with careful attention to follow-up and a little luck, at the end of third grade we have measured vocabulary achievement at five different times for most of the 331 students. For some others, children who have missed one or more testing sessions but who are still in one of the 12 schools, we have measures on several—two, three, four—different occasions.

The same, moreover, will be true of many students lost to attrition. We may not have measures for every testing occasion, but we are likely to have collected vocabulary achievement data for a subset of the five testing periods. For each student measured, then, we have test scores nested within individual students.

11.2 ANALYZING LONGITUDINAL DATA: PRETEST–POSTTEST

At one time or another, many of us have encountered data similar to those just described. An obvious, time-honored, and informative way to analyze the post-Head Start program data is through regression-based analysis of covariance (ANCOVA).

Depending on the data set, there are a variety of ways to specify the regression model. In this example, we will simply use the end-of-third-grade vocabulary test score as the dependent variable. Independent variables will be limited to the beginning-of-kindergarten test score as a pretest (X_{PRE}), and dummy variables representing participation in Head Start (X_{HEAD}) and participation in a post-Head Start program ($X_{PROGRAM}$). Measures of duration of participation in the program being evaluated would be more informative than a dummy variable, but we will use what we have. As things stand, 62.7% of the students in the data set participated in Head Start, and 54.2% participated in the post-Head Start program.

After centering the Head Start and post-Head Start program variables, we create a same-level multiplicative interaction term ($X_{HEAD} * X_{PROGRAM}$). This term is especially useful in our analysis, because 52.2% of Head Start participants were enrolled in the post-Head Start program, while the remaining 47.8% received no additional services.

Finally, as additional independent (control) variables, we add family income (X_{INCOME}), parent respondent's level of educational attainment ($X_{EDUCATION}$), and neighborhood quality (X_{HOOD}).

The results reported in Table 11.1 indicate that Head Start (X_{HEAD}) makes no difference, that the program being evaluated ($X_{PROGRAM}$) makes no difference, and that the $X_{HEAD} * X_{PROGRAM}$ interaction effect is also inconsequential. The pretest, of course, has a substantial relationship with the posttest: For each 1-point increase in the pretest score, posttest scores, on average, increased by 0.940 points.

TABLE 11.1. ANCOVA for Vocabulary Achievement

$$Y_{POST} = 37.149 + 0.940X_{PRE} - 0.675X_{HEAD} - 0.556X_{PROGRAM} + 1.587X_{HEAD} * X_{PROGRAM}$$
$$\quad\;(0.384)\;\;(0.095)\qquad(0.904)\qquad\;\;(0.805)\qquad\qquad(1.591)$$

$$+\; 0.289X_{EDUCATION} - 0.064X_{INCOME} + 0.069X_{HOOD}$$
$$\quad(0.253)\qquad\qquad\;\;(0.193)\qquad\;\;(0.058)$$

$$R^2 = 35.9\%$$
$$N = 258$$

11.3 NESTED MEASURES: GROWTH IN STUDENT VOCABULARY ACHIEVEMENT

Notice, however, that our sample size is only 258. Due to attrition and missing data, we have lost 73 cases.

Furthermore, the question being asked and answered—is vocabulary achievement at the end of third grade related to post-Head Start program participation?—ignores a good deal of data. Specifically, test scores at the end of kindergarten, at the end of first grade, and at the end of second grade have been excluded. If we had measures on all variables in the analysis for the specified occasions, we could use well-known time series procedures. But the available data are not adequate to that task.

Perhaps we should simply ignore the additional data. After all, we have provided a tentative answer to the question posed—the program makes no difference—and test score data for intervening outcome variables seem not to have been needed. Just what may we be missing by making this choice?

Suppose we select one case at random. (In our program evaluation data set, it is case number 280.) We find that this student had a vocabulary test score of 11 at the beginning of kindergarten and 37 at the end of third grade. This means that student number 280 gained, on average, 6.5 points per year. Since the standard deviation for vocabulary achievement at the beginning of kindergarten is 4.28, this is, on average, just over 1.5 standard deviations per year. It all seems perfectly straightforward and at first look, it is not clear that we have lost anything by excluding the intervening scores.

But let's look more closely at the progress of student number 280 over the four years from the beginning of kindergarten until the end of third grade. If we plot test scores year by year, as in Figure 11.1, we see that growth in vocabulary achievement represents a fairly clear-cut departure from linearity.

If we limit our analysis to the posttest score as a function of the pretest score and a commonplace complement of other independent variables, as in Table 11.1, we completely overlook the S-shaped pattern that is evident in Figure 11.1. But perhaps this is for the best. After all, there is no good reason to believe that case 280 provides a useful typification of the entire data set. It may be, moreover, that departures from linearity with regard to this case are due to random error (Singer & Willett, 2003).

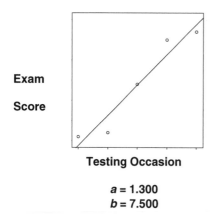

Exam

Score

Testing Occasion

$a = 1.300$
$b = 7.500$

FIGURE 11.1. Case number 280: Growth in Woodcock–Johnson 22 vocabulary test scores.

We can, however, easily select another case at random and see what we get. This time we select case number 87 (see Figure 11.2). This is certainly a very different pattern, and one wonders how to account for the sharp drop in test-taking performance at the end of first grade. Perhaps the data were mispunched. Maybe the child was ill. It could be that he or she misunderstood the test administrator's directions. Or perhaps the child actually suffered a rather dramatic achievement decline throughout the kindergarten year. Whatever the explanation, scores for this case do not suggest the S-shaped pattern we very tentatively discerned in Figure 11.1.

As it turns out, we have scores for the same students on four other tests administered during the same testing sessions for the same program evaluation purpose. Two of these—the Peabody Picture Vocabulary Test (Dunn & Dunn, 1981) and the Woodcock–Johnson 23 passage comprehension test (Woodcock & Johnson, 1990)—have also been commonly used as measures of verbal achievement. We can easily graph changes in the performance of student number 87, using these tests (see Figure 11.3 and 11.4). Though the three tests are not directly comparable, it is instructive to see that the dramatic drop in measured achievement for case number 87 is peculiar to the Woodcock–Johnson 22. Whatever the explanation for this dramatic decline, it is not manifest in related test scores for the same student.

If we select another case at random (number 166) and plot growth in vocabulary achievement as measured by the Woodcock–Johnson 22, we get the results in Figure 11.5. In this instance, all points are clustered very close to the regression line.

We could continue randomly selecting individual cases and graphing achievement growth student by student, and, as we have been doing, using OLS to estimate intercepts and slopes. This would be a tedious exercise, to be sure, and it is not at all clear that we would learn much more than is suggested by the few cases we have examined: For vocabulary achievement as measured by the Woodcock–Johnson 22, OLS estimates of intercepts and slopes vary substantially from case to case. Furthermore, there seems not to be a nonlinear functional form that is consistently better-fitting than a straight regression line.

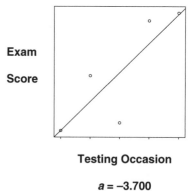

Exam

Score

Testing Occasion

$a = -3.700$
$b = 3.700$

FIGURE 11.2. Case number 87: Growth in Woodcock–Johnson 22 vocabulary test scores.

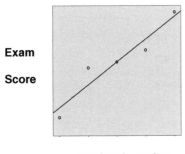

$a = 39.600$
$b = 7.800$

FIGURE 11.3. Case number 87: Growth in Peabody Picture Vocabulary Test scores.

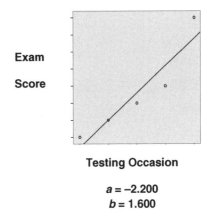

$a = -2.200$
$b = 1.600$

FIGURE 11.4. Case number 87: Growth in Woodcock–Johnson 23 passage comprehension test scores.

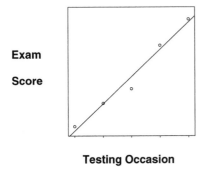

$a = -5.000$
$b = 9.400$

FIGURE 11.5. Case number 166: Growth in Woodcock–Johnson 22 vocabulary test scores.

Still, we might try developing this example further by being more purposeful in selecting cases. Suppose we select two cases at random, but we specify that one student (case number 45) will be a White female from a rural county, with parents whose education and income levels are in the top quartile; the other (case number 72) will be a Black male from a nonrural county, with parents whose education and income levels are in the bottom quartile. Having selected two students to assure they are different on high-profile variables—race, gender, place of residence, family income, and parents' education—we get the vocabulary achievement growth results in Figures 11.6 and 11.7.

With these additional examples, we continue to get very different intercepts and slopes from one student to another, and it remains the case that consistently patterned departures from linearity are not evident. Our examples show a tight clustering of observations about the regression line, and the S-shaped growth curve suggested by case number 280, while again intimated in Figure 11.6, seems likely to have been due to chance.

The dramatic differences in intercepts and slopes are instructive in themselves. They suggest, moreover, that even when a growth curve is best construed as linear, use of a simple pretest–posttest analysis hides a lot of valuable information. Students may start at very different achievement levels, and by the end of the third grade may be at a similar place. And the converse is also true. Understanding the achievement growth pro-

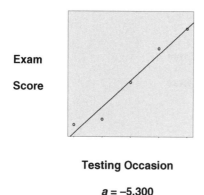

a = -5.300
b = 9.300

FIGURE 11.6. Case number 45: Growth in Woodcock–Johnson 22 vocabulary test scores.

a = 7.600
b = 3.800

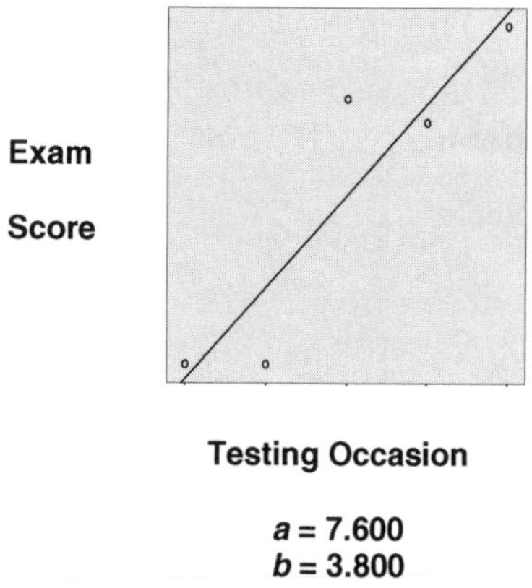

FIGURE 11.7. Case number 72: Growth in Woodcock–Johnson 22 vocabulary test scores.

cess, as a result, requires a good deal more information than is provided by a pretest–posttest design.

The slope and intercept differences we have just seen should be remembered when we examine a relationship such as that displayed in Figure 11.8. Here we have used all information available for the Woodcock–Johnson 22 vocabulary test for each of the five testing occasions.

Figures 11.1 through 11.8 enable us to visualize what we mean by the claim that observations are *nested* within individual students. In this instance, depending on the number of testing sessions for which a student was present, each was measured one to five times over a period of 4 years.

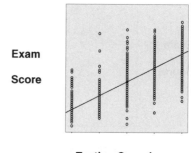

a = 1.182
b = 7.270

FIGURE 11.8. All cases: Growth in Woodcock–Johnson 22 vocabulary test scores.

11.4 NESTED MEASURES: GROWTH IN NCLEX PASS RATES

Though we have learned a lot from examining the graphical descriptions of achievement growth, it is important that we not be misled by the tidy relationships so far depicted. Yes, intercepts and slopes varied sharply, but in case after case we saw remarkably little variation around the regression line. In each instance, moreover, growth meant growth! In addition, each of the individuals whose performance was graphed had been measured on all five test-taking occasions. None of the students whose scores provided our examples had failed to take one or more tests.

Figures 11.9 through 11.12 below, however, illustrate growth in institutional pass rates on the national nursing certification exam, commonly referred to as NCLEX (National Council of State Boards of Nursing, 2006). The cases include all 21 institutions—whether these were universities, 4-year colleges, community colleges, vocational–technical schools, or hospitals—that offered registered nursing programs in West Virginia at any time during the 10-year period from 1985 to 1994.

We have purposefully selected three of those institutions to further illustrate the meaning of the nesting of measures within level-one cases, and to clarify the meaning of **growth** as we are using that term. In Figure 11.9 we see that institution 15 reported pass rates for 9 of the 10 years. For those nine measures, an upward-sloping linear regression line seems quite fitting.

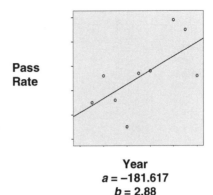

Pass Rate

Year
a = −181.617
b = 2.88

FIGURE 11.9. Institution 15: Growth in NCLEX pass rate.

In Figure 11.10 we see that institution 12 reported pass rates for all 10 years. In this instance, the scatter of points corresponding to the pass-rate-by-time relationship clearly suggests no change. The OLS estimate of the slope of the regression line is almost exactly zero.

In Figure 11.11 we see that institution 21 reported pass rates for 9 of 10 years. In this case, points are scattered widely, but the pass-rate-by-time relationship is clearly negative. Calling the regression line in Figure 10.11 a *growth curve* manifests a linguistic convention. *Change curve* would be a better way to put it, but so long as we recognize that repeated measures growth curves may manifest loss or constancy as well as growth, conventional terminology will do the job well enough.

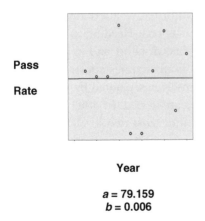

Pass

Rate

Year

a = 79.159
b = 0.006

FIGURE 11.10. Institution 12: Growth in NCLEX pass rate.

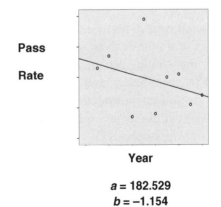

Pass

Rate

Year

a = 182.529
b = −1.154

FIGURE 11.11. Institution 21: Growth in NCLEX pass rate.

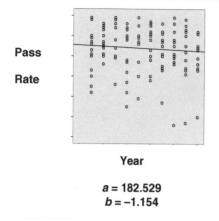

Pass

Rate

Year

a = 182.529
b = −1.154

FIGURE 11.12. All institutions:
Growth in NCLEX pass rate.

In Figure 11.12 we have graphed all 21 institutions in terms of the relationship between time and NCLEX pass rate from 1985 to 1994. We find a very weak average relationship represented by an OLS regression line that has a slight downward slope with a great deal of scatter. Figures 11.9 through 11.12 suggest a marked lack of consistency in the pass-rate-by-time relationship from institution to institution. However, since we have no reason to think that the relationship is nonlinear for any institution, the intercepts and slope, while quite different from case to case, are directly comparable.

Note, by the way, that whether we used vocabulary achievement test scores or NCLEX pass rates to construct growth curves, measures were taken on *fixed* occasions—at the beginning of kindergarten or at the end of a subsequent year of elementary school; or at the end of a year of operation of a nursing education program during from 1985 to 1994. Even if measurement occasions are not fixed, however, multilevel regression growth models may be used in much the same way as when measurement occasions are fixed (Hox, 2002, pp. 74–93).

11.5 DEVELOPING MULTILEVEL REGRESSION GROWTH MODELS

Now that we have provided another series of examples of observations' being nested within level-one units, how do we use this information to describe and explain growth more informatively? With regard to evaluating the post-Head Start program, for example, can we get regression results more useful than those reported in Table 11.1? As it turns out, by studying multilevel regression models, we have already learned most of what we need to know about growth models—a more informative alternative to traditional pretest–posttest designs evaluating programs such as post-Head Start.

Let's think about it. We have just devoted a good deal of effort and exposition to demonstrating that growth models with repeated measures are manifestations of nesting. This immediately gives us two levels: the measures themselves separated by time intervals, and the individual cases within which the measures are nested. In other words, we have set the stage for a multilevel regression model with **at least** two levels.

The emphasis on at least two levels is quite pertinent here. Observations within students are at level one, where we place our measure of time as a predictor. The individual student is at level two, where student-level predictors such as family income, parents' educational level, and Head Start participation are located. But what about the post-Head Start program that we want to evaluate?

As it turns out, the post-Head Start program ($X_{PROGRAM}$) is at level three, the school level. This is because the 12 schools involved were randomly assigned to program participation–nonparticipation status, with six schools in each category. As a result, in evaluating the post-Head Start program, we will use a *three-level growth model*.

Since our objective is primarily pedagogical rather than evaluative, however, we will begin with simpler two-level models and work our way up. When we have acquired a reasonable degree of skill in specifying and testing two-level growth models, we will specify and test the three-level growth model needed for evaluating the post-Head Start program. Along the way, we will be introducing predictors that will be needed as constituents of that three-level model.

Data sets with repeated measures are commonly set up with each case corresponding to one record, one row of data. To estimate growth curves, the data set has to be *reorganized* so that the *repeated measures* (in this case, vocabulary test scores) *are arranged in a column*. This means that each case will now have as many rows of data or records as there are testing occasions. For most of us, this is a very unfamiliar procedure, but it can be done simply by looking at the computer screen and following the instructions listed in SPSS Routine 11.1.

SPSS Routine 11.1. Restructuring a Data File for Growth Modeling

1. Open an SPSS data file.
2. Click on DATA and then click on RESTRUCTURE.
3. At the top of the screen, you will see WELCOME TO THE RESTURUCTURE DATA WIZARD!
4. Beneath WHAT DO YOU WANT TO DO?, stay with the default option RESTRUCTURE SELECTED VARIABLES INTO CASES.
5. At the bottom of the RESTRUCTURE DATA WIZARD box, click on NEXT.
6. At the top of the screen, you will see VARIABLES TO CASES: NUMBER OF VARIABLE GROUPS. Beneath that you will see HOW MANY VARIABLES DO YOU WANT TO RESTRUCTURE? For now, choose the default option ONE (FOR EXAMPLE, W1, W2, W3).
7. At the bottom of the screen, click on NEXT.
8. At the top of the screen, you will see VARIABLES TO CASES: SELECT VARIABLES. Move the variables that will used to estimate the growth curve into the VARIABLES TO BE TRANSPOSED box beneath TARGET VARIABLE.
9. Move time-independent variables to be used as predictors into the FIXED VARIABLE(S) box. (Time-independent variables may be factors such as gender, ethnicity, or parent's level of education. They are independent variables that have the same value at each measurement occasion.)
10. At the bottom of the screen, click on NEXT.
11. At the top of the screen, you will see VARIABLES TO CASES: CREATE INDEX VARIABLES. Use the default option ONE.
12. At the bottom of the screen, click on NEXT.
13. At the top of the screen, you will see VARIABLES TO CASES: CREATE ONE INDEX VARIABLE. Click on FINISH.
14. Remove the contents of the OUTPUT VIEWER from the screen, and you will see the restructured data set. It is currently UNTITLED, so save it, using any name you like.

The first few times I restructured a data set to accommodate a growth model, I felt very uncertain about the process. Just remember that SPSS does all the work. When the data set has been restructured, with repeated measures arranged in a column, it is suitable for doing multilevel regression analysis with growth curves.

In Table 11.2, we have specified level-one, level-two, and full models for growth in vocabulary achievement, using the West Virginia data set that includes the post-Head Start data. In this example, the intercept and the slope for TIME1 are random, and the slope for the student-level predictor X_{HEAD2} is fixed. As with our other applications of multilevel regression, all independent variables are grand-mean-centered.

TIME1 is measured in terms of testing sessions. As we will see in subsequent examples, however, we will usually measure time in a more purposeful way. Depending on research objectives, time might be reckoned in terms of age, grade level, span of program participation, or other substantively interesting time-varying factors.

In contrast to presentations that adopt distinctive notation for growth models, we have used the same notation that we used with other multilevel regression models (see, e.g., Raudenbush & Bryk, 2002; Singer & Willett, 2003). This is part of our ongoing effort to find useful commonalities among statistical procedures. After all, if multilevel analysis is just regression under specific circumstances, perhaps the same is true of multilevel growth modeling.

The within-student or level-one predictor, TIME1, is measured simply by numbering the testing sessions from 1 to 5. The between-student or level-two contextual variable, X_{HEAD2}, is a dummy variable coded 1 for those who participated in the Head Start program and 0 for those who did not.

It is important to emphasize again that the level-one independent variable TIME1 refers to repeated measures taken *within each student*. Variability in the random component for TIME1 occurs *between students*. *The student constitutes level two.* As a result, the level-two variable X_{HEAD2} is a characteristic of students—they participated in Head Start or they did not. It sounds odd, to be sure, but the individual student is the context. Level-one measures occur within students.

TABLE 11.2. Vocabulary Achievement Growth: Multilevel Regression Growth Model

Level-one model

$$Y = \beta_{0J} + \beta_{1J}TIME1 + e_{IJ}$$

Level-two model

$$\beta_{0J} = \gamma_{00} + \gamma_{01}X_{HEAD} + u_{0J}$$
$$\beta_{1J} = \gamma_{10} + \gamma_{11}X_{HEAD2} + u_{1J}$$

Full model

$$Y = \gamma_{00} + \gamma_{01}X_{HEAD2} + \gamma_{10}TIME1 + \gamma_{11}X_{HEAD2} * TIME1 + (u_{1J} * TIME1 + u_{0J} + e_{IJ})$$

As we develop this model, it will become more realistic, including a level-three predictor for the post-Head Start program ($X_{PROGRAM}$). We will then be able to replicate and improve upon the ANCOVA evaluation model in Table 11.1, this time using a three-level regression growth model.

We will, however, start simply. Empirical results for the model specified in Table 11.2 are reported in Tables 11.3 and 11.4. They have almost exactly the same form and content as our other tabular accounts of multilevel regression. Interpretation of the fixed components in Table 11.3 proceeds very much like interpretation of fixed components in any other multilevel analysis:

1. For each 1-unit increase in time, vocabulary achievement growth increases, on average, by 7.128 points.
2. Head Start participants' vocabulary achievement is, on average, diminished by 1.710 points when compared to that of nonparticipants.

This analysis is easy to do with SPSS Mixed Models. Just follow the steps in SPSS Routine 11.2.

In the pretest–posttest ANCOVA in Table 11.1, we found no Head Start effect, but here we find that Head Start participation actually *diminishes* achievement. This is not an impossible finding, but it certainly seems implausible. When the signs of coefficients go in unexpected directions, multicollinearity is a usual suspect. When the analysis reported in Table 11.3 is run as an OLS regression equation, however, each of the variance inflation factors is 1.000 and the Condition Index is 1.110. Multicollinearity is not the problem.

TABLE 11.3. Vocabulary Achievement Growth: Multilevel Regression Growth Equation; Fixed Components

$$Y_{GROWTH} = 8.508 + 7.128TIME1 - 1.710X_{HEAD2} - 0.345X_{HEAD2} * TIME1$$
$$\phantom{Y_{GROWTH} = } (0.242)\ (0.101) (0.619) (0.227)$$

$$Pseudo\text{-}R^2 = 87.9\%^a$$

Note. [a]Pseudo-R^2 is a summary measure used here as an alternative to R_1^2. Its interpretation is given in the next section.

TABLE 11.4. Vocabulary Achievement Growth: Multilevel Regression Growth Equation; Estimates of Covariance Parameters

Parameter	Estimate	Std. error	Wald Z	Sig. level
Residual	13.902	0.673	20.667	.000
INTERCEPT1	10.671	1.553	6.871	.000
INTERCEPT1 by TIME1	2.296	0.449	5.115	.000
TIME1	1.445	0.256	5.645	.001

SPSS Routine 11.2. Multilevel Growth Model for Vocabulary Achievement

1. Open the SPSS data file and click on ANALYZE.
2. Go to MIXED MODELS and click on LINEAR.
3. Since the student is the level-two grouping variable in which measures are nested, insert the student identifier into the SUBJECTS box.
4. Click on CONTINUE, and insert vocabulary achievement as a repeated measures variable into the DEPENDENT variable box. Then insert our measure of time, TIME1, along with the other independent variable, X_{HEAD2}, and the cross-level interaction term, X_{HEAD2} * TIME1, into the COVARIATES box.
5. Click on FIXED at the bottom of the screen. In the small box in the middle of the screen, change FACTORIAL to MAIN EFFECTS. Move the independent variables and the cross-level interaction term from the FACTORS AND COVARIATES box to the MODEL box.
6. Click on CONTINUE.
7. Click on the RANDOM button at the bottom of the screen. The student identifier is already in the SUBJECTS box, and now we also insert it into the COMBINATIONS box.
8. In the small box in the middle of the screen, change FACTORIAL to MAIN EFFECTS.
9. Near the top of the screen, click on INCLUDE INTERCEPT, and move the measure of time, TIME1, into the MODEL box.
10. Just above INCLUDE INTERCEPT, select UNSTRUCTURED.
11. Click on CONTINUE and click on the STATISTICS button.
12. On the left, under MODEL STATISTICS, select PARAMETER ESTIMATES and TESTS FOR COVARIANCE PARAMETERS.
13. Click on CONTINUE and click on OK.

Too often, I must admit, I have *misrepresented* a finding such as that pertaining to X_{HEAD2} by saying something like "Program participants' vocabulary achievement *growth* is, on average, diminished by 1.710 points. . . . " *This interpretation is patently incorrect.* Since the X_{HEAD2} dummy variable is a main effect, it may shift the growth curve up or down, but it is not implicated in the growth process itself. X_{HEAD2} may affect achievement, but *not* achievement *growth*.

On the other hand, *if* the negative coefficient for X_{HEAD2} * TIME1 had been statistically significant, we would have interpreted it as follows: "For program participants, the relationship between verbal achievement growth and TIME1 is diminished, on average, by 0.345 points when compared with that for nonparticipants." Since the coefficient is not statistically significant, however, it needs no further interpretation. It will be useful to keep these main-effect and interaction-effect interpretations in mind as we continue working with multilevel growth models.

Having clarified the interpretation of level-two coefficients, we can also see that our multilevel growth model is misspecified. There are obvious and consequential independent (control) variables such as family income that should be included in a multilevel regression model designed to answer the question posed here.

TABLE 11.5. Vocabulary Achievement Growth: Multilevel Regression Growth Equation; Variability with Respect to a Random Slope

$$b_{\text{FIXED}} - t_{.05}(b_{\text{RANDOM}})^{1/2} \text{ to } b_{\text{FIXED}} + t_{.05}(b_{\text{RANDOM}})^{1/2}$$

$$7.128 - 1.960(1.445)^{1/2} \text{ to } 7.128 + 1.960(1.445)^{1/2}$$

$$4.772 \text{ to } 9.484$$

Observers familiar with the voluminous and conflicting literature that has characterized the history of Head Start since its inception in 1965 will not be astonished by negative results (Spatig, Bickel, Parrot, Dillon, & Conrad, 1998). The same applies to no Head Start effects or positive Head Start effects (see, e.g., Gilliam & Zigler, 2000; Garces, Thomas, & Currie, 2000; U.S. Department of Health and Human Services, Administration for Children and Families, 2005).

Previous analyses with this West Virginia data set have simply reported no Head Start effects (Bickel & McDonough, 1998). None of those analyses, however, was done with a multilevel growth model. We shall see what happens as we further develop the model, making it more realistic and defensible. We will bear in mind, moreover, that we are working toward a three-level growth model—one sufficiently complex to permit evaluation of the post-Head Start program.

Table 11.3 does make clear, however, that our multilevel growth equation has explained a substantial amount of the variability in the vocabulary achievement dependent variable. Substantial growth occurs with the passage of time from one testing occasion to another.

With a linear functional form for our growth curve, we may use the fixed component of the slope for TIME1 as reported in Table 11.3 and the random component variance for TIME1 as reported in Table 11.4 to construct the interval in Table 11.5. As these things go, this is a fairly narrow interval—one enabling us to say that 95% of the achievement-by-TIME1 slopes for the students in the data set fall within the range from 4.772 to 9.484. Nevertheless, we see quite clearly that achievement growth over time is not uniform from one student to another, but displays substantial variability. Surely it makes a good deal of sense to assign a random coefficient to TIME1.

Notice, by the way, that the information in Table 11.4 includes random component variances and a random component covariance. This means that we have used an unstructured covariance structure, just as we have done many times in previous examples. Both random component variances and the random component covariance are statistically significant.

11.6 SUMMARY STATISTICS WITH GROWTH MODELS

The R_1^2 summary statistic that we have used with cross-sectional data can also be applied to multilevel growth models. As with simpler multilevel models, however, realistic growth model specification usually includes acknowledgment that random component variances may differ from group to group, and that they may be correlated. Why else introduce the complexity that comes with application of the unstructured option for covariance structure? Under these circumstances, calculation of R_1^2 for growth models becomes labor-intensive (Snijders & Bosker, 1999, pp. 173–180). Consequently, we will adopt a conceptually similar statistic called *pseudo-R²* (Singer & Willett, 2003)—one of a family of summary measures that is also well known to analysts who use logistic regression (Menard, 2002).

Tables 11.6 and 11.7 provide the information we have become accustomed to using for computing R_1^2. As we know, R_1^2 is easy to compute. All we need is the residual variance and the intercept variance for the unconditional model (as in Table 11.6) and the residual variance and intercept variance for the conditional model with all slopes fixed (as in Table 11.7).

$$R_1^2 = (1 - [(17.265 + 23.409)/(142.227 + 5.250)]) * 100 = 72.4\%$$

Pseudo-R^2, our growth model alternative to R_1^2, is even easier to compute. We just divide the residual variance from the unconditional model by the residual variance for the conditional model, subtract the result from 1, and multiply by 100. In this instance, that gives us the following:

$$\text{Pseudo-}R^2 = (1 - [(17.265)/(142.227)]) * 100 = 89.9\%$$

This is the percentage of reduction in level-one residual variance when the unconditional model is compared with the conditional model.

One troublesome limitation of this easy-to-compute, easy-to-interpret measure is that in some instances introduction of an additional independent variable may yield a

TABLE 11.6. Vocabulary Achievement Growth: Multilevel Regression Growth Equation; Unconditional (Null) Model; Estimates of Covariance Parameters

Parameter	Estimate	Std. error	Wald Z	Sig. level
Residual	142.227	5.975	23.804	.000
INTERCEPT1	5.250	2.342	2.027	.027

TABLE 11.7. Vocabulary Achievement Growth: Multilevel Regression Growth Equation; Conditional Model with Fixed Slopes; Estimates of Covariance Parameters

Parameter	Estimate	Std. error	Wald Z	Sig. level
Residual	17.265	0.721	23.956	.000
INTERCEPT1	23.409	2.129	10.994	.000

decreased rather than increased pseudo-R^2 value. This is because computation of the unconditional model, which gives us the denominator for pseudo-R^2, tends to underestimate the residual variance component and overestimate the level-two variance component (Hox, 2002). An anomalous decrease in pseudo-R^2 is typically due to model misspecification, in the form of introduction of predictors unrelated to the dependent variable in the population from which the sample is selected.

The foregoing cautionary comment applies to all multilevel models, but it is an issue we were able to avoid until now because of the ease with which we could calculate R_1^2 when working with cross-sectional data. We have compromised between labor-intensivity and precision by using pseudo-R^2 as an alternative to R^2 when working with growth models.

On the other hand, the –2 log likelihood statistic or deviance and the information criteria, all estimated with ML, are used in exactly the same way with growth models as they are with other multilevel models. The versatility and accuracy of information criteria and the deviance difference statistic explain why they are used so often and in so many different kinds of analyses.

By way of illustration, we might compare the growth model specified in Table 11.3 with the unconditional or intercept-only model. After reestimating both equations with ML, we get the results in Table 11.8.

$$\text{Deviance difference} = 9675.8 - 8824.3 = 851.5$$
$$df = 8 - 3 = 5$$

Each of the five smaller-is-better measures indicates that the conditional model provides the better fit. In addition, with three parameters estimated for the unconditional model (the fixed component and the random component for the intercept and the level-one residual) and eight parameters estimated for the conditional model (fixed components for the intercept and three slopes, the random components for the intercept and one slope, and the level-one residual), the deviance difference is statistically significant at any conventionally used alpha level.

TABLE 11.8. Vocabulary Achievement Growth: Information Criteria for Unconditional and Conditional Growth Models

Criterion	Unconditional	Conditional
–2 log likelihood	9675.8	*8824.3*
Akaike's Information Criterion	9685.8	*8840.3*
Hurvich and Tsai's Criterion	9685.9	*8840.4*
Bozdogan's Criterion	9717.3	*8890.7*
Schwarz's Bayesian Criterion	9712.3	*8862.7*

Note. The smaller value for each measure is boldfaced and italicized.

11.7 SAMPLE SIZES

In addition to the difference manifest in reporting pseudo-R^2 rather than R_1^2, Table 11.3 differs from previous reports of multilevel regression analyses in that it does *not* report nominal sample sizes. The level-one sample size is the number of repeated measures occurring within each student. In the example at hand, student vocabulary achievement was measured on five occasions. However, the actual number of measures on each student shows a good deal of variability from one test-taking session to another: beginning of kindergarten, 331; end of kindergarten, 331; end of first grade, 281; end of second grade, 273; end of third grade, 258. Furthermore, SPSS reports that the valid number of cases with listwise deletion of missing data is 246, meaning that some students skipped a testing session but appeared again later. Finally, the mean number of tests completed by the 331 students is 2.86.

In conventional analyses, such as the pretest–posttest ANCOVA reported in Table 11.1, we would be obliged to report that we had lost 22% of our cases due to attrition and missing data. This is because we would be working with the data collected in the first and last testing sessions.

With multilevel growth models, however, SPSS uses whatever data are available to estimate the best-informed growth curve for each student. For example, Figures 11.13 and 11.14 report OLS estimates of growth curves for students who were present for four of the five testing sessions. Student number 302 has no test score for the end-of-second-grade testing session, and student number 58 has no test score for the end-of-third-grade testing session.

The slope of the growth curve in Figure 11.14 seems much steeper than its reported value of 5.500 would suggest, because the SPSS software ties the metric for the vertical axis to maximum and minimum test scores. Since the end-of-third-grade score (usually

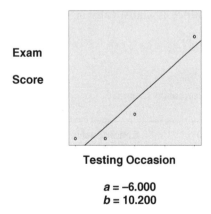

Testing Occasion

$a = -6.000$
$b = 10.200$

FIGURE 11.13. Case number 302: Growth in Woodcock–Johnson 22 vocabulary test scores.

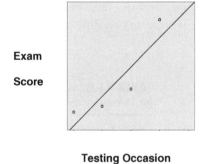

Testing Occasion

$a = 1.300$
$b = 5.500$

FIGURE 11.14. Case number 58: Growth in Woodcock–Johnson 22 vocabulary test scores.

the highest) is missing for case number 58, the vertical axis has been shortened. This visually exaggerates the steepness of the slope. The growth curve in Figure 11.15 was estimated with only three test scores, and the growth curve in Figure 11.16 was drawn with data from only two testing sessions. As a result, the graphed steepness of these slopes is further exaggerated. Nevertheless, the OLS intercepts and slopes recorded beneath each graph are accurate for the data at hand.

Though confusion may result from the way in which SPSS draws growth models with missing values, Figures 11.13 through 11.16 still make an important point: Even with one or more missing test scores, individual growth curves are estimated and used in constructing the overall or average growth curve. This holds, moreover, even for cases such as number 302 in Figure 11.13, in which a student missed one testing session but was present for the next.

In instances where we have reason to suspect that growth curves depart from linearity, however, missing data, if they exist in abundance, may have more serious consequences. In Figure 11.16, for example, with only beginning-of-kindergarten and end-of-kindergarten test scores, we can estimate an intercept and a slope, but departures from linearity cannot occur. In general, the more measurement occasions the better, and the fewer missing data the better.

This flexible procedure for estimating growth curves when data are complete or some measures are missing is extremely useful. As explained in detail by Singer and Willett (2003), however, missing data still pose the usual inferential problems. The nature and number of missing data may badly compromise our analysis, so that inferences from sample to population become dubious. As with so many other issues, exactly the same sorts of questions arise when we are working with more conventional applications of regression analysis or any other statistical procedure (Little & Rubin, 2002).

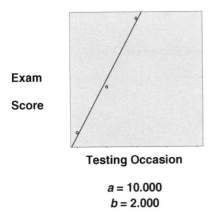

Exam

Score

Testing Occasion

a = 10.000
b = 2.000

FIGURE 11.15. Case number 177: Growth in Woodcock–Johnson 22 vocabulary test scores.

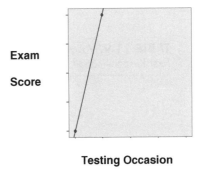

Exam

Score

Testing Occasion

a = –1.000
b = 7.500

FIGURE 11.16. Case number 149: Growth in Woodcock–Johnson 22 vocabulary test scores.

We can now see, however, that reporting level-one and level-two sample sizes for multilevel regression growth models is complicated by the fact that due to missing data, the number of measures available varies from student to student. In addition, in the presence of missing data, the number of students corresponding to each subset of measures also exhibits variability. Singer and Willett's (2003, pp. 156–159) discussion of types of missing data and their consequences is certainly worth reading.

11.8   THE MULTILEVEL REGRESSION GROWTH MODEL RESPECIFIED

At this point we may move toward more adequately replicating and improving upon the ANCOVA in Table 11.1. We will, of course, be using individual student growth curves as the dependent variable rather than end-of third-grade posttest scores. In addition to the Head Start independent variable (X_{HEAD2}), we will introduce family income ($X_{INCOME2}$) and parent's educational level ($X_{EDUCATION2}$) as predictors at level two.

We will, moreover, modify the way we understand time, construing it in a substantively more interesting way. Recall that testing sessions occurred at the beginning and end of kindergarten, and at the end of first, second, and third grades. This enables us to measure time in terms of years of schooling completed: 0 for the beginning of kindergarten, 1 for the end of kindergarten, 2 for the end of first grade, 3 for the end of second grade, and 4 for the end of third grade. Our measure of time in terms of years of schooling completed, YEARS1, will have a random slope, permitting it to vary from student to student.

Years of schooling completed is certainly a more substantively appealing measure than testing occasions. In addition, since YEARS1 has an unambiguous zero, it lends itself more readily to informative interpretation. Seventeen students were retained one or more grades, and they have been removed from the data set. The respecified model is shown in Table 11.9.

Interpretation of the fixed components (see Table 11.10) is again straightforward:

TABLE 11.9. Vocabulary Achievement Growth: Multilevel Regression Growth Model; First Respecification

Level-one model

$$Y = \beta_{0J} + \beta_{1J}\text{YEARS1} + e_{IJ}$$

Level-two model

$$\beta_{0J} = \gamma_{00} + \gamma_{01}X_{HEAD2} + \gamma_{02}X_{INCOME2} + \gamma_{03}X_{EDUCATION2} + u_{0J}$$
$$\beta_{1J} = \gamma_{10} + \gamma_{11}X_{HEAD2} + \gamma_{12}X_{INCOME2} + \gamma_{13}X_{EDUCATION2} + u_{1J}$$

Full model

$$Y = \gamma_{00} + \gamma_{01}X_{HEAD2} + \gamma_{02}X_{INCOME2} + \gamma_{03}X_{EDUCATION2} + \gamma_{10}\text{GRADE1} + \gamma_{11}X_{HEAD2} * \text{YEARS1}$$
$$+ \gamma_{12}X_{INCOME2} * \text{YEARS1} + \gamma_{13}X_{EDUCATION2} * \text{YEARS1} + (u_{1J} * \text{YEARS1} + u_{0J} + e_{IJ})$$

TABLE 11.10. Vocabulary Achievement Growth: Multilevel Regression Growth Equation; First Respecification; Fixed Components

$$Y_{GROWTH} = 8.508 - 0.245X_{HEAD2} + 0.507X_{INCOME2} + 0.477X_{EDUCATION2} + 7.126YEARS1$$
$$\quad\quad (0.233)\ (0.667)\quad\quad (0.137)\quad\quad\quad (0.190)\quad\quad\quad\quad (0.110)$$

$$\quad - 0.194X_{HEAD2} * YEARS1 + 0.031X_{INCOME2} * YEARS1 + 0.116X_{EDUCATION2} * YEARS1$$
$$\quad\quad (0.230)\quad\quad\quad\quad\quad (0.047)\quad\quad\quad\quad\quad (0.065)$$

$$\text{Pseudo-}R^2 = 83.6\%$$

TABLE 11.11. Vocabulary Achievement Growth: Multilevel Regression Growth Equation; First Respecification; Estimates of Covariance Parameters

Parameter	Estimate	Std. error	Wald Z	Sig. level
Residual	13.896	0.672	20.671	.000
INTERCEPT1	9.315	1.447	6.438	.000
INTERCEPT1 by YEARS1	2.124	0.430	4.934	.000
YEARS1	1.384	0.250	5.542	.000

1. For each year of schooling completed, vocabulary achievement growth increases, on average, by 7.126 points.
2. For every one-level increase in family income, vocabulary achievement increases, on average, by 0.507 points.
3. For every one-level increase in parent's education, vocabulary achievement increases, on average, by 0.477 points.

Now that the multilevel growth model is approximating a more defensible specification, the negative Head Start effect that we acknowledged in reference to Table 11.3 has been explained away. This is not surprising, since we are now controlling for family income and the respondent parent's educational level—independent variables typically confounded with Head Start participation–nonparticipation.

The slope of the vocabulary achievement growth curve has been affected very little by model respecification. In Table 11.11, however, we see that the level-one intercept variance (INTERCEPT1) and the covariance between the intercept and the slope for our measure of time (INTERCEPT1 by YEARS1) have been substantially diminished when compared with the parameter estimates in Table 11.4. The variance of the YEARS1 slope, however, is only slightly smaller.

11.9 THE MULTILEVEL REGRESSION GROWTH MODEL: FURTHER RESPECIFICATION

In Table 11.12, we have two additional level-two predictors: neighborhood quality (X_{HOOD2}) and ethnicity (X_{BLACK2}, coded 1 if Black and 0 if White). Each of the addi-

TABLE 11.12. Vocabulary Achievement Growth: Multilevel Regression Growth Model; Second Respecification

Level-one model

$Y = \beta_{0J} + \beta_{1J}\text{YEARS1} + e_{IJ}$

Level-two model

$\beta_{0J} = \gamma_{00} + \gamma_{02}X_{\text{HEAD2}} + \gamma_{02}X_{\text{INCOME2}} + \gamma_{03}X_{\text{EDUCATION2}} + \gamma_{04}X_{\text{HOOD2}} + \gamma_{05}X_{\text{ETHNIC2}} + u_{0J}$

$\beta_{1J} = \gamma_{10} + \gamma_{11}X_{\text{HEAD2}} + \gamma_{12}X_{\text{INCOME2}} + \gamma_{13}X_{\text{EDUCATION2}} + \gamma_{14}X_{\text{HOOD2}} + \gamma_{15}X_{\text{ETHNIC2}} + u_{1J}$

Full model

$Y = \gamma_{00} + \gamma_{01}X_{\text{HEAD2}} + \gamma_{02}X_{\text{INCOME2}} + \gamma_{03}X_{\text{EDUCATION2}} + \gamma_{04}X_{\text{HOOD2}} + \gamma_{05}X_{\text{ETHNIC2}} + \gamma_{10}\text{YEARS1}$

$\quad + \gamma_{11}X_{\text{HEAD2}} * \text{YEARS} + \gamma_{12}X_{\text{INCOME2}} * \text{YEARS} + \gamma_{13}X_{\text{EDUCATION2}} * \text{YEARS} + \gamma_{14}X_{\text{HOOD2}} * \text{YEARS}$

$\quad + \gamma_{15}X_{\text{ETHNIC2}} * \text{YEARS} + (u_{1J} * \text{YEARS1} + u_{0J} + e_{IJ})$

tional independent variables has a fixed slope, and each is used to account for variability in the level-one dependent variable, the random intercept and the random slope for YEARS1, and for the INTERCEPT1-by-YEARS1 covariance. Inclusion of these additional student-level contextual factors also yields two more implied cross-level interaction terms: $X_{\text{HOOD2}} * \text{YEARS1}$ and $X_{\text{EDUCATE2}} * \text{YEARS1}$. The cross-level interaction terms have fixed slopes. All level-two variables are centered with respect to their grand means.

Statistically, there is nothing new or unusual about this model; it is just a bit more complex than the multilevel growth model specified in Table 11.9. As it turns out, however, the model specified in Table 11.12 will serve a useful instructional purpose, enabling us to illustrate interpretation of a statistically significant cross-level interaction term created with the level-two predictor $X_{\text{EDUCATION2}}$ and our level-one measure of time, YEARS1.

Interpretation of the fixed components (see Table 11.13) goes as follows:

TABLE 11.13. Vocabulary Achievement Growth: Multilevel Regression Growth Equation; Second Respecification; Fixed Components

$Y_{\text{GROWTH}} = 8.464 - 0.257X_{\text{HEAD2}} + 0.360X_{\text{INCOME2}} + 0.402X_{\text{EDUCATION2}} + 0.130X_{\text{HOOD2}}$
$\qquad\quad (0.234)\ (0.693)\qquad\quad (0.146)\qquad\qquad (0.198)\qquad\qquad (0.044)$

$\qquad + 0.455X_{\text{ETHNIC2}} + 7.137\text{YEARS1} - 0.142X_{\text{HEAD2}} * \text{YEARS1} + 0.023X_{\text{INCOME2}} * \text{YEARS1}$
$\qquad\quad (0.840)\qquad\quad (0.104)\qquad\quad (0.243)\qquad\qquad\qquad (0.051)$

$\qquad + 0.116X_{\text{EDUCATION2}} * \text{YEARS1} + 0.016X_{\text{HOOD2}} * \text{YEARS1} + 0.353X_{\text{ETHNIC2}} * \text{YEARS1}$
$\qquad\quad (0.069)\qquad\qquad\qquad (0.017)\qquad\qquad\qquad (0.366)$

Pseudo-R^2 = 83.7%

1. For each year of schooling completed, student vocabulary achievement growth increases, on average, by 7.137 points. This value has changed very little from one specification to another.
2. For each one-level increase in family income, student vocabulary achievement increases, on average, by 0.360 points.
3. For each one-level increase in parent respondent's educational level, student vocabulary achievement increases, on average, by 0.402 points.
4. For each one-level increase in neighborhood quality, vocabulary achievement increases, on average, by 0.130 points.
5. If we use a one-tailed t test for the slope corresponding to $X_{EDUCATE2} * YEARS1$, the effect on achievement *growth* of each additional year of schooling completed is increased, on average, by 0.116 points. Given the nature of the variables involved, use of a one-tailed test makes sense. The more important point for instructional purposes, however, is that we can see how a level-two predictor can serve as a moderator variable and modify the relationship between YEARS1, our measure of time, and achievement growth.

When we compare Table 11.14 with Table 11.11, we see that the additional level-two predictors and cross-level interaction terms have contributed little to explaining the random component variances and covariance. The intercept variance has been modestly diminished, while the random component covariance and the slope variance have slightly increased.

In Table 11.15 we compare the simpler multilevel regression growth equation from Table 11.10 with the more complex respecification from Table 11.13. The deviance difference is statistically significant at any alpha level we might reasonably select, indicating that the more complex model provides the better fit. Each information criterion is consistent with this judgment.

$$\text{Deviance difference} = 8795.8 - 8216.0 = 579.8$$

$$df = 16 - 12 = 4$$

TABLE 11.14. Vocabulary Achievement Growth: Multilevel Growth Equation; Second Respecification; Estimates of Covariance Parameters

Parameter	Estimate	Std. error	Wald Z	Sig. level
Residual	13.941	0.697	19.997	.000
INTERCEPT1	8.604	1.442	5.965	.000
INTERCEPT1 by YEARS1	2.152	0.440	4.893	.000
YEARS1	1.422	0.262	5.427	.000

TABLE 11.15. Vocabulary Achievement Growth: Information Criteria for Comparing Respecifications

Criterion	Table 11.10	Table 11.13
−2 log likelihood	8795.8	*8216.0*
Akaike's Information Criterion	8819.8	*8248.0*
Hurvich and Tsai's Criterion	8820.0	*8248.4*
Bozdogan's Criterion	8895.3	*8347.6*
Schwarz's Bayesian Criterion	8883.3	*8331.6*

Note. The smaller value for each measure is boldfaced and italicized.

11.10 RESIDUAL COVARIANCE STRUCTURES

We have paid a lot of attention to covariance structures for random components. Through there are many other choices, we have consistently used the unstructured option. The unstructured option permits random components to vary, and it permits them to be correlated as well. But why raise the long-since-settled issue of covariance structures here and now? What is the point?

Let's think about some of the usual regression assumptions that we have been taking for granted. Specifically, do homoscedasticity and the absence of autocorrelation characterize the level-one *residuals*? In other words, *should we model the level-one residuals in much the same way that we have modeled the random components?* In the form of a question, that is the point.

Without saying so, in the growth models estimated above we have been using the scaled identity option for the level-one residuals. Scaled identity constrains residuals to have a homogeneous variance and be uncorrelated. Does this seem realistic?

Given that we are using repeated measures (the same test administered on five different occasions), there is good reason to be guided by the possibility that the residuals do not have uniform variance from one testing occasion to another and that they are correlated. If we want to estimate a multilevel growth model from the specification in Table 11.12 *while allowing for violations of the assumption of homoscedasticity for level-one residuals*, the SPSS instructions are again pretty easy to follow (see SPSS Routine 11.3).

The results of this analysis, with the error term modeled to accommodate heteroscedasticity, are reported in Tables 11.16 and 11.17. Interpretation of fixed components for Table 11.16 is similar to that for Table 11.13. In Table 11.16, however, each of the slopes for each of the statistically significant main effects is a bit smaller than in Table 11.13, and the slope for the cross-level interaction term $X_{EDUCATION2} * YEARS1$ is no longer statistically significant.

1. For each year of schooling completed, student vocabulary achievement growth increases, on average, by 6.702 years.
2. For each one-level increase in family income, student vocabulary achievement increases, on average, by 0.336 points.

SPSS Routine 11.3. Growth Model
with a Diagonal Residual Covariance Structure

1. Open the SPSS data file and click on ANALYZE.
2. Go to MIXED MODELS and click on LINEAR.
3. Since the individual student is the level-two or grouping variable, insert the student identifier into the SUBJECTS box.
4. Insert the INDEX NUMBER (INDEX1) into the REPEATED box. The INDEX NUMBER was created when we restructured the data set. By inserting INDEX1 into the REPEATED box, we indicate that we are using repeated measures.
5. Beneath the REPEATED box, you will see the REPEATED COVARIANCE TYPE box. The default option is DIAGONAL. Structurally this is equivalent to the covariance structure that we have used to illustrate random components, but here it is applied to level-one residuals. It permits residual variances to vary from one repeated measure to another, but it constrains the residuals to be uncorrelated.
6. Click on CONTINUE, insert vocabulary achievement as the dependent variable into the DEPENDENT VARIABLE box, and insert YEARS1 into the COVARIATE(S) box. YEARS1 in the COVARIATE(S) box is our level-one measure of time.
7. Insert all the level-two independent variables and cross-level interaction terms into the COVARIATE(S) box: X_{HEAD2}, $X_{INCOME2}$, $X_{EDUCATION2}$, X_{HOOD2}, $X_{INCOME2}$, $X_{ETHNIC2}$, X_{HEAD2} * YEARS1, $X_{INCOME2}$ * YEARS1, $X_{EDUCATION2}$ * YEARS1, X_{HOOD2} * YEARS1, and $X_{ETHNIC2}$ * YEARS1.
8. Click on FIXED at the bottom of the screen. In the small box in the middle of the screen, change FACTORIAL to MAIN EFFECTS. Move the level-one independent variable INDEX1, all the level-two independent variables, and all the cross-level interaction terms from the FACTORS AND COVARIATES box to the MODEL box.
9. Click on CONTINUE.
10. Click on the RANDOM button at the bottom of the screen. The student identifier is already in the SUBJECTS box, and now we also insert it into the COMBINATIONS box. Move YEARS1 from the FACTORS AND COVARIATES box to the MODEL box.
11. In the small box in the middle of the screen, change FACTORIAL to MAIN EFFECTS.
12. Near the top of the screen, click on INCLUDE INTERCEPT, and insert YEARS1 into the MODEL box.
13. Just above INCLUDE INTERCEPT and to the right of COVARIANCE TYPE, select UNSTRUCTURED.
14. Click on CONTINUE, and then click on the STATISTICS button.
15. On the left, under MODEL STATISTICS, select PARAMETER ESTIMATES and TESTS FOR COVARIANCE PARAMETERS.
16. Click on CONTINUE and click on OK.
17. Near the bottom of the SPSS output, values for the INTERCEPT and SLOPE, along with their standard errors, appear in the ESTIMATE and STD. ERROR columns of the box labeled ESTIMATES OF FIXED EFFECTS.
18. Just below the ESTIMATES OF FIXED EFFECTS box, values of the variances for the repeated measures of reading achievement appear in the ESTIMATES column of the box labeled ESTIMATES OF COVARIANCE PARAMETERS. Beneath values of the variances for the repeated measures of reading achievement, we find values for the variances and covariances of random components.

TABLE 11.16. Vocabulary Achievement Growth: Multilevel Regression Growth Equation; Diagonal Residual Covariance Structure; Fixed Components

$$Y_{GROWTH} = 9.935 - 0.060X_{HEAD2} + 0.336X_{INCOME2} + 0.375X_{EDUCATION2} + 0.131X_{HOOD2}$$
$$(0.228)\ (0.682) \qquad (0.143) \qquad\quad (0.195) \qquad\qquad (0.043)$$

$$+\ 0.542X_{ETHNIC2} + 6.702YEARS1 - 0.088X_{HEAD2} * YEARS1 - 0.004X_{INCOME2} * YEARS1$$
$$(0.811) \qquad\quad (0.094) \qquad\quad (0.220) \qquad\qquad\qquad (0.047)$$

$$+\ 0.083X_{EDUCATION2} * YEARS1 + 0.014X_{HOOD2} * YEARS1 + 0.376X_{ETHNIC2} * YEARS1$$
$$(0.063) \qquad\qquad\qquad (0.014) \qquad\qquad\qquad (0.331)$$

Pseudo-R^2 = 83.7%

3. For each one-level increase in parent's educational level, vocabulary achievement increases, on average, by 0.375 points. (This holds only if we use a one-tailed test for the slope for $X_{EDUCATION2}$.)
4. For each one-level increase in neighborhood quality, vocabulary achievement increases, on average, by 0.131 points.

In Table 11.17, we have an estimate of the level-one residual variance for each testing occasion (INDEX1 = 1 through INDEX1 = 5). It is clear that residual variances are quite different from one testing occasion to another. Our tacit assumption of homogeneous variances for the level-one residuals was obviously in error. For this reason, use of the diagonal residual covariance structure rather than scaled identity represents an improvement in regression model specification.

When we compare information criteria in Table 11.18, we see that permitting the residuals to have a nonuniform variance has improved the model fit. The deviance difference and each of the smaller-is-better information criteria indicate that modeling the error term to accommodate heteroscedasticity has been the right thing to do.

Deviance difference = 8216.0 − 8138.8 = 77.2

df = 20 − 16 = 4

TABLE 11.17. Vocabulary Achievement Growth: Multilevel Regression Growth Equation; Diagonal Residual Covariance Structure; Estimates of Covariance Parameters

Parameter	Estimate	Std. error	Wald Z	Sig. level
INDEX1 = 1	2.406	1.246	1.932	.053
INDEX1 = 2	23.033	2.142	10.753	.000
INDEX1 = 3	17.215	1.776	9.696	.000
INDEX1 = 4	17.367	1.771	9.807	.000
INDEX1 = 5	2.395	1.637	1.463	.143
INTERCEPT1	14.099	1.911	7.379	.000
INTERCEPT1 by YEARS1	0.396	0.458	0.865	.367
YEARS1	2.010	0.230	8.723	.000

TABLE 11.18. Vocabulary Achievement Growth: Information Criteria for Scaled Identity and Diagonal Residual Covariance Structures

Criterion	Scaled identity	Diagonal
–2 log likelihood	8216.0	*8138.8*
Akaike's Information Criterion	8248.0	*8178.8*
Hurvich and Tsai's Criterion	8248.4	*8179.4*
Bozdogan's Criterion	8347.6	*8303.3*
Schwarz's Bayesian Criterion	8331.6	*8283.3*

Note. The smaller value for each measure is boldfaced and italicized.

We have also acknowledged, however, the possibility that the residuals may be correlated. To model *both* heteroscedasticity *and* autocorrelation in the level-one error term, we would make one simple change in SPSS Routine 11.3: In step 5, instead of selecting DIAGONAL, we select AR(1): HETEROGENEOUS. In other words, we will use a heterogeneous autoregressive residual covariance structure.

The fixed component estimates in Table 11.19 are very similar to those in Table 11.16. Of the random component variances and covariance in Table 11.20, only the vari-

TABLE 11.19. Vocabulary Achievement Growth: Multilevel Regression Growth Equation; AR(1): Heterogeneous Residual Covariance Structure; Fixed Components

$$Y_{\text{GROWTH}} = 10.195 - 0.129X_{\text{HEAD2}} + 0.334X_{\text{INCOME2}} + 0.375X_{\text{EDUCATION2}} + 0.133X_{\text{HOOD2}}$$
$$\phantom{Y_{\text{GROWTH}} = } (0.183)\ (0.679) \qquad (0.143) \qquad (0.194) \qquad (0.043)$$

$$+ 0.571X_{\text{ETHNIC2}} + 6.592\text{YEARS1} - 0.080X_{\text{HEAD2}} * \text{YEARS1} - 0.003X_{\text{INCOME2}} * \text{YEARS1}$$
$$ (0.651) \qquad\quad (0.121) \qquad\quad (0.284) \qquad\qquad (0.060)$$

$$+ 0.082X_{\text{EDUCATION2}} * \text{YEARS1} + 0.015X_{\text{HOOD2}} * \text{YEARS1} + 0.333X_{\text{ETHNIC2}} * \text{YEARS1}$$
$$ (0.081) \qquad\qquad\quad (0.018) \qquad\qquad (0.427)$$

$$\text{Pseudo-}R^2 = 83.7\%$$

TABLE 11.20. Vocabulary Achievement Growth: Multilevel Regression Growth Equation; AR(1): Heterogeneous Residual Covariance Structure; Estimates of Covariance Parameters

Parameter	Estimate	Std. error	Wald Z	Sig. level
INDEX1 = 1	1.326	0.838	1.581	.114
INDEX1 = 2	22.680	2.954	7.675	.000
INDEX1 = 3	19.343	2.013	9.609	.000
INDEX1 = 4	17.188	2.571	6.686	.000
INDEX1 = 5	1.201	1.184	1.014	.311
Rho	0.167	0.043	3.868	.000
INTERCEPT1	5.408	4.376	1.236	.216
INTERCEPT1 by YEARS1	1.520	1.057	1.438	.150
YEARS1	1.187	0.280	4.225	.000

ance for YEARS1 remains statistically significant, and its magnitude has been substantially diminished

The repeated measures variances again show substantial variability from one testing occasion to another. Furthermore, the value of rho, a measure of the strength of the association among the level-one residuals, is statistically significant. The level-one residuals are correlated, and the added complexity that comes with modeling a heterogeneous autoregressive residual covariance structure, including estimation of rho, is warranted. The heterogeneous autoregressive error covariance structure seems the right choice.

When we compare information criteria for an equation estimated with the diagonal residual covariance structure to information criteria for the same equation estimated with the heterogeneous autoregressive residual covariance structure, we get the results in Table 11.21. The deviance difference is statistically significant, and each of the information criteria indicates that the more complex covariance structure provides the better fit. This is certainly consistent with the statistically significant rho value.

$$\text{Deviance difference} = 8216.0 - 8106.3 = 109.7$$
$$df = 21 - 20 = 1$$

Having made this decision, moreover, we will forgo the opportunity to consider an even more complex residual covariance structure. Yes, the unstructured option is available for modeling residuals, just as it is available for modeling random component variances and covariances. We have just seen, however, that the gain in goodness of fit that came with the heterogeneous autoregressive residual covariance structure, while real, was quite small. Furthermore, the unstructured residual covariance option requires *nine* additional parameter estimates. This is one of those instances in which, even though greater complexity is possible, we have done enough.

At this point, it is useful to recall all the specification decisions we are obliged to make with a conventional multilevel model: selection of predictors; assuring proper functional form; determining if the intraclass correlation is sufficiently large to warrant use of a multilevel model; deciding which coefficients should be fixed and which should be permitted to vary across higher-level groups; determining which contextual factors

TABLE 11.21. Vocabulary Achievement Growth: Information Criteria for Diagonal and AR(1): Heterogeneous Covariance Structures

Criterion	Diagonal	AR(1): Heterogeneous
–2 log likelihood	8216.0	*8106.3*
Akaike's Information Criterion	8248.0	*8148.3*
Hurvich and Tsai's Criterion	8248.4	*8149.0*
Bozdogan's Criterion	8347.6	*8279.0*
Schwarz's Bayesian Criterion	8331.6	*8258.0*

Note. The smaller value for each measure is boldfaced and italicized.

and cross-level interaction terms should be used to explain variability in the random components; deciding if random components should be independent or should be permitted to vary together; and deciding whether or not a third or higher level should be included.

Now, with multilevel regression repeated measures growth models, we have yet *another* specification decision: selecting the proper residual covariance structure. Each of these decisions can be statistically and substantively consequential, and each is best made with reference to richly informative substantive and theoretical knowledge. As we know all too well, however, such knowledge is often not available in the social and behavioral sciences.

11.11 MULTILEVEL REGRESSION GROWTH MODELS WITH THREE LEVELS

Multilevel regression growth models are always complex. Just as conventional multilevel models may, moreover, a growth model may have more than two levels. The example we have been working with has so far been restricted to the within-student level and the between-student level. As we know from previous work with this data set, however, the school is also available as a third level. Since there are only 12 schools, this West Virginia data set is not ideal for constructing a three-level growth model, but it can still be useful for illustrative purposes.

In the process of working toward specification of this three-level growth model, we may have lost sight of the basic question that prompted it all: Does the post-Head Start program work? Does it contribute to student achievement? Even more specifically, does it maintain Head Start gains? In the analyses we have seen so far, there are no Head Start gains to maintain. Nevertheless, we can introduce the post-Head Start categorical variable at level three in our three-level growth model and evaluate the results.

With the repeated measures at level one, student characteristics at level two, and school characteristics at level three, the post-Head Start variable (X_{PROGRAM3}) belongs at the school level. After all, *schools* were randomly assigned to participation–nonparticipation in the program. For this reason, we need a three-level model.

It would, of course, be useful if we had a more informative measure of X_{PROGRAM3} than that provided by a dummy variable. A measure of level of implementation would be helpful. Acknowledging that the post-Head Start program was poorly implemented in all 12 schools does not help, however, and a participant–nonparticipant school-level dummy variable is the best that we can do.

The basic three-level growth model is specified in Table 11.22, and the fixed component results for this model with a scaled identity structure are reported in Table 11.23. In the three-level equation reported in Table 11.23, the intercept is random at levels two and three, and the slope for YEARS1 is random at level two. An obvious and useful modification to this specification would assign a random slope to YEARS1 at both levels two

TABLE 11.22. Vocabulary Achievement Growth: Multilevel Regression Growth Model with Three Levels

<hr>

Level-one model

$$Y_{IJK} = \beta_{0JK} + \beta_{1JK}YEARS1 + e_{IJK}$$

Level-two model

$$\beta_{0JK} = \beta_{00K} + \gamma_{010}X_{HEAD2} + \gamma_{020}X_{INCOME2} + \gamma_{030}X_{EDUCATION2} + \gamma_{040}X_{HOOD2} + \gamma_{050}X_{ETHNIC2} + u_{0JK}$$

$$\beta_{1JK} = \gamma_{100} + \gamma_{110}X_{HEAD2} + \gamma_{120}X_{INCOME2} + \gamma_{130}X_{EDUCATION2} + \gamma_{140}X_{HOOD2} + \gamma_{150}X_{ETHNIC2} + u_{1JK}$$

Level-three model

$$\beta_{00K} = \gamma_{000} + \gamma_{001}X_{PROGRAM3} + u_{00K}$$

Full model

$$Y = \gamma_{000} + \gamma_{001}X_{PROGRAM3} + \gamma_{010}X_{HEAD2} + \gamma_{020}X_{INCOME2} + \gamma_{030}X_{EDUCATE2} + \gamma_{040}X_{HOOD2} + \gamma_{050}X_{ETHNIC2}$$
$$+ \gamma_{100}YEARS1 + \gamma_{110}X_{HEAD2} * YEARS1 + \gamma_{120}X_{INCOME2} * YEARS1 + \gamma_{130}X_{EDUCATE2} * YEARS1$$
$$+ \gamma_{140}X_{HOOD2} * YEARS1 + \gamma_{150}X_{ETHNIC2} * YEARS1 + (u_{00K} + u_{0JK} + u_{1JK} * YEARS1 + e_{IJK})$$

<hr>

TABLE 11.23. Vocabulary Achievement Growth: Multilevel Regression Growth Equation; Three-Level Model; Unstructured; Fixed Components

<hr>

$$Y_{GROWTH} = 8.792 + 0.682X_{HEAD2} + 0.265X_{INCOME2} + 0.570X_{EDUCATION2} + 0.107X_{HOOD2} + 0.124X_{ETHNIC2}$$
$$\quad\quad (0.652)\ (0.754)\quad\quad (0.156)\quad\quad\quad (0.213)\quad\quad\quad\quad (0.047)\quad\quad\quad\quad (0.821)$$

$$\quad + 7.123YEARS1 - 0.144X_{HEAD2} * YEARS1 + 0.023X_{INCOME2} * YEARS1$$
$$\quad\quad (0.128)\quad\quad\quad (0.298)\quad\quad\quad\quad\quad\quad (0.063)$$

$$\quad + 0.105X_{EDUCATION2} * YEARS1 + 0.016X_{HOOD2} * YEARS1 + 0.339X_{ETHNIC2} * YEARS1$$
$$\quad\quad (0.085)\quad\quad\quad\quad\quad\quad (0.019)\quad\quad\quad\quad\quad\quad (0.445)$$

$$\quad - 1.515X_{PROGRAM3} - 0.577X_{PROGRAM3} * X_{HEAD2}$$
$$\quad\quad (1.285)\quad\quad\quad\quad (0.989)$$

Pseudo-R^2 = 83.8%

<hr>

and three. Recall, however, that we have only 12 schools—only 12 observations at level three—so we will proceed cautiously.

In Table 11.23 we see that neither $X_{PROGRAM3}$ nor $X_{PROGRAM3} * X_{HEAD2}$ has a statistically significant slope. $X_{PROGRAM3} * X_{HEAD2}$ is a cross-level interaction term not implied by the model, but added at our discretion. It is intended to respond directly to this question: "Does the relationship between vocabulary achievement and Head Start participation vary from category to category of $X_{PROGRAM3}$?" In this specification of our three-level growth model, there is no evidence that the program works.

Random component variances and covariances are reported in Table 11.24. Since this is a three-level model, we have an estimate of the intercept variance at level three. In this example, it is statistically nonsignificant.

TABLE 11.24. Vocabulary Achievement Growth: Multilevel Regression Growth Equation; Three-Level Model; Unstructured; Estimates of Covariance Parameters

Parameter	Estimate	Std. error	Wald Z	Sig. level
Residual	18.860	0.779	24.207	.000
INTERCEPT1 variance at level two	3.552	1.318	2.695	.007
INTERCEPT1 by YEARS1 covariance at level two	2.878	0.614	4.685	.000
YEARS1 variance at level two	2.332	0.633	3.687	.000
INTERCEPT1 variance at level three	3.841	2.389	1.608	.108

In Table 11.25, we have reestimated the three-level growth equation specified in Table 11.22, this time using the heterogeneous autoregressive residual covariance structure rather than scaled identity. The fixed components in Table 11.25 are approximately the same as in Table 11.23. SPSS Routine 11.4 provides instructions for estimating a three-level growth model with the AR(1): Heterogeneous covariance structure.

The random component estimates in Table 11.26 indicate that there is substantial variability in the residual variance from one testing occasion to another, indicating violation of the assumption of homoscedasticity for the residuals at level one. The rho value, moreover, is statistically significant, meaning that the level-one residuals are autocorrelated. Based on our work with the two-level model specified in Table 11.12, we suspected that both heteroscedasticity and autorcorrelation would characterize the distribution of our level-one residuals, and in this instance we were right. As with Table 11.24, the intercept variance at level three is statistically nonsignificant, and the other covariance parameter estimates are largely unchanged.

In Table 11.27, we use the four information criteria routinely provided by SPSS to compare multilevel regression equations based on the three-level model specified in Table 11.22. The equations differ only with regard to residual covariance structure. Each information criterion indicates that the model with heterogeneous autoregressive resid-

TABLE 11.25. Vocabulary Achievement Growth: Multilevel Regression Growth Equation; Three-Level Model; AR(1): Heterogeneous; Fixed Components

$$Y_{\text{GROWTH}} = 10.312 - 0.575X_{\text{HEAD2}} + 0.215X_{\text{INCOME2}} + 0.486X_{\text{EDUCATION2}} + 0.090X_{\text{HOOD2}}$$
$$\quad (0.553) \quad (0.676) \quad\quad (0.141) \quad\quad\quad (0.192) \quad\quad\quad\quad (0.043)$$

$$\quad - 0.098X_{\text{ETHNIC2}} + 6.668\text{YEARS1} - 0.077X_{\text{HEAD2}} * \text{YEARS1} + 0.009X_{\text{INCOME2}} * \text{YEARS1}$$
$$\quad (0.844) \quad\quad\quad (0.094) \quad\quad\quad (0.219) \quad\quad\quad\quad\quad (0.046)$$

$$\quad + 0.076X_{\text{EDUCATION2}} * \text{YEARS1} + 0.014X_{\text{HOOD2}} * \text{YEARS1} + 0.391X_{\text{ETHNIC2}} * \text{YEARS1}$$
$$\quad (0.062) \quad\quad\quad\quad (0.014) \quad\quad\quad\quad (0.330)$$

$$\quad - 1.610X_{\text{PROGRAM3}} - 0.009X_{\text{PROGRAM3}} * X_{\text{HEAD2}}$$
$$\quad (1.093) \quad\quad\quad (0.939)$$

Peudo-R^2 = 83.7%

SPSS Routine 11.4. Three-Level Growth Model for Vocabulary Achievement with AR(1) Heterogeneous Covariance Structure

1. Open the SPSS data file and click on ANALYZE.
2. Go to MIXED MODELS and click on LINEAR.
3. Since the individual student is the level-two grouping variable, insert the student identifier into the SUBJECTS box. Since the school is the level-three grouping variable, insert the school identifier into the SUBJECTS box.
4. Insert the INDEX NUMBER (INDEX1) into the REPEATED box. The INDEX NUMBER was created when we restructured the data set. By inserting INDEX1 into the REPEATED box, we indicate that we are using repeated measures.
5. Beneath the REPEATED box, you will see the REPEATED COVARIANCE TYPE box. Replace the default option, DIAGONAL, with AR(1): HETEROGENEOUS. This models the residual variance to vary from one measurement occasion to another, and to be autocorrelated.
6. Click on CONTINUE; insert vocabulary achievement as the dependent variable into the DEPENDENT VARIABLE box; and insert the independent variables X_{HEAD2}, $X_{INCOME2}$, $X_{EDUCATION2}$, X_{HOOD2}, $X_{ETHNIC2}$, $X_{PROGRAM3}$, and YEARS1, and the cross-level interaction terms $X_{EDUCATION2}$ * YEARS1, X_{HOOD2} * YEARS1, $X_{ETHNIC2}$ * YEARS1, and $X_{PROGRAM3}$ * X_{HEAD2} into the COVARIATES box.
7. Click on FIXED at the bottom of the screen. In the small box in the middle of the screen, change FACTORIAL to MAIN EFFECTS. Move all the independent variables and cross-level interaction terms from the FACTORS AND COVARIATES box to the MODEL box.
8. Click on CONTINUE.
9. Click on the RANDOM button at the bottom of the screen. The student identifier is already in the SUBJECTS box, and now we also insert it in the COMBINATIONS box.
10. In the small box in the middle of the screen, change FACTORIAL to MAIN EFFECTS.
11. Near the top of the screen, click on INCLUDE INTERCEPT and move the independent variable YEARS1, our measure of time, into the MODEL box.
12. Just above INCLUDE INTERCEPT, select UNSTRUCTURED.
13. In the upper right corner of the screen, click on NEXT.
14. Near the top of the screen, click on INCLUDE INTERCEPT.
15. Just above INCLUDE INTERCEPT, select UNSTRUCTURED.
16. Click on CONTINUE, and then click on the STATISTICS button.
17. On the left, under MODEL STATISTICS, select PARAMETER ESTIMATES and TESTS FOR COVARIANCE PARAMETERS.
18. Click on CONTINUE and click on OK.

TABLE 11.26. Vocabulary Achievement Growth: Multilevel Regression Growth Equation; Three-Level Model; AR(1): Heterogeneous; Estimates of Covariance Parameters

Parameter	Estimate	Std. error	Wald Z	Sig. level
INDEX1 = 1	3.787	2.236	1.693	.090
INDEX1 = 2	25.243	2.259	11.174	.000
INDEX1 = 3	54.353	4.886	11.125	.000
INDEX1 = 4	18.993	1.843	10.306	.000
INDEX1 = 5	0.652	1.216	0.537	.591
Rho	0.175	0.487	3.586	.000
INTERCEPT1 variance at level two	9.886	2.529	3.910	.000
INTERCEPT1 by YEARS1 covariance at level two	0.873	0.628	1.391	.164
YEARS1 variance at level two	1.974	0.257	7.681	.000
INTERCEPT1 variance at level three	2.786	1.581	1.762	.078

TABLE 11.27. Vocabulary Achievement Growth: Information Criteria for Scaled Identity, Diagonal, and AR(1): Heterogeneous Residual Covariance Structures

Criterion	Scaled identity	Diagonal	AR(1): Heterogeneous
−2 log likelihood	8652.7	8373.7	*8323.7*
Akaike's Information Criterion	8690.7	8421.7	*8369.7*
Hurvich and Tsai's Criterion	8691.2	8422.6	*8370.5*
Bozdogan's Criterion	8809.0	8571.2	*8512.9*
Schwarz's Bayesian Criterion	8790.0	8547.2	*8489.9*

Note. The smaller value for each measure is boldfaced and italicized.

ual covariance structure provides the best fit. This means that we should model the residuals to have nonuniform variance and to be autocorrelated. This is consistent with the statistically significant rho value in Table 11.26. The fixed coefficients in Tables 11.25 and 11.28, however, are quite similar, and the same applies to random components when we compare Tables 11.26 and 11.29. As a practical matter, then, it is of little or no consequence if we use a diagonal or heterogeneous autoregressive residual covariance structure.

We have already presented the regression results obtained with the scaled identity residual covariance structure in Tables 11.23 and 11.24, and the same information obtained with the heterogeneous autoregressive residual covariance structure is reported in Tables 11.25 and 11.26. The regression results obtained with a diagonal covariance structure are presented in Tables 11.28 and 11.29.

We have worked with various specifications of the three-level growth model needed to evaluate the post-Head Start program. The program's objective was to maintain Head Start gains throughout the first 4 years of elementary school, but in the West Virginia analysis, there were no Head Start gains to maintain. The most we can say, then, is that the post-Head Start program itself did not improve vocabulary achievement or promote vocabulary achievement growth.

TABLE 11.28. Vocabulary Achievement Growth: Multilevel Regression Growth Equation; Three-Level Model; Diagonal; Fixed Components

$$Y_{\text{GROWTH}} = 10.151 - 0.571X_{\text{HEAD2}} + 0.217X_{\text{INCOME2}} + 0.485X_{\text{EDUCATION2}} + 0.090X_{\text{HOOD2}}$$
$$\quad (0.558)\ (0.674) \qquad (0.140) \qquad\quad (0.191) \qquad\qquad (0.043)$$

$$- 0.097X_{\text{ETHNIC2}} + 6.713\text{YEARS1} - 0.073X_{\text{HEAD2}} * \text{YEARS1} + 0.006X_{\text{INCOME2}} * \text{YEARS1}$$
$$\quad (0.838) \qquad\quad (0.094) \qquad\quad (0.221) \qquad\qquad\quad (0.047)$$

$$+ 0.076X_{\text{EDUCATION2}} * \text{YEARS1} + 0.015X_{\text{HOOD2}} * \text{YEARS1} + 0.384X_{\text{ETHNIC2}} * \text{YEARS1}$$
$$\quad (0.063) \qquad\qquad\qquad (0.014) \qquad\qquad\quad (0.332)$$

$$- 1.584X_{\text{PROGRAM3}} - 0.038X_{\text{PROGRAM3}} * X_{\text{HEAD2}}$$
$$\quad (0.102) \qquad\qquad (0.934)$$

Pseudo-R^2 = 83.7%

TABLE 11.29. Vocabulary Achievement Growth: Multilevel Regression Growth Equation; Three-Level Model; Diagonal; Estimates of Covariance Parameters

Parameter	Estimate	Std. error	Wald Z	Sig. level
INDEX1 = 1	2.578	1.226	2.104	.035
INDEX1 = 2	23.484	2.002	11.732	.000
INDEX1 = 3	53.210	4.668	11.400	.000
INDEX1 = 4	18.243	1.637	11.143	.000
INDEX1 = 5	0.901	1.681	0.536	.592
INTERCEPT1 variance at level two	10.885	1.324	8.223	.000
INTERCEPT1-by-YEARS1 covariance at level two	0.550	0.413	1.332	.183
YEARS1 variance at level two	2.124	0.228	9.323	.000
INTERCEPT1 variance at level three	2.852	1.711	1.667	.096

11.12 NONLINEAR GROWTH CURVES

At the beginning of our discussion of vocabulary achievement growth, we entertained the possibility that this growth was not linear. In response to data from case number 280 in Figure 11.1, we briefly considered a cubic relationship—one that changed direction twice in roughly S-shaped fashion—as providing the best descriptive account of vocabulary growth over five testing occasions. After examining growth curves for more randomly selected students, however, we decided that the complexity of a cubic functional form was not warranted. All told, a linear growth curve seemed a better choice, and certainly one providing statistical results that were easier to interpret.

When we use the same West Virginia data set and examine *math* achievement growth for its 331 students over the same time span, from the beginning of kindergarten until the end of third grade, the existence of a roughly consistent and identifiable departure from linearity seems just a bit easier to discern. Using the same five randomly selected illustrative cases as in our vocabulary achievement example, Figures 11.17 through 11.21 below suggest that the relationship, on average, may be nonlinear.

Yielding to the temptation to fish or dredge data, we will then examine two additional cases, appearing in Figures 11.22 and 11.23. Figure 11.22 suggests a nonlinear relationship, very roughly approximating a sine wave. Figure 11.23, however, looks like the usual unpatterned scatter around a linear regression line.

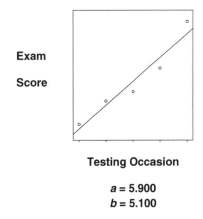

Exam

Score

Testing Occasion

a = 5.900
b = 5.100

FIGURE 11.17. Case number 280: Growth in Woodcock–Johnson 25 math test scores.

In Figure 11.17, the growth curve for case number 280 increases, decelerates, and then accelerates. This description may represent an overinterpretation of the five data points in this figure, but it's a start.

Figures 11.18 and 11.19 are not consistent with our interpretation of Figure 11.17. Again, although we are perhaps overinterpreting random fluctuations, each curve seems to open upward in parabolic fashion and then either decelerate or actually slope downward. Since Figure 11.19 includes measures of math achievement at only four times, with a score for the fourth testing occasion missing, it is especially difficult to describe this curve in functionally specific terms.

Figure 11.20, however, is similar to Figure 11.17: increasing, decelerating or leveling off, and than accelerating. Figures 11.21 and 11.22 begin with a shallow slope, then accelerate, and then decelerate, both very roughly approximating a sine wave.

Figure 11.23, however, exhibits the sort of distribution of points we expect to find with a linear functional form accompanied by a random scatter of observations about the growth curve. Perhaps each of our efforts to discern identifiable nonlinear growth curves

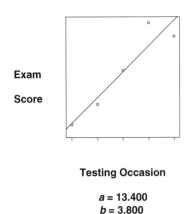

Exam

Score

Testing Occasion

a = 13.400
b = 3.800

FIGURE 11.18. Case number 87: Growth in Woodcock–Johnson 25 math test.

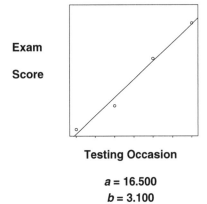

Exam

Score

Testing Occasion

a = 16.500
b = 3.100

FIGURE 11.19. Case number 166: Growth in Woodcock–Johnson 25 math test scores.

in Figures 11.17 through 11.21 has been nothing more than overinterpretation of random error.

Finally, in Figure 11.24 we examine math achievement growth for all students. In the aggregate, it appears that an S-shaped cubic functional form *may* prove useful. If this is the case, however, the troughs and peaks that characterize a cubic function appear only in *very* shallow form. What do we do?

Lacking a theoretical rationale for any particular functional form, and faced with thoroughgoing empirical uncertainty, it seems best to opt for the straightforward interpretability and simplicity of a linear function. This is consistent with Singer and Willett's (2003) informative discussion of linear and nonlinear growth curves. They add that it is seldom necessary to work with a functional form more complex than quadratic.

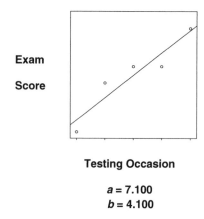

Testing Occasion

a = 7.100
b = 4.100

FIGURE 11.20. Case number 45: Growth in Woodcock–Johnson 25 math test scores.

For instructional purposes, we will begin by specifying a linear functional form for math achievement growth. We will then use the information criteria to test this against quadratic and cubic functional forms to determine which seems best suited to math achievement growth. While engaged in this exercise, we will bear in mind that we hope to avoid the interpretative complexity that comes with a cubic growth curve. Whatever functional form we settle on, we will remember that individual growth curves typically exhibit a great deal of variability. We have seen this with respect to intercepts and slopes in our examples using reading achievement growth. The same applies to the *shape* of

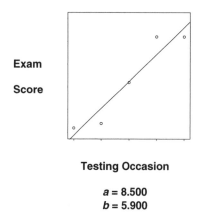

Testing Occasion

a = 8.500
b = 5.900

FIGURE 11.21. Case number 172: Growth in Woodcock–Johnson 25 math test scores.

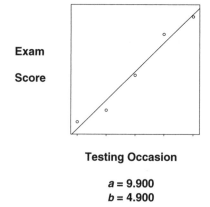

Testing Occasion

a = 9.900
b = 4.900

FIGURE 11.22. Case number 201: Growth in Woodcock–Johnson 25 math test scores.

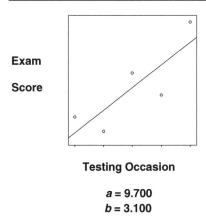

$a = 9.700$
$b = 3.100$

FIGURE 11.23. Case number 161: Growth in Woodcock–Johnson 25 math test scores.

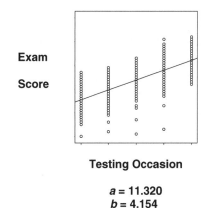

$a = 11.320$
$b = 4.154$

FIGURE 11.24. All cases: Growth in Woodcock–Johnson 25 math test scores.

each individual curve. Whatever functional form we choose for our analysis of math achievement growth, it will represent an overall *average*.

Tables 11.30 through 11.40 below report the results of analyses aimed at deciding on a suitable functional form—linear, quadratic, or cubic—for the math achievement growth curve. After we have made a decision on functional form, we will use individual student growth curves as the dependent variable, and introduce level-two predictors, beginning in Table 11.41.

In Table 11.30 we have specified a two-level model for math achievement growth in which a linear growth curve is specified. At level one, our measure of time, years of schooling completed (YEARS1), is incorporated into a linear function. Both the intercept and the slope are treated as random coefficients, varying among individuals at level two. Since there are no level-two contextual factors to account for this variability, we have specified a random coefficient growth model with a linear functional form. This model

TABLE 11.30. Math Achievement Growth: Multilevel Regression Growth Model; Linear Functional Form

Level-one model

$$Y = \beta_{0J} + \beta_{1J}\text{YEARS1} + e_{IJ}$$

Level-two model

$$\beta_{0J} = \gamma_{00} + u_{0J}$$

$$\beta_{1J} = \gamma_{10} + u_{1J}$$

Full model

$$Y = \gamma_{00} + \gamma_{10}\text{YEARS1} + (u_{0J} + u_{1J}\text{YEAR} + e_{IJ})$$

has exactly the same form as two-level growth models that we have specified previously. Results for fixed components and random components are reported in Tables 11.31 and 11.32.

This model specified in Table 11.33 is a straightforward extension of the model in Table 11.30. We have added the quadratic term YEARS1^2 to the level-one model; the random slope β_{2J} is included in the level-two model; and the full model, complete with its more complex error term, has been modified accordingly. A quadratic growth curve can be estimated only if there are at least three measurement occasions: one for the change in direction of the curve, and two for each section of the curve that precedes or follows the change in direction.

TABLE 11.31. Math Achievement Growth: Multilevel Regression Growth Equation; Linear Functional Form; Fixed Components

$$Y_{\text{GROWTH}} = 15.454 + 4.189\text{YEARS1}$$
$$(0.230)\quad (0.105)$$

$$\text{Pseudo-}R^2 = 68.7\%$$

TABLE 11.32. Math Achievement Growth: Multilevel Regression Growth Equation; Linear Functional Form; Estimates of Covariance Parameters

Parameter	Estimate	Std. error	Wald Z	Sig. level
Residual	16.234	0.837	19.396	.000
INTERCEPT1 variance at level one	7.347	1.444	5.089	.000
INTERCEPT1-BY-LINEAR TERM covariance at level two	−0.073	0.507	−0.143	.886
LINEAR TERM variance at level two	1.469	0.334	4.400	.000

TABLE 11.33. Math Achievement Growth; Multilevel Regression Growth Model; Quadratic Functional Form

Level-one model

$$Y = \beta_{0J} + \beta_{1J}\text{YEARS1} + \beta_{2J}\text{YEARS1}^2 + e_{IJ}$$

Level-two model

$$\beta_{0J} = \gamma_{00} + u_{0J}$$
$$\beta_{1J} = \gamma_{10} + u_{1J}$$
$$\beta_{2J} = \gamma_{20} + u_{2J}$$

Full model

$$Y = \gamma_{00} + \gamma_{10}\text{YEARS1} + \gamma_{20}\text{YEARS1}^2 + (u_{0J} + u_{1J}\text{YEAR} + u_{2J}\text{YEARS1}^2 + e_{IJ})$$

Results for fixed components and random components are reported in Tables 11.34 and 11.35.

Table 11.36 is a straightforward modification of the linear and quadratic specification in Tables 11.30 and 11.33. The cubic term YEARS1^3 has been added as an additional predictor at level one; the random term β_{3j} is included in the level-two model; and the full model, complete with its more complex error term, has been modified accordingly. A cubic growth curve, whatever its value in this instance, can be estimated only if there are at least five testing occasions: two testing occasions for each change of direction in the cubic growth curve, and three for each section of the curve that precedes or follows each change of direction.

Results for fixed components and random components are reported in Tables 11.37 and 11.38. The most conspicuous feature of the estimates of covariance parameters reported in Table 11.38 is the frequency with which random component variances and covariances are too small to measure. The warning at the top of the SPSS printout reads as follows: "Iteration was terminated but convergence has not been achieved. . . . " The REML algorithm, in other words, cannot settle on a specific value for the unmeasured parameter estimate.

It is easy to prompt SPSS to work through additional iterations, and this sometimes results in more useful output. In this instance, however, with additional iterations the warning changes to the following: "The final Hessian matrix is not positive definite

TABLE 11.34. Math Achievement Growth; Multilevel Regression Growth Equation; Quadratic Functional Form; Fixed Components

$$Y_{\text{GROWTH}} = 14.609 + 4.115\text{YEARS1} + 0.503\text{YEARS1}^2$$
$$\quad\;\; (0.214)\;\; (0.064) \qquad\qquad (0.045)$$

Pseudo-R^2 = 70.0%

TABLE 11.35. Math Achievement Growth: Multilevel Regression Growth Equation; Quadratic Functional Form; Estimates of Covariance Parameters

Parameter	Estimate	Std. error	Wald Z	Sig. level
Residual	12.828	0.809	15.859	.000
INTERCEPT1 variance at level one	15.987	2.258	7.082	.000
INTERCEPT1-by-LINEAR TERM covariance at level two	−1.316	0.555	−2.370	.018
LINEAR TERM variance at level two	1.211	0.295	4.103	.000
QUADRATIC TERM variance at level two	−2.532	0.494	−5.128	.000
QUADRATIC TERM-by-INTERCEPT1 covariance at level two	0.586	0.133	−4.403	.000
QUADRATIC TERM-by-LINEAR TERM covariance at level two	0.677	0.162	4.178	.000

TABLE 11.36. Math Achievement Growth: Multilevel Regression Growth Model; Cubic Functional Form

<u>Level-one model</u>

$$Y = \beta_{0J} + \beta_{1J}\text{YEARS1} + \beta_{2J}\text{YEARS1}^2 + \beta_{3J}\ \text{YEARS1}^3 + e_{IJ}$$

<u>Level-two model</u>

$$\beta_{0J} = \gamma_{00} + u_{0J}$$
$$\beta_{1J} = \gamma_{10} + u_{1J}$$
$$\beta_{2J} = \gamma_{20} + u_{2J}$$
$$\beta_{3J} = \gamma_{30} + u_{3J}$$

<u>Full model</u>

$$Y = \gamma_{00} + \gamma_{10}\text{YEARS1} + \gamma_{20}\text{YEARS1}^2 + \gamma_{30}\text{YEARS}^3 + (u_{0J} + u_{1J}\text{YEARS1} + u_{2J}\text{YEARS1}^2 + u_{2J}\text{YEARS1}^3 + e_{IJ})$$

TABLE 11.37. Math Achievement Growth: Multilevel Regression Growth Equation; Cubic Functional Form; Fixed Components

$$Y_{\text{GROWTH}} = 12.465 + 5.244\text{YEARS1} + 0.575\text{YEARS1}^2 - 0.349\text{YEARS1}^3$$
$$\phantom{Y_{\text{GROWTH}} = }(0.308)\ \ (0.192)(0.085)(0.077)$$

Pseudo-R^2 = 70.6%

TABLE 11.38. Math Achievement Growth: Multilevel Regression Growth Equation; Cubic Functional Form; Estimates of Covariance Parameters

Parameter	Estimate	Std. error	Wald Z	Sig. level
Residual	7.057	0.315	22.392	.000
INTERCEPT1 variance at level one	1.197	0.000	—	—
INTERCEPT1-by-LINEAR TERM covariance at level two	−0.267	0.721	−0.370	.711
LINEAR TERM variance at level two	4.027	0.873	4.614	.000
QUADRATIC TERM variance at level two	1.033	0.659	1.569	.117
QUADRATIC TERM-by-INTERCEPT1 covariance at level two	−0.884	0.698	−1.265	.206
QUADRATIC TERM-by-LINEAR TERM covariance at level two	1.412	0.000	—	—
CUBIC TERM variance at level two	−0.432	0.419	−1.031	.302
CUBIC TERM-by-INTERCEPT1 covariance at level two	−0.342	0.000	—	—
CUBIC TERM-by-LINEAR TERM covariance at level two	0.329	0.000	—	—
CUBIC TERM-by-QUADRATIC TERM covariance at level two	1.253	0.000	—	—

Note. A dash (—) indicates a value too small to measure.

although all convergence criteria are satisfied. The MIXED procedure continues despite this warning. Validity of subsequent results cannot be ascertained."

In other words, given the data at hand, a cubic functional form is unduly complex, resulting in a misspecified growth model. This is consistent with the information criteria in Table 11.39. When linear, quadratic, and cubic functional forms are compared, the best fit is provided by the quadratic curve, and the worst fit to the data comes with the cubic specification.

We can remedy lack of convergence if we assign fixed rather than random coefficients to one or more of the terms in the cubic function. In the absence of a compelling theoretical or substantive rationale, there is no reason not to do so. The consequences of changing some of the random terms to fixed are reported in Table 11.40. Note, however, that when we compare information criteria for alternative specifications of the cubic growth curve with the information criteria in Table 11.39, the quadratic functional form still provides the best fit.

Now that we have settled on a quadratic functional form, we begin trying to account for student-to-student differences with respect to math achievement growth. In Table 11.41 we use some of the same individual-level predictors we have used with vocabulary achievement growth models.

Results for fixed and random components are reported in Tables 11.42 and 11.43. With a quadratic functional form for our measure of time, interpretation of the fixed components is a bit more complex than with the other growth models we have studied.

TABLE 11.39. Math Achievement Growth: Information Criteria for Linear, Quadratic, and Cubic Functional Forms

Criterion	Linear	Quadratic	Cubic
−2 log likelihood	8888.5	7917.9	9116.1
Akaike's Information Criterion	8900.5	7931.9	9146.1
Hurvich and Tsai's Criterion	8900.6	7932.0	9146.4
Bozdogan's Criterion	8938.3	7976.0	9240.5
Schwarz's Bayesian Criterion	8932.3	7969.0	9225.5

Note. The smaller value for each measure is boldfaced and italicized.

TABLE 11.40. Math Achievement Growth: Information Criteria for Cubic Functional Form; Fixed and Random Coefficient Combinations

Criterion	All fixed	Linear	Linear and quadratic
−2 log likelihood	8879.8	8796.2	8738.9
Akaike's Information Criterion	8891.8	8812.2	8752.9
Hurvich and Tsai's Criterion	8891.9	8813.3	8753.0
Bozdogan's Criterion	8929.6	8862.5	8797.0
Schwarz's Bayesian Criterion	8923.6	8854.5	8789.0

Note. The smaller value for each measure is boldfaced and italicized.

TABLE 11.41. Math Achievement Growth: Multilevel Regression Growth Model; Quadratic Functional Form; Level-Two Predictors Added

Level-one model

$$Y = \beta_{0J} + \beta_{1J}YEARS1 + \beta_{2J}YEARS1^2 + e_{IJ}$$

Level-two model

$$\beta_{0J} = \gamma_{00} + \gamma_{01}X_{INCOME2} + \gamma_{02}X_{EDUCATION2} + \gamma_{03}X_{HOOD2} + u_{0J}$$

$$\beta_{1J} = \gamma_{10} + \gamma_{11}X_{INCOME2} + \gamma_{12}X_{EDUCATION2} + \gamma_{13}X_{HOOD2} + u_{1J}$$

$$\beta_{2J} = \gamma_{20} + \gamma_{21}X_{INCOME2} + \gamma_{22}X_{EDUCATION2} + \gamma_{23}X_{HOOD2} + u_{2J}$$

Full model

$$Y = \gamma_{00} + \gamma_{01}X_{INCOME2} + \gamma_{02}X_{EDUCATION2} + \gamma_{03}X_{HOOD2} + \gamma_{10}YEARS1 + \gamma_{11}X_{INCOME2} * YEARS1$$

$$+ \gamma_{12}X_{EDUCATION2} * YEARS1 + \gamma_{13}X_{HOOD2} * YEARS1 + \gamma_{20}YEARS1^2 + \gamma_{21}X_{INCOME2} * YEARS1^2$$

$$+ \gamma_{22}X_{EDUCATION2} * YEARS1^2 + \gamma_{23}X_{HOOD2} * YEARS1^2 + (u_{0J} + u_{1J}YEARS1 + u_{2J}YEARS1^2 + e_{IJ})$$

TABLE 11.42. Math Achievement Growth: Multilevel Regression Growth Equation; Quadratic Functional Form; Level-Two Predictors Added; Fixed Components

$$Y_{GROWTH} = 22.805 + 0.226X_{INCOME2} + 0.249X_{EDUCATION2} + 0.058X_{HOOD2} + 4.238YEARS1$$
$$\quad\quad (0.269) \quad (0.122) \quad\quad\quad (0.178) \quad\quad\quad\quad (0.040) \quad\quad\quad (0.103)$$

$$+ 0.110X_{INCOME2} * YEARS1 + 0.146X_{EDUCATION2} * YEARS1 - 0.024X_{HOOD2} * YEARS1$$
$$\quad (0.047) \quad\quad\quad\quad\quad (0.068) \quad\quad\quad\quad\quad\quad (0.015)$$

$$+ 0.506YEARS1^2 + 0.029X_{INCOME2} * YEARS1^2 + 0.040X_{EDUCATION2} * YEARS1^2$$
$$\quad (0.078) \quad\quad\quad (0.035) \quad\quad\quad\quad\quad (0.051)$$

$$- 0.038X_{HOOD2} * YEARS1^2$$
$$\quad (0.332)$$

Pseudo-R^2 = 71.4%

TABLE 11.43. Math Achievement Growth: Multilevel Regression Growth Equation; Quadratic Functional Form; Level-Two Predictors Added; Estimates of Covariance Parameters

Parameter	Estimate	Std. error	Wald Z	Sig. level
Residual	13.188	0.849	15.536	.000
INTERCEPT1 variance at level one	15.156	1.967	7.714	.000
INTERCEPT1-by-LINEAR TERM covariance at level two	0.357	0.615	0.581	.561
LINEAR TERM variance at level two	1.470	0.299	4.908	.000
QUADRATIC TERM variance at level two	0.734	0.175	4.191	.000
QUADRATIC TERM-by-INTERCEPT1 covariance at level two	−1.582	0.475	−3.332	.001
QUADRATIC TERM-by-LINEAR TERM covariance at level two	0.794	0.159	5.061	.000

Recall, however, our work with quadratic relationships in OLS regression from Chapter 6: The coefficient for YEARS1 represents the best-fitting linear relationship, and the coefficient for YEARS1^2 measures departures from linearity over time.

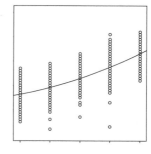

Testing Occasions

1. For each year of schooling completed, individual student math achievement growth increases, on average, by 4.238 points.
2. For each year of schooling completed, the rate of change for math achievement growth increases, on average, by 0.506 points. This is a measure of the upward curve of the relationship graphed in Figure 11.25. The best-fitting linear relationship is adjusted to conform better to the data.

FIGURE 11.25. Growth in Woodcock–Johnson 25 math test scores: Quadratic functional form.

3. For each one-level increase in family income, math achievement increases, on average, by 0.226 points. This finding holds only with use of a one-tailed t test.
4. For each one-level increase in parent's level of educational attainment, the effect of YEARS1 on math achievement growth increases, on average, by 0.146 points. This is due to the $X_{EDUCATION2}$ * YEARS1 interaction term.
5. For each one-level increase in family income, math achievement growth increases, on average, by 0.110 points. This is due to the $X_{INCOME2}$ * YEARS1 interaction term.

11.13 NCLEX PASS RATES WITH A TIME-DEPENDENT PREDICTOR

In Figures 11.9 through 11.12, we found an enormous amount of variability in growth in pass rates for the 21 nursing education programs operating in West Virginia during all or part of the period from 1985 to 1994. Referring specifically to Figure 11.12, which includes an overall growth curve for all programs for all years, we see that use of the term *growth* might easily be misconstrued because, on average, there was a very modest *decline* in pass rates over time. Having made that cautionary observation, we can specify a multilevel regression growth model for pass rates, as in Figure 11.25.

YEAR1 is a level-one predictor defined by subtracting 85, the value for the first year, from all entries for time. This produces a range of values from 0 to 9, indicating the number of years for which a program has been reporting NCLEX information to the state. We will use this as a crude proxy for level of organizational maturity or development.

The institutions that certify registered nurses may be categorized in a variety of ways. In this instance, we will create a set of dummy variables corresponding to the kind of certification offered: certification with a diploma but no degree ($X_{DIPLOMA2}$), certification with an associate's degree (X_{ASSOC2}), or certification with a bachelor's degree. Dummy variables for the first two categories were created by using the usual 1-if-yes, 0-if-no coding scheme. The third category is suppressed and provides a basis for comparison.

In addition, percentage of faculty members with a doctorate ($X_{PCTDOC1}$) is used as another level-one independent variable. This variable too has been centered with respect to its mean.

Throughout our discussion of multilevel growth models, all the independent variables except time have been measured at one occasion only: at the beginning of data collection. From year to year, all level-two and level-three explanatory variables have had fixed values. As such, they are referred to as *time-independent* predictors. In our nursing education example, the level-two variables $X_{DIPLOMA2}$ and X_{ASSOC2} are time-independent. The status of each program in terms of these two variables has been constant from one year to the next over the time span for which we have data.

The level-one predictor $X_{PCTDOC2}$, however, *varies* from one measurement occasion to another. As faculty members come and go, faculty composition changes in a variety of ways, and one of these is the percentage of instructors who have a doctorate. As such, $X_{PCTDOC2}$ is a *time-dependent* predictor, and it becomes a component of our level-one model.

The role of a time-dependent predictor in analyzing growth curves is the same as that for a time-independent predictor. We are still trying to account for differences in the way entities (in this case, nursing education programs) change over time. The comparability of time-independent and time-dependent predictors makes sense if we recall how the data set has been restructured (Hox, 2002). Each value of the dependent variable corresponds to a value on each independent variable. With time-independent predictors, the values of the independent variable do not change over time. With time-dependent predictors, they may differ from one measurement occasion to another.

The multilevel regression growth model that we will use in accounting for differences in institutional change over a 10-year period in terms of NCLEX pass rates is specified in Table 11.44. Results of applying the model to the West Virginia data set are reported in Tables 11.45 and 11.46.

The only independent variables with statistically significant coefficients are the time-dependent predictor, $X_{PCTDOC2}$, and the cross-level interaction term, $X_{DIPLOMA2}$ * YEAR1. As we see, for every 1% increase in $X_{PCTDOC2}$, growth in NCLEX pass rate is diminished by 0.267%. In addition, with each 1-unit increment in YEAR1, pass rates for diploma programs increase by 2.264% relative to those for bachelor's degree programs.

How do we explain the unexpected negative relationship between change in pass rate and percentage of instructors with a doctorate? This finding has been robust in unpublished analyses of the same data done in different ways (Stevens, 1996). It may be due to the fact that instructors with doctorates are more likely than others to be interested in nursing research, which is not covered in the NCLEX, than in nursing practice. In addition, nurses with doctorates may be more likely to work in settings where research is valued and clinical practice is given less attention.

TABLE 11.44. NCLEX Pass Rate: Multilevel Regression Growth Model; Diagonal Residual Covariance Structure

<u>Level-one model</u>

$$Y = \beta_{0J} + \beta_{1J}YEAR1 + {}_{20}X_{PCTDOC1} + e_{IJ}$$

<u>Level-two model</u>

$$\beta_{0J} = \gamma_{00} + \gamma_{01}X_{DIPLOMA2} + \gamma_{02}X_{ASSOC2} + u_{0J}$$

$$\beta_{1J} = \gamma_{10} + \gamma_{11}X_{DIPLOMA2} + \gamma_{12}X_{ASSOC2} + u_{1J}$$

<u>Full model</u>

$$Y = \gamma_{00} + \gamma_{01}X_{DIPLOMA2} + \gamma_{1J}YEAR + \gamma_{02}X_{ASSOC2} + \gamma_{11}X_{DIPLOMA2} * YEAR1$$

$$+ \gamma_{12}X_{ASSOC2} * YEAR1 + \gamma_{20}X_{PCTDOC1} + (u_{1J} * YEAR1 + u_{0J} + e_{IJ})$$

TABLE 11.45. NCLEX Pass Rate: Multilevel Regression Growth Equation; Diagonal Residual Covariance Structure; Fixed Components

$$Y_{CHANGE} = 85.338 + 6.688X_{DIPLOMA2} - 0.350YEAR1 + 0.081X_{ASSOC2} - 0.267X_{PCTDOC2}$$
$$(1.645) \quad (7.669) \qquad (0.248) \qquad (3.727) \qquad (0.119)$$

$$+ 2.264X_{DIPLOMA2} * YEAR1 + 0.1932X_{ASSOC2} * YEAR1 + 0.034X_{PCTDOC2} * TIME1$$
$$(1.243) \qquad\qquad (0.616) \qquad\qquad (0.035)$$

Pseudo-R^2 = 4.7%

TABLE 11.46. NCLEX Pass Rate: Multilevel Regression Growth Equation; Diagonal Residual Covariance Structure; Estimates of Covariance Parameters

Parameter	Estimate	Std. error	Wald Z	Sig. level
INDEX1 = 1	98.932	45.247	2.187	.029
INDEX1 = 2	18.241	12.640	1.443	.149
INDEX1 = 3	37.317	18.384	2.030	.042
INDEX1 = 4	125.179	51.933	2.410	.016
INDEX1 = 5	96.846	43.946	2.204	.028
INDEX1 = 6	45.959	22.069	2.082	.037
INDEX1 = 7	18.607	10.928	1.703	.089
INDEX1 = 8	111.020	45.149	2.459	.014
INDEX1 = 9	118.313	44.687	2.648	.008
INDEX1 = 10	24.011	15.130	1.587	.113
INTERCEPT1	42.060	18.796	2.238	.439
INTERCEPT1 by YEAR1	1.744	2.254	0.774	.000
YEAR1	0.300	0.403	0.745	.456

TABLE 11.47. NCLEX Pass Rate: Multilevel Regression Growth Equation; Information Criteria for Comparing Residual Covariance Structures

Criterion	Scaled identity	Diagonal	AR:1 Heterogeneous	Unstructured
−2 log likelihood	1032.7	*993.5*	1022.1	1094.9
Akaike's Information Criterion	1040.7	*1019.5*	1068.1	1211.0
Hurvich and Tsai's Criterion	1041.0	*1022.6*	1077.6	1295.5
Bozdogan's Criterion	*1056.4*	1070.1	1158.8	1439.6
Schwarz's Bayesian Criterion	*1052.4*	1057.1	1135.8	1381.6

Note. The smaller value for each measure is boldfaced and italicized.

Table 11.46 shows us the repeated measures variances from year to year, as well as random component variances and the covariance for INTERCEPT1 and YEAR1. This information is provided because we selected the diagonal residual covariance structure option, and the unstructured option for random components. Again, we have permitted residuals for the repeated measures to have nonuniform variances, but we have constrained the residuals to be uncorrelated.

If we want to make sure that we have made the correct choice, we may use the information criteria in Table 11.47, where we see results obtained with a variety of residual covariance structures, from the simplest to the most complex. (To save space, fixed and random components for analyses using scaled identity, heterogeneous autoregressive, and unstructured residual covariance structures are not reported.) Clearly, the relatively simple diagonal residual covariance structure provides a better fit than more complex structures.

11.14 SUMMING UP

In this chapter we have tried to make the case that the admonition "It's just regression!" applies not only to conventional multilevel models, but to multilevel growth models as well. After all, repeated measures taken on the same set of units, such as repeated achievement scores calculated for individual students, can readily be construed as measures taken at level one, while the students or other units are located at level two. Still higher-level units, such as classrooms, schools, and school districts, may then be treated as located at levels three, four, and five. In this way, the multilevel framework is maintained.

The primary difference between conventional multilevel models estimated with cross-sectional data and multilevel growth models, of course, is the way time is treated. Given the nature of cross-sectional data, time has to be ignored. When repeated measures are available, however, change over time may be profitably studied. More to the point, *change* over time becomes available for close scrutiny.

As we have seen, multilevel growth models permit us to estimate individual growth curves displaying the nature of change over time for each person or other unit in our data set. This is accomplished by treating measures as nested within individuals. The individual growth curves provide a basis for estimating an overall or average growth curve, summarizing the time-dependent pattern over all individuals.

Beyond that, level-two explanatory factors may be used to explain differences in change over time among individuals. The level-two explanatory variables may have fixed or random coefficients, and variability in random components may be explained with level-three variables, if a third level is available.

In short, multilevel growth models enable us to describe the nature of measured change, and to explain why patterns of change differ from one individual to another. They represent a substantial advance over conventional before-and-after or pretest–posttest designs.

11.15 USEFUL RESOURCES

Singer, J., & Willett, J. (2003) *Applied Longitudinal Data Analysis*. New York: Oxford University Press.

Gamoran, A. (2005) *Using Multilevel Growth Models to Assess the Impact of the Urban Systemic Initiative in Texas, 1994–2000*. Retrieved from htttp://facstaff.wcer.wisc.edu/norman/Tech%20Report%Texas/7%20GAMORAN.pdf

Zaidman-Zat, A., & Zumbo, B. (2005) *Multilevel (HLM) Models for Modeling Change with Incomplete Data: Demonstrating the Effects of Missing Data and Level-1 Model Mis-specification*. Paper presented at the American Educational Research Association Conference, Montreal, April 11–15.

The first 300 pages of Singer and Willett's text provide an excellent introduction to multilevel growth modeling. The material is very well written and unusually accessible. An analyst who has acquired a good understanding of multilevel regression will be able to work through this material without the usual enormous amount of difficulty, and will soon be able to construct and estimate informative models of change over time. Coverage of important topics is extremely thorough, and there are numerous carefully worked-out examples.

Until reading Singer and Willett, I was troubled by uncertainty as to the best way to make analytical sense of the distinction between time-independent and time-dependent explanatory variables. The authors clarify this distinction in a way that makes it readily applicable in applied work. Moreover, Singer and Willett's discussion of error covariance structures facilitates drawing useful parallels with random component covariance structures; this makes a complex topic comparatively easy to understand. Finally, the authors devote a great deal of attention to alternative ways of construing time and to nonlinear growth curves. As with other difficult issues, this material is presented in readable fashion.

Gamoran's brief account of using multilevel growth models to assess the achievement effects of district-level urban systemic initiatives is useful because of the clarity of its objectives and the straightforward way in which a three-level model—within-student, student, district—is presented. Achievement growth in Gamoran's evaluation is curvilinear, with growth slowing as time passes. Comparison of students from selected Texas school districts suggests that implementation of the urban systemic initiative enhances achievement growth for all students. Differences in level of implementation, however, make no difference. Gamoran's discussion of data problems, especially measuring level of implementation, is instructive.

The material is presented as part of a larger but unspecified document, and the nature of systemic initiatives is not explained. I am assuming that Gamoran is studying an example of the systemic initiatives fostered by the National Academy of Sciences to promote achievement in science and math. In spite of this uncertainty, the clarity of Gamoran's methodological account makes this document well worth reading.

The brief paper by Zaidman-Zat and Zumbo is of interest for much the same reason as Gamoran's: clearly explained application of a relatively simple model to an issue of real interest. The authors' objective is to examine the effects of missing data on fixed coefficients estimated to explain differences among individuals with regard to verbal achievement.

Recall that one of the commonly cited virtues of multilevel growth models is that even if one or more observations on the dependent variable are missing, the procedure makes best use of information available, rather than deleting the case. Zaidman-Zat and Zumbo provide evidence consistent with this desirable characteristic, but they offer a caveat: If the level-one model is misspecified, missing data constitute much more of a problem than has commonly been recognized. With proper level-one specification as manifest in use of the correct functional form, however, the efficacy of multilevel models of change in handling missing data is remarkable, indeed.

Clearly, this paper is intrinsically interesting. For one new to the specification and estimation of multilevel growth models, however, the primary virtue of Zaidman-Zat and Zumbo's work is the clarity with which they present it.

References

Abdulnabi, R. (1999) *Using Model Fitting Information and PROC PLOT to Select the Type of Variance–Covariance Structure for Repeated Measures.* Ann Arbor, MI: Clinical Biostatistics, Pfizer.

Aguinis, H. (2004) *Regression Analysis for Categorical Moderators.* New York: Guilford Press.

Alford, R. (1998) *The Craft of Inquiry.* New York: Oxford University Press.

Alford, R., & Friedland, R. (1985) *Powers of Theory: Capitalism, the State, and Democracy.* Cambridge, UK: Cambridge University Press.

Alicias, E. (2005) Toward an Objective Evaluation of Teacher Performance: The Use of Variance Partitioning Analysis. *Education Policy Analysis Archives, 13.* Retrieved from http://epaa.asu.edu/epaa/v13n30

Anatolyev, S. (2002) Electoral Behavior of U.S. Counties: A Panel Data Approach. *Economics Bulletin, 3,* 1–10.

Andersen, B. (2004) *Mixed Models for Independent Data.* Retrieved from http://socserv.mcmaster.ca/andersen/ICPSR/12.Mixed.pdf

Andersen, R. (2004) *Regression III: Advanced Methods.* PowerPoint Presentation at the ICPSR Summer Program in Quantitative Methods, University of Michigan, Ann Arbor, June 28–July 23.

Angeles, G., & Mroz, T. (2001) *A Guide to Using Multilevel Models for the Evaluation of Program Impacts.* Chapel Hill: Carolina Population Center, University of North Carolina.

Annie E. Casey Foundation (2004) *Kids Count 2004 Data Book Online: Raw Data.* Retrieved from www.aecf.org/kidscount/databook

Arrow, K., Bowles, H., & Durlauf, S. (Eds.) (2000) *Meritocracy and Economic Inequality.* Princeton, NJ: Princeton University Press.

Barr, R., & Dreeben, R. (1983) *How Schools Work.* Chicago: University of Chicago Press.

Beale, C. (2004) *Measuring Rurality: Rural–Urban Continuum Codes.* Washington, DC: Economic Research Service, U.S. Department of Agriculture.

Beck, N. (2003) *What Do Random Coefficient (or Hierarchical) Models Buy? (And What Do They Cost?): Applications to Cross-National Survey and Cross-National Political Economy Data.* La Jolla: Department of Political Science, University of California, San Diego.

Beck, P., Dalton, R., & Greene, S. (2001) *The Social "Calculus" of Voting: Media, Organization, and Interpersonal Influences on Presidential Choices.* Retrieved from http://psweb.sbs.ohio-state.edu/faculty/pbeck/soccal.focc.301.pdf

Becker, G. (1964) *Human Capital*. New York: National Bureau of Economic Research.

Becker, G. (1993) *Human Capital: A Theoretical and Empirical Analysis, with Special Reference to Education* (3rd ed.). Chicago: University of Chicago Press.

Belanger, P., & Eagles, M. (2005) *The Geography of Class and Religion in Canadian Elections*. Paper Presented at the Canadian Political Science Association Conference, University of Western Ontario, London, Ontario, June 2–4.

Belsley, D., Kuh, E., & Welsh, R. (1980) *Regression Diagnostics: Identifying Influential Data and Sources of Collinearity*. New York: Wiley.

Benveniste, L., Carnoy, M., & Rothstein, R. (2003) *All Else Equal: Are Public and Private Schools Different?* London: Falmer.

Berliner, D., & Biddle, B. (1995) *The Manufactured Crisis*. Reading, MA: Addison-Wesley.

Berry, W. (1993) *Understanding Regression Assumptions*. Newbury Park, CA: Sage.

Betebenner, D. (2004) *An Analysis of School District Data Using Value-Added Methodology*. Los Angeles: Center for the Study of Evaluation, National Center on Evaluation, Graduate School of Education and Information Studies, University of California, Los Angeles.

Bickel, R. (1987) Practical Limitations of the Input–Output Model for Research and Policymaking. *Educational Policy, 1*, 271–287.

Bickel, R. (1989) Post-High School Prospects and High School Completion Rates in an Appalachian State: A Near-Replication of Florida Research. *Youth and Society, 21*, 61–84.

Bickel, R., & Dufrene, R. (2001) Community, Opportunity, and Crime on School Property: A Quantitative Case Study. *Educational Foundations, 15*, 19–39.

Bickel, R., & Howley, C. (2000) The Influence of Scale on School Performance: A Multi-Level Extension of the Matthew Principle. *Education Policy Analysis Archives, 8*. Retrieved from http://epaa.asu.edu/epaa/v8n22

Bickel, R., & Howley, C. W. (2003) Math Achievement and the Development of Poor Rural Areas: Effects of Contextual Factors Intrinsic to the Modern World. *Educational Foundations, 17*, 83–105.

Bickel, R., Howley, C., Williams, T., & Glascock, C. (2001) High School Size, Achievement Equity, and Cost: Robust Interaction Effects and Tentative Results. *Education Policy Analysis Archives, 9*. Retrieved from http://epaa.asu.edu/epaa/v9n40.html

Bickel, R., & Lange, L. (1995) Opportunities, Costs, and High School Completion in West Virginia. *Journal of Educational Research, 88*, 363–370.

Bickel, R., & Maynard, A. (2004) Group and Interaction Effects with "No Child Left Behind: Gender and Reading in a Poor Appalachian District." *Education Policy Analysis Archives, 12*. Retrieved from http://epaa.asu.edu/epaa/v12n4

Bickel, R., & McDonough, M. (1998) No Effects to Fade: Head Start in Two West Virginia Counties. *Educational Foundations, 12*, 69–89.

Bickel, R., McDonough, M., & Williams, T. (1999) Opportunity, Community, and Early Adolescent Pregnancy: A Replication of Research with Older Teenaged Girls. *Educational Foundations, 37*, 47–72.

Bickel, R., & Papagiannis, G. (1988) Post-High School Prospects and District-Level Dropout Rates. *Youth and Society, 20*, 123–147.

Bickel, R., Smith, C., & Eagle, T. (2002) Poor Rural Neighborhoods and Early School Achievement. *Journal of Poverty, 6*, 89–108.

Blalock, H. (1960) *Social Statistics*. New York: McGraw-Hill.

Blalock, H. (1964) *Causal Inferences in Non-Experimental Research*. Chapel Hill: University of North Carolina Press.

Blalock, H. (1972) *Social Statistics* (2nd ed.) New York: McGraw-Hill.

Blalock, H. (1982) *Conceptualization and Measurement in the Social Sciences*. Beverly Hills, CA: Sage.

Bland, J. (2000) Sample Size in Guidelines Trials. *Family Practice, 17,* S17–S20.

Blau, P. (1960) Structural Effects. *American Sociological Review, 25,* 175–193.

Blau, P. (1964) *Exchange and Power in Social Life.* New York: Wiley.

Blau, P. (1994) *Structural Contexts of Opportunity.* Chicago: University of Chicago Press.

Blau, P., & Duncan, O. (1967) *The American Occupation Structure.* New York: Wiley.

Boggess, J., & Roulet, M. (2001) *Welfare Reform and Family Conflict among Low-Income, Never-Married Parents.* Madison: Center for Family Policy and Practice, University of Wisconsin.

Borgatta, E., & Bohrnstedt, G. (Eds.) (1969) *Sociological Methodology, 1969.* San Francisco: Jossey-Bass.

Boudreau, J., & Boswell, W. (1997) *Employee Attitudinal Effects of Perceived Performance Appraisal Use.* Ithaca, NY: Center for Advanced Human Resource Studies, School of Industrial and Labor Relations, Cornell University.

Bowerman, B., & O'Connell, R. (1993) *Forecasting and Time Series: An Applied Approach.* Belmont, CA: Duxbury.

Boyd, L., & Iversen, G. (1979) *Contextual Analysis: Concepts and Statistical Techniques.* Belmont, CA: Wadsworth.

Brasington, D., & Haurin, D. (2005) *Educational Outcomes and House Values: A Test of the Value-Added Approach* (Working Paper No. 2005-03). Baton Rouge: Department of Economics, Louisiana State University.

Bryk, A., & Raudenbush, S. (1992) *Hierarchical Linear Models.* Newbury Park, CA: Sage.

Bryk, A., & Thum, Y. (1989) The Effect of High School Organization on Dropping Out: An Exploratory Investigation. *American Education Research Journal, 26,* 353–383.

Burnham, K., & Anderson, D. (2002) *Model Selection and Multi-Model Inference.* New York: Springer-Verlag.

Burnham, K., & Anderson, D. (2004) Multimodel Inference: Understanding AIC and BIC in Model Selection. *Sociological Methods and Research, 33,* 261–304.

Byrne, B. (2001) *Structural Equation Modeling with Amos: Basic Concepts, Applications, and Programming.* Mahwah, NJ: Erlbaum.

Campbell, D., & Kenny, D. (1999) *A Primer on Regression Artifacts.* New York: Guilford Press.

Card, D. (1995) Using Geographic Variation in College Proximity to Estimate the Return to Schooling. In Christophides, E., Grant, E., & Swidinsky, R. (Eds.), *Aspects of Labor Market Behavior: Essays in Honor of Jan Vanderkamp.* Toronto: University of Toronto Press, pp. 201–222.

Carnoy, M. (2001) *Sustaining the New Economy.* Cambridge, MA: Harvard University Press.

Cavanaugh, J. (2005) *The Application of Model Selection Criteria.* Iowa City: Department of Biostatistics, College of Public Health, University of Iowa.

Chatfield, C. (2003) *The Analysis of Time Series: An Introduction.* London: Chapman & Hall.

Chatterjee, S., Hadi, A., & Price, B. (2000) *Regression Analysis by Example.* New York: Wiley.

Chevalier, A., Harmon, C., & Walker, I. (2002) *Does Education Raise Productivity, or Just Reflect It?* Dublin: Policy Evaluation and Governance Programme, Institute for the Study of Social Change.

Chubb, J., & Moe, T. (1992) *Politics, Markets, and America's Schools.* Washington, DC: Brookings Institution.

Cliff, N. (1983) Some Cautions Concerning the Application of Causal Modeling Methods. *Multivariate Behavioral Research, 18,* 115–126.

Cohen, M. (1998) Determining Sample Size for Surveys with Data Analyzed by Hierarchical Linear Models. *Journal of Official Statistics, 14,* 267–275.

Cohen, P., Cohen, J., West, S., & Aiken, L. (2002) *Applied Multiple Regression/Correlation Analysis for the Behavioral Sciences.* Mahwah, NJ: Erlbaum.

Coleman, J. (1986) Social Theory, Social Research, and a Theory of Action. *American Journal of Sociology, 91*, 1309–1335.

Coleman, J., & Hoffer, T. (1987) *Public and Private High Schools: The Impact of Communities.* New York: Basic Books.

Coleman, J., Hoffer, T., & Kilgore, S. (1982) *High School Achievement.* New York: Basic Books.

Conley, D. (1999) *Being Black, Living in the Red.* Berkeley: University of California Press.

Coser, L. (1975) Presidential Address: Two Methods in Search of a Substance. *American Sociological Review, 40*, 691–700.

Dallal, G. (2005) *The Little Handbook of Statistical Practice.* Boston: Jean Mayer USDA Human Nutrition Research Center on Aging, Tufts University.

Davis, J. (1985) *The Logic of Causal Order.* Beverly Hills, CA: Sage.

De Leeuw, J. (2003) Review of Joop Hox, *Multilevel Analysis,* Erlbaum, 2002. Retrieved from http://preprints.stat.ucla.edu/358/hox.pdf

Diez-Roux, A. (2002) A Glossary for Multilevel Analysis. *Journal of Epidemiology and Community Health, 56*, 588–594.

Draper, N., & Smith, H. (1998) *Applied Regression Analysis.* New York: Wiley.

Duncan, O. (1966) Path Analysis: Sociological Examples. *American Journal of Sociology, 72*, 1–16.

Duncan, O. (1975) *Introduction to Structural Equation Models.* New York: Academic Press.

Dunn, L., & Dunn, L. (1981) *Peabody Picture Vocabulary Test—Revised.* Circle Pines, MN: American Guidance Service.

Economic Research Service (ERS) (2004a) Rural Income, Poverty, and Welfare: Rural Child Poverty. Retrieved from www.ers.usda.gov/Briefing/IncomePovertyWelfare/ChildPoverty/

Economic Research Service (ERS) (2004b) Rural Income, Poverty, and Welfare: Rural Poverty. Retrieved from www.ers.usda.gov/Briefing/incomepovertywelfare/ruralpoverty

Ezekiel, M. (1930) *Methods of Correlation Analysis.* New York: Wiley.

Ezekiel, M. (1930) *Methods of Correlation and Regression Analysis: Linear and Curvilinear.* New York: Wiley.

Ezekiel, M., & Fox, K. (1959) *Methods of Correlation and Regression Analysis: Linear and Curvilinear* (3rd ed.) New York: Wiley.

Falk, R., & Miller, N. (1992) *A Primer on Soft Modeling.* Akron, OH: University of Akron.

Farkas, G. (1996) *Human Capital or Cultural Capital?* New York: Aldine de Gruyter.

Fielding, D. (2004) How Does Monetary Policy Affect the Poor?: Evidence from The West African Economic and Monetary Union. *Journal of African Economies, 13*, 563–593.

Fitzgerald, J., Gottschalk, P., & Moffitt, R (2002) *An Analysis of Sample Attrition in Panel Data: The Michigan Panel Study of Income Dynamics.* Baltimore: Department of Economics, Johns Hopkins University.

Flanigan, W., & Zingale, N. (2002) *Political Behavior of the American Electorate.* Washington, DC: CQ Press.

Fox, J. (1991) *Regression Diagnostics.* Newbury Park, CA: Sage.

Fox, J. (1997) *Applied Regression Analysis, Linear Models, and Related Methods.* Thousand Oaks, CA: Sage.

Freckleton, R. (2002) On the Misuse of Residuals in Ecology: Regression of Residuals vs. Multiple Regression. *Journal of Ecology, 71*, 542–545.

Freedman, D. (1987) As Others See Us: A Case Study in Path Analysis. *Journal of Educational Statistics, 12*, 108–128.

Furstenburg, F., Cook, T., Eccles, J., Elder, G., & Samerhoff, A. (1999) *Managing to Make It: Urban Families and Academic Success.* Chicago: University of Chicago Press.

Gamoran, A. (2005) *Using Multilevel Growth Models to Assess the Impact of the Urban Systemic Initiative in Texas, 1994–2000.* Retrieved from http://facstaff.wcer.wisc.edu/norman/Tech%20Report%Texas/7%20GAMORAN.pdf

Garces, E., Thomas, T., & Currie, J. (2000) *Longer Term Head Start Effects.* Santa Monica, CA: RAND.

Gewirtz, S. (1997) *Can All Schools Be Successful?* Paper Presented at the British Educational Research Association Annual Conference, York, September 11–14.

Gill, J., & King, G. (2003) *What to Do When Your Hessian is Not Invertible.* Retrieved from http://gking.harvard.edu/files/help.pdf

Gilliam, W., & Zigler, E. (2000) A Critical Meta-Analysis of All Evaluations of State-Funded Preschool Programs from 1977–1998. *Early Childhood Research Quarterly, 125,* 441–473.

Goldberger, A. (1991) *A Course in Econometrics.* Cambridge, MA: Harvard University Press.

Goldfield, S., & Quandt, R. (1972) *Nonlinear Methods of Econometrics.* Amsterdam: North-Holland.

Goldstein, H. (1998) *Bootstrapping for Multilevel Models.* London: Institute of Education, University of London, Multilevel Models Project.

Goldstein, H. (1999) *Multilevel Statistical Models.* London: Institute of Education, University of London, Multilevel Models Project.

Goldstein, H. (2000) *School Effectiveness Critiques: Update November 2000.* London: Institute of Education, University of London, Multilevel Models Project.

Goldstein, H. (2003) *Multilevel Statistical Models* (3rd ed.) London: Arnold.

Goldstein, H., Huiqi, P., Rath, T., & Hill, N. (2000) *The Use of Value Added Information in Judging School Performance.* London: Institute of Education, University of London.

Gorard, S. (2000) *Education and Social Justice.* Cardiff, UK: University of Wales Press.

Greene, J., & Mellow, N. (1998) *Integration Where It Counts: A Study of Racial Integration in Public and Private School Lunchrooms.* Paper Presented at the American Political Science Association Conference, Boston, September.

Greenland, S. (2000) Principles of Multilevel Modeling. *International Journal of Epidemiology, 29,* 158–167.

Gresham, F., & Elliott, S. (1989) Social Skills Deficits as a Primary Learning Disability. *Journal of Learning Disabilities, 22,* 141–152.

Gresham, F., & Elliott, S. (1990) *Social Skills Rating System Manual.* Circle Pines, MN: American Guidance Service.

Grusky, D. (Ed.) (2001) *Sociological Stratification: Class, Race, and Gender in Sociological Perspective.* Boulder, CO: Westview Press.

Gujarati, D. (2003) *Basic Econometrics.* New York: McGraw-Hill.

Gujarati, D. (2006) *Essentials of Econometrics.* New York: McGraw-Hill.

Haavelmo, T. (1943) The Statistical Implications of a System of Simultaneous Equations. *Econometrica, 11,* 1–12.

Halcoussis, D. (2005) *Understanding Econometrics.* Mason, OH: Thomson/South-Western.

Halsey, A., Lauder, H., Brown, P., & Wells, A. (Eds.) (1997) *Education: Culture, Economy, and Society.* New York: Oxford University Press.

Hamilton, L. (1999) *Regression with Graphics.* Pacific Grove, CA: Brooks/Cole.

Hardy, M. (1993) *Regression with Dummy Variables.* Newbury Park, CA: Sage.

Hausman, J. (1978) Specification Tests in Econometrics. *Econometrica, 46,* 1251–1271.

Hayashi, F. (2000) *Econometrics.* Princeton, NJ: Princeton University Press.

Hayduk, L. (1987) *Structural Equation Modeling with LISREL: Essentials and Advances.* Baltimore: Johns Hopkins.

Hayes, A., & Cai, L. (2005) *Using Heteroscedasticity-Consistent Standard Error Estimator in OLS Regression: An Introduction and Software Implementation.* Columbus: School of Communication, Ohio State University.

Heck, R., & Thomas, S. (2000) *An Introduction to Multilevel Modeling Techniques.* Mahwah, NJ: Erlbaum.

Heckman, J. (1978) Endogenous Dummy Variables in a Simultaneous Equation System. *Econometrica, 46*, 931–959.

Heckman, J. (1979) Sample Selection Bias as a Specification Error. *Econometrica, 47*, 153–161.

Heckman, J., & Krueger, A. (Friedman, B., Ed.) (2003) *Inequality in America: What Role for Human Capital Policies?* Cambridge, MA: MIT Press.

Herrnstein, R., & Murray, C. (1994) *The Bell Curve: Intelligence and Class Structure in American Life.* New York: Free Press.

Hershberg, T., Simon, V., & Lea-Kruger, B. (2004) The Revelations of Value-Added. *The School Administrator.* Retrieved from www.aasa.org/publications/sa/2004/hershberg_12.htm

Hilden-Minton, J. (1995) *Multilevel Diagnostics for Mixed and Hierarchical Linear Models.* Unpublished Doctoral Dissertation, University of California, Los Angeles.

Hoffmann, J. (2003) *Generalized Linear Models: An Applied Approach.* Boston: Allyn & Bacon.

Hofmann, D. (2005) *Hierarchical Linear Modeling.* Chapel Hill: University of North Carolina, CARMA Webcast. Retrieved from www.pubinfo.ncu.edu/carma/webcasts.asp

Homans, G. (1974) *Social Behavior.* New York: Harcourt Brace Jovanovich.

Hoover, H., Dunbar, S., & Frisbie, D. (2001) *Iowa Tests of Basic Skills.* Itasca, IL: Riverside.

Hosmer, D., & Lemeshow, S. (1989) *Applied Logistic Regression.* New York: Wiley.

Howe, H. (2005) *Urban–Rural Gradients in Cancer Incidence and Mortality in the United States.* Springfield, IL: North American Association of Cancer Registries.

Howley, A., & Howley, C. (2006) Small Schools and the Pressure to Consolidate. *Education Policy Analysis Archives, 14.* Retrieved from http://epaa.asu.edu/epaa/v14n10.html

Howley, C., & Howley, A. (2004) School Size and the Influence of Socioeconomic Status: Confronting the Threat of Size Bias in National Data Sets. *Education Policy Analysis Archives, 12.* Retrieved from http://epaa.asu.edu/epaa/v12n52.html

Hox, J. (1995) *Applied Multilevel Analysis.* Amsterdam: TT-Publikaties.

Hox, J. (1998) Multilevel Modeling: When and Why? In Balderjahn, R., & Schader, M. (Eds.), *Classification, Data Analysis, and Data Highways.* New York: Springer-Verlag, pp. 147–154.

Hox, J. (2002) *Multilevel Analysis: Techniques and Applications.* Mahwah, NJ: Erlbaum.

Hox, J. (in press) Multilevel Analysis of Grouped and Longitudinal Data. In Little, T., Schnabel, K., & Baumert, J. (Eds.), *Modeling Longitudinal and Multiple Group Data.* Mahwah, NJ: Erlbaum.

Hox, J., & Maas, C. (2002) *Sample Size and Robustness Issues in Multilevel Regression Analysis.* Paper Presented at the XV World Congress of Sociology, Brisbane, Australia, July 7–13.

Huang, G. (2000) Mathematics Achievement by Immigrant Children: A Comparison of Five English Speaking Countries. *Education Policy Analysis Archives, 8.* Retrieved from http://epaa.asu.edu/epaa/v8n2

Ilbo, C. (2000) *The New Shape of the Presidential Election of 2000.* Washington, DC: Governance Studies Program, Brookings Institution.

Inkeles, A., & Smith, D. (1974) *Becoming Modern.* Cambridge, MA: Harvard University Press.

Institute for Social Research, University of Michigan (2003) *The Child Development Supplement: Panel Study of Income Dynamics.* Ann Arbor: Author.

Iversen, G. (1991) *Contextual Analysis.* Newbury Park, CA: Sage.

Jaccard, J., & Turrisi, R. (2003) *Interaction Effects in Multiple Regression* (2nd ed.). Thousand Oaks, CA: Sage.

Jaccard, J., Turrisi, R., & Wan, C. (1990) *Interaction Effects in Multiple Regression.* Newbury Park, CA: Sage.

Jencks, C., Smith, M., Acland, H., Band, M., Cohen, D., Gintis, H., et al. (1972) *Inequality.* New York: Basic Books.

Johnson, J. (2005) *Et in Arcadia Matheus?: An Investigation of Educational Equity in Kentucky's Public Schools.* Unpublished Doctoral Dissertation, Ohio University, Athens.

Johnson, J., Howley, C., & Howley, A. (2002) *Size, Excellence, and Equity: A Report on Arkansas Schools and Districts.* Washington, DC: Rural School and Community Trust.

Johnston, R., Hagen, M., & Jamieson, K. (2004) *The 2000 Presidential Election and the Foundations of Party Politics.* New York: Cambridge University Press.

Joreskog, K. (1973) A General Method for Estimating a Linear Structural Equation System. In Goldberger, A., & Duncan, O. (Eds.), *Structural Equation Models in the Social Sciences.* New York: Academic Press.

Kaiser, R. (2005) Inauguration: Instant Analysis. *The Washington Post,* January 20. Retrieved from www.washingtonpost.com.com/wp-dyn/articles/a10435-2005jan14.html

Kalton, G. (1983) *Introduction to Survey Sampling.* Beverly Hills, CA: Sage.

Kennedy, B., Kawachi, I, Glass, R., & Prothro-Stith, D (1998) Income Distribution, Socioeconomic Status, and Self-Rated Health in the United States: A Multilevel Analysis. *British Medical Journal, 317,* 917–921.

Kennedy, P. (1979) *A Guide to Econometrics.* Cambridge, MA: MIT Press.

Kennedy, P. (1998) *A Guide to Econometrics* (4th ed.). Cambridge, MA: MIT Press.

Kennedy, P. (2003) *A Guide to Econometrics* (5th ed.). Cambridge, MA: MIT Press.

Kenny, D. (1979) *Correlation and Causality.* New York: Wiley.

Kerlinger, D., & Pedhazur, E. (1973) *Multiple Regression in Behavioral Research.* New York: Holt, Rinehart & Winston.

Kish, L. (1989) *Deffs: Why, When, and How? A Review.* Ann Arbor: University of Michigan.

Kish, L. (1995) *Survey Sampling.* New York: Wiley-Interscience. (Original work published 1965)

Klees, S. (1999) *Privatization and Neo-Liberalism: Ideology and Evidence in Rhetorical Reforms* (Current Issues in Comparative Education). New York: Teachers College, Columbia University.

Klein, K., & Kozlowski, S. (Eds.) (2000) *Multilevel Theory, Research, and Methods in Organizations: Foundations, Extensions, and New Directions.* San Francisco: Jossey-Bass.

Kleinbaum, D. (1996) *Survival Analysis.* New York: Springer.

Kline, R. (2005) *Principles and Practices of Structural Equation Modeling* (2nd ed.). New York: Guilford Press.

Kmenta, J. (1997) *Elements of Econometrics* (2nd ed.). Ann Arbor: University of Michigan Press.

Knoke, D., Bohrnstedt, G., & Mee, A. (2002) *Statistics for Social Data Analysis.* Belmont, CA: Wadsworth.

Kreft, I. (1996) *Are Multilevel Techniques Necessary? An Overview, Including Simulation Studies.* Los Angeles: California State University, Los Angeles.

Kreft, I., & De Leeuw, J. (1998) *Introducing Multilevel Modeling.* Thousand Oaks, CA: Sage.

Kreft, I., De Leeuw, J., & Aiken, L. (1995) The Effect of Different Forms of Centering in Hierarchical Linear Models. *Multivariate Behavioral Research, 30,* 1–21.

Kuha, J. (2004) AIC and BIC: Comparison of Assumptions and Performance. *Sociological Methods and Research, 33,* 118–229.

Kunovich, R. (2004) Social Structural Position and Prejudice: An Exploration of Cross-National Differences in Regression Slopes. *Social Science Research, 33,* 20–44.

Lamy, C., Barnett, W., & Jung, K. (2005) *The Effects of West Virginia's Early Education Program on Young Children's School Readiness.* New Brunswick, NJ: National Institute for Early Childhood Education, Rutgers University.

Lareau, A. (2003) *Unequal Childhoods.* Berkeley: University of California Press.

Lazarsfeld, P., & Menzel, H. (1969) On the Relationship between Individual and Collective Properties. In Etzioni, A. (Ed.), *A Sociological Reader on Complex Organizations.* New York: Holt, Rinehart & Winston, pp. 499–516.

Leamer, E. (1983) Let's Take the Con Out of Econometrics. *American Economic Review, 73,* 31–43.

Lee, V. (2004) Effects of High School Size on Student Outcomes: Response to Howley and Howley. *Education Policy Analysis Archives, 12.* Retrieved from http://epaa.asu.edu/epaa/v12n52.html

Levin, J., & Fox. J. (2002) *Elementary Statistics in Social Research* (9th ed.). Boston: Allyn & Bacon.

Lewis-Beck, M. (1980) *Applied Regression: An Introduction.* Beverly Hills, CA: Sage.

Leyland, A. (2004) *A Review of Multilevel Modeling in SPSS.* Glasgow, UK: University of Glasgow.

Leyland, A., & McCleod, A. (2000) *Mortality in England and Wales, 1979– 2000: An Introduction to Multilevel Modeling Using MlwiN.* Glasgow, UK: MRC Social and Public Health Services Unit, University of Glasgow.

Little, R., & Rubin, D. (2002) *Statistical Analysis with Missing Data* (2nd ed.). Hoboken, NJ: Wiley.

Lochman, J. (2004) Contextual Factors in Risk and Prevention Research. *Merrill–Palmer Quarterly, 50,* 311–325.

Longford, N. (1993) *Random Coefficient Models.* New York: Oxford University Press.

Lonigan, C., Wagner, R., Torgesen, J., & Rashotte, C. (2002) *Preschool Comprehensive Test of Phonological and Print Processing (Pre-CTOPPP).* Tallahassee: Department of Psychology, Florida State University.

Lowery, C., Petty, M., & Thompson, J. (1995) Employee Perceptions of Effectiveness of a Performance-Based Pay Program in a Large Public Utility. *Public Personnel Management, 24,* 475–492.

Lubienski, S., & Lubienski, C. (2005) A New Look at Public and Private Schools: Student Background and Mathematics Achievement. *Phi Delta Kappan, 86.* Retrieved from www.pdkintl.org/kappan/k_v86/k0505lub.htm

Luke, D. (2004) *Multilevel Modeling.* Thousand Oaks, CA: Sage.

Maas, C., & Hox, J. (2004) Robustness Issues in Multilevel Regression Analysis. *Statistica Neerlandica, 58,* 127–137.

Maas, C., & Hox, J. (2005) Sufficient Sample Sizes for Multilevel Modeling. *Methodology, 1,* 86–92.

Maxwell, S. (2000) Sample Size and Multiple Regression Analysis. *Psychological Methods, 4,* 434–458.

Mayer, J. (2002) *Running on Race: Racial Politics in Presidential Campaigns, 1960–2002.* New York: Random House.

Mayer, S., & Jencks, C. (1989) Growing Up in Poor Neighborhoods: How Much Does It Matter? *Science, 243,* 1441–1445.

McCaffery, D., Lockwood, J., Koertz, D., & Hamilton, L. (2004) *Evaluating Value-Added Models for Teacher Accountability.* Santa Monica, CA: RAND.

McDonough, S. (2004) 2004 Not the Breakout Year for Youth Vote After All. *San Francisco Chronicle,* November 2. Retrieved from www.sfgate.com/cgibin/article.cgi?f=/news/archive/2004/11/02/politics2059EST0779.DTL

McMurrer, D., & Sawhill, I. (1998) *Getting Ahead: Economic and Social Mobility in America.* Washington, DC: Urban Institute.

Menard, S. (2002) *Applied Logistic Regression Analysis.* Thousand Oaks, CA: Sage.

Mincer, J. (1974) *Schooling, Earnings, and Experience.* New York: National Bureau of Economic Research.

Mirer, T. (1995) *Economic Statistics and Econometrics* (3rd ed.). Englewood Cliffs, NJ: Prentice Hall.

Mok, M. (1995) Sample Size Requirements for 2-Level Designs in Educational Research. *Multilevel Modelling Newsletter, 7,* 11–15.

Montgomery, D., Peck, E., & Vining, G. (2001) *Introduction to Linear Regression Analysis*. New York: Wiley.

MoveOn.org (2005) MoveOn.org: Democracy in Action. Retrieved from www.moveon.org/front

Murtazashvilli, I., & Wooldridge, J. (2005) *Fixed Effects Instrumental Variables Estimation in Correlated Random Coefficient Panel Data*. East Lansing: Department of Economics, Michigan State University.

National Council of State Boards of Nursing (2006) *NCLEX Examination*. Chicago: Author.

National Evaluation Systems. (2002) *California Basic Educational Skills Test*. Sacramento, CA: Author.

Newman, K. (1994) *Declining Fortunes*. New York: Basic Books.

Newman, K. (1999) *Falling from Grace*. Berkeley: University of California Press.

Niemi, R., & Weisberg, H. (2001) *Controversies in Voting Behavior*. Washington, DC: CQ Press.

Nezlek, J. (2001) Multilevel Random Coefficient Analysis of Event- and Interval-Contingent Data in Social and Personality Psychology Research. *Personality and Social Psychology Bulletin, 27*, 771–785.

Nunnally, J., & Bernstein, I. (1994) *Psychometric Theory*. New York: McGraw-Hill.

Oberwittler, D. (2004) A Multilevel Analysis of Neighbourhood Contextual Effects on Serious Juvenile Offending. *European Journal of Criminology, 1*, 201–235.

Office of the Secretary (1994) *Biographical Memoirs* (Vol. 64). Washington, DC: National Academies Press, pp. 438–470.

Paccagnella, O. (2006) Centering or Not Centering in Multilevel Models? The Role of the Group Mean and the Assessment of Group Effects. *Evaluation Review, 30*, 66–85.

Pedhazur, E., & Schmelkin, L. (1991) *Measurement, Design, and Analysis: An Integrated Approach*. Hillsdale, NJ: Erlbaum.

Penn, H. (2004) *Childcare and Early Childhood Development Programs and Policies: Their Relationship to Eradicating Child Poverty*. London: Childhood Poverty Research and Policy Center.

Poston, D. (2002) The Effects of Human Capital and Cultural Characteristics on the Economic Attainment Patterns of Male and Female Asian-Born Immigrants in the United States: A Multilevel Analysis. *Asian and Pacific Migration Journal, 11*, 197–220.

Preacher, K. (2003) *A Primer on Interaction Effects in Multiple Regression Analysis*. Chapel Hill: University of North Carolina.

Raudenbush, S., & Bryk, A. (2002) *Hierarchical Linear Models* (2nd ed.). Thousand Oaks, CA: Sage.

Retherford, R., & Choe, M. (1993) *Statistical Models for Causal Analysis*. New York: Wiley.

Riordan, C. (2004) *Equality and Achievement* (2nd ed.). Upper Saddle River, NJ: Prentice Hall.

Robinson, W. (1950) Ecological Correlation and the Behavior of Individuals. *American Sociological Review, 15*, 351–357.

Romano, E., Tremblay, R., Boulerice, B., & Swisher, R. (2005) Multilevel Correlates of Childhood Physical Aggression and Prosocial Behavior. *Journal of Abnormal Child Psychology, 33*, 565–578.

Rosenberg, M. (1968) *The Logic of Survey Analysis*. New York: Basic Books.

Rothstein, R., Carnoy, M., & Benveniste, L. (1999) *Can Public Schools Learn from Private Schools?* Ithaca, NY: Economic Policy Institute, Cornell University.

Rubin, L. (1994) *Families on the Fault Line*. New York: HarperCollins.

Rumberger, R., & Palardy, G. (2004) Multilevel Models for School Effectiveness Research. In Kaplan, D. (Ed.), *Handbook of Quantitative Methods for the Social Sciences* (pp. 235–258). Thousand Oaks, CA: Sage.

Santos, N., & Freedman, A. (2004) *Adjusting Dairy Yield from 3 Times to 2 Times Milking Using a Random Regression Model* (Animal Industry Report No. R1895). Ames: Iowa State University.

SAS Institute (1999) *SAS/STAT User's Guide: The Mixed Procedure.* Cary, NC: Author.

Satterthwaite, F. (1946) An Approximate Distribution of Estimates of Variance Components. *Biometrics Bulletin, 2,* 110–114.

Schroeder, L., Sjoquist, D., & Stephan, P. (1986) *Understanding Regression Analysis: An Introductory Guide.* Beverly Hills, CA: Sage.

Schultz, T. (1960) Capital Formation by Education. *Journal of Political Economy, 68,* 571–583.

Schwarz, J. (1997) *Illusions of Opportunity.* New York: Norton.

Shields, M., & Snyder, A. (2005) *Using the Web to Better Understand Local Social and Economic Conditions.* Harrisburg: Pennsylvania Department of Labor and Industry, Center for Workforce Information and Analysis.

Shier, Y., & Fouladi, Y. (2003) The Effect of Multicollinearity on Multilevel Modeling Parameter Estimates and Standard Errors. *Educational and Psychological Measurement, 63,* 951–985.

Singer, J. (1987) An Intraclass Correlation for Analyzing Multilevel Data. *Journal of Experimental Education, 18,* 219–228.

Singer, J. (1998) Using SAS PROC MIXED to Fit Multilevel Models, Hierarchical Models, and Linear Growth Models. *Journal of Educational and Behavioral Statistics, 24,* 323–355.

Singer, J., & Willett, J. (2003) *Applied Longitudinal Data Analysis.* New York: Oxford University Press.

Smelser, N. (2001) *Organizations in the 21st Century: Knowledge and Learning—The Basis for Growth.* Berlin: Social Science Research Center.

Snedecor, G., & Cochran, W. (1989) *Statistical Methods* (8th ed.). Ames: Iowa State University Press.

Snijders, T., & Bosker, R. (1999) *Multilevel Analysis.* Thousand Oaks, CA: Sage.

Solon, G., Page, M., & Duncan, G. (2000) Correlations between Neighboring Children in Their Subsequent Educational Attainment. *Review of Economics and Statistics, 82,* 383–393.

Sousza-Poza, A. (2000) *Labor Market Segmentation and the Gender Wage Differential: An Industry-Level Analysis Using Data from the 1998 Swiss Wage Structure Survey.* Paper Presented at the Southern Economic Association Annual Conference, Tampa, FL, November 16–19.

Spatig, L., Bickel, R., Parrot, L., Dillon, A., & Conrad, K. (1998) Developmentalism Meets Standardized Testing: Do Low-Income Children Lose? In Ellsworth, J., & Ames, L. (Eds.), *Critical Perspectives on Project Head Start.* Albany: State University of New York, pp. 260–290.

SPSS (2003) *The Linear Mixed Models Procedure.* Chicago: Author.

SPSS (2005a) *Linear Mixed-Effects Modeling in SPSS: An Introduction to the MIXED Procedure.* Chicago: Author.

SPSS (2005b) *Statistical Support—Algorithms.* Chicago: Author.

Steenbergen, M., & Bradford, S. (2002) Modeling Multilevel Data Structures. *American Journal of Political Science, 46,* 218–237.

Stemler, S., Sternberg, R., Grigorenko, E., Jarvin, L., & Macomber, D. (2003) *Policy Brief on Data Analyses and Their Implications for School Policy* (Publication Series No. 7). New Haven, CT: Yale University.

Stevens, B. (1996) *A Study of the Relationships between Faculty Qualifications, Program Attributes, and Student Outcomes in Schools of Nursing in West Virginia from 1985–1994.* Morgantown: Department of Educational Leadership Studies, West Virginia University.

Strange, M., Howley, C., & Bickel, R. (2001) *Research about School Size in Impoverished Rural Neighborhoods.* Charleston, WV: ERIC Clearinghouse on Rural Education and Small Schools.

Swamy, P. (1970) Efficient Inference in a Random Coefficient Regression Model. *Econometrica, 38,* 311–323.

Swamy, P. (1971) *Statistical Inference in Random Coefficient Regression Models.* Berlin: Springer-Verlag.

Tabachnick, B. (2005) *Multilevel Modeling with SPSS*. San Bernardino: Psychology Department, California State University, San Bernardino.

Tacq, J. (1997) *Multivariate Analysis Techniques in Social Science Research*. Thousand Oaks, CA: Sage.

Tanner, H., Jones, S., & Treadway, M. (2000) *The Role of Middle Managers in Raising Standards in Mathematics*. Sydney: Australian Association for Research in Education.

Tate, R. (2004) A Cautionary Note on Shrinkage Estimates of School and Teacher Effects. *Florida Journal of Educational Research, 42,* 1–21.

Teachman, J., Duncan, G., Yeung, W., & Levy, D. (2001) Covariance Structure Models for Fixed and Random Effects. *Sociological Methods and Research, 30,* 271–288.

Thompson, R. (2000) Voters, Candidates Vague on Family Values. *Cincinnati Enquirer,* October 16. Retrieved from www.enquirer.com/editions/2000/10/16//loc_voters_candidates.html

Thrupp, M. (1999) *Schools Making a Difference: Let's Be Realistic! School Mix, School Effectiveness and the Social Limits of Reform*. Philadelphia: Open University Press.

Thum, Y. (2004) *Measuring Progress towards a Goal: Estimating Teacher Productivity Using a Multivariate Multilevel Model for Value-Added Analysis*. Los Angeles: Graduate School of Education and Information Studies, University of California, Los Angeles.

Thurow, T. (1983) *Dangerous Currents: The State of Economics*. New York: Random House.

Uchitelle, L. (2006) *The Disposable American*. New York: Knopf.

UCLA Academic Technology Services (2006) *Statistical Computing Seminar: Introduction to Multilevel Modeling Using SAS*. Retrieved from www.ats.ucla.edu/STAT/seminars/sas_mlm/mlm_sas_seminar.htm

U.S. Department of Health and Human Services, Administration for Children and Families (2005) *Head Start Impact Study: First Year Findings*. Washington, DC: Author.

U.S. Politics (2005) *Educational Attainment and 2004 Vote*. Retrieved from http://uspolitics.about.com/library/bl_education_vote.htm

USA Today (2004) Election 2004. November 16. Retrieved from www.usatoday.com/news/politicselections/vote2004/countymap.htm

Varanian, T., & Gleason, P. (1999) Do Neighborhood Conditions Affect High School Dropout and College Graduation Rates? *Journal of Socioeconomics, 28,* 21–42.

Vogt, W. (1999) *Dictionary of Statistics and Methodology*. Thousand Oaks, CA: Sage.

Watson, S. (2004) *Value Added: The Costs and Benefits of College Preparatory Programs*. Washington, DC: Educational Policy Institute.

Weisberg, H., & Wilcox, C. (Eds.). (2004) *Models of Voting Behavior in Presidential Elections: The 2000 U.S. Election*. Stanford, CA: Stanford Law and Politics.

Wiggins, R., Joshi, H., Bartley, M., Gleave, S., Lynch, K., & Cullis, A. (2002) Place and Personal Circumstances in a Multilevel Account of Women's Long-Term Illness. *Social Science and Medicine, 54,* 827–838

Williams, L. (2002) The Prophecy of Place: A Labor Market Study of Young Women and Education. *American Journal of Sociology and Economics, 61,* 681–712.

Wittink, D. (1988) *The Application of Regression Analysis*. Boston: Allyn & Bacon.

Wolfinger, R. (1993) Covariance Structure Selection in General Mixed Models. *Communications in Statistics, Simulation and Computation, 22,* 1079–1106.

Wolfle, L. (2003) The Introduction of Path Analysis to the Social Sciences, and Some Emergent Themes: An Annotated Bibliography. *Structural Equation Modeling: A Multidisciplinary Journal, 2003,* 1–34.

Wonnacott, T., & Wonnacott, R. (1984) *Introductory Statistics for Business and Economics* (4th ed.). New York: Wiley.

Wonnacott, T., & Wonnacott, R. (1990) *Introductory Statistics* (5th ed.). New York: Wiley.

Woodcock, R., & Johnson, M. (1990) *Woodcock–Johnson Psycho-Educational Battery—Revised.* Allen, TX: DLM Teaching Resources.

Woodhall, M. (1997) Human Capital Concepts. In Halsey, A., Lauder, H., Brown, P., & Wells, A. (Eds.), *Education: Culture, Economy, and Society.* New York: Oxford University Press, pp. 219–223.

Wooldridge, J. (2002) *Introductory Econometrics* (2nd ed.). Cincinnati, OH: South-Western.

Wooldridge, J. (2004) *Fixed Effects and Related Estimators for Correlated Random Coefficient and Treatment Effect Panel Data Models.* East Lansing: Department of Economics, Michigan State University.

Wooldridge, J. (2006) *Introductory Econometrics* (3rd ed.). Mason, OH: Thomson/South-Western.

Wright, R., Dielman, T., & Nantell, T. (1977) *Analysis of Stock Repurchases with a Random Coefficient Regression Model* (Working Paper No. 149). Ann Arbor: Division of Research, Graduate School of Business Administration, University of Michigan.

Wright, S. (1920) The Relative Importance of Heredity and Environment in Determining the Piebald Pattern of Guinea-Pigs. *Proceedings of the National Academy of Sciences, 6,* 320–332.

Wright, S. (1960) Path Coefficients and Path Regressions: Alternative or Complementary Concepts? *Biometrics, 16,* 189–202.

Yang, M., Goldstein, H., Rath, T., & Hill, N. (1999) The Use of Assessment Data for School Improvement Purposes. *Oxford Review of Education, 25,* 469–483.

Yuan, W., & Loi, L. (1996) *Misuse of Statistical Methods in Business Applied Research Projects.* Singapore: Division of Actuarial Science and Insurance, School of Accountancy and Business, Nanyang Technological University.

Zaidman-Zat, A., & Zumbo, B. (2005) *Multilevel (HLM) Models for Modeling Change with Incomplete Data: Demonstrating the Effects of Missing Data and Level-1 Model Mis-Specification.* Paper Presented at the American Educational Research Association Conference, Montreal, April 11–15.

Author Index

343

Subject Index

Kits for Web Professionals
from SitePoint

Available exclusively from
http://www.sitepoint.com/